D0340844

How Rights
Went Wrong

*Why Our Obsession with Rights
Is Tearing America Apart*

Jamal Greene

HOUGHTON MIFFLIN HARCOURT
BOSTON   NEW YORK
2021

Copyright © 2021 by Jamal Greene

All rights reserved

For information about permission to reproduce selections from this book, write
to trade.permissions@hmhco.com or to Permissions, Houghton Mifflin Harcourt
Publishing Company, 3 Park Avenue, 19th Floor, New York, New York 10016.

hmhbooks.com

Library of Congress Cataloging-in-Publication Data
Names: Greene, Jamal, author.
Title: How rights went wrong : why our obsession with rights is tearing America apart /
Jamal Greene.
Description: Boston : Houghton Mifflin Harcourt, 2021. | Includes bibliographical
references and index.
Identifiers: LCCN 2020034165 (print) | LCCN 2020034166 (ebook) |
ISBN 9781328518118 (hardcover) | ISBN 9780358450245 |
ISBN 9780358450443 | ISBN 9781328518149 (ebook)
Subjects: LCSH: Civil rights — United States. | United States. Constitution. 1st–10th
Amendments. | Affirmative action programs — United States. | Discrimination —
Law and legislation — United States.
Classification: LCC KF4749 .G74 2021 (print) | LCC KF4749 (ebook) |
DDC 342.7308/5 — dc23
LC record available at https://lccn.loc.gov/2020034165
LC ebook record available at https://lccn.loc.gov/2020034166

Book design by Chloe Foster

Printed in the United States of America
DOC 10 9 8 7 6 5 4 3 2 1

For Mom and Dad

Contents

Foreword

T he problem of the twenty-first century," Jamal Greene argues, echoing
W. E. B. DuBois, "is the problem of the rights line." Rights talk has become the driving force of American political discourse, a chief source of the
contortion of American courts, and an engine of American political polarization. Rights wars are battles of all against all, absolute and unrelenting. It
is the argument of this important book that until Americans can reimagine
rights, there is no path forward, and there is, especially, no way to get race
right. No peace, no justice.

Claiming that your rights have been violated has become the best and in
many cases the only way to pursue your political interest. Instead of seeking
political change in pursuit of my interest in the realm of political debate and
the making of law — where my interest will compete with your interest, and
we will likely arrive at a compromise — my remedy is to claim that my interest is not an interest but a right. You do that, too. And then we go to court.
As a result, conflicts that don't need to be settled in the courts are settled in
the courts, where the winner takes all. In a contest between your rights and
my rights, the courts decide whose rights win based on each judge's preferences. This is neither fair nor democratic. And, as Greene writes searingly,
"it divides us into those who have rights and those who don't."

Greene is not the first legal scholar to point out that rights claims have
run amok. In 1991, in *Rights Talk: The Impoverishment of Political Discourse,*

Mary Ann Glendon argued that "discourse about rights has become the principal language that we use in public to discuss weighty questions of right and wrong, but time and again it proves inadequate, or leads to a standoff of one right against another." Under this regime, Glendon argued, "a tendency to frame nearly every social controversy in terms of a clash of rights (a woman's right to her own body vs. a fetus's right to life) impedes compromise, mutual understanding and the discovery of common ground." Glendon saw the much-vaunted "rights revolution" as having begun in the 1960s. But, as Greene argues here, it has a much longer and more complicated history, calling for different solutions. It is one of the hallmarks of Greene's work that he looks to other countries for those solutions, finding, in their different rights discourses, a world of possibilities. And he looks, as well, to the past.

Like Glendon, Greene finds the origins of the hardening of rights discourse in the 1960s. But he begins his inquiry in the eighteenth century, because he's particularly keen to figure out exactly when and how and why things went awry. "American courts draw firm lines, often in morally arbitrary ways, between the interests they consider rights and those they don't," Greene writes. "The interests that courts count, they protect robustly from democratic politics, while those that they don't count remain wholly at the government's mercy. We sometimes describe this fetishism about rights — but just some rights — as foreordained by the Founding Fathers, but America wasn't born this way." It was only born this way in this sense: to be a human being held as property is to be a person without *any* rights. Dividing people into those with rights and those without began at the beginning.

Read this book to find out what Greene means about how rights went wrong and what he proposes, and then decide whether you agree. But I suggest keeping your eye on the ball, which is racial injustice. The oldest national organization in the United States founded to pursue constitutional rights is the National Association for the Advancement of Colored People, which began in 1909. Six years later, the NAACP concluded that the Supreme Court "has virtually declared that the colored man has no rights." The NAACP embarked on a strategy to seek fundamental rights, as guaranteed under the Fourteenth and Fifteenth Amendments. Led by this organization, the Progressive movement marked a turning point in the history of rights seeking by way of lawsuits, down through *Brown v. Board of Education* in 1954 and the criminal justice cases addressed by the Warren Court in the 1960s. Rights asserted by way of a remedy to rights for so long and so violently denied did not end the battle of rights but instead turned it into a war when, beginning in the 1970s, modern conservatives, adopting methods used by liberals, asserted not liberal claims to rights, but *conservative* claims to rights. Rights fights became politics by other means.

How Rights Went Wrong is an essential and fresh and vital history of constitutional law and American politics. It is also a cautionary tale, with a sober warning for judges and lawyers. "Courts should be reminding litigants of what they have in common, not encouraging them to view their opponents in the worst conceivable light," Greene writes. *How Rights Went Wrong* is an argument against judicial supremacy, in the interest of justice.

The courts in plenty of other countries avoid this mess. One of the most valuable contributions of this book is its comparative approach, looking especially at the resolution of rights conflicts in Germany and the United Kingdom as models of rights mediation. Those courts aren't perfect, and Greene doesn't pretend that they are. But he wants to shake Americans loose from the fiction that the courts own the Constitution. It is, instead, ours.

Jill Lepore

Introduction

You have the right to remain silent, and the right to free speech. The right to go out, and the right to stay home. The right to worship, and the right to doubt. The right against racial or sex discrimination, and the right to hate. The right to marry and to have children. The right to divorce and to terminate a pregnancy. The right not to be tortured. The right to die. The right to vote, and the right not to. The right to education, and the right to homeschooling. The right to health, and to refuse health insurance. The right to eat, and to stop eating. The right to clean air and water. The right to smoke cigarettes. The right to buy what you need. The right to hoard. The right to work. The right to party.

A performance artist named Karen Finley, best known for smearing chocolate over her naked body, claimed a right to National Endowment for the Arts funding. She lost. A conservative advocacy group called Citizens United claimed the right to use its corporate treasury funds to produce an anti–Hillary Clinton movie during her first presidential run. They won. Two Orthodox Jewish merchants in Philadelphia claimed the right to keep their stores open on Sundays. They lost. Jack Phillips, a Colorado baker, claimed the right to refuse to make a cake for a same-sex wedding. He won. Two Missouri women, Ndioba Niang and Tameka Stigers, claimed the right to braid hair without completing a 1,500-hour training course and obtaining a cosmetology license. They lost. A group of neo-Nazis claimed the right to unite, armed with racist propaganda and semiautomatic rifles, in a public park in Charlottesville, Virginia. They won. A Louisiana man named Gregory Sibley claimed the right to food, clothing, and shelter. He lost. A Long Island man, James Maloney, claimed the right to use his homemade nunchucks to teach the "Shafan Ha Lavan" karate style, which he made up, to his children. He won.

Rights have gone viral. We debate policy in the language of rights. We speak solemnly of soldiers heading to battle to defend them. We wave the dog-eared constitutions that enumerate them. We kiss the hems of the robes of judges who recognize and elevate them. The Frenchman Alexis de Tocqueville wrote in 1835 that "scarcely any political question arises in the United States that is not resolved, sooner or later, into a judicial question." That was hyperbole in his time, but it rings true in our own. Rights are the commandments of our civic religion. This book is about how to get them right, and why it matters.

Taking Rights Literally

Just after 10 a.m. on the morning of Sunday, May 31, 2009, a fifty-one-year-old airport shuttle driver named Scott Roeder rose from a pew at the Reformation Lutheran Church in Wichita, Kansas, rested a .22-caliber handgun against the temple of an usher, Dr. George Tiller, and pulled the trigger. A prominent provider of late-term abortions, Dr. Tiller had survived the bombing of his clinic in 1986. He had survived being shot in both arms in 1993. He did not survive Scott Roeder's bullet. He died before paramedics arrived.

At his murder trial, Roeder admitted that he had killed Dr. Tiller, but he claimed a "necessity" defense. A murder defendant can claim necessity if he killed to prevent a greater harm to others, like the trolley switchman in the old philosophy dilemma. For Roeder, the "others" whose rights he said he was protecting were fetuses, or, as he called them, "unborn children."

Private violence begins where the law runs out. Pimps, hit men, and mob goons enforce contracts the government refuses to back through its police and courts. Terrorists turn to violence when they see ordinary politics as fruitless or hostile to their agendas. Vigilantes promise security or justice to those the state is unable or unwilling to protect. Roeder believed it was for him to defend those whose rights the law would not recognize.

Roeder's act was grievously wrong, but he was right about one thing. In *Roe v. Wade,* the Supreme Court said fetuses do not have constitutional rights. Justice Harry Blackmun, *Roe*'s author, thought denying fetal rights was the price of saying women had the right to control their bodies. Either women had constitutional rights or fetuses did. There was no middle ground, no room for compromise or negotiation. The fight over abortion has since become a war, with people like Scott Roeder anointing themselves as its noble guerrillas.

The story of abortion rights sets into tragic relief a common but unrecognized problem in American law: in striving to take rights seriously, we take them too literally. We believe that holding a right means getting a judge to let us do whatever the right protects. A right to racial equality means no segregated public schools. A right to vote means no property requirements. A right to free speech means no sedition laws. For Blackmun, a right to abortion meant minimal abortion regulation.

This attitude might make sense in a world in which rights are few and therefore precious. *Fiat justitia, ruat caelum:* Let justice be done, though the heavens fall. But in a modern, cosmopolitan society, rights are not few and precious. They are many and ubiquitous. Racial equality isn't just about segregated schools but also race-based affirmative action and single-family zoning laws and prison overcrowding. Voting rights are not just about property requirements but also voter ID laws and butterfly ballots and partisan gerrymanders. Free speech is not just about McCarthyism but also corporate electioneering and 8kun manifestos and deep fakes. Abortion is not just about a woman's destiny but also matters of life and death. Rights are everywhere, but we disagree, intensely and in good faith, about what rights protect. Both rights and disagreement about rights are inevitable. They need somehow to coexist.

"The problem of the twentieth century," W. E. B. DuBois wrote in 1903, "is the problem of the color-line." That same year, the Democratic candidate for Mississippi governor, James Vardaman, ran on a platform of racial terrorism. "If it is necessary," he announced, "every Negro in the state will be lynched." He won and was later elected to the U.S. Senate. In neighboring Alabama, a Black Montgomery janitor named Jackson Giles submitted his case to the U.S. Supreme Court. Giles had been denied the right to vote under the 1901 Alabama Constitution, which gave limitless discretion to local registrars to deny ballots to Black voters. John B. Knox, who presided over the state constitutional convention, had announced that the convention's goal was "to establish white supremacy in this State." But the Court denied Giles's claim. Writing for the majority, the sainted Justice Oliver Wendell Holmes Jr. told Giles that, in the face of a state-ordered racial conspiracy, a mere court order would be nothing more than "an empty form."

Racial discrimination of the kind the brilliant but deeply flawed Justice Holmes and so many of his fellow judges let stand in cases like Giles's left a stain on the U.S. Constitution. Strong rights helped to scrub that stain away. Cases such as *Brown v. Board of Education,* affirming a right to racially integrated public schools, and *Loving v. Virginia,* striking down bans on interracial marriage, calcified the courts' formal commitment to the right of racial equality. Rights had to be resilient to weather the massive resistance embodied in Jim Crow. Rights had to be absolute, or close to it, lest they succumb to ever more ingenious devices of racial subordination. Rights had to be decided by federal judges with life tenure, because politicians have publics and can't be trusted with something so dear. Justice Holmes's casual dismissal of Jackson Giles's rights was shameful. It deserves our scorn.

But the problem with Giles's case isn't that the Supreme Court justices didn't take rights seriously; it's that they didn't take white supremacy seriously. As rights claiming has grown, our courts have badly misunderstood this lesson. Strong rights protection is far from harmless. The proliferation of strong rights can frustrate the democratic will and erode the solidarity of communities. Judicial dominion over constitutional rights can absolve the rest of us of our responsibility to take rights seriously, leading our moral intuitions to atrophy and eventually to decay. Rights can breed resentment of those who win the Constitution's favor at the expense of others.

Where perceived as absolute, rights take poorly to conflict. When recognizing our neighbor's rights necessarily extinguishes our own, a survival instinct kicks in. Our opponent in the rights conflict becomes not simply a fellow citizen who disagrees with us, but an enemy out to destroy us. Law becomes reducible to winners and losers, to which side you are on, which tribe you affiliate with. With stakes this high, polarization should not just be expected but is indeed the only sensible response. *If only one side can win, it might as well be mine.* Conflict over rights can encourage us to take aim at our political opponents instead of speaking to them. And we shoot to kill.

The problem of the twenty-first century, in short, is the problem of the rights line. Human beings and the societies they populate are different from one another. We have different tastes; look different; speak different languages; eat different foods; entertain ourselves differently; worship different gods; form different familial and social bonds; hold different acts, images, symbols, and historical figures and episodes as beautiful, contemptuous, humorous, obscene, sacred, or ridiculous. When different people come into contact with each other and must live together, we preserve our values and avoid debilitating erasure by claiming rights.

Fights about rights, then, are a byproduct of human pluralism, an inescapable symptom of the human condition. It's no accident that "complaint," the term for the filing that begins a legal case, finds a synonym in the word "gripe." "Gripe" comes from the verb "grip," meaning "to seize firmly," as when the flu virus — "the grippe" — constricts the throat. Rights conflicts, like diseases, are forms of pain. The treatment courts prescribe can help ameliorate that pain — or make it much, much worse.

Mediating Rights

The law can respond to the proliferation of competing rights in one of three ways: it can *minimize* rights, it can *discriminate* between them, or it can *mediate* them. Only the last of these choices makes sense in a diverse and complex society. Only rights mediation fits this precarious moment in our collective life.

Minimizing rights is the strategy once associated with social conservatives. Their subsequent abandonment of this strategy attests that it doesn't work. A rights minimizer believes that only the barest, most fundamental of rights deserve constitutional recognition. Justice Holmes was this way. For minimizers like him, the few rights the Constitution protects might be identified by what is most specific in the constitutional text — the right to freedom of speech or the right against racial discrimination, perhaps. Or else judges might choose to preserve those rights that have an unbroken tradition of constitutional protection, such as the right to a jury trial.

The strategy of minimizing rights is harder to pull off than it might seem. The U.S. Constitution is not just the world's oldest written constitution but is also very nearly its shortest. (Monaco has us beat, alas.) Many of the rights it provides are couched vaguely in terms of "due process of law" and "equal protection of the laws." Most of the rights that anyone disagrees about are barely mentioned in the Constitution. This is true even of core rights like freedom of speech, which doesn't self-evidently apply, say, to running a super PAC or burning a flag and which the Constitution only textually shields from Congress, not state or local officials or courts or the president. The Constitution also, for example, doesn't specifically forbid racial discrimination or provide for the right to vote. It doesn't specify that criminal defendants be found guilty beyond a reasonable doubt, nor does it specifically prohibit warrantless searches or coerced confessions. Denial of these rights might be perfectly rational or fit within long traditions of intolerant or abusive behavior by the government.

Truly protecting constitutional rights requires more than staring intently at the document or staging a dramatic reading on the House floor. The Constitution requires interpretation, and interpretation seems to require courts to *discriminate* between those rights the vague text captures and those it doesn't.

Discriminating between rights is the dominant strategy across the political spectrum in the United States. For many conservatives, the rights to be protected are those the Framers or those in their generation would have thought encompassed within the Constitution. Progressives typically reject this "originalist" approach, which seems inconsistent with the right to birth control or abortion or even racially integrated schools. But like conservatives, progressives also feel compelled to discriminate between rights they deem more fundamental and those, such as the right to commercial advertising or to carry firearms, that they see as insubstantial or destructive. Everyone's a little bit "rightsist."

But "rightsism" gives judges much more power than they deserve in a democracy. For the rightsist, whether education or abortion rights, gun rights or rights against police brutality, religious conscience or same-sex marriage, are protected depends on the judge's interpretive philosophy or political background. Given the backgrounds of judges, it should come as no surprise that many of the problems invested with the solemnity of constitutional rights are the worries of First World men — access to politicians, to pornography, or to open-shop workplaces. Rights more essential to the poor, such as the right to food or shelter or health care, are left out altogether within our system. Judges do not justify their decisions to recognize some rights but not others through the moral reflection that these choices seem to demand. Rather, driving the judges' analysis are their skill and creativity with historical research or textual exegesis and their ability to apply their legal training to the parsing of previously decided cases. Judges treat disagreements about rights as little more than a mystery to be solved by good lawyering, as if it is their business, like that of another Holmes, to know what other people do not.

But rights conflicts are not mystery novels. They are principled, often reasonable disagreements about political morality that affect the intimate lives, the hopes and dreams, of actual people. We don't disagree about rights because some of us are correct about the rights we have and others of us are wrong, lacking the clues needed to solve the mystery. We disagree about rights because we are human beings who are different from one another and yet must live together.

We need a different strategy for responding to competing rights, a strategy of rights *mediation.* U.S. courts recognize relatively few rights, but strongly. They should instead recognize more rights, but weakly. In determining that someone holds a constitutional right, judges should be more generous, more respectful of the differences among us, of the idiosyncrasies of our personal values and commitments. But that same respect should lead judges to be more discerning in deciding how far my right goes as it comes predictably into conflict with the rights of others. Mediation is not about deciding, for all time, which side of a rights conflict is right and true — the campus speaker or the student, the baker or the same-sex couple, the shop owner or the protester. Mediation is also not about simply "balancing" one side against the other or maximizing social welfare in the way of a crude economic formula. Mediation is about paying unwavering attention to the *facts* of the parties' dispute.

Mediating rights would mean shifting our collective emphasis from whether the Constitution includes particular rights to what the government is actually doing to people and why. Courts should devote less time to parsing the arcane legalisms — probes of original intentions, pedantic textual analysis, and mechanical application of precedent — that they use to discriminate between the rights they think the Constitution protects and the ones they think it doesn't, and spend more time examining the facts of the case before them: What kind of government institution is acting? Is there good cause, grounded in its history, procedures, or professional competence, to trust its judgments? What are its stated reasons? Are those reasons supported by evidence? Are there alternatives that can achieve the same ends at less cost to individual freedom or equality? Knowing that courts will ask these kinds of questions makes other government actors ask them, too, as they craft their own policies and structure their own behavior. It makes rights recognition and enforcement a shared enterprise, one that is of, by, and for all the people and not just the judges.

None of which is to say that rights shouldn't matter. Of course they should. But the one indispensable right in a democracy is the right to participate in one's own governance. That is the right a state denies when, for example, it keeps Blacks from voting or participating equally in civil society; when the government investigates college professors or prosecutes labor organizers for espousing communism; or when a state outlaws birth control, keeping women permanently homebound. But acting through its judges, the state can also deny us the right to govern ourselves when it too easily allows an individual claim of a right to spoil the fruits of self-governance — the law.

A twenty-first-century court shouldn't earn its keep by *declaring* rights but rather by *reconciling* them. The American experiment rests on the audacious belief that liberalism and pluralism are not just compatible but also mutually constitutive. Until we can turn the language of rights that dominates our politics into a language of reconciliation, the experiment will remain in peril. The last century gave us the constitutional tools to fight political exclusion. In this century, we need the tools to build a politics of pluralism.

The benefits of this approach don't end at self-governance. A strategy of rights mediation also would bring U.S. rights in line with those of the rest of the world, while at the same time recovering the most essential lessons of the American Founding. It would reforge the necessary connection between rights and justice, so that whether rights are given effect depends on the real world rather than legal fictions. It would accommodate conflicts among rights instead of erasing the values and commitments of one side or the other. In doing so, it would lower the stakes of those conflicts, enabling us more readily to see each other as friends who disagree instead of enemies who must annihilate each other. And it would treat judges, legislators, and other legal decision-makers as human beings who, because they are prone to error, should treat their decisions about matters of dignity and democracy, of life and death, with a measure of humility that they too often lack.

The Wrong Kind of Exceptionalism

Americans often take great pride in their exceptionalism. They cite the unique features of the U.S. system as the reason it has so long endured. Americans are suspicious of what Supreme Court justice Clarence Thomas has called "foreign moods, fads, or fashions." That suspicion is justified at times, but not when it comes to rights. The American embrace of strong rights husbanded by federal judges is foreign to most of the country's history. The years since its advent have been marked by rising polarization and deteriorating levels of trust in government and in one another.

Adopting a strategy of rights mediation could help mitigate these unfortunate trends and pull American rights into the modern world. The approach this book urges has been adopted by virtually all the constitutional systems of the developed world, save that of the United States. And yet it is less foreign than it might seem. The Framers' vision of rights has more in common with modern Canada than it does with the modern United States.

For the Framers, constitutional rights were not primarily intended to protect minorities or unpopular dissenters from the tyranny of the majority, as we so often describe them today. Rather, rights were meant to protect that very majority from factional capture or executive overreach. The statesmen of the Founding generation saw the right to participate in self-government, via the vote and the jury, as sacrosanct. But for them, the substantive rights that we today associate with the Supreme Court's docket — freedom of speech, the right to bear arms, rights of equality, due process of law, and so forth — were best protected by legislatures and juries, not judges. This reflected the Framers' understanding that other local institutions besides courts — institutions such as churches, families, and even the militia — also had a role in self-governance, and thus also had a role both in defining rights and in deciding how rights could be limited in the public interest. Rights lived less in judicial chambers than in meetinghouses and jury rooms, at the ballot box and in the streets.

Indeed, the Bill of Rights didn't even originally apply against state and local officials. This wasn't an oversight. It reflected a considered view that responsive, accountable, democratic governments grant and preserve rights; they don't threaten them. Individuals and minority groups using the power of federal courts to upset community judgments wasn't what the Bill of Rights protected — it was what it protected *against*.

Today, an approach called "proportionality," though exotic in the United

States, dominates courts around the world. A structured way of setting rights against government interests, proportionality would have resonated with America's Founders but today is more commonly associated with Canadians and Germans. Courts that adopt proportionality tend to recognize a wide range of rights — far wider than in the United States — but the courts' attention trains on the ways in which government can, or can't, limit those rights. In these other countries, limiting rights is not just something the government can do in an emergency, when the time bomb is ticking. Rather, rights are *inherently* limited.

The widespread refusal of many U.S. judges and lawyers to accept proportionality has deeply American roots, but those roots don't run to the Founding. The American legal profession's aversion to proportionality emerged out of a shortsighted attempt to correct a tragic, peculiarly American mistake — indeed, the defining mistake of the twentieth century: we protected the wrong rights. During the same period in which courts were shamefully disregarding the rights of Black citizens, they were routinely deploying the Fourteenth Amendment to shield businesses from health, safety, and labor regulations. In 1905, two years after Oliver Wendell Holmes Jr. and his fellow justices blithely allowed Alabama to deny Jackson Giles his right to vote, the Supreme Court struck down a New York law that capped the number of hours bakers could work in bakeries, saying it violated the shop owners' right to contract.

The decision, called *Lochner v. New York,* would come to define four decades of constitutional law, and not in a good way. During the so-called *Lochner* era, courts struck down minimum wage and maximum hour laws; they invalidated bans on child labor and efforts to protect workers' collective bargaining rights; and, in the 1930s, they redlined significant chunks of President Roosevelt's New Deal and threatened to kneecap many of the landmark laws — Social Security and unemployment insurance, the National Labor Relations Act, and the Fair Labor Standards Act — that have come to define the modern welfare state.

The Supreme Court overruled *Lochner* in 1937 following Roosevelt's landslide victory in the 1936 election, and the case has since become an epithet among mainstream judges and lawyers, held up to this day as an example of exactly how *not* to do constitutional law. The legal establishment's rejection of *Lochner* rests on the idea that courts should trust democratic governments to make sensitive decisions in complex regulatory environments.

But the *Lochner* era wasn't just about the overprotection of the right to contract. Courts during this period were equally conspicuous in their indifference to basic civil rights and civil liberties. The state can't always be trusted. In particular, a government that racially segregates its citizens or jails them for opposing a war or sympathizing with the Communist Party is in the grips of a pathology. We cannot and should not defer to such a government when it makes decisions, sensitive or otherwise, about its people.

The Civil War and its long-simmering aftermath stand as violent testament to the inadequacy of the Framers' original vision of rights to confront racial discrimination or other forms of systemic, intentional subordination. Sometimes your political opponent really is out to destroy you — to use the violence of the state to preserve your subservience, to deny your citizenship, to enshrine your social and economic inferiority in law. When, as during the Jim Crow era, local governments threaten rights flagrantly and in bad faith, courts are called upon to respond with courage and resolve, to condemn the injustice of the government's actions with clarity. The idea that rights are sacred, to be interfered with in only the most emergent of circumstances, is premised on this kind of pathological government, one that makes itself the enemy of its citizens.

And so a stark division emerged within the courts, later spreading beyond. On the one hand were challenges to the ordinary operation of the regulatory and welfare state — wage and hour laws, occupational licensing, social insurance, safety regulations, and the like. Following the lead of Holmes, who dissented forcefully in the *Lochner* case, twentieth-century courts would simply refuse to entertain rights challenges to these laws. On the other hand were core civil rights violations, such as racial discrimination and freedom of speech and religion. Courts would come to frame the interests these laws implicated in the lofty language of rights — unassailable, nearly absolute, and the peculiar province of the judicial branch. Violations of these rights represented a breach of trust. Identifying rights came to take on a solemnity that demanded complete vindication. If rights claimers aren't going to win, judges seemed to say, what they're claiming must not be rights.

These categories persist today, but they are far too crude for the modern world. The 1960s and 1970s witnessed a mushrooming of rights challenges that fit neither the traditional civil rights model nor the kinds of contract or property rights Holmes has been celebrated for rejecting: rights to gender equality and sexual freedom; criminal justice rights; free speech rights for college students, war protesters, and civil rights advocates; rights arising out of the provision of government services such as Aid to Families with Dependent Children (AFDC) and Social Security; rights to racial justice in public accommodations and housing. A struggling family's right not to be kicked off a state's welfare rolls arbitrarily, a criminal defendant's right to a government lawyer, a white college applicant's right not to have race used in admissions, a woman's right to have an abortion: none of these fit neatly into the binary categories of the mid-twentieth century.

In each case, the government might be pursuing a perfectly legitimate interest. The government's funds are limited; it might not be able to give welfare to everyone who wants it or fancy lawyers to every criminal defendant. A college admissions office might implement an affirmative action plan not to preserve white supremacy but to dismantle it. A community might ban abortion not to subordinate women but because it believes in good faith that abortion devalues human life. The government's goals in such cases aren't the dehumanizing ends of the Jim Crow South. But it also makes neither moral nor constitutional sense to say, with Holmes, that no rights are at issue at all. The binary approach to rights that sought to correct for the mistakes of the twentieth century is deeply unstable in the twenty-first. Getting race wrong early has led courts to get everything else wrong since.

Rights in a modern constitutional democracy are not the glass we break in the emergency of a government captured by bigots or morons. They are the predictable byproducts of ordinary governance in a pluralistic society in which we disagree with one another about important matters. Rights are not precious. They are all around us.

Rights and Justice

I have my rights, and you have yours. If they conflict, the stakes will be high. The winner will have a nearly absolute claim against the government, and the loser will remain at its mercy. Reaching a decision under these circumstances requires a keen sense of justice. Yet the rights that U.S. courts actually recognize bear little relationship to what justice requires.

Take two real cases.

In one case, an information processing firm called IMS Health wanted to scrape data from pharmacies, including the prescription practices of individual doctors, which it could then sell to drug companies wanting to better tailor their marketing to physicians. Vermont wanted to protect the privacy of doctors and their patients, so it passed a law banning the sale of prescription data. The Supreme Court struck the law down, saying it invaded the *free speech* rights of drug companies.

In the other case, a Black man named Warren McCleskey was sentenced to death for shooting a white police officer in Atlanta. His lawyers presented persuasive evidence that murder defendants were more than four times as likely to be sentenced to death when their victims were white than when they were Black. The lawyers told the Supreme Court that racial bias infests the death penalty process all the way from prosecutors' charging practices to jurors' assessments of witness credibility to judges' sentencing decisions. McCleskey lost. Writing for the majority, Justice Lewis Powell worried openly that a win for McCleskey meant judges would need to excise racism from the entire criminal justice system. Four years later, the State of Georgia electrocuted him.

No reasonable person believes IMS Health's right to sell prescription data to drug companies is more important than Warren McCleskey's right to an unbiased death sentence. The Constitution says nothing about selling prescription data, but it does say states can't deny "equal protection of the laws." So why is IMS Health now able to sell that data in Vermont, while McCleskey is dead? It's because faced with a novel rights claim in each case, the Supreme Court chose to discriminate between rights instead of mediating them.

This approach to rights has shattered the Court's moral compass. The justices placed IMS Health's rights claim into a *category*—freedom of speech—they were able to recognize. Under the U.S. approach, this meant Vermont's effort to protect the medical privacy of its citizens had to be treated with the same skepticism as if the state were tossing a political prisoner in the clink.

The justices drew very different lines in McCleskey's case. Unlike most courts around the world, the U.S. Supreme Court refuses to see government acts that produce racial or sex disparities—like McCleskey's death sentence—as raising *any* constitutional concern unless the government specifically intends to cause the disparity. The Court's austerity in this area is a hangover from the *Lochner* debacle. Acknowledging these "disparate impact" claims would, the Court has said, require that it invalidate just about every law, and so it has said that no such rights may be recognized constitutionally. It means, for example, that race-conscious remedies for structural racial inequality draw the Court's ire, whereas the underlying inequality itself does not. McCleskey's complaint of lethal racial bias thus wound up in the same anemic constitutional category as a driver's complaint about street-cleaning rules.

This perverse pattern recurs throughout American constitutional law. Like an insurance company that reimburses a face-lift but not chemo treatments, U.S. courts discriminate between rights with all the sensitivity of a corporate algorithm. According to the Supreme Court, a wealthy partisan has a *right* to form a corporation that spends unlimited sums on political campaigns. A schoolteacher has a *right* to avoid contributing to the union's cost of negotiating her collective bargaining agreement. Modern-day Nazis clad in SS uniforms and proudly waving swastika flags have a *right* to march in an Illinois suburb that thousands of Holocaust survivors call home. But Americans have no right to food, to shelter, or to health care. Having no strategy for *mediating* rights, the justices have steadfastly insisted that any rights that can't be protected absolutely aren't rights at all. As Justice William Brennan wrote in dissent in McCleskey's case, his fellow justices seemed worried about "too much justice."

That's not hyperbole. Disparate impact claims like McCleskey's lose out because, in the Supreme Court's words, acknowledging such rights might require the Court to invalidate any tax and welfare laws that "may be more burdensome to the poor and to the average black than to the more afflu-ent white." Affirmative rights like the right to education lose out because, in the Court's words, they would call into question gross inequities in basic municipal services such as policing and firefighting. Rights for people with disabilities lose out because, the Court says, the same logic would apply not just to physical handicaps but also, for example, to mental illness, addiction, and old age. Even the most robotic indifference to the dignity of people with disabilities bucks no constitutional prohibition, yet we hold sacred James Maloney's right to his nunchucks.

This should be no one's idea of justice. It needn't be the Constitution's either. The question for courts shouldn't be *whether* Warren McCleskey or a poor schoolchild or a disabled American has constitutional rights. It should be what the government is obligated to do in virtue of those rights. The degree of amelioration or investment required of the government shouldn't depend on cold dissections of commas or resurrections of ancient scrolls. It should depend on the real-world burdens on the people claiming rights and on the government's real-world motives, behavior, and constraints in denying them.

A more proportional approach to rights wouldn't just be more fair; it would be more sustainable, too. A litigant who loses today need not, like McCleskey or like Americans with disabilities, simply be erased from the Constitution. On different facts, with different burdens on the plaintiff or weaker justifications for the law, they might win tomorrow. They therefore have reason to stay invested in the constitutional project.

Putting the Politics Back in Political Conflict

The purpose of politics is to negotiate over disagreement. The purpose of law is to set the ground rules for that negotiation. But negotiation requires that each side have leverage. The American approach to rights conflicts makes that impossible.

Conflicting rights can't both be absolute, and so when U.S. judges face a conflict of rights, they cancel one right or the other. Abortion laws pit the rights of women to sovereignty over their bodies and to equal opportunity to participate in civil society against the right of fetuses to life; courts have chosen to say that fetuses have no rights. A baker, florist, or photographer who refuses, on religious grounds, to participate in a same-sex wedding claims a right to religious freedom that competes with the right of gays and lesbians to be served without discrimination; courts have chosen not to see the right against sexual orientation discrimination as bearing constitutional weight. Both sides in the battles over race-based affirmative action policies at colleges and universities claim to be vindicating the right to an unbiased admissions process; courts have insisted on seeing only the rights of the rejected applicant.

American courts' failure to acknowledge the presence of rights on multiple sides of conflicts wreaks havoc on politics. Nowhere is this more obvious or with a less happy ending than in the abortion area. The Supreme Court's declaration in *Roe* that fetuses have no constitutional rights and that abortion can be only lightly regulated before the third trimester realigned abortion politics. Prior to *Roe,* the anti-abortion movement was a big tent that included, for example, birth control advocates, Great Society liberals, and Black evangelicals. This makes sense for a movement that tries to accomplish its ends primarily through legislative politics. After *Roe,* the movement splintered as anti-abortion advocates pursued a constitutional amendment, incremental court victories, and changes in the composition of the Supreme Court. Abortion rights advocates strategically adopted the language of "choice," aligning abortion rights with a classically liberal premise that lent itself to judicial rather than political enforcement. Abortion politics in the United States today plays out in the Supreme Court's shadow, making the very idea of legislative compromise seem profoundly naïve.

This realignment was not inevitable. The best evidence of that is the parallel universe in Germany. In 1975, West Germany's constitutional court heard that country's own momentous abortion case at nearly the same time as *Roe,* approaching it from a startlingly different perspective. Abortion was illegal in almost all circumstances until the Social Democrats tried to pass a decriminalization law in 1974. The question before the West German court was not whether restrictions on abortion infringed the rights of women but rather whether liberalizing abortion interfered with the rights of fetuses. The court struck down the law for this reason. But rather than structure abortion jurisprudence around the rights of either women or fetuses alone, the court has consistently structured the law around *both* sets of rights.

In practice, this has meant that the German government must take seriously both the constitutional value of women's autonomy and its commitment to fetal life. There, as in the United States, the best way to protect fetal life is not to outlaw abortion (which only drives the practice underground) but rather to provide women with meaningful alternatives to termination. How women actually behave in the shadow of abortion laws isn't a platitude about the country's founders or a monologue about privacy. It's a fact about the world. And by emphasizing the constitutional status of fetal life, the German court has forced political actors to account for that fact. The balance the Germans have struck is that abortion is decriminalized only in the first trimester or when indicated for particular reasons, but the state must provide prenatal care, childcare, and employment guarantees that encourage women to choose life rather than termination.

Abortion has become, in Germany, a subject of intense political negotiation among parties proceeding from radically different policy views. Remarkably, abortion politics in Germany today is less controversial than it was in the 1970s, and far less controversial than it is here. What's more, although the West German court started from a premise of fetal rights, today it is easier (and often much cheaper) for women to obtain abortions in Germany than in much of the United States.

We can't say for sure whether the German model could have worked in the United States, but it does suggest that violent, apocalyptic conflict over abortion rights isn't inevitable. Even the most fiercely contested, most deeply personal debates can be influenced by the legal rules courts put in place. When courts shape those rules by trying to mediate rights rather than minimize or discriminate among them, those differences have space to remain principled, strongly felt, and yet surmountable.

Rights mediation can channel conflicts of rights away from courts, which are ill-suited to open balancing, and into politics, where negotiation is both possible and clear-eyed. Americans have seen this dynamic firsthand in other electric debates over rights — only to see their political compromises undermined by rightsism in the courts.

For example, in the early race-based affirmative action cases of the 1970s, public institutions with politically accountable leadership were open about the perceived need to protect the rights of African-American applicants who found themselves at the business end of structural inequality. Typically, the policies that school administrators and public employers implemented were contrary to the interests of the racial groups to which the administrators and government officials themselves belonged. Often public officials faced political pressure from civil rights advocates to institute or continue such programs. Skeptics of affirmative action were also able, through politics, to voice their disapproval or question the burdens on white applicants. This is a healthy form of disagreement. There is little reason for courts to be especially skeptical of the resulting political arrangement.

Rejected applicants have nonetheless turned to the courts to protect their interests. In the Supreme Court's hands, an ordinary policy disagreement has been framed as a conflict between the "rights" of those (typically white) applicants, which the Court sees as sacred, and the "choices" of school officials to place unfair burdens on those applicants. The Supreme Court has seen those choices as purely discretionary and inherently suspicious.

But rights populate both sides of conflicts over race-based affirmative action — those of rejected applicants and those of admissions candidates suffering under the weight of structural inequality. The Supreme Court's failure to acknowledge this basic symmetry has produced a hot mess. The

Court has declared that a school's interest in "diversity," which conspicuously accrues to the benefit of white students, is its only constitutionally acceptable motivation. In service of this rationale, the Court has required schools to treat every applicant individually rather than as a member of a racial group, even though group disadvantage is what schools are trying to combat. This has led schools to be opaque about their motives and methods, undermining the basis for political negotiation. That lack of transparency then itself becomes a reason not to trust school administrators.

Judicial interventions in this area, as in so many others, have made us more suspicious of each other while correcting no particular injustice. We don't need another institution to remind us of our divisions, to tell us whether we have rights or not. Cable news and social media do that job well enough. What we need instead is for courts to call us to the table — kicking and screaming if need be, but at the table all the same.

Rights and Polarization

Americans are deeply fractured. Party polarization in Congress has reached heights not seen in at least a century. While there is mixed evidence of rising policy or ideological cleavage among voters, studies show that when people disagree with us, we *dislike* them at levels not seen since at least the Vietnam War era. The anemic response to the rights explosion has made these trends worse.

Rightsism has victims. Treating a rights conflict as a question of who has rights and who doesn't degrades our relationship to the law and to each other. By denying the loser any claim of rights, the court tells him not just that he has lost but that *he does not matter*. Although the loser's interests and projects remain important — perhaps even essential — to him, he is made an outsider to the law. He may become suspicious of political institutions. He may choose to participate in civic life sparsely or even subversively. He may, like Roeder, come to see those with divergent commitments or values as his mortal enemies rather than his fellow citizens.

A case about a wedding cake offers a striking study in how judges and litigants in the grips of rightsism can needlessly raise the temperature of political conflict. As courts and legislatures have extended marriage rights to same-sex couples, some artisans, such as photographers, florists, and bakers, have refused to serve same-sex weddings, claiming religious objections. In the first of the wedding cases to reach the Supreme Court, a Colorado baker refused to bake a custom cake for a same-sex wedding, citing his devout Christianity. To hear the parties, some pundits, and some of the amici who submitted briefs to the Supreme Court tell it, the baker was just like Jim Crow–era segregationists who put "Whites Only" signs in their windows, and the engaged couple were just like tin-pot dictators who force believers to submit to false gods. In this framing, the wedding cake case was a naked clash of rights, a battle for the soul of the country.

Except that it wasn't. The baker and the couple actually agreed on a surprising amount. They agreed that it would be illegal under state law for the baker to refuse service to a gay couple, for religious or other reasons, based on their sexual orientation. They also agreed that a professional baker need not sell his wares to all comers, indeed that he may refuse to sell to customers whose beliefs he disagrees with. The reason you likely didn't know any of that is because the modern American approach to rights encourages not just the parties but also the rest of us to tie our opponents' claims to the most extreme possible position. When a court flattens textured rights conflicts into a facile question of which side has rights, when it sidelines the particular facts, motives, and evidence that are actually before it in favor of *interpretive* questions about text or intent or historical values, it pays for lawyers and advocates to paint the rights their opponents seek as leading to absurd or destructive consequences. We blind ourselves to the dignity in each other's claims.

By divesting rights fights of their *righteousness,* mediation equips courts to mitigate rather than exacerbate polarization. They can thereby make progress even in conflicts that seem beyond saving. Ideological clashes between college students, for example, particularly around speaker invitations or campus harassment policies, are among the most visible emblems of the polarized state of American society. Conservative student groups court professional racists and provocateurs to make a point about freedom of speech, and their opponents deploy increasingly aggressive tactics to deny a platform to certain speakers. The crude language of rights adds unneeded fuel to these conflicts.

Courts confronted with harassment codes or cancel culture at public colleges are too easily seduced by the fact that schools are regulating the content of student speech and even the viewpoints embedded within it. The U.S. approach to rights can't easily distinguish these practices from *Nineteen Eighty-Four*–style Thought Police, leading courts to elevate drunken racial slurs or performative racism to the tracts of freedom fighters. But no less than the rights of individuals to expression, the Constitution also protects universities' freedom to determine how to educate their students, including just how to filter the information students engage with.

A court that views its role through the lens of mediation would pay less attention to jejune questions of whether schools are discriminating between content and viewpoint — which is, after all, what educators *do* — and more attention to contextual, factual questions of the schools' motives, methods, sanctions, exemptions, and track records in applying them to actual cases. Creating a civil campus environment is a high calling for a university, no less so than its commitment to academic freedom. The modern information environment calls for institutions that can play the role of curator; educators should be on the front lines, and they need discretion to do their jobs. A rightsist approach prevents schools from meeting this challenge. The next generation will pay the price.

On Humility and Healing

The spell of rights is an ancient problem. You might (or might not) recall from high school the core conflict of Sophocles's *Antigone*, between the title character, who wishes to bury her fallen brother Polynices, and her uncle

Creon, the ruler of Thebes, who refuses an honorable burial to a man who took up arms against the kingdom. Antigone is too wedded to "the bond of kinship" to allow for exceptional cases or the validity of a royal command. Creon is too stubborn about his exercise of public power to respect "the sacred tie of blood." Antigone ends up hanging herself in prison, and Creon loses his wife and his son to suicide. It was for good reason that *Antigone* was the German philosopher G. W. F. Hegel's main text when he described a conflict between two diametrically opposed sides, each with a strong justification, as the "essence of tragedy."

We, too, are hurtling toward tragedy. The Constitution claims to spring from the mouths of "We the People of the United States." Its deepest flaw was its drafters' failure to understand that "the people" never speak with just one voice. They didn't then, and they don't now. Getting the Constitution right by the lights of some of those people means getting it wrong by the lights of others. The challenge, then, is to resolve conflicts under the Constitution without erasing some of the people in whose name it speaks.

The Framers sought an answer to this problem in political institutions that could seek justice through mediation: legislatures and juries, churches and families. But those institutions excluded and marginalized women and people of color. American lawyers, judges, and ordinary citizens eventually came to appreciate what the Framers refused to see, but we have stumbled toward an equally untenable extreme — one in which unelected judges choose the rights we have and enforce them at full throttle against bad-faith bigots and good-faith legislatures alike, while allowing the government free rein over whatever rights judges happen to leave behind. This, too, courts tragedy.

A constitution for the modern world asks judges neither to ignore nor to supplant politics, but rather to structure it, to push it, and to police it, giving the people of this country the tools to resolve our own disputes in a way that respects one another's legitimate ends. For the U.S. Constitution isn't just built for lawyers. It is built for citizens and aliens, for lovers and haters, for laborers and bosses, for partyers and essential workers. It is built for Karen

Finley and her chocolate body paint, for Jack Phillips and his wedding cakes, and for the couples Phillips refuses to serve. It is built for veterans and hippies, for atheists and priests, for Dr. George Tiller and even, for all his sins, for Scott Roeder. It is, to paraphrase James Madison, for everyone but the angels.

Part I

How Rights
Became Trumps

IN 1984, A WISCONSIN MAN named Randy DeShaney beat his four-year-old son, Joshua, into a coma, causing brain damage that left Joshua profoundly intellectually disabled for the rest of his life. County officials had been aware of Randy's abusive behavior but had failed to remove Joshua from his father's custody. Joshua's mother sued the county and lost. The Supreme Court said there is no constitutional right to be protected from private violence.

Four months later, the same Supreme Court unanimously struck down a federal law for violating a dial-a-porn company's right to sell phone sex recordings to horny guys.

We've come to a strange place. American courts draw firm lines, often in morally arbitrary ways, between the interests they consider rights and those they don't. The interests that courts count, they protect robustly from democratic politics, while those that they don't count remain wholly at the government's mercy. We sometimes describe this fetishism about rights — but just some rights — as foreordained by the Founding Fathers, but America wasn't born this way. This hard-edged rights discrimination was a shortsighted, contingent response to the explosion of rights in the 1960s, and it has failed us.

The Framers of the U.S. Constitution cared deeply about rights, but not in the way most Americans do today. The men who wrote rights into the Constitution did not view rights as a shield for individuals against the oppressive laws of their communities. Rather, rights were the freedoms that enabled a productive life. Communities made laws in order to protect these rights. The Bill of Rights, the Constitution's iconic collection of original rights, is best understood less as a charter of individual liberty than as a paean to self-government.

But American self-government died in the womb. The Framers did not count African slaves or their descendants as equal citizens and gave them no hand in governance. That form of discrimination was wounded at Appomattox, only to be supplemented by another. The post–Civil War constitutional amendments were meant to correct the Constitution's original sin but instead were repurposed by businesses claiming rights against health, safety, and labor regulations.

The middle of the twentieth century saw a momentous reversal. On the one hand, Progressives such as Felix Frankfurter and his legion of disciples amplified the message most memorably delivered decades earlier by Justice Oliver Wendell Holmes Jr. Dissenting from a 1905 decision invalidating a maximum hour law for bakery workers, Holmes counseled nearly complete deference to the state in the realm of economic regulation. On the other hand, the mid-century civil rights and civil liberties movements pushed for vigilance to combat Jim Crow, McCarthyism, and religious discrimination against Catholics and Jews, among others. What resulted was a two-track regime in which courts have been largely permissive of state regulation but have kicked into high gear once they have identified a "true" right.

The problem is that in a diverse and complex world, rights do not sort easily into the ones that are "true" and the ones that aren't. So when rights claiming exploded in the 1960s, American courts had no good answers to some very good questions. Does a welfare recipient have a right to a hearing before having her benefits cut? Does a Vietnam War protester have a right to burn his draft card? Does a Boston kindergartner have a right to be bused to an integrated elementary school? Does a teenager have a right to purchase a diaphragm? Does a murder defendant have a right to be read his rights?

In matters of gender equality, sexual privacy, reproductive freedom, social welfare, criminal justice, expressive freedom, and many other areas of public and private life, Americans advocated forcefully for their rights in the 1960s and 1970s, and they continue to do so today. American judges, lawyers, and legal scholars, whether conservative or progressive, activist or strict constructionist, originalist or living constitutionalist, keep searching for the correct rubric, the skeleton key that will reveal which rights are "true" rights and which are not. We're still looking for ways to discriminate.

Before we can figure out how to do better, we first need to understand how we got here.

1

Getting the Bill of Rights Right

A mericans see rights as our national inheritance. The Declaration of Independence speaks grandly, after all, of the "unalienable" rights to "Life, Liberty and the pursuit of Happiness." The Constitution's first ten amendments represent the first bill of rights ever to be written into a national constitution. The suggestion that rights have limits, and that those limits should be determined by democratic politics, feels foreign to many Americans. We are exceptional here for good reason, they say. America was born of strong rights, and America has worked.

In fact, America was not born of strong rights, and the America the Founders created did not work. Americans today typically associate rights with several key features: rights are meant to protect minorities and dissenters from the tyranny of the majority, they are enforced coercively by judges, and they are presumptively absolute, yielding only in special circumstances, if at all. These features better reflect the legacy of the 1960s than the 1780s. Early Americans believed deeply in "rights," but within Founding-era political thought, the institutions best suited to reconcile the competing demands of rights bearers were not courts but rather state and local political bodies: juries, churches, families, and legislatures. Democracy was not a tool of majoritarian oppression but rather was the means through which a community prevented oppression from the outside.

This vision of rights protection failed, obliterated in a savage war whose aftermath produced a very different vision of human freedom. The white statesmen of the Founding era drew the boundaries of community membership too narrowly, excluding African slaves and their descendants, women, and the indigenous population. What followed the Civil War was a more liberal-minded understanding of rights, tied to individuals flourishing in the face of potential state oppression.

Still, the Founders had a point. A rights culture too focused on individuals outsources rights recognition and enforcement to judges, who are not well suited to performing the sensitive mediation needed to reconcile the rights of diverse citizens. The more of our rights we hand to judges, the less of them we keep within the kinds of social and political institutions that are accustomed to — and usually better at — optimizing competing values. The Framers understood that well.

Rights as Self-Government

One year to the day before Americans declared their independence from Great Britain, a Presbyterian minister named John Joachim Zubly delivered a sermon from the sweltering floor of his Savannah, Georgia, meetinghouse. Zubly was Swiss by birth (né Hans Joachim Züblin), but since moving to Savannah at age seventeen, he had become not just a minister but a pamphleteer of some renown. No minister in pre-Revolutionary Georgia was more influential; Zubly would later be one of five Georgians selected as delegates to the Second Continental Congress in Philadelphia. His agitations against the Stamp Act and other British indignities formed no small part of the story that had brought that day in Savannah about. Delegates to Georgia's Second Provincial Congress had gathered there to decide whether to join the Association, an illegal colonial network formed to implement a trade ban against Great Britain. Georgia's eventual decision to join was an important step in the march to war.

"There was a time when there was no king in Israel, and every man did what was good in his own eyes," Zubly's sermon began. "The consequence was a civil war in the nation, issuing in the ruin of one of the tribes, and a considerable loss to all the rest." Law, the minister seemed to be saying, is needed to prevent a breakdown in the social order. But he continued: "And there was a time when there was a king in Israel, and he also did what was right in his own eyes." Foolish and imprudent, the king failed "to redress the grievances of the nation" and harshly treated "those who applied for relief." This king, too, "brought on a civil war." Law is essential, Zubly was telling his fellow patriots, but law cannot survive without justice.

Zubly titled his sermon "The Law of Liberty," but it wasn't about freedom of speech, or equal protection of the laws, or due process, or much else that modern Americans tie to the idea of rights. It was, singularly, about the importance of responsible representative government. "Liberty and law are perfectly consistent," Zubly exhorted. "Liberty does not consist in living without all restraint; for were all men to live without restraint, as they please, there would soon be no liberty at all . . . : Well regulated liberty of individuals is the natural offspring of laws, which prudentially regulate the rights of whole communities; and as laws which take away the natural rights of men, are unjust and oppressive, so all liberty which is not regulated by law, is a delusive phantom, and unworthy of the glorious name."

Zubly's vantage was typical of statesmen of his era. The colonists' demand was less for particular rights than for the right to decide for themselves, to forge their own path to liberty *through* law. As Zubly later wrote, "Let the Americans enjoy, as hitherto, the privilege to GIVE and GRANT by their own representatives, and they will give and grant liberally." The sermon was published in Philadelphia, the incipient nation's largest and most important city, and it circulated widely in the year leading up to the Declaration of Independence.

Americans today have forgotten Zubly's message. We have come to see lawmaking and rights as opposed to each other. According to this view, it is the peculiar province of a judge to uphold the constitutional rights of minorities, dissenters, and the oppressed against the majoritarian preferences of the legislature or the executive. Absent some emergency or other compelling reason for rights to be limited by law, rights are absolute. A right's very raison d'être, Americans today believe, is to exempt the rights holder from the law's reach.

No matter how often we tell ourselves otherwise, this vision of rights has no basis in the Founding era. Rights were a gift to the Constitution from its opponents. The document that emerged from the secret Philadelphia convention on September 17, 1787, granted few explicit rights. Neither states nor Congress were to pass bills of attainder (criminal laws that targeted an individual) or ex post facto laws (those that made a crime of conduct that had already occurred). Congress could not suspend access to the writ of habeas corpus except in cases of "rebellion or invasion." States could not unilaterally cancel contracts or discriminate against anyone based on his or her out-of-state citizenship. Some special rules relating to proof applied to treason prosecutions. Most significantly, all federal crimes (except impeachment crimes) had to be tried by jury. But that was it. Many prominent Framers, including Alexander Hamilton, James Madison, and James Wilson, believed a bill of rights was unnecessary and would be ineffective. Worse still, including a bill of rights in the Constitution might carry the ominous implication that the federal government retained whatever powers the bill of rights did not specifically limit.

The paucity of rights in the original Constitution lit a flame under the state ratifying conventions. The state constitutions that began to dot the colonial landscape throughout the 1770s typically contained their own bills of rights — the first written into a constitution anywhere in the world — modeled on rights available to Englishmen at common law. At the Virginia ratifying convention, Governor Edmund Randolph, who would become the country's inaugural attorney general, and George Mason, author of the Virginia Declaration of Rights, spoke early on and claimed that the lack of rights provisions were among the main reasons they had refused to sign the Constitution as delegates in Philadelphia. Several states, including the crucial states of Virginia and New York, ratified the Constitution only on the understanding that a bill of rights would promptly be added. Writing to Madison from Paris, where he was serving as ambassador to France, Thomas

Jefferson listed "the omission of a bill of rights" as his main gripe against the newly drafted Constitution. It is tempting, then, to date our modern zeal for rights to the ultimatums of that era. The colonists seemed to declare in 1787, as they had in 1776, that it was rights or bust.

Maybe it was. But we should not ascribe to Founding-era charters our own modern understandings of *what it means* to hold a right. It was well understood that many rights, including the "natural" right to pursue one's livelihood, could be limited by valid laws aimed at the public welfare. State bills of rights took the 1689 English Bill of Rights as their inspiration. The English model was a bold declaration of parliamentary supremacy, of the power of the people to have a hand in their own lawmaking. Indeed, it wasn't until Massachusetts became among the last states to adopt a constitution, in 1780, that any state bill of rights even used words of government obligation ("shall not") rather than mere aspiration ("ought not"). The colonists weren't just rebelling against a king, as when the English dethroned James II in the Glorious Revolution of 1688. Americans' complaint was as much against a parliament sitting in Westminster that did not *represent* them. To their minds, King George III's sin was not in denying those famous "unalienable" rights directly but rather in denying the colonists' right to self-determination. It was equally "self-evident," as Jefferson wrote in the Declaration of Independence, echoing Reverend Zubly, "that to secure these rights, Governments are instituted among Men, deriving their just powers from the consent of the governed."

Rights were a defense against arbitrary actions by an executive, his agents, or a distant sovereign. Holding a right did not necessarily mean holding an exemption from what would later be called the community's "police power" — its power to pass laws regulating the health, safety, and welfare of the citizenry. In passing laws, the state or local governments were exercising and indeed protecting the rights of the people as a whole.

For confirmation, we need only to think about who was insisting on constitutional rights in the 1780s. Adding a bill of rights to the Constitution was a strident (if perhaps disingenuous) demand of constitutional detractors, such as Virginians Patrick Henry, Richard Henry Lee, and George Mason. The concern of the Virginians and other anti-Federalists was not the familiar twentieth-century fear of tyranny of the majority. All had served in the state or colonial legislature. Henry had been born into a prominent Virginia family. Lee was the son of a Virginia governor. Mason's father served in Virginia's House of Burgesses, and his maternal grandfather was the colony's attorney general. Within the commonwealth, as propertied white men to the manor born, they were well positioned to resist policies they deemed oppressive. Colonial judges, appointed by the king or his loyal agents, weren't the heroes of independence, and judges' role under the new constitution was uncertain and below the fold. The men sent as delegates to the state ratifying conventions who insisted on the addition of a bill of rights thought *themselves* to be better guardians of liberty.

Americans believed deeply in "rights," then, but within Founding-era political thought, the institutions best suited to reconcile the competing demands of rights bearers were not courts but local representative bodies: legislatures and juries. Indeed, juries were considered a vital democratic body on a par with the assembly. Every one of the twelve states that had a written constitution at the time the Bill of Rights was ratified protected the right to trial by jury. (By contrast, only two protected freedom of speech.) The legislature and jury together, wrote John Adams twenty-five years earlier, in 1766, hold "wholly, the liberty and security of the people." Comprising ordinary citizens who, through their votes, had the power to nullify executive actions by construing the law or the facts in line with community norms, juries were a people's congress. "[The people] have no other fortification against wanton, cruel power," wrote Adams, "no other indemnification against being ridden like horses, fleeced like sheep, worked like cattle, and fed and cloathed like swine and hounds: No other defence against fines, imprisonments, whipping posts, gibbets, bastenadoes [*sic*] and racks."

The Constitution itself was built, deliberately, on the assumption that rights would reside more in these local political bodies than in courts. Madison's conception of the separation of powers contemplated rule at the federal level by neither a majority nor a minority but rather by minori*ties*, each in control of an important lever of government yet none in control of too many. "The great security against a gradual concentration of the several powers in the same department consists in giving those who administer each department the necessary constitutional means and personal motives to resist encroachments of the others," Madison wrote in Federalist No. 51. "Ambition must be made to counteract ambition. The interest of the man must be connected with the constitutional rights of the place." The backers of the Bill of Rights were not interested in protecting minorities from majority tyranny. They were interested in protecting their own governing majorities from others who might have different interests or agendas.

Rethinking the Bill of Rights

Fashioning a bill of rights was among the first orders of business for the First Congress of the United States. Though initially an opponent of such a bill, Madison made good on a Federalist promise to constitutional skeptics and took up the quill himself. Madison wrote twenty amendments, twelve of which were sent to the states for ratification and ten of which became the law of the land on December 15, 1791.

Yet the men who debated and ratified the rights codified in the first ten amendments to the Constitution were not primarily concerned with "rights" as we understand them today — protective of politically powerless dissenters, enforced by courts against majorities, and presumptively absolute. Rather, they cared about preserving the primacy of local representative bodies. Each of the provisions of the Bill of Rights — whether about freedom of speech, the right to bear arms, or the right to a jury trial — is best viewed as protecting self-governance, not individual liberty from the majority. Once we understand that, America's foundational charter of rights comes into sharper focus.

The First Amendment: Speech, Press, and Religion

Americans often view the First Amendment as sacred and inviolable. There is something to this. Speech is essential to politics and to the formation of the democratic culture on which politics depends. But that doesn't mean that every act that might count as "speech" is equally deserving of judicial protection. Modern courts have interpreted freedom of speech to extend nearly absolute constitutional protection to, among other things, selling drugs to doctors, filming sex acts for profit, contributing to super PACs, yelling racial slurs at one's college roommate, and paying union dues. The Framers would be appalled.

The First Amendment provides that "Congress shall make no law . . . abridging the freedom of speech, or of the press." And yet, less than seven years after the Bill of Rights was ratified, Congress passed and President John Adams signed into law the Sedition Act, which made it a federal crime to "write, print, utter or publish" any "false, scandalous and malicious writings" against the government, Congress, or the president. The first indictment brought under the act was brought against Vermont congressman Matthew Lyon for complaining in a letter to the editor of *Spooner's Vermont Journal* that under Adams, "every consideration of public welfare [was] swallowed up in a continual grasp for power, in an unbounded thirst for ridiculous pomp, foolish adulation, and selfish avarice." Supporters of the Sedition Act didn't think they were violating the Constitution. For them, freedom of speech and of the press didn't protect someone from being held liable for injuries their speech caused to others.

During the debates over the Sedition Act, Massachusetts congressman Harrison Gray Otis took to the House floor to describe freedom of speech in terms familiar from English common law and memorialized in Sir William Blackstone's famous *Commentaries on the Laws of England*: freedom of speech meant "nothing more than the liberty of writing, publishing, and speaking one's thoughts, under the condition of being answerable to the injured party, whether it be the Government or an individual, for false, malicious, and seditious expressions." Freedom of the press simply meant "an exemption from all previous restraints." The government could not interfere with a citizen's right to speak before the speech happened, as with a licensing requirement, and it couldn't do so just because public officials didn't agree with what the speaker was saying. But it could punish speech to protect against the many ways — such as fraud, defamation, or incitement

— in which words cause real harm. The Sedition Act was passed during an undeclared war with France and was sparked by fears that populist dissent could precipitate the kind of anarchic violence that characterized the early years of the French Revolution. As Connecticut's Samuel Dana put it during the House debate over the Sedition Act, "Can it, in the nature of things, be one of the rights of freemen to do injury?"

Of course, not everyone agreed that the Sedition Act was lawful. The act has become one of the most notorious historical instances of congressional overreach. It was famously resisted by the state legislatures of Virginia and Kentucky in resolutions ghostwritten, respectively, by James Madison and Thomas Jefferson. But for Madison and Jefferson, the main problem with the Sedition Act wasn't that freedom of speech or of the press necessarily protected the right to publish seditious views, but that the act was passed by Congress and not by a state. What the First Amendment demonstrated, Jefferson wrote, was a determination on the part of "the states or the people . . . *to retain to themselves* the right of judging how far the licentiousness of speech and of the press may be abridged without lessening their useful freedom, and how far those abuses which cannot be separated from their use should be tolerated."

Indeed, both the Virginia Declaration of Rights and the Kentucky Constitution specifically protected freedom of the press, and yet prosecutions for the common-law crime of seditious libel continued to be legal in both states, as in every other. In December 1792, Virginia's general assembly passed a law making it a felony to urge "by writing or speaking" the creation of a government other than Virginia's. At the time Madison was writing the Virginia Resolutions, the commonwealth had on its books a law against cursing.

The Federalists' firm distinction between prior restraint and punishment of speech after the fact sounds nitpicky to modern ears. If the First Amendment means to safeguard individual expressive autonomy or an open "marketplace of ideas," it is offended at least as much by a sedition prosecution as it is by a licensing regime. But an important difference between pre-publication restraint and post-publication punishment comes into focus when we think about the role of the jury. Every educated American at the time of the Bill of Rights knew the case of New York newspaper publisher John Peter Zenger. Zenger had been prosecuted for seditious libel after being critical of the British royal governor, William Cosby, including calling him a "Nero" and an "idiot." The judge, handpicked by Cosby, directed the jury to find for the state, but Zenger's renowned lawyer, Andrew Hamilton, urged the jury to ignore his instructions. Zenger was acquitted. Zenger's example is among those that led the colonists to appreciate the importance not only of a free press but of the jury as a site of political resistance.

Prior restraints left freedom of speech and of the press in the hands of the executive and his judges. Punishing speech after the fact enabled a defendant to appeal to the sense of the community. Indeed, part of the reason libel prosecutions were rare in eighteenth-century America — there appear to have been fewer than seven prosecutions and just two convictions for seditious libel during the entire colonial period — is because printers who published allegedly scandalous material were often more popular than their victims. Freedom of speech and of the press started off as protections for *majorities*.

So, too, with the First Amendment's religion provisions. The First Amendment begins by prohibiting Congress from passing laws "respecting an establishment of religion." The modern Supreme Court has put an individualistic gloss on this language, reading the ban on religious establishment as protecting religious dissenters from being offended by the government's endorsement of religion or of any particular religion. But as with the Constitution's speech and press provisions, the Framers viewed the religion provisions as protecting local majoritarian institutions, namely state churches and local congregations, from federal interference.

Recall that the Georgia Provincial Assembly convened on its first day in Reverend Zubly's meetinghouse and opened its session with a Calvinist sermon. Churches in colonial America were not just places of worship but also were typically the centers of town social and political life. State-church ministers were taxpayer supported. New York and Boston banned most traffic on the Sabbath. "The idiom of religion penetrated all discourse, underlay all thought, marked all observances, gave meaning to every public and private crisis," writes historian Patricia Bonomi of eighteenth-century America. "There was hardly a day of the week, to say nothing of the Sabbath, when colonial Americans could not repair to their churches for some occasion or other, all of which gave a certain tone to everything they did in their collective and communal capacity." Sermons were, by far, the most widely read colonial publications, and in the years preceding the Declaration of Independence, they often had overtly political content. As historian Jon Butler notes, "The most common denominator among pro-Revolution ministers was a state church pulpit."

It's not that American religious practice was especially tolerant or ecumenical. It's that it was especially *local*. Resistance to a centralized church was bound up with the same suspicion of interloping from a politically distant power that led to the Revolution. As Bonomi notes, "Because the colonies possessed no single established church that was perceived as being in league with the government, the American revolutionaries did not have to overthrow a church along with the state." The Church of England had priests throughout the colonies, with its biggest strength being in Virginia, but it was not the dominant religious force. There was no Anglican bishop for America, and religion in the colonies was highly diverse and decentralized — Puritans in New England, Dutch Reformers in New York, Presbyterians and Baptists in the Delaware Valley, Quakers in Pennsylvania, Episcopalians in Virginia, with great local variation both within cities and from town to town.

New England, for example, was dominated by the "parish system." Parishes could vary from town to town, from Presbyterian to Congregational to Baptist, but the parishes themselves were highly controlling. Selectmen would canvass the streets of Boston, enjoining people to go to church on pain of the stocks. The parish minister, writes Butler, "assumed responsibility for propagating and maintaining Christian practice and belief among the entire population, not just among a few knowledgeable and loyal believers." Local parishes were permitted to flout the laws of the state in deference to local customs and traditions. Dissenters didn't stick around to lodge their dissent; they had to find a more hospitable community.

This history makes plain that protections against religious establishment and protections of religious freedom were understood as shields for community-based churches, not for individual dissenters. State churches were publicly funded, with at least six states maintaining established churches when the Bill of Rights was drafted. Connecticut kept its church until 1818, Massachusetts until 1833. Those states that included disestablishment provisions in their constitutions did so primarily to enable local congregations to incorporate, thereby providing a measure of protection for church administrators over congregational assets, not to protect the rights of individual worshippers. As Supreme Court justice Joseph Story wrote in his celebrated 1833 constitutional treatise, *Commentaries on the Constitution,* "Probably at the time of the adoption of the Constitution, and of [the First Amendment], the general, if not the universal, sentiment in America was, that Christianity ought to receive encouragement from the state." The First Amendment was designed to shield local political institutions — which churches were — from those who would diminish or destroy them.

The Second and Third Amendments: The Well-Regulated Militia

The Second and Third Amendments have enjoyed very different receptions from modern advocates and courts. The Second Amendment's protection of the right to bear arms has become a rallying cry for an entire political party. A politician's National Rifle Association (NRA) "score" on Second Amendment issues can make or break their electoral prospects. The gun lobby takes the amendment as its brand, and its hold on the legal and political culture makes basic firearms regulation off-limits even in the face of intolerable levels of private gun violence.

By contrast, the Third Amendment is the runt piglet of the Bill of Rights. The Supreme Court has never applied or interpreted it, and even educated Americans can't tell you what it says or why it's in the Constitution. Supreme Court justice Samuel Miller, in an 1893 book on the Constitution, could offer little more in the way of analysis than that "this amendment seems to have been thought necessary."

For all their differences in notoriety, when we view the Second and Third Amendments through the lens of local representative institutions, the common object both were designed to preserve comes into focus: the militia. The text of the Second Amendment announces its purpose. It begins not with the famous "right to bear arms" but with a preamble: "A well regulated Militia, being necessary to the security of a free State, . . ." Manned by ordinary, armed citizens, the militia was a premodern form of policing. It could be — and very much was — limited by the state in furtherance of that goal. The amendment meant simply that the militia couldn't be similarly limited by the federal government.

The modern NRA opposes virtually all gun control as a threat to the Second Amendment. It opposes banning guns for individuals on terrorism watch lists, for people convicted of violent felonies, and for people facing temporary restraining orders. It opposes laws restricting concealed carry in elementary schools, airports, and bars. It opposes all registration, licensing, and training requirements. It opposes a United Nations treaty that bans the sale of weapons to governments and armed groups that have committed war crimes or genocide. The NRA and its supporters typically link their views to the Founding Fathers. As NRA chief Wayne LaPierre said a month after a shooter killed twenty young children and six adults at Sandy Hook Elementary School in Connecticut, "We are as absolutist as the Founding Fathers and framers of the Constitution. And we're proud of it."

This is rubbish. At the time the Second Amendment was written into the federal Constitution, several state constitutions included analogous provisions guaranteeing the right to keep and bear arms. And yet restrictions on firearms were commonplace. Less than two years after enacting a constitution that guaranteed the people's "right to bear arms for the defence of themselves and the state," Pennsylvania passed a law providing for confiscation of weapons from anyone who refused to pledge allegiance to the state or to the United States. Massachusetts included a right to bear arms in its constitution of 1780 and still saw fit, just three years later, to forbid Boston residents to bring loaded weapons into "any Dwelling-House, Stable, Barn, Out-house, Ware-house, Store, Shop or other Building" and, in 1792, to regulate the transporting of gunpowder in the capital. Tennessee, whose 1796 constitution guaranteed "that the freemen of this State have a right to Keep and to bear Arms for their common defence," banned concealed carry in 1821. As historian Saul Cornell has noted, passage of the Second Amendment heralded more, not less, regulation of guns.

The need to temper the reach of rights is more obvious in the Second Amendment area than in most. Restrictions on who may bear arms, of what kind, and where they may brandish them cannot be completely off-limits in a functioning society. It is also clear, and too easily ignored by gun rights zealots, that gun control is not simply the edict of a tyrant looking to snuff out challenges to his authority. Supporters of gun regulation fear for their safety and for the safety of their families, friends, and fellow citizens. They are traumatized by show-and-tell being supplanted by active shooter drills in schools. They understand themselves as having a powerful personal interest — that is, a *right* — to be substantially free of private violence. They protect that right not primarily by going to court and invoking the Second Amendment but rather by passing laws. The fact that gun laws protect rights to personal safety does not negate the fact that Americans also have a right to bear arms. It simply means that rights populate both sides of the battle over gun control.

Not just that, but the Second Amendment was specifically crafted as an adjunct to law and order, not an exception to it. For Americans of the Founding era, legislatures and juries were the most significant institutions of local political control, but they were not the only ones. An inheritance from the English Bill of Rights, the right to bear arms is sewn from the same cloth as the right to a jury trial. In the absence of an organized police force in England, detective work fell to members of the community who might have had special knowledge about the circumstances of an offense or civil dispute — this was the precursor of the grand jury. Apprehension of fugitives or suppression of riots — workaday police work in modern times — relied on the "hue and cry" and other forms of private organizing. Groups of citizens banded together to help the sheriff solve crimes and keep the peace. A white man had not just a right but a duty to be armed.

The right to bear arms was thus a common feature of colonial charters and later state constitutions. This right was not primarily protected in order to wage war on the federal government or to resist some shadowy tyranny, but rather in anticipation of quite specific threats to public order — from common criminals to political rioters to revolting slaves to hostile indigenous tribes — that armed white citizens might be called upon to resist. As Akhil Reed Amar notes, the "militia" did not at the time refer to what we might think of today as the National Guard, but to the full body of arms-bearing citizens.

This understanding makes sense of the numerous state and local regulations of guns at the time. States' ability to regulate firearms was inseparable from their dominion over the militia. The most common regulation of firearms in the eighteenth century involved controlling the militia itself. Thus the government could keep a registry of who had firearms. It could require citizens to report for inspection of their weapons. Several states restricted Black Americans from carrying guns. Founding-era Americans were committed less to a bunker mentality or private self-defense than to white communal self-reliance, what Jefferson called the "boldness, enterprise and independence of mind" that gun ownership could help nurture.

The Third Amendment was also meant to safeguard the primacy and independence of the militia. Its ban on peacetime quartering of soldiers without consent has the feel of a historical footnote, belonging to a time when the U.S. homeland was not just an imaginable theater of war but a likely one. The abuses it was intended to repel evoke invasions of privacy, which today we associate with the Fourth Amendment's barrier to unreasonable searches and seizures. But fresh insight into this forgotten amendment emerges when we view the Bill of Rights as primarily about *who* gets to protect rights: the white community, via the militia, and the white male head of household.

The amendment's quartering ban was a backdoor assault on a standing federal army. Federalist supporters of the Constitution succeeded in allowing for the possibility of a standing army (so long as it was reauthorized every two years), but it would be more difficult to maintain such an army if soldiers had no place to stay. By contrast, the militia comprised local citizens who had no need for housing. The Third Amendment, like the Second, was therefore a means of protecting the militia and the local autonomy it conferred.

The Third Amendment was also, of course, about the sanctity of the home, but perhaps not in the way most obvious to modern Americans. The expression "A man's house is his castle" was in wide circulation at the time and was frequently invoked in connection to the ban on quartering. The saying is just as gendered as it sounds. It contemplates a degree of social control that unsettles the modern listener.

Consider some of the complaints memorialized in a series of newspaper articles called the "Journal of the Times" or "Journal of Occurrences," Samuel Adams's published diary of Boston's legal, social, and political affairs in 1768 and 1769. The journal, otherwise comprising banal descriptions of this or that festival and detailed accounts of such wonders as the flax-spinning prowess of the ladies of Beantown, is peppered liberally with numerous gripes about the behavior of the British soldiers who occupied the city at the time. Two complaints in particular loomed large: the soldiers' treatment of women and their interactions with slaves.

For example, two women had to take "refuge" in a house to evade a soldier's "solicitations," only to be followed inside by the soldier, who then stabbed the homeowner with his sword. A local magistrate tried to break up a riot started by a soldier claiming a female passerby as his wife ("as usual with those people"). A young woman passing through Long-Lane was "stopt and very ill-treated by some soldiers," who "seiz'd her as their prey" before her husband came to the rescue. A soldier entered the house of an "aged woman" on the pretense of discussing the Bible with her and then tried to rape her, "notwithstanding her years." Some two weeks later, a "girl at New-Boston" was "knock'd down and abused by soldiers for not consenting to their beastly proposal." A "married niece of a distinguished ship builder" was stalked by soldiers and "treated . . . with great rudeness" until she could "recover the shelter of her uncle's house." A "worthy old gentleman" found a soldier in bed with "a favourite grand-daughter." The soldier refused to leave, "saying she was his wife," having earlier absconded with her and married her before "a person drest as a priest." A woman was reported as having collapsed and died of her wounds on her way to a fish market after having "been recently ravished." An ensign followed a woman home and tried to break into her house. He later returned and, told by her husband that she was married, said, "I don't care whose wife she is . . . for by G–d you shan't keep her long, and if you don't put your head into the window immediately, I'll be d — d if I don't blow your brains out." The husband went for his pistol but was kept from firing it "by the fright and intreaties of his wife."

Colonial Bostonians also protested the British regulars' efforts to sow disorder among Boston's slave population. Massachusetts had about five thousand slaves, roughly half of whom lived in and around Boston, with its teeming commercial shipbuilding, fishing, and distilling industries. Boston slaves were typically domestic servants rather than field laborers, and so they were intimately embedded in their masters' home lives. Adams's October 29, 1768, entry describes several physical assaults by officers on local residents, noting that "the most atrocious offense and alarming behaviour" was that of a captain who tried to "persuade some Negro servants to ill-treat and abuse their masters, assuring them that the soldiers were come to procure their freedoms, and that with their help and assistance they should be able to drive all the Liberty Boys to the devil." One night, three officers were overheard saying, "'If the Negroes could be made freemen, they should be sufficient to subdue these damn'd rascals.'" A week later, a group of soldiers entered a judge's house and "were very free with the blacks, to whom they declared a liking," before being forced out by armed neighbors. The selectmen were so alarmed by these incidents that they instituted a curfew for "Negro servants."

These reports betray a concern less with privacy in the modern sense than with social control. The problem wasn't having to share a bathroom. It was that a white man, king of his castle, had to compete with other men for the women and girls of his home, for the loyalty and service of his servants and slaves, for control over the care and upbringing of his children. The words of Joseph Galloway, a Pennsylvania politician who tried to stave off the Revolution, are instructive. He warned that the Continental Army would "[travel] over your estates, [enter] your houses — your castles, . . .

[seize] your property, . . . [ravish] your wives and daughters, and afterwards [plunge] the dagger into their tender bosoms." The injury the British regulars inflicted fell upon an institution — the white family — as much as upon any individual. The Third Amendment, like the rest of the Bill of Rights, was meant to prevent an institutional injury.

The Fourth Through Eighth Amendments: The Jury

The jury sits at the heart of the Bill of Rights. Each of the five amendments numbered four through eight regulates an aspect of the civil or criminal justice process, and each takes special care to safeguard the jury's role in those processes. These amendments protect defendants and other targets of the criminal justice system, yes, but the way they do so is by entrusting defendants' rights to juries rather than to judges or the executive.

Before the thirteenth century, English criminal disputes were typically settled by ordeal. For a range of crimes, from murder to forgery to witchcraft, the accused might be forced to walk three paces carrying a hot iron. If his wound was "clean" three days later, he was innocent; pus or discoloration was a sign of guilt. Or a suspected offender might be bound and immersed in a cold stream; sinking to the bottom testified to her innocence. Trial by battle was typically reserved for civil cases, in which the battle was fought by hired "champions." In cases of private criminal charges ("appeals of felony"), the accused would fight the accuser personally and to the death. If the defendant was beaten but not killed, he would be hanged on the spot.

King Henry II did the world a favor by offering trial by jury as an alternative to battle in property disputes. The jury took on added significance after the Fourth Lateran Council of 1215, at which Pope Innocent III forbade clerical participation in ordeals. With priests no longer available to sacralize the irons or the water, ordeals declined in popularity, leaving the jury trial as an available replacement in criminal trials. The fate of the accused would rest not on divine intervention but, more sensibly, on the community's local knowledge of the facts.

Jury service is lampooned today as an ordeal of a different sort, a tedious and thankless imposition best avoided by the savvy. Modern jurors are less actors than acted upon. They sit in a sterile room beneath flickering fluorescent lighting waiting for their name to be called, hoping it isn't. They endure inscrutable interrogations by lawyers and judges during voir dire, with some sent off and others forced to stay, for reasons unknown. Those selected for trial spend half the time watching the attorneys huddle in private with the judge and the other half wondering about lunch. A studiously observed distance between the lay juror and the legal professional has become the dominant reality of the American jury system. It can feel quite pointless.

It wasn't always so. Jurors once ran the show. Medieval juries were chosen because, as locals, they were likely to have first- or secondhand information about the facts of the case. They came not to listen but to speak. The self-informing function of the jury declined in significance in subsequent centuries, owing in no small part to the Black Death, which killed 40 percent of the English population and reoriented communal policing along the way. But well into the eighteenth century in the colonies, juries routinely decided both the law and the facts, undisciplined by judges, who were often clergy or farmers or blacksmiths, not professionals trained in the law.

The first ten amendments to the U.S. Constitution brim with jury protections. The Fifth Amendment protects the grand jury directly. The Sixth Amendment guarantees a petit jury in criminal cases, and the Seventh Amendment preserves the right to a jury in civil cases. Although Article III of the Constitution guarantees a jury trial in criminal cases, the Bill of Rights strengthened the guarantee by requiring that a trial be held not just in the state but in the federally defined "district" in which the crime was committed. As the Virginia Ratifying Convention delegate William Grayson said in protesting the inadequacy of the Article III guarantee, federal officials could select jurors "from any part of the state" and thereby "can hang any one they please, by having a jury to suit their purpose." An act allowing for treason trials to be held anywhere in the British Empire had been the subject of intense pre-Revolutionary opposition in the colonies. The more local the exercise of political power the jury represented, the better.

The other rights that appear in the Sixth Amendment also relate to protection of the jury's role in the administration of criminal justice. Trials needed to be "speedy" to prevent pretrial executive detention from substituting for a jury trial. The right to confront and to call witnesses ensured that the accused had a right equal to the state's to make sure the jury was well-informed about the facts. The Sixth Amendment also guarantees a right to counsel, whose expertise could safeguard the integrity of the jury's deliberation and verdict. The right to counsel wasn't a right under English common law, but in England the assumption was that judges were experts in the law and so needed no help. This wouldn't do in the United States, where the judge might be a blacksmith.

The importance of juries makes sense not just of the grand jury but of the whole mélange of rights thrown together in the Fifth Amendment. The amendment is fundamentally about the process that attends a loss of life, liberty, or property, and in each instance the Framers relied on the safeguard of a jury. Thus the right against double jeopardy ensures that the petit jury's verdict cannot later be revised through a subsequent prosecution. The right against self-incrimination preserves the jury's role in determining the facts. The right was first recognized under English common law in response to inquisitorial practices modeled on Roman law. An executive could circumvent the jury if he could coerce the accused into a confession. The requirement of due process of law had its origins in the Magna Carta's admonition that "no freeman is to be taken or imprisoned or disseised of his free tenement or of his liberties . . . save by lawful judgment of his peers or by the law of the land." This meant that the legislature had to authorize any executive action and that certain deprivations couldn't occur without a jury's agreement. Even the Takings Clause, which isn't about criminal law, interjects a civil jury between the individual and the state by requiring "just compensation" before property can be seized by the government. Payment isn't determined by the official taking one's property but instead by a jury of one's peers.

Even the Fourth Amendment, which seems to be about executive overreach into the privacy of an individual home, is more community-oriented than it might appear at first blush. The current Supreme Court takes a judge-centered view of the amendment, holding that any government act that qualifies as a search requires a judicial warrant. The standard for issuing a warrant is a demanding one, requiring "probable cause" to believe the search will reveal evidence of a crime. The Supreme Court has accordingly created a series of exceptions to the warrant requirement, as, for example, in searching your luggage before you board an airplane, in searching the pockets of a suspect who is being arrested, and in so-called Terry stops — brief delays of motorists or pedestrians based ostensibly on suspicion of a crime.

The text and history of the Fourth Amendment reveal something like the opposite of this judge-centered view. The amendment contains two different sets of commands. First, *searches and seizures* must not be "unreasonable." Second, *warrants* must satisfy probable cause, must be sworn, and must be specific. These constraints are puzzling at first blush. It appears that police have more leeway to carry out a warrantless search, which need only be reasonable, than they have to obtain a search warrant, which must meet the more stringent test of probable cause. Why would a police officer seek a warrant if it will only make it harder to execute the search? The riddle has led the Supreme Court to collapse the two sets of commands into one, but for the ad hoc exceptions, warrantless searches are per se unreasonable under the modern cases. This makes some sense if we assume, along with the modern Court, that the Fourth Amendment means to empower independent judges to protect individuals threatened by overreaching police.

But what if we instead see the Fourth Amendment as designed to protect "the people" — whom it refers to explicitly — from an executive whom judges at the time were more likely to be in league with than opposed to? The rights of the people were thought best protected by legislatures, juries, and other local institutions. The command that a search not be "unreasonable" — a classic jury question — invites the search's target to appeal to the good sense of the people as a constraint on the executive. Someone whose home was invaded could sue the government for trespassing on his property, and it would be for a jury to assess whether the search was reasonable or not. A warrant, on the other hand, is analogous to a prior restraint in the First

Amendment context. It is issued in advance, without the jury's intervention, and is authorized by a magistrate who is in the pay of the federal government rather than beholden to the local community. From this perspective, it makes sense that the standard the police and the judge must meet is much higher than for a warrantless search.

Finally, there's the Eighth Amendment, which prohibits "cruel and unusual punishments." The amendment parrots the language of the 1689 English Bill of Rights. Though gentle by European standards, seventeenth-century England was a vicious, barbarous place in which criminal punishment for even minor offenses could consist of branding, flogging, or slitting the perpetrator's nostrils. In 1765, when Blackstone's *Commentaries on the Laws of England* was published, death was an authorized punishment for some 160 specific offenses. Titus Oates, the Anglican cleric whose case is said to have inspired the "cruel and unusual punishments" language of the English Bill of Rights, was convicted of perjury and ordered to be whipped "from Aldgate to Newgate," a distance of a mile and a half, and then — after a day's break — to be whipped for another two miles, from Newgate to Tyburn. The whipping was but a prelude to a life sentence in which he was to be pilloried four times a year. In eighteenth-century England, traitors could be burned alive or disemboweled. Punishments on the Yankee side of the Atlantic were typically more lenient than in England. Public flogging and mutilation were common, but women accused of witchcraft were hanged rather than burned. (That fate was reserved for men accused of the special atrocity of conspiring in slave revolts.)

Americans today tend to think of the Eighth Amendment ban as a way for judges to protect individual criminal defendants from barbarous or excessive punishments authorized by state legislatures. This is because the modern Supreme Court has repeatedly — and in recent decades nearly exclusively — used the amendment to police states' application of their death penalty laws. States may not, for example, authorize execution of the intellectually disabled, minors, rapists, and so on. But in the colonial era, the bans on cruel and unusual punishments placed not just in the Eighth Amendment but in nine state constitutions were as significantly a protection of defendants, and of the jury's verdict, from sentencing judges.

The Ninth and Tenth Amendments: The Rights of the People

The last two Amendments in the Bill of Rights both refer not to judges but to "the people." The Ninth Amendment provides that the enumeration of rights in the Constitution "shall not be construed to deny or disparage others retained by the people." The Tenth Amendment focuses not on rights but on powers, saying that those that aren't delegated by the Constitution to the federal government are generally "reserved to the States respectively, or to the people." "The people" did not mean an aggregation of disparate individuals holding rights against the government. The Framers of the Bill of Rights were referring, rather, to the community in its collective capacity.

Madison and many others worried that the Bill of Rights could improperly imply the absence of certain rights or the presence of certain federal powers. These twin fears led to the Ninth and Tenth Amendments. Both amendments are fundamentally defensive; they anticipate and rebut hypothetical arguments that a judge, public official, or ordinary citizen might make about rights or powers. Neither amendment guarantees any particular rights, or even rights in general. The Ninth Amendment responds precisely to the problem that birthed it: the listing of rights is not in itself a reason to say "the people" lack other rights. In parallel, the Tenth Amendment means to prevent anyone from inferring the existence of additional federal government powers from the bare existence of the Bill of Rights.

Which is to say that both the Ninth and Tenth Amendments preserve a certain residual power of "the people" and "the states" to identify, develop, and enforce rights and exercise power. The point of those amendments was not primarily to recognize new substantive rights, but rather to emphasize that state and local actors, tied to their communities, were the ones tasked with doing so.

The Founders' vision of rights recognized that the capacity to identify and enforce the rights of the people rested with the people themselves: local citizens acting through legislatures and local assemblies; through juries; through militias, churches, and families. That vision did not primarily connect rights to minorities dissenting from majorities. Rather, as Alexander Hamilton wrote, "One object of a bill of rights [is] to declare and specify the political privileges of the citizens in the structure and administration of the government." Rights, therefore, were congenial with rather than opposed to the lawmaking function of the state. Rights came from inside the house.

Relatedly, and crucially, the Founding vision also did not rest primarily on the role of independent judges drawing on their legal training and their unique access to the American rights tradition. It's not that judges didn't matter. They did, of course. In introducing the Bill of Rights to Congress, Madison referred to the significance of "independent tribunals of justice" in protecting rights. But the rights to be protected were themselves grounded in political participation and self-governance via local community institutions.

The difference between tying rights to judges and tying them to "the people" acting through local institutions affects the substance of the rights themselves. The decision-making process of a legislature or even a jury typically involves negotiation and the open balancing of competing interests. By contrast, American constitutional judges are socialized to draw on a very different set of resources in adjudicating rights disputes: they zero in on the text of the Constitution, existing judicial precedent, and the original intentions or understandings of the Founding generation.

Federal judges are not elected, and they generally are not selected on the basis of their political instincts. Self-conscious about their weak democratic credentials, judges often treat matters of great moral urgency — abortion rights, affirmative action, presidential power — in just the way they treat disputes over a property line or an addendum to a business contract. Rather than concede a significant role for interest balancing or moral deliberation as essential to rights adjudication, they fall back on their narrow professional training. To give a judge the primary role in adjudicating rights disputes is, therefore, to subject rights recognition and enforcement to the limits of that professional training. Legislatures and juries are not so limited, and that turns out to matter a great deal. Managing the mass proliferation of rights claims requires institutions well suited to reconciling competing values.

The Framers' vision of rights failed for good reason. Preserving local political institutions meant preserving chattel slavery. Minorities and women were subject to forms of domination that local empowerment exacerbated and supported rather than cured. And yet there is great value in a vision of rights recognition and enforcement that recognizes the compatibility between rights and law. Recovering that vision, but not all of it, is the problem of the twenty-first century.

Requiem

Reverend Zubly's fame in Revolutionary America didn't last. His tenure in the Second Continental Congress was brief. Two months in, the irascible Samuel Chase, representing Maryland at the Congress, openly accused Zubly of deception for sending reports of the proceedings to Georgia's loyalist governor, James Wright. Six months later, Zubly was arrested for refusing to take an oath of allegiance to the states. He was eventually banished from Georgia, and half his property was confiscated, including his beloved library. Zubly died poor and bitter, largely lost to history.

For all his prescience in seeing how law and liberty must be made compatible, Zubly's inflexibility was his downfall. Accommodation with the government is not always appropriate or possible. There comes a time when moderation and reconciliation must yield to principle, even to war. But law and liberty need not, should not, be perpetually at war. That posture reflects a different kind of inflexibility, as dangerous as the good reverend's.

We have forgotten Zubly, but we forget his lesson at our peril.

2

Rights Meet Race

There's a lot to admire in the Framers' approach to rights. For the states-men of the Founding generation, rights weren't just *for* the people, handed down to them from unelected guardians in robes and wigs. Rights, rather, were *of* the people, grounded in the imperatives of communal life. Conflicts between rights and governance were resolved by appealing to the community's judgment, and this made some sense. A just and reasonable society protects rights because rights protect everyone in the society.

The problem is that the Framers' society was neither just nor reasonable — not to everyone, at least. Chief Justice Roger Taney has been vilified for writing, in the infamous *Dred Scott* case, that Black Americans at the Found-ing "had no rights which the white man was bound to respect," but he had a point. On the day the Constitution was signed, nearly 700,000 of the roughly 750,000 African descendants living in America were held as slaves. The slave population would more than quintuple by the time of the Civil War. For another century after emancipation, most Blacks in America lived under an apartheid system in which they were denied voting rights and other benefits of citizenship. A community defining the rights of its members alone does nothing for the excluded others.

Race, then, upended the Framers' vision of rights. State and local institu-tions couldn't be trusted to protect the rights of Black Americans. A different vision was needed, one that eventually would have two features that endure today. First, under a vision of constitutional rights trained on protecting minorities from the "tyranny of the majority," it made sense to treat rights as essentially absolute. To allow rights to succumb to the general will of the people would reinforce the tyranny that minority rights were meant to resist. Second, the new vision of rights ultimately would rely on judges to seize unprecedented control over the scope and substance of constitutional rights. The fact that federal judges were not elected meant that, even as they were often of the majority community and equally capable of bias, they could not easily be intimidated or controlled.

This new vision of rights didn't arrive overnight, though. And what happened in the interim profoundly shaped what that vision would look like. The Fourteenth Amendment, ratified three years after Robert E. Lee's surrender at Appomattox, granted unprecedented rights of equality and due process of law to all Americans. But air-dropped into a deeply racist society on the eve of wrenching changes in U.S. economic life, the new set of rights embodied in the Fourteenth Amendment were almost immediately repurposed to protect American industry instead of the country's Black underclass.

This was a bait and switch, of course. The Civil War wasn't fought over the right to pay poverty wages or crush labor unions. But pinning the failure of Reconstruction on the excesses of the Gilded Age is too easy. Not all rights claimants are robber barons or venture capitalists. Neither are all rights claimants besieged racial minorities or political dissidents. Confronting the challenge of rights proliferation requires us to understand that most rights live in the wide gulf between those extremes. Our failure to shape our constitutional law to that reality has roots in the first half of the twentieth century, when a little case about New York bakeshops became one of the most reviled in the American legal tradition.

The Constitutional Anticanon

Every discipline has its canon. *Moby-Dick* and *The Grapes of Wrath* in American literature. The works of Kant and Hegel in continental philosophy. Within neuroscience, everyone knows the tale of Phineas Gage, the sober-minded Vermont railroad worker whose frontal lobe was impaled by an iron rod with such precision that it caused minimal outward disturbance but made him into a profane, insufferable asshole — healthy by appearances but, friends said, "no longer Gage." Canons are the raconteurs of their disciplines. They are the vehicles through which disciples tell the story of their craft. A canon can act as an argot, a shorthand gesture at a subject's history, its central claims and commitments.

Lawyers train by learning cases, and so court decisions lie at the heart of the legal canon. By their second year, law students are on a first-name basis with *Marbury,* with *Brown,* with *Roe.* At least rudimentary knowledge of these cases stands as a measure of basic legal literacy.

Certain cases within the American legal canon, like *Brown,* are famously correct: no one who said *Brown* was wrong could be appointed to a U.S. court. Other decisions are famously *wrong,* forming an "anticanon" of cases that all mainstream lawyers must reject. In the United States, the anticanon includes three cases above all others: *Dred Scott v. Sandford, Plessy v. Ferguson,* and *Lochner v. New York.* The story these cases tell forms the crucial bridge from the Founders' understanding of rights to our own. Two of the three cases are about America's original sin and continuing burden: race. To understand how rights in America have gone so wrong, we need to understand what the two cases that are about race have to do with the one that isn't.

Dred Scott v. Sandford

In the earliest of the cases, Dred Scott, an enslaved Missourian, had been taken by his owner, John Emerson, to Illinois and then to Wisconsin Territory. There, Scott met his wife, Harriet, and they lived together for two years near what is now St. Paul, Minnesota. The Scotts were subsequently moved to Louisiana and eventually resettled, with their daughter Eliza, in Missouri. But Illinois was a free state, and slavery was banned in Wisconsin Territory. The Scotts argued that by taking them to live in free areas of the country, Emerson had emancipated them.

Under the Constitution, plaintiffs have the right to sue in federal court when they are citizens of a different state than the defendant. In the Scotts' case, Emerson had since died, and his widow had transferred ownership of the Scotts to her brother, John Sanford, a New York City resident. (The reporter for the Supreme Court misspelled Sanford's name, hence the denomination of the case as *Dred Scott v. Sandford*.) Scott argued that the "diversity" of citizenship between him and Sanford gave him access to federal court. The case would eventually make it to the Supreme Court, which had to decide two separate questions: Did Scott have a right to bring his case in federal court, and if so, was he free?

It would be difficult to construct a set of questions that better encapsulate the American rights dilemma as the Civil War drew near. The Founders understood rights in terms of participation in self-governance. Rights under the U.S. Constitution were designed primarily to keep the federal government from interfering with state and local representative institutions — legislatures, juries, militias, churches, and families. But, of course, most of the people living in antebellum America had no right to participate in the governance of those institutions. Women had no right to vote, serve on juries, or hold office. Under the doctrine of coverture, a married woman's legal personhood was subsumed within that of her husband. At the time of Dred Scott's case, slavery was permitted in fifteen of the thirty-two states, and even free Blacks were beneath the law's protection in most of the rest. The Jim Crow laws we typically associate with the postwar South, and indeed the term itself, were seeded in the prewar North, where, historian Leon Litwack writes,

> blacks were either excluded from railway cars, omnibuses, stagecoaches, and steamboats or assigned to special "Jim Crow" sections; they sat, when permitted, in secluded and remote corners of theaters and lecture halls; they could not enter most hotels, restaurants, and resorts, except as servants; they prayed in "Negro pews" in the white churches, and if partaking of the sacrament of the Lord's Supper, they waited until the whites had been served the bread and wine. Moreover, they were often educated in segregated schools, punished in segregated prisons, nursed in segregated hospitals, and buried in segregated cemeteries.

Black voting rights eroded in many northern states over the first half of the nineteenth century such that by the time of the war, Blacks had the vote in only six states. New York was the only state outside New England that allowed them the franchise, but it subjected potential Black voters to onerous property restrictions that did not apply to whites. No African American appears to have served on a jury in any state until two served in Worcester, Massachusetts, in 1860. In five western states, a Black man could not testify in a case in which a white man was a party. In Indiana, Illinois, and Oregon, Blacks were forbidden to enter or settle in the state. And under an 1842 Supreme Court decision, a slave owner had a constitutional right to enter a free state and kidnap anyone he deemed to be an escaped slave without any interference from the state. White supremacy was a constitutional promise to slaveholders.

At stake in *Dred Scott* were the boundaries of the political community entitled to the law's protection and able to claim rights under it. The ability to sue in court was what nineteenth-century Americans would have referred to as a basic civil right. Civil rights also included the power to make and enforce contracts, to hold and transfer property, to appear as a witness in court, and to ply one's trade. Civil rights were the accoutrements of legal personhood. Holding civil rights entitled a citizen to the benefits and obligations of the social contract that underwrote the Constitution itself. The question for the justices in *Dred Scott,* then, was this: Who was included in "We the People"?

The majority answered that question with ferocious clarity. Chief Justice Roger Taney acknowledged that the Declaration of Independence had emphasized the "self-evident" truth "that all men are created equal." But, Taney continued, "it is too clear for dispute, that the enslaved African race were not intended to be included, and formed no part of the people who framed and adopted this declaration." No descendants of African slaves could be citizens, Taney said, and so Scott lacked the "diversity" of citizenship needed for him to access the federal courts.

Taney then decided to add injury to insult. Even if the Court had jurisdiction, he said, any law declaring that slaves taken into free territory were free would violate the Constitution because it would constitute the taking of property from slave owners without due process of law.

That holding threw national politics into disarray. The nascent Republican Party had called for the abolition of slavery in all federal territories. Northern Democrats such as Stephen Douglas, the party's nominee for president in 1860, believed the residents of federal territories should determine for themselves whether slavery was permitted or not. Many southerners, including Vice President John Breckinridge, the standard-bearer for the Southern Democrats, the faction that splintered off from the Douglas wing of the party, believed slavery had to be allowed from sea to shining sea. Under *Dred Scott,* only this more radical proposition was constitutionally permitted. Republican Abraham Lincoln took less than 40 percent of the vote in the 1860 election, enough to defeat the divided Democrats, and the war came.

The Civil War began as a battle over the indivisibility of the Union, but it ended, emphatically, as a referendum on the morality and legality of slavery. The war killed 600,000 Americans, 2 percent of the country's population, and wounded nearly 500,000 others. We can measure the Civil War's legacy in the slaves it emancipated, in the women it widowed, in the men whose bodies it spared but whose minds it haunted with the sights, sounds, and smells of death. Its legal legacy is a revolution in the Constitution's protection of rights.

At war's end, Congress amended the Constitution to overturn the *Dred Scott* decision in both letter and spirit. The Fourteenth Amendment declared that any person born or naturalized in the United States was a citizen, repudiating Taney. The Fourteenth Amendment also, for the first time, constitutionalized a robust set of rights applicable against state and local governments and not just the Feds. States could not deprive anyone of their life, liberty, or property without due process of law, nor could they deny the equal protection of the laws to anyone within their jurisdiction.

The Framers had viewed rights through the lens of state and local lawmaking, juries, militias, churches, and families. But the plight of Blacks taught white Americans that rights had to protect persecuted minorities and that these state and local institutions weren't up to the task. The very community the Framers had relied on to embody and protect people's rights were oppressing much of the rest of the population. The Fourteenth Amendment deputized new institutions: Congress and the federal courts. Both were granted the power to enforce the amendment's new rights guarantees.

But simply saying that someone has rights does not make it so. The Fourteenth Amendment had to be interpreted. It didn't take long for judges to forget the people this new set of rights was made for and to put the rights to other uses. That fateful choice haunts us today. The rights challenge we face in the twenty-first century arises out of confusion over how to apply the Fourteenth Amendment's majestic promises to a wide range of political conflicts, many of which have nothing to do with slavery or Jim Crow.

Plessy v. Ferguson

In the cases most directly involving race, courts stripped the Fourteenth Amendment bare. *Plessy v. Ferguson,* an 1896 case out of Louisiana, is Jim Crow's avatar. It was a test case cooked up to challenge the Separate Car Act, a state law requiring that Blacks ride in "equal, but separate" railway cars. A thirty-year-old Black shoemaker named Homer Plessy was enlisted to buy a first-class ticket on the East Louisiana Railroad from New Orleans to the city of Covington, in St. Tammany Parish, and then attempt to sit in a car reserved for white passengers. It was prearranged that he would be confronted by the conductor and arrested by a private detective hired by his recruiters for the specific purpose of challenging the Separate Car Act. The law had been passed in 1890 as part of a tsunami of segregation laws pushed out of former Confederate states after Reconstruction collapsed.

The centennial year of 1876 had seen yet another momentous compromise with white supremacy. The presidential election between Republican Rutherford B. Hayes and Democrat Samuel Tilden was bitterly fought. Tilden was a New York Democrat who would go on to win his home state as well as neighboring Connecticut and New Jersey, and so Hayes's electoral strategy ran through those reconstructed southern states that had not yet been "redeemed" — that is, they had not yet fallen back into the hands of white supremacists who would never vote for a candidate of Lincoln's party. South Carolina, Florida, and Louisiana were Hayes's targets, and their Republican political machinery could be counted on to deliver their electoral votes to Hayes.

The cost of doing so, however, was a thinly veiled promise that the new administration would put a formal end to Reconstruction. During the campaign, Hayes pledged to bring to the South "the blessings of honest and capable local self government," an obvious dog whistle even by nineteenth-century standards. Tilden took the popular vote by three percentage points, but once the party machines had worked their magic, Hayes appeared to have a razor-thin edge in the Electoral College. The horse-trading that followed resulted in a Hayes presidency and a more explicit commitment to ending Reconstruction. "I think the policy of the new administration will be to conciliate the white men of the South," wrote the prominent Kansas Republican John A. Martin, who would later become governor. "Carpetbaggers to the rear, and niggers take care of yourselves."

The *Plessy* Court obliged. The legislature, wrote Justice Henry Billings Brown, a northern Republican, "is at liberty to act with reference to the established usages, customs and traditions of the people." Mr. Plessy's perception that this particular custom "stamps the colored race with a badge of inferiority" was, Brown said, a figment of his imagination: "If this be so, it is not by reason of anything found in the act, but solely because the colored race chooses to put that construction upon it." The late legal scholar Charles Black's measure of Justice Brown's words gets it just right: "The curves of callousness and stupidity intersect at their respective maxima." The *Plessy* decision gave the Supreme Court's official blessing to a system of racial segregation that would not be dismantled until the middle of the twentieth century.

It's easy to see why mainstream constitutional lawyers feel that they need to renounce *Dred Scott* and *Plessy*. Never again can an account of rights under the U.S. Constitution miss the now obvious fact that members of a despised minority group don't have the luxury of viewing rights as the Framers did. Majorities — *especially local ones* — can be every bit as tyrannical as a king, and then some. Unless independent courts had a hand in naming and enforcing rights, what Martin Luther King Jr. called the "promissory note" of the Declaration of Independence would continue to be in default. *Dred Scott* and *Plessy* embody Dr. King's "bad check." They are justly reviled for that reason.

The third anticanonical case is not like the others, though. The Supreme Court's early lack of interest in racial equality shouldn't be mistaken for a lack of interest in rights. The Fourteenth Amendment meant something, after all, and although it was motivated by the need to afford civil equality to emancipated slaves, neither slavery nor race is mentioned in the text of its crucial first section. More-litigious readers will at once see the potential for mischief. Instead of protecting racial minorities, the courts quickly lost sight of the original animating purpose behind the Fourteenth Amendment and applied it most forcefully to businesses seeking to escape health, safety, and labor laws. Shame over that turn of events haunts and distorts the law to this day.

But what the courts got wrong wasn't rights; it was race. We've taken the wrong lesson from their overzealous support of the wrong rights at the turn of the century.

Lochner v. New York

The Supreme Court in the *Lochner* case struck down a law that capped the hours of New York bakery employees at sixty hours per week and ten hours per day. Justice Rufus Peckham, writing for the majority, said the law violated the bakery owners' and employees' "right to make a contract" for the conditions of their work, a right not specifically mentioned in the Constitution.

This seems deeply wrong in retrospect, but much rides on just *how* it is wrong. The sin of *Lochner* isn't that the Court identified *a right to contract,* protected by judges — a common view of its error — but rather that it didn't also see *a right to labor,* protected through politics.

The Fourteenth Amendment arrived during an era of industrialization on a world-historic scale. The nineteenth-century United States remained what historian Robert Wiebe has called "a society of island communities" that relied on a substantial degree of local autonomy and provincial authority. That largely agrarian society was quickly being superseded in the century's climax by one "derived from the regulative, hierarchical needs of urban industrial life." More than three times as many Americans were working in manufacturing at the turn of the twentieth century as at the end of the Civil War. Despite two major economic depressions in the interim, the number of sweatshops nearly quadrupled over that same period. These factories typically required employees to work long hours for little pay and under physically demanding and dangerous working conditions.

As farms consolidated under shifting economic realities, men flocked to cities for work within the new economy. But city life was dramatically more transient, lacking established community institutions such as churches and professional associations, and also lacking an established middle class or a social order that could sustain public morality or political ethics. Opportunistic and corrupt urban political machines stepped into the breach. "Lawmakers by the score came to expect cash and whiskey as their due," Wiebe writes. Those who succeeded financially, of whom titans like Andrew Carnegie and John D. Rockefeller were most emblematic, did so relentlessly.

Among those attracted to the opportunities of urban life, moreover, were unprecedented numbers of immigrants, whose languages, religions, and patterns of work, leisure, and political engagement felt distant and threatening. For many Anglo-Saxon men, then, industrialization brought with it and made more visceral the economic inequality, financial instability, and alienation from communal political life that had long been a fact of life for women, immigrants, and racial minorities.

Jacob Riis's shocking 1890 portrait of New York City tenement life, *How the Other Half Lives,* exposed the roots of the rights dilemma the Fourteenth Amendment helped seed. Riis quotes a report of the Society for the Improvement of the Condition of the Poor that painted a sober picture of early tenement life: "Crazy old buildings, crowded rear tenements in filthy yards, dark, damp basements, leaking garrets, shops, outhouses, and stables converted into dwellings, though scarcely fit to shelter brutes, are habitations of thousands of our fellow-beings in this wealthy, Christian city." The report at once captured the lowly state of the tenements, the stark inequality they announced, and the failure of Protestant values they represented.

But in the very same section of his book, Riis writes astutely that the tenement builders' "one excuse" is that "[such] . . . is the lack of house-room in the city that any kind of tenement can be immediately crowded with lodgers, if there is space offered." A landlord seeking a return on his investment can attract tenants who decide it's in their best interest to live in a slum. A pub owner can attract customers even if his kitchen is infested with rats. A railroad owner can attract workers willing, for the pay, to risk the fate of poor Phineas Gage. The market logic of such transactions is inescapable but socially disastrous. Who holds rights in these situations? Is it individuals as autonomous market participants, or is it the community that decides to intervene and alter the market status quo for the greater good?

One might think that America's laboring classes stood to gain from the Constitution's refashioning of rights to equality and to certain basic freedoms. Even if the Fourteenth Amendment didn't protect Homer Plessy from racial segregation, maybe it could keep Lehigh Valley's anthracite miners from unsecured mineshafts or protect the mill children of Chester, South Carolina, from fourteen-hour days at the cotton gin. Legislatures seeking to shield vulnerable members of the community from the new dangers of the industrial age were attending to the rights of their citizens in just the way the Bill of Rights seemed to contemplate, most explicitly via the Ninth and Tenth Amendments.

Understanding turn-of-the-century labor and safety laws as *rights protective* could have helped align new thinking about equality and the basic trappings of a well-lived life with old thinking about legislatures rather than courts as the primary sites for turning those ideas into reality. But in the first seventy years after the Fourteenth Amendment, courts didn't see things that way. Indeed, they could hardly have seen things more differently.

The New York legislature unanimously passed its maximum hour law for bakers in 1899. A Utica bakery owner named Joseph Lochner challenged the law as a violation of his freedom to make whatever contracts he wished with his employees. A lot rides on how we think about a claim like Lochner's. The Fourteenth Amendment has the potential to place a federal court between state legislatures and an individual's freedom of action, whether to attend the school of one's choice, to use birth control, to take a low-wage job, to braid hair in the style of one's Senegalese ancestors, or to leave one's home, unmasked, during a pandemic. A citizen or corporation that loses in the churn of the legislative process can lawyer up and take a second bite of the apple through the courts. Without a strategy for managing these kinds of claims, the courts could be deluged with pleas to second-guess legislation and regulation of all kinds. But in 1905, the Supreme Court agreed with Lochner. It struck down the New York bakery law in a 5–4 ruling.

Mainstream lawyers today, from across the political spectrum, see the *Lochner* decision as disastrously wrong. Nearly every member of the Supreme Court over the past half century has publicly repudiated the decision. In consecutive confirmation hearings in the early 1990s, one of the Court's most conservative judges, Clarence Thomas, and one of its most liberal, Ruth Bader Ginsburg, each affirmed that, in Ginsburg's words, *Lochner*'s "line of authority has been so discredited by so many Supreme Court decisions, that if anything is well established, it is well established that the *Lochner* era is over."

But the consensus over *Lochner*'s wrongness obscures deep disagreement over *why* it is wrong. On one view, the decision is wrong because Joseph Lochner had *no constitutional right* to contract with his bakers. On another view, the decision is wrong because the legislature, in consideration of the labor rights of its citizens, *had properly limited* Lochner's constitutional right to contract.

This is not a semantic point. Understanding that the *Lochner* decision can be wrong in more than one way is essential to understanding Americans' wrong turn on rights. *Dred Scott* and *Plessy* were about how American courts should think about rights against white supremacy. *Lochner* was about how courts should think about rights against *everything else*. But as crucial as the case has been, its warning to modern Americans is ambiguous. Do we have a small number of unconstrained constitutional rights or a large number of limited ones?

The two judges who wrote dissents in *Lochner* differed radically on what they thought was wrong with it. Those differences modeled two separate ways of viewing rights, only one of which works in the modern world.

One of the dissenting judges, Oliver Wendell Holmes Jr., was a thrice-wounded Civil War hero who would gain a reputation as the greatest judge of the English-speaking world. He believed, as most modern U.S. judges and lawyers do, that Joseph Lochner had no right to contract. He is the bad guy in this tale.

The other dissenting judge, John Marshall Harlan, was a slaveholder into adulthood who condemned the Emancipation Proclamation, campaigned against Lincoln's reelection, and opposed Black suffrage. He believed Lochner had a right to contract, but that the people's right to govern should have defeated it. He's the good guy.

These two men's examples continue to show different ways courts can address rights conflicts in the complex world the twentieth century inaugurated. The problem is that in the United States, the bad guy won.

An "Abstract Conviction"

Every American law student has heard of Holmes. His 1881 book, *The Common Law,* is impenetrable to first-years but is nonetheless considered required reading for budding lawyers. He sat on the Supreme Court for three decades, following a long stint on the Massachusetts Supreme Judicial Court, the most prestigious state court in the country at the time.

His father and namesake was a locally famous physician and a nationally famous poet and essayist. As a doctor, the elder Holmes was, for a time, the dean of Harvard Medical School and played a key role in establishing the contagiousness of puerperal fever, a potentially lethal postpartum uterine infection. As a writer, he was credited with originating the term "Boston Brahmin" in an essay in the *Atlantic Monthly*. Holmes Sr. enabled his son's intimate acquaintance with the likes of Ralph Waldo Emerson and Henry Wadsworth Longfellow, as well as young "Wendie's" childhood friendships with, for example, the acclaimed psychologist William James and his equally famous brother, the novelist Henry James. Herman Melville lived just down the road. Holmes Jr.'s elevated social status and his love of an audience would play a part in his enduring influence on U.S. law.

But Holmes was an odd cat. He was a committed cynic, if there is such a thing. That cynicism found its tidiest expression in his support for eugenics. Many American lawyers are familiar with his too-blasé, too-savage quip — in a decision upholding the sterilization of a woman who was alleged to be "feeble-minded" and whose mother and daughter had been similarly diagnosed — that "three generations of imbeciles is enough." Fewer recognize that Holmes wasn't joking. Holmes was always eerily unsentimental, but early in his adult life, toward the end of the Civil War, he came to believe that the mentally unfit were destined to spawn paupers and knaves. In time, he hoped, science would advance to a point where such unfortunate people could be quickly identified and euthanized. Holmes was attracted to the Australian racist Charles Henry Pearson, who feared that the white Anglo-Saxon lifestyle would be stifled, and white people perhaps overpowered altogether, by the rapid expansion of the "black and yellow races" of the tropics.

Holmes's social Darwinism is crucial to understanding the later development of the American rights tradition. He believed that political combatants were best left fighting it out; for him, judicially enforced rights distorted the playing field.

More surprisingly, Holmes's Malthusian sensibility also affected his war service. By all appearances, Holmes was a patriot of startling derring-do. He didn't have to fight, but when the Civil War broke out in April 1861, two months before his graduation from Harvard College, Holmes dropped out to volunteer without so much as a word to the registrar. Propelled, he later said, by "abstract conviction," he thrice returned to the fight after near-fatal injuries.

The first came in his very first battle, in September of 1861 at Ball's Bluff, where his regiment was routed, then pushed into the Potomac to drown. Holmes was hit twice, in the stomach and chest, but was saved from certain death by the accident of a ball glancing off his rib and passing out on the other side. He returned to the front lines the next year and was nearly killed again at the Battle of Antietam, shot in the back of the neck and left for dead behind the Confederate line. Again, Providence guided the bullet, this time just to the left of his windpipe and out the front of his neck. Holmes eventually recovered and returned to the field, only to be shot again, in the heel just outside Fredericksburg, in May. By now a captain, he was given the courtesy this time of being carried from the field.

Holmes's injuries saved his life. His regiment, the Massachusetts Twentieth, suffered the most losses of any in the state and the fifth most in the entire Union army. Nearly every officer in the so-called Harvard regiment — named for the number of young Harvard officers who, like Holmes, received sinecure commissions at the start of the war — ended the war as a casualty. This included Ned Paine, who took command of Holmes's company after the Fredericksburg incident, only to fall at Gettysburg two months later.

Holmes, for his part, returned again to the field in 1864 and finally ended his service a few months later when the Twentieth was disbanded for lack of surviving officers. When he wasn't being shot, Holmes contracted body lice, bowel disorders, scurvy, and a case of dysentery that nearly took his life. To call such a man indifferent to others or to the war's cause seems an insult to his service.

And yet Holmes was strangely ambivalent toward abolition. Many of his friends when he was growing up in Boston and attending Harvard were committed abolitionists (among them the famous Garrisonian Wendell Phillips), but Holmes's prewar interest in the slavery question appears to have been limited to a 25-cent donation in 1861 to the Massachusetts

Anti-Slavery Society. During the war, several officers in the Harvard regiment, including Holmes's best friend, Pen Hallowell, took officer commissions in the Massachusetts Fifty-Fourth — the country's first Black regiment — but Holmes himself declined repeated invitations to join them.

In later describing his initial reasons for volunteering, Holmes emphasized "the principle that the Union is indissoluble," and then added: "Many of us, at least, also believed that the conflict was inevitable, and that slavery had lasted long enough." *Long enough.* "Perhaps they disliked slavery, and were fighting a slave-holding nation," Holmes's biographer Sheldon Novick notes of him and some of his fellow Harvard officers, "but the slaves themselves had no call on their passions." Holmes's letters reveal a bitter argument with his parents, while he was on leave in January 1863 — the month of the Emancipation Proclamation — over the aims of the war. His mother had long been an abolitionist, and his father had become one over the course of the fighting, but Holmes insisted that his duty wasn't to emancipate but "simply to fight."

If it wasn't abolition that led this Boston Brahmin to embark on what amounted to a series of suicide missions to the South, then what was it? Love of country, yes, but not all of it. Holmes was a man of letters, an elitist of the highest order, and, by his own description, a "devout Malthusian." Thomas Malthus believed that sustained world population growth was incompatible with human subsistence. War plays a crucial role in the Malthusian worldview as what Malthus called a "positive check" on population growth that enables the survival of the species. It has been observed that while many of Malthus's positive checks — famine, disease, infant mortality — have tended to decline over time, humans have steadily improved their skill at mass extermination through violence.

Holmes joined the army on a lark. No one in April 1861 anticipated four years of fighting and 600,000 dead men. Long after the war, he would speak of his "naïve idea of a gentleman strolling, as if down the steps of the State House on a sunny afternoon, after a good dinner, pulling on his gloves, to ride into battle on the Common." Indeed, he and his Harvard "clique" (Massachusetts governor John Andrew's term) were criticized for leaving the enlisted men in their barracks to have dinner at Delmonico's, the famed New York City steakhouse, while on their way to join the Army of the Potomac.

But the war coarsened Holmes's boyish insouciance. He had never liked southerners. At Harvard, he was aghast at southern students' boasts of sexual adventures with enslaved girls. In a letter written late in life to Indiana senator Albert Beveridge, Holmes noted "half-educated" southerners' "comparatively primitive intellectual condition" and referred to "the southern gentlemen" as "an arrogant crew who knew nothing of the ideas that make the life of the few thousands that may be called civilized." Can it be surprising that Holmes, the social Darwinist, found himself "indifferent" to their deaths, as he put it in a December 1862 letter to his parents? "Perhaps," he wrote, it is because "one gets aristocratic and don't value much a common life — then they are apt to be so dirty it seems natural — 'Dust to dust.'" The mass death of the Civil War was, for Holmes, a Malthusian project. The soldier's duty was "simply to fight."

The law can become grotesque in the hands of such a person. Holmes was morally committed to nothing but the law's lack of moral commitments. He famously described the law as "a bad man, who cares only for the material consequences which [knowledge of the law] enables him to predict, not as a good one, who finds his reasons for conduct, whether inside the law or outside of it, in the vaguer sanctions of conscience." For Holmes, for example, someone who entered into a contract owed no legal duty to perform under the contract. His only obligation was to pay damages if he didn't keep his promise. This is not how most socialized people think of the ethics of promises, but Holmes insisted against the law tracking our social duties. The law simply is what it is.

Holmes showed off his detachment from the law's moral core in one of his first opinions as a Supreme Court justice. In 1902, Jackson Giles, a Black citizen of Montgomery, Alabama, was turned away when he tried to register to vote. Giles had been registered for years, but under the newly enacted Alabama Constitution, local registrars could refuse to re-register voters for lack of "good character." Whereas white voters usually passed this test, Black voters never did. The reason for the new registration requirements wasn't mysterious. In opening the 1901 state constitutional convention, John B. Knox, the convention's president, openly declared "white supremacy" to be the aim of the gathering.

Denying the right to vote on the basis of race violates the Fifteenth Amendment. The Alabama Constitution had the intent to do just that, and it was effective. Between Reconstruction and the turn of the century, Black Alabamians voted in large numbers, with greater than 60 percent turnout in each of the key elections in the 1890s. But by 1902, registration of Black Alabamians had dropped to 1.3 percent. Black turnout between the presidential elections of 1900 and 1904 dropped by 96 percent. So why did Holmes rule against Giles?

He offered two reasons. First, Giles's argument was that Alabama's entire voting scheme was a racial conspiracy, invalid on its face. If that was so, Holmes said, the Court couldn't simply order that Giles be registered, or the Court itself would be participating in the illegal scheme. Second, the sheer scale of the conspiracy Giles was alleging exceeded the Court's power to remedy it. "The [complaint] imports that the great mass of the white population intends to keep the blacks from voting," Holmes wrote. "To meet such an intent something more than ordering the plaintiff's name to be inscribed upon the [registration lists] will be needed. If the conspiracy and the intent exist, a name on a piece of paper will not defeat them. Unless we are prepared to supervise the voting in [Alabama] by officers of the court, it seems to us that all that the plaintiff could get from equity would be an empty form."

Holmes's opinion in *Giles* is startling in its callousness. Holmes's response to the open, state-sponsored extinction of Black voting rights was a lecture on the limits of the common law. He might not have been wrong about those limits. Rights have remedies, and Holmes didn't see a way for the Supreme Court to solve Giles's problem. It wouldn't, in fact, be solved until Congress passed the Voting Rights Act more than sixty years later, in 1965. But Holmes didn't even try. His opinion is written with all the urgency of a slip-and-fall case, an indifference that he carefully cultivated. "The importance of things we [on the Supreme Court] have to deal with makes me shudder from time to time," he wrote, "but I don't lie awake over them — and try to think of them merely as problems to be handled in just the same way whether they involve $25 — or the welfare of a state or a people."

We often celebrate this approach to legal reasoning. The law, on this view, is a set of texts, court precedents, and rules of decision that are indifferent to the world that surrounds them. It is, if you will, the product of "abstract conviction." It should take no account of the legislature's particular intentions, of the care it took in drafting a law or in considering the perspectives of those the law affects, or of the equities in applying the law to a particular case. What matters to the judge is the integrity of the rule itself, not the consequences of applying it to a case that cannot escape the rule's logic.

Holmes's short, punchy dissent in *Lochner* is famous for just this attitude. Writing for the majority, Justice Rufus Peckham observed, correctly, that the Supreme Court's prior cases had held that the Constitution protects the right to contract. The government could overcome the right, but only if it was legitimately regulating the health, safety, or general welfare of the public *as a whole*. Peckham didn't buy the evidence that a baker's work was especially laborious or dangerous. What he saw instead was special-interest legislation, pure favoritism for bakers over shop owners, rather than laws passed in the general interest.

For Holmes, the problem with this ruling was that there was no reason to give any special weight to the right to contract, which the Constitution does not specifically protect. "It is settled by various decisions of this court," he wrote, "that state constitutions and state laws may regulate life in many ways which we as legislators might think as injudicious or if you like tyrannical, as this, and which equally with this, interfere with the liberty to contract." As examples, he referred to laws requiring that businesses be closed or that alcohol not be sold on Sundays, or laws preventing lenders from charging usurious interest rates, or compulsory schooling laws, or the (then in vogue) prohibition on lotteries. If these laws were acceptable, so, too, was a law regulating the hours of bakers. "The Fourteenth Amendment," Holmes said, "does not enact Mr. Herbert Spencer's *Social Statics*." That famous 1851 tract defending laissez-faire competition as natural to the social order was a favorite of social Darwinists. Ask Holmes how he knew.

Holmes had no patience, then, for the claim that the Constitution gives Americans a general "liberty right" to do or contract as they please. "The word 'liberty,'" he said, "is perverted when it is held to prevent the natural outcome of a dominant opinion, unless it can be said that a rational and fair man necessarily would admit that the statute proposed would infringe fundamental principles as they have been understood by the traditions of our people and our law." Holmes's dissent presages one face of modern rights review. For rights claims that fall within this rule, the government wins so long as the judge perceives any "rational basis" for the challenged law to be passed. Rational basis review is the lightest, most deferential standard known to American constitutional law. The Constitution didn't enact *Social Statics,* but it would allow a winner-take-all "survival of the fittest" in the *political* process: an individual's claim of a right generally shouldn't "prevent the natural outcome of a dominant opinion."

Of course, this can't be the rule for *all* rights. Holmes recognized that; he would later write another famous dissent defending freedom of speech. And the reason *Dred Scott* and *Plessy* are so discredited today is that racial discrimination is now thought to be a special concern of courts. Holmes's *Lochner* dissent, taken together with the lessons of the other anticanonical cases, suggests a two-track system: specific constitutional rights and those involving racial discrimination receive special treatment from courts; all others receive none.

This two-track understanding of constitutional rights review frames American constitutional law to this day. But it is completely inadequate, even dangerous, under modern conditions.

John Marshall Harlan's *Lochner* dissent, more celebrated than Holmes's at the time but largely forgotten since, contains the seeds of a better approach. Although Americans' rejection of Harlan's dissent and acceptance of Holmes's might have made some sense in the middle of the twentieth century, it should not have survived the 1960s.

"Let It Be Said That I Am Right
Rather Than Consistent"

Holmes and Harlan shared service in the Union army, nine years on the Supreme Court, and little else. Both were born into prominent families — Harlan's father, James, was a Kentucky congressman and state legislator — but inherited fame and wealth carried a very different meaning in nineteenth-century Boston than it did in the rural villages of central Kentucky. Whereas a young Boston Brahmin went to Harvard, broke bread with Emerson, and befriended abolitionists, a prominent Kentucky scion like John Harlan attended Centre College, five miles from his home, in Danville, and owned slaves into adulthood.

The Harlans were ambivalent about slavery before the war. They had inherited about a dozen slaves, refusing on principle to buy or sell human beings. James also believed strongly in treating slaves with kindness, though not to the point of manumission. This was a view John inherited, warts and all. He didn't back native Kentuckian Abraham Lincoln in the 1860 presidential election (Lincoln received less than 1 percent of the Kentucky vote), but he supported the preservation of the Union above all else. He initially served as a captain in the Crittenden Zouaves, a loyal Louisville militia, and then, as the war gained steamed, he raised his own regiment, the Kentucky Tenth, and was promoted to colonel. He served with distinction until resigning in 1863 to provide for his newly widowed mother. Still, whether to support his incipient Kentucky political career — he successfully ran for attorney general in 1863 — or for some other reason, Harlan publicly opposed the Emancipation Proclamation and became a vocal critic of Lincoln. He backed Democrat George McClellan in the 1864 presidential contest.

Harlan didn't mourn emancipation, but he didn't try to bring it about either, and he opposed the Thirteenth Amendment, which made slavery unconstitutional. As attorney general, he opposed civil rights measures for Blacks, at one point supporting the indictment of the commander of Union forces in Kentucky, John Palmer, for helping Blacks escape their masters after the war. At a speech in New Albany, Indiana, a month before the 1864 presidential election, Harlan reaffirmed his support for the war but argued that Lincoln had "perverted" the "high and noble goal" of preserving the Union in favor of "warring chiefly for the freedom of the African race." Harlan also opposed Black suffrage and the granting of ordinary political rights such as jury service to Blacks.

And yet something changed in Harlan during Reconstruction. Harlan was a Unionist but a conservative, a compromise position that left him increasingly isolated in postwar Kentucky politics. Like the centrist Republicans of today, conciliators like Harlan had by 1866 become an endangered species in the Bluegrass State. Soon after the war, the state repealed its Expatriation Act of 1862, which had excluded rebels from the franchise. This swelled the ranks of the Democratic Party with Confederate sympathizers who were hostile to Unionists like Harlan. At the same time, Republicans in Congress had become more radical, voting to exclude from the body southern legislators who resisted civil rights for emancipated slaves. Harlan left the Democratic Party in 1867 and was booted, hard, from his seat as attorney general. His biographer Tinsley Yarbrough reports a letter Harlan's friend and fellow conservative Unionist B. S. Sinclair wrote to him just after the election: "As there are nationally but the 2 parties," he wrote, "we will be compelled to go with one or the other, which virtually disenfranchises me." The following year, Harlan decided to support his former general, Ulysses Grant, for the presidency. He soon became a loyal Republican.

Harlan didn't have the luxury Holmes did of viewing race from afar. He started a Louisville law practice shortly after being unseated as attorney general, and his cases increasingly involved Black Kentuckians who had been beaten or terrorized by the incipient Ku Klux Klan. Harlan's half brother, Robert, had (it appears) been born of a sexual encounter between his then-teenage father and a mulatto slave girl, just the kind of "adventure" Holmes's classmates had bragged about, to Holmes's disgust. Harlan, whom Holmes privately called "the last of the tobacco-spittin' judges" and more publicly (and condescendingly) "my lion-hearted friend," was indeed the embodiment of Holmes's "southern gentleman." He was not widely read and left little in the way of papers, but his convictions were anything but abstract.

Harlan's personal inheritance and proximity to the brutality of slavery shaped his views on the peculiar institution, from the wary but unquestioning support of his youth to his fierce opposition during Reconstruction. "It is true fellow-citizens that almost the entire people of Kentucky, at one period in their history, were opposed to freedom, citizenship and suffrage [for] the colored race," Harlan said in an 1871 speech during a failed gubernatorial run. "It is true that I was at one time in my life opposed to conferring these privileges upon them, but I have lived long enough to feel and declare, as I do this night, that the most perfect despotism that ever existed on this earth was the institution of African slavery . . . Let it be said that I am right rather than consistent."

In 1877, President Hayes nominated Harlan to the Supreme Court, where he quickly became known as "the Great Dissenter." He dissented when the Court struck down Congress's effort to prohibit racial discrimination in "public accommodations" such as inns, theaters, and modes of transportation. He dissented from an opinion upholding his native Kentucky's right to prosecute a private school for accepting both Black and white students. He filed a lonely dissent in *Plessy*, famously writing that "our Constitution is color-blind, and neither knows nor tolerates classes among citizens." He dissented from Holmes's opinion denying Jackson Giles's effort to register to vote in Alabama. And he dissented in the New York bakery case.

Even though both Holmes and Harlan dissented in *Lochner*, neither joined the dissenting opinion of the other. The two men's views reflected very different attitudes toward constitutional rights. For Holmes, the Constitution protected very few rights — and certainly not the right to contract — but those it protected, such as freedom of speech, it protected strongly. Harlan, by contrast, began his dissenting opinion by acknowledging, just as the majority had, that the Constitution protects the right to contract. "Speaking generally," he wrote, "the State . . . may not unduly interfere with the right of the citizen to enter into contracts that may be necessary and essential in the enjoyment of the inherent rights belonging to everyone."

There's nothing peculiar, for good or ill, about such a right. It would take no leap of legal imagination to say that a law that, for no good reason, prevented people from selling shoes or buying bread or, for that matter, purchasing first-class railway tickets would be an unconstitutional infringement of their liberty. By contrast, a ban on contract killing bucks no constitutional prohibition. And so for Harlan, the bakers' case wasn't really about whether there is a special right to contract in the Constitution. It was about *how far the right goes.* The right to contract "is subject to such regulations as the state may reasonably prescribe for the common good and the well-being of society."

What were the state's reasons for limiting bakers' contracts in New York in 1895? Were they more like the reasons for limiting contract killing — i.e., *good, supported reasons* — or more like the reasons for limiting the sale of shoes — i.e., *bad, unsupported reasons*? A judge deciding this case doesn't need to dust off the records of the Constitutional Convention or the congressional debates from the 1860s, when the Fourteenth Amendment was ratified. The judge doesn't need to read Locke, or Madison, or Herbert Spencer. He needs to know the facts.

As it turns out, there were plenty of good, supported reasons for the New York bakery law. Harlan noted the common knowledge that bakers breathe air less "pure and healthful" than the air breathed outside or by other workers. He cited the German scholar Ludwig Hirt's treatise *Die Krankheiten der Arbeiter* (The diseases of the workers), which described bakers' work as "among the hardest and most laborious imaginable." He quoted another treatise writer at length on bakers' susceptibility to rheumatism, on their "palefaced" visages and short life spans, on the 1720 Marseilles plague, which it is said killed every baker in the city. He related statistics showing that the average number of working hours in thirteen Western countries was less than or equal to the maximum hours set out in the New York law. Whether or not there is a right to contract was beside the point. States get to legislate for the public good, and the facts showed that there was ample basis for doing so here. For Harlan, the judge's job wasn't to decide whether a right existed in the abstract. The judge's job was to assess the legislature's balance of individual rights against the common good. Both were worth caring about. Both were of constitutional dimension. Neither was beneath the Constitution.

Two Models of Rights

The Holmes dissent and the Harlan dissent represent competing models for deciding individual rights cases. On the Holmes model, the judge decides whether a right is special, like racial equality or free speech. If it is, the judge looks skeptically at laws infringing the right. If it isn't, the government can do what it wants. Faithfully practiced, this model has the benefit of predictability, at least among the professional class. Most rights won't make the cut. The ones that do will, in theory, be those that the constitutional text specifies, that the Framers recognized, or that the common law, rightly reasoned, supports. In practice, the Constitution will rest in the hands of lawyerly judges who, like Holmes, have the professional training to parse texts and analyze cases, but who invariably bring their own backgrounds and assumptions to which rights they recognize and which they don't. The Holmes model enables a judge to "get aristocratic and [not] value much a common life."

On the Harlan model, the judge doesn't focus on whether a right is special. Instead, the judge always asks what the government's reasons for infringing the right are. The government wins if the law is reasonable in light of the asserted right. On this model, the legislature and the courts are shared custodians of our constitutional rights. Faithfully practiced, this model has the benefit of accuracy more than predictability. Different factual contexts, different stakes, and different legislative motives call for different outcomes. A problem involving $25 is *different* from a problem involving the welfare of a state or a people, and a judge should treat both accordingly. Sometimes it is better to be right than to be consistent.

Americans chose Holmes's model, and the rest of the world chose Harlan's. We had our reasons, but the choice leaves us frozen in the headlights of modern pluralism. Harlan was a border-state politician, a slave owner who became a champion for Black civil rights. There was nothing abstract about the southern redeemers or the Klan. Their actions helped Harlan see that there are times when one must remain "lion-hearted." The warning of *Dred Scott* and *Plessy* was that rights in America had to account for race in America, something Harlan understood better than Holmes.

But Harlan also had an inbred understanding of *disagreement*. He understood that not just laws but rights themselves often involve negotiation and compromise, even internal contradiction, not unlike the judges who interpret and apply them. Our celebration of Holmes's more elegant but less nuanced *Lochner* dissent obscures the essential warning the case offers: the law can infringe rights, it can protect them, or it can do *both*.

3

Rightsism

Americans are more than a little bit rightsist. They discriminate firmly between those rights that count — and which judges must therefore apply vigorously against public officials — and those that don't count — which the government may therefore ignore.

The U.S. Constitution doesn't require rightsism of this sort. The Framers didn't practice it, and for most of American history, neither did judges. Rather, rightsism emerged in the 1930s and 1940s as a way of reconciling a Progressive vision of unburdened regulation of the economy with a burgeoning judicial commitment to civil rights enforcement. At the time, discriminating among rights seemed the best way to protect rights while avoiding the excesses typified by the *Lochner* case. The serious shortcomings of this approach became evident in the 1960s, when rights claiming became a vital national pastime.

None of this was inevitable. In the thirtieth article of the first constitution for the state of Massachusetts in 1780, John Adams famously wrote that government under the new constitution should be one "of laws, and not of men." But a government of laws is, always has been, and always will be an inescapably human endeavor. In the law, as in so much of human experience, relationships matter. Tempting though it may be to attribute American rightsism to our constitutional DNA, our liberty-loving Founders, or our indomitable liberal spirit, what has mattered just as much is who lived, who died, whose story was told and by whom.

Justice Holmes's opinion in the New York bakery case, the prototype for the American approach to rights, is the most famous dissent ever written. It became so not because of some peculiar tie to the American rights tradition but through the hard work of Holmes's disciples and friends. Harlan, whose more measured dissent offers a path away from our all-or-nothing rightsist system, succumbed to pneumonia six years after the bakery case was decided. He was more famous than Holmes at the time, and his dissent received more coverage in the newspapers than Holmes's. But Holmes stayed on the Court for another two decades after Harlan's death. The period extending from that moment in 1911 to Holmes's own death in 1935 bookends the ascension of the Progressive legal movement. Holmes was not himself a Progressive, but the young intellectuals of that movement who would largely determine the path of American law in the twentieth century viewed Holmes as their patron saint.

No one was more responsible for the ascendancy of Holmes's thinking than Felix Frankfurter. Harvard law professor, New Deal consigliere, Supreme Court justice, operator par excellence, Frankfurter is second to none (save perhaps Holmes himself) in his influence on twentieth-century American constitutional thinking. That claim may surprise anyone who knows Frankfurter primarily through his disappointing tenure as a justice. But the long arm of Frankfurter's constitutional thought reached far beyond the opinions he authored. In particular, Frankfurter's adoration of Holmes — and of Holmes's *Lochner* dissent above all else — would frame the Court's misguided response as it struggled to manage a wave of new, unfamiliar rights claims in the 1960s and 1970s.

The House of Holmes

Frankfurter lived the American dream. Born in Vienna, he sailed to the United States in steerage on an immigrant boat in August of 1894, at the age of eleven. The Frankfurters settled on New York's Lower East Side, where Felix's father, Leopold, sold linens. Felix soon became a star student in City College's joint high school–college program. He attended Harvard Law School, where he graduated first in his class, then carried the briefcase of Henry Stimson, who was the U.S. attorney in Manhattan. When Stimson became William Taft's secretary of war in 1911, he took the twenty-eight-year-old Frankfurter with him to D.C. to serve as a legal adviser in the Bureau of Insular Affairs, which managed the country's overseas territories of Puerto Rico and the Philippines.

Frankfurter was "that guy." An inveterate sycophant and social climber, he craved proximity to power. As the child of working-class Jewish immigrants, he also craved acceptance, and he was prepared to work his tail off to get it. Holmes, the Boston Brahmin, became an early target. Frankfurter lived in a Dupont Circle boardinghouse with a dozen or so other young bachelors then working in the Taft administration. The roommates hosted dinners, cocktail parties, and salons, mixing drinks with verve and chatting up the D.C. intelligentsia, among whom Holmes was the *ne plus ultra*. Holmes was "the gay soldier who can talk of Falstaff and eternity in one breath, and tease the universe with a quip," recalled journalist Walter Lippmann, a boarder with Frankfurter at what came to be known as the House of Truth. "A sage with the bearing of a cavalier . . . he wears wisdom like a gorgeous plume, and likes to tickle the sanctities between the ribs."

Frankfurter excelled in this environment. Standing just five feet, five inches tall but gifted with a quick wit and preternatural self-confidence, he could charm and dominate in equal measure. He would grab firm hold of his listener's arm, squeezing tightly as he spoke to — or at — him. (Kiss up and kick down, as they say.) Eventually, Frankfurter became a frequent caller at Holmes's Northwest D.C. home, and the two grew close. Frankfurter wrote a great many letters to Holmes over the years, always fawning, almost nauseatingly obsequious. Holmes was, for Frankfurter, "the King" before whom all others were "creeping worms," as he wrote *to Holmes* in one missive.

Though never waning in adulation, Frankfurter's letters to Holmes grew more intimate in tone with the passage of time. "To know you is to have life authenticated not through you but in my own rich increase of life," he wrote in March 1921. "I count it as one of my ultimately precious benedictions to have you be — for so I feel — be part of me." He continued what can only be described as a florid love letter to the old jurist: "When I saw you from the very first I knew it was *there* — the answer to life that needeth no 'answer', that accepts without fatalism, that questions without humorous arrogance. Above all there is the beauty and the gay valor of you, for me forever. You give me the exhilaration, the life-intoxicated ferment that no other man does."

Holmes was (by necessity) more measured in his replies, but he did not object to Frankfurter's flattery. "It will be many years before you have occasion to know the happiness and encouragement that comes to an old man from the sympathy of the young," Holmes told his young suitor in 1912, early in Frankfurter's courtship. "That, perhaps more than anything else, makes one feel as if one had not lived in vain, and counteracts the eternal gravitation toward melancholy and doubt." Holmes seems to have regarded Frankfurter as the son he never had, fit to protect and enlarge his legacy.

He wasn't wrong. Shortly after Holmes's death in 1935, Frankfurter penned an encomium in which he declared that Holmes's "conception of the Constitution must become part of the political habits of the country, if our constitutional system is to endure." The "expression of his views," Frankfurter insisted, "must become part of our national culture."

And so it has. American courts continue to frame rights as all or nothing. Frankfurter devoted much of his professional life to ensuring that Holmes's dissent in the New York bakery case anchored the "nothing."

Felix's Happy Hot Dogs

In 1914, Frankfurter became, at thirty-one, the first Jewish professor at Harvard Law School. Once there, he set about imprinting Holmes's constitutional views on the hearts and minds of the legions of students who would seek Frankfurter's favor over the years. Frankfurter told Holmes as much. "Much of our labor these days is bringing bricks to the building of the structures for which you long ago sketched the blue prints," he wrote to Holmes early in his tenure at Harvard. Within two years of arriving in Cambridge, Frankfurter published a glowing study of Holmes's constitutional opinions in the *Harvard Law Review*, in which he claimed that Holmes's dissent in the bakery case had decisively turned away a "tide" of activist thinking at the Supreme Court. This is a bizarre assertion to make of a dissent, particularly one that had never been cited in a federal court opinion. It was also wrong. Holmes's dissent wouldn't be vindicated for another two decades.

Frankfurter was undeterred. In a 1928 treatise on federal jurisdiction, Frankfurter argued that, in *Lochner*'s wake, "the philosophy behind the constitutional outlook of Mr. Justice Holmes . . . appeared to be vindicated by demonstration in detail." This, again, was wrong. Just five years earlier, the Supreme Court had struck down a D.C. law setting a minimum wage for women and children. The opinion, which quoted *Lochner* at length, was written by Justice George Sutherland in his first term on the Court, over Holmes's dissent. Still, there was Frankfurter, five years later, celebrating the eighty-seven-year-old Holmes's consistently losing views as if they were the law. Ten years later, in a lecture on Holmes that he would later turn into a hagiographic monograph, Frankfurter wrote that "Mr. Justice Holmes' classic dissent will never lose its relevance." Not if Frankfurter had a say in it, anyway.

Well, he did have a say. Frankfurter returned to Washington in 1917 to serve as a special assistant to the secretary of war, Newton Baker, and later as chairman of the War Labor Policies Board, whose mandate, in part, was to prevent labor unrest that could disrupt wartime production. The board also included the assistant secretary of the navy, a fellow named Franklin Delano Roosevelt, and the two ambitious men became close professional acquaintances in D.C. Frankfurter rekindled the relationship when Roosevelt became governor of New York in 1929, offering frequent advice via letters, phone calls, and personal visits to "Frank's" Hyde Park estate. When Roosevelt became president in 1933, Frankfurter became one of his most trusted advisers.

It is difficult to gauge Frankfurter's precise influence within the Roosevelt administration, but it was undoubtedly substantial. He tended to be circumspect about his role, but by reputation Frankfurter became an operator of nearly supernatural powers. Some newspapers offered unflattering comparisons to Shakespeare's Iago or to Rasputin, the Russian mystic and tsar whisperer. Raymond Moley, the Roosevelt brain truster who coined the term "New Deal," called Frankfurter a "patriarchal sorcerer" to his "apprentice[s]" within the brain trust, such as Ben Cohen and "Tommy the Cork" Corcoran. Hugh Johnson, the original head of the National Recovery Administration, called Frankfurter "the most influential single individual in the United States" in the 1930s.

Frankfurter earned these lofty appellations not just by doling out his own advice to the president, though he did plenty of that, but by staffing the growing federal bureaucracy with students and friends whom he had mentored and who owed him loyalty. Thus it was that Agricultural Adjustment Administration head George Peek complained of the "plague" of young Washington lawyers who "all claimed to be friends of somebody or other and mostly of Felix Frankfurter." These disciples, whom Frankfurter called his "boys" and whom others called his "happy hot dogs," numbered in the hundreds. They would check in regularly with Frankfurter to receive their marching orders on pain of excommunication from his network.

If Holmes was the patron saint of the Progressive legal movement, Frankfurter was its high priest. His fingerprints were everywhere in the federal government during the New Deal era. Corcoran, a former student whom Frankfurter had placed in a clerkship with Holmes, was a de facto chief of staff to Roosevelt and an important drafter of several key pieces of New Deal legislation, including the Securities Act of 1933 and the Fair Labor Standards Act of 1938. A long career in public service followed, including as a key adviser to President Lyndon Johnson. Cohen, another seminal member of FDR's brain trust, drafted the New Deal's most important corporate oversight measures and had Frankfurter's nod to thank for his clerkship with the esteemed judge Learned Hand. Frankfurter's coauthor on that 1928 treatise celebrating Holmes's *Lochner* dissent was his former student James Landis, whom Frankfurter had awarded a coveted clerkship with Louis Brandeis. Five years later, Frankfurter brought Landis to Washington to help draft the

Securities Act. Landis then served as an inaugural commissioner and later chair of the Securities and Exchange Commission. He became dean of Harvard Law School after he left Washington in 1937.

Other former students of Frankfurter's in high administration positions included Charles Wyzanski (Labor Department solicitor), David Lilienthal (head of the Tennessee Valley Authority), Nathan Margold (Interior Department solicitor), Nathan Witt (secretary of the National Labor Relations Board), and Lee Pressman (the top lawyer in the Works Progress Administration). Before Alger Hiss became notorious for being an alleged Soviet spy, he was a student of Frankfurter's, a clerk for Holmes (at Frankfurter's behest), and a lawyer placed by Frankfurter in the Agricultural Adjustment Administration. Future secretary of state Dean Acheson, who helped create NATO and draft the Marshall Plan, was a Frankfurter protégé who was placed in a Brandeis clerkship and in Roosevelt's Treasury Department.

Frankfurter himself never took a formal administration position, declining Roosevelt's offer to serve as his first solicitor general. This enabled him to run a Sunday salon out of his house on Brattle Street, to which, Joseph Lash writes, "for men concerned with the intellectual aspects of law and politics, a pilgrimage . . . was obligatory." From Cambridge, Frankfurter could continue to cultivate apprentices without having to hold a day job arguing cases before the Supreme Court. As the career paths of his happy hot dogs attest, Frankfurter's good graces could mean a law clerkship with Holmes, Brandeis, or Hand, perhaps the three most renowned American judges of the twentieth century.

And it wasn't just the men who would come to dominate the administrative state who were in Frankfurter's web. At least as important to the spread of Frankfurter's thinking were the former students of his who would become the century's preeminent academics. Paul Freund, one of the leading constitutional law scholars of his generation, owed his Brandeis clerkship, his government service, and his teaching career to Frankfurter. Henry Hart, godfather of the famed "legal process" school of jurisprudence and coauthor of the most influential casebook in all of American law — *The Federal Courts and the Federal System,* which birthed the field of "federal jurisdiction" — was a Frankfurter disciple who was gifted a Brandeis clerkship. The legendary Harvard Law School dean Erwin Griswold, after whom the building housing the dean's suite today is named, owed his job in the solicitor general's office in the 1930s to his old professor Frankfurter.

Charles Fairman, who would teach at Harvard and Stanford and who would become perhaps the best-known Fourteenth Amendment scholar of the twentieth century, was firmly in the fold of Frankfurter, his former adviser. Frankfurter recruited Fairman to write an article tearing down Justice Hugo Black's theory (and supporting Frankfurter's) of how to apply the Fourteenth Amendment to the acts of states. The piece became one of the most cited law review articles ever written. Fairman's 1948 undergraduate casebook, *American Constitutional Decisions,* devotes substantial attention to *Lochner,* which was not nearly as famous then as it is now. Astoundingly, eight of Fairman's ten paragraphs on the case pay tribute to Holmes's dissenting opinion. "An entire philosophy is compressed into three paragraphs," Fairman writes, parroting his mentor with uncanny precision. "His point of view has now become a part of the accepted doctrine of the court." Frankfurter's hustle had paid off.

Roosevelt's appointment of Frankfurter to the Court didn't end his tutelage. Frankfurter made it a point to get to know clerks in other justices' chambers, grabbing them by the arm and squeezing as he pressed his point. And his own clerks weren't slouches, of course. Some would go on to become legendary professors at the nation's top law schools: Albert Sacks at Harvard, Alexander Bickel at Yale, Louis Henkin at Columbia, David Currie and Philip Kurland at Chicago. These men, who became the leading law professors of the 1960s and 1970s, would help make Frankfurter feel, to paraphrase Holmes, as if he had not lived in vain.

The Footnote

Amplified by Frankfurter, Holmes's famous New York bakery dissent suggests two "tracks" for U.S. rights claims. One track would come to be known as "rational basis review," a form of judicial scrutiny whereby judges defer almost entirely to the government. The case setting out the basic rule emerged from a challenge to the Filled Milk Act of 1923, a federal law that prevented the interstate shipment of certain milk substitutes. In upholding the act, the Court said that laws affecting "ordinary commercial transactions" — which is most laws — will be upheld so long as there is any conceivable rational reason to pass them. Congress did not have to hold hearings or prove to a court that milk substitutes were unhealthy; it was enough that legislators might have rationally believed they were. Likewise, in the *Lochner* case, the New York legislature should not have had to produce evidence that bakery work was especially strenuous or dangerous; it was enough that, as Holmes said in his dissent, "a reasonable man might think it a proper measure on the score of health."

The second track is set out in the fourth footnote of the filled milk case. There, Justice Harlan Fiske Stone described three *categories* in which the rational basis standard might not apply: (1) when the law interferes with a right the Constitution specifically protects, (2) when the law restricts the political process itself, or (3) when the law discriminates against particular religious or racial minorities. In other words, the Court committed itself to highly deferential review of laws regulating commercial markets, while reserving a place for stricter review of laws that fell within specific constitutional language, laws that made it more difficult to engage in politics, or laws that discriminated against what the opinion called "discrete and insular minorities." In Professor John Hart Ely's later, influential description of this standard, the Court would resort to heightened review when it found that the political process was undeserving of *trust,* whether because it was trying to limit the channels of political change (think voter suppression laws) or was not inclusive of certain minorities (think Jim Crow).

This two-track approach largely vindicated Holmes's *Lochner* dissent. Courts should generally let the political process play out unless the Constitution specifically instructs them not to. The further caveats in that footnote describe situations in which the "natural outcome of a dominant opinion" that Holmes celebrated was, in reality, *unnatural* because of inappropriate interference with the political process. The footnote marries a Progressive approach to political economy, one that authorizes political control over economic markets, to a burgeoning understanding of the need to protect African Americans from Jim Crow and to protect Catholics, Jews, and Jehovah's Witnesses from the kind of religious bigotry that was conspicuous in 1938, the year of Kristallnacht. Judicial review was usually to have a light touch, but when authorized it was meant to protect minorities and other political outsiders.

This was a victory for Frankfurter and, through him, for Holmes. In case after case in the mid-century years and since, U.S. courts have shown nearly total deference to states and the federal government in cases deemed to involve "ordinary commercial transactions." In one well-known case, an Oklahoma optician challenged a state law that permitted only optometrists or ophthalmologists to fit lenses to glasses, arguing (correctly) that it was just protectionism for eye doctors. The Supreme Court held that it was obligated to uphold the law so long as it could think of any rational reason for passing the law, *even if it wasn't the state's actual reason.* This approach to economic legislation simply abdicates the Court's reviewing function, just as Holmes would have wanted.

There were exceptions, of course, but for a time these were relatively straightforward to apply. For example, all the justices save Frankfurter blessed a 1943 decision upholding the right of Jehovah's Witness children to refuse to salute the flag. And although some groused behind the scenes, the justices were unanimous in virtually every case in the 1940s, 1950s, and 1960s that challenged segregation in schools or other public facilities, including *Brown v. Board of Education.* Jim Crow was, after all, the heart of footnote 4.

But the heart wasn't where the trouble was. A decade after *Brown,* courts would need to figure out just how far the footnote could be stretched before it snapped.

The Right to Birth Control

Frankfurter suffered a stroke that forced him to retire in 1962. His last significant majority opinion showed the limits of footnote 4.

The State of Connecticut had banned the use of contraceptives ever since 1879, when it joined a wave of states passing decency laws pushed by the anti-vice advocate Anthony Comstock. Connecticut's own "Comstock law" was written in part by the circus entrepreneur P. T. Barnum, then a state representative from Bridgeport. The law, enforced but once in the next eighty-six years, might have been Barnum's greatest con.

The plaintiffs in the case that reached the Supreme Court in 1961 as *Poe v. Ullman* were two married couples. Their doctors had reported that a pregnancy would likely result in either fatal genetic abnormalities for the fetus or the death of the woman. Though no one had sought or threatened to prosecute them, they argued that the state's prohibition against contraceptive use violated their right to liberty without due process of law.

A birth control ban is an unusually invasive law. Its enforcement would wedge the state in between consenting sexual partners, including married couples, such as the carefully selected plaintiffs in *Poe.* Sometimes, as in *Poe,* that interference could have devastating physical and psychological consequences. More broadly, the right to make family-planning decisions is deeply personal, and the curtailment of that right seemed not to vindicate any especially important interest of the State of Connecticut.

To put this right into the first "track" of American rightsism — total deference to the government — seems tone-deaf and cruel. Yet the footnote in the filled milk case isn't very helpful either. The Constitution does not specifically provide a right to use contraception. A birth control ban doesn't curtail the political process, at least not directly. Those affected by a birth control ban, typically poor women, are not "discrete and insular minorities." Indeed, women are not a minority at all. Holding for the plaintiffs in *Poe* seemed to require either stretching the old categories or creating a new one.

Faced with this dilemma, Frankfurter decided to punt. His opinion in *Poe* denied the couples' claims on the ground that they did not have "standing" to challenge the Connecticut law because it was never going to be enforced against them. Birth control devices were openly sold in Connecticut drugstores despite the Comstock law. In fact, the only time the state had initiated a prosecution, in 1939, the state's attorney moved to dismiss the case after winning in the Connecticut Supreme Court. With no recorded prosecutions or prospects for any in the future, Frankfurter said, one had to question whether the Comstock law was even the law at all.

The Planned Parenthood League of Connecticut, which had been behind the *Poe* lawsuit, had to regroup. What its executive director, Estelle Griswold, did next would alter the course of American history. Frankfurter's opinion in *Poe* said that Connecticut didn't arrest people for violating its birth control laws, but Griswold would see about that. Soon after the *Poe* decision came down, Griswold announced that Planned Parenthood would be opening a birth control clinic in New Haven that fall.

The clinic began operations on November 1, 1962, and held a press conference the following day. When news of the clinic's opening splashed across the papers, a local grumpalump named James Morris called as many police officers as he could find until finally two New Haven detectives agreed to pay a visit to the clinic's second-floor offices on Trumbull Street. Griswold, thrilled to see them, offered the officers the clinic's literature and told them that the doctors in the office were busy fitting illegal diaphragms and giving out contraceptive jelly. She even asked the officers to dip their fingers into some Emko vaginal foam that she had on hand. She volunteered to provide the detectives with patients who could provide witness statements to assist in her own prosecution.

They fell for it. An arrest warrant was issued a few days later, and Griswold, now a criminal defendant, had the court case she was craving.

A Rights Explosion

A new era was upon the country and its courts. Griswold's case wasn't just about birth control. It was about every law that rested on little more than the

moral sense of the community. It was about every law that disproportionately burdened an identifiable class of citizens, in this case women. It was
about every law that exposed intimate decisions to government scrutiny, every law that hit the poor much harder than the rich, every law that someone
sincerely and reasonably believed infringed their rights and that someone
else sincerely and reasonably believed did not. It was, in short, about every
law. The judicial minimalism of Holmes's New York bakery dissent wouldn't
do for these rights assertions, but neither would the maximalism of *Brown*.
The courts would need a new approach to a host of constitutional rights
claims that were unthinkable in Holmes's time, or even in Frankfurter's.

The four years between Frankfurter's punt in *Poe* and the Supreme Court's
June 1965 decision in *Griswold v. Connecticut* were among the most tumultu-
ous in the nation's history. In areas from race to politics, social welfare to gender, criminal justice to civil liberties, the kinds of rights conflicts that reached
courts involved ever less the banal, state-sanctioned bigotry of the Jim Crow
era or Joseph McCarthy's casual authoritarianism and ever more the workaday
churn of political disagreement. Responding to these claims pushed courts out
of the comfort zone of legal formalism and into more overtly political domains.

Race

At the time of *Poe,* Jim Crow remained resilient in the Deep South. Although
many public facilities were slowly desegregating, privately owned hotels
and restaurants still could and often did ban Black customers. The sit-in
movement that began with North Carolina lunch counters in the 1960s and
quickly expanded to theaters, hotels, parks, swimming pools, beaches, and
other public places needed creative courts to come up with reasons to void
trespass prosecutions. The Civil Rights Act of 1964, which President Kennedy originally proposed after Birmingham, Alabama, police commissioner
Bull Connor used attack dogs and fire hoses on peaceful protesters in the
spring of 1963, catalyzed both southern school integration and the demise

of Jim Crow in public accommodations such as hotels and restaurants. But the act needed the Supreme Court's blessing to survive.

Southerners were continuing their fierce resistance against *Brown's* desegregation mandate. In 1964, on the eve of the passage of the Civil Rights Act and a decade after *Brown*, 99 percent of Black students in the eleven Deep South states attended schools that had *no* white students. States and counties resisted *Brown* not just by openly refusing to enroll Black students in integrated schools but also by putting in place seemingly neutral policies that they knew would have the same effect. Prince Edward County in Virginia, for example, simply shut down its public school system for five years, busing white students to private schools whose discriminatory policies didn't violate the Constitution. Many other states and counties enacted "freedom of choice" plans that enabled students to "choose" their schools. Social pressure, intimidation, and inertia meant that these policies would simply reproduce existing racial segregation.

Too facile an approach to rights would mean victory for this kind of cynical compliance. The Supreme Court would eventually forbid "freedom of choice" plans for school districts that were under desegregation orders, but how much further should it go? Geographic zoning replaced freedom of choice but also reliably produced segregated schools based on white flight and other ostensibly private residential housing choices. Courts in the 1970s found themselves ordering kids bused around town, or even into other counties, to produce integration. Whatever the wisdom of these desegregation efforts, it's impossible to fit them into a two-track system of all-or-nothing rights.

Gender

Griswold's case wasn't just about sex. It was also about . . . *sex.* Up until the 1970s, women consistently lost sex equality cases brought to the Supreme Court. In 1873, the Court held that the State of Illinois could refuse to admit women lawyers to its state bar. In 1948, Frankfurter wrote a majority opinion holding that Michigan could ban women from working as bartenders. As late as 1961, a unanimous Supreme Court upheld a Florida rule requiring men but not women to serve on juries, on the ground that "woman is still regarded as the center of home and family life."

A creative reading of footnote 4 could perhaps meet the challenge of sex discrimination. Birth control bans, sex discrimination on the job, and the exclusion of women from jury service could certainly curtail the ordinary operation of the political process. Women whose lives were artificially constrained by discrimination could not fully participate in civil society. Still, women were a majority, not a minority, much less an "insular" one, and they had had the vote since 1920, should they be willing and able to exercise it.

As today, sex discrimination in the 1960s relied not simply on male beliefs that women were inferior or of a lower caste, but on deeply embedded beliefs about familial roles. Some of those beliefs about role differentiation were consistent with believing in the substantive equality of the sexes. The President's Commission on the Status of Women, headed by Eleanor Roosevelt, issued a report in 1963 that maintained as a "fact of life" that is "not debatable" that "the care of the home and the children remain [women's] unique responsibility."

Title VII of the Civil Rights Act of 1964 banned sex discrimination by employers, but it did so almost by accident. The language was added to the bill at the eleventh hour by a dogged opponent of the civil rights bill, Virginia representative Howard W. Smith, probably as a poison pill to make its passage less likely. Even after the sex discrimination ban passed, the Equal Employment Opportunity Commission, which was responsible for its implementation, tried to neutralize it, issuing guidance saying that the act didn't prohibit employers from advertising jobs for just men or just women. A judge conditioned by Frankfurter and his progeny to avoid "activism" could easily have been thrown off by the prospect that he should henceforth treat sex discrimination with the same care as racial discrimination.

But the Civil Rights Act tapped into something that had been hiding there all along. Its sex discrimination ban quickly became one of its most litigated provisions. Betty Friedan's *The Feminine Mystique,* which questioned the culturally dominant assumption that being a housewife was a woman's best route to a well-lived life, had spent six weeks on the *New York Times* bestseller list after its 1963 release. The government's shoddy enforcement of Title VII's sex discrimination language is what led Friedan and others to found the National Organization for Women in 1966. At the time of the Civil Rights Act, Hawaii and Wisconsin were the only states that banned sex discrimination in employment. Within a decade, nearly every state had such a ban.

And yet our social experience of sex discrimination and racial discrimination remains quite distinct. We tolerate sex-segregated bathrooms, dorm rooms, and schools. Most Americans, from pedestrians to beachgoers to movie raters, treat male and female nudity differently. Many religious leaders refuse to marry same-sex couples. As a matter of casual nomenclature, we distinguish parents, children, and other relatives based on their sex. Swapping out sex for race in any of those examples would be irredeemably scandalous. But failing to acknowledge sex differences at all seems to miss something about how human and other animal societies behave. Sex discrimination isn't the same as racial discrimination, but neither is it the same as discriminating between natural and filled milk. It needs a different language of rights resolution.

Politics

Federal supervision of state elections was almost nonexistent prior to the 1960s. Over a series of cases running from the 1920s through the 1950s, the Supreme Court had eliminated all-white primary elections, but more-subtle forms of voter suppression continued unabated. Griswold's case was argued two weeks after Bloody Sunday, when Selma police officers and Alabama state troopers brutally assaulted peaceful civil rights marchers on the Edmund Pettus Bridge. Ten days after Bloody Sunday, the Voting Rights Act (VRA) was introduced into Congress. The act would immediately halt literacy and "good character" tests in the Deep South and would subject all the voting rules in six southern states and in numerous counties throughout the country to supervision by the Department of Justice and federal courts. This was the biggest federal intervention into local politics since Reconstruction.

Court supervision of elections wasn't limited to racial discrimination. The year after the VRA passed, the Supreme Court held that states couldn't collect poll taxes, no matter how small. This raised questions of how closely the Court would scrutinize other forms of wealth discrimination, which is both pernicious and inevitable in a capitalist society. The year before the VRA, the Court had announced the rule of "one man, one vote," which would commit federal courts for the first time to overseeing states' sorting of voters into legislative districts. Frankfurter's last significant opinion was a dissent from the Supreme Court's declaration that such cases were fit to be resolved by judges. Holmesian minimalism in this area passed with Frankfurter.

Criminal Justice

The first half of the 1960s was a momentous time for criminal justice rights. Until 1961, the state could use illegally seized evidence against criminal defendants in trials. Until 1963, a felony defendant too poor to afford a lawyer would simply be tried without one. Until 1964, state and local police officers could refuse criminal suspects' request to have a lawyer present during their interrogation. *Miranda v. Arizona* and its famous "right to remain silent" would come two years later.

Some of the revolutionary changes in constitutional criminal procedure were intertwined with the civil rights movement, as a disproportionate number of criminal suspects were African-American, and Black defendants were more likely to see their rights disregarded. Another factor was that mass use of automobiles had forever changed policing. As traffic stops came to be citizens' most common point of contact with law enforcement — one experienced by whiter, wealthier Americans as well as others — standards for criminal suspicion were recalibrated in revolutionary ways.

Freedom of Speech

The civil rights movement helped deepen the Court's appreciation for freedom of speech. In March 1960, a group headed by A. Philip Randolph was raising money for Martin Luther King Jr.'s legal defense against trumped-up Alabama perjury charges. The group placed a full-page ad in the *New York Times* headed "Heed Their Rising Voices." The ad contained a number of trivial factual errors. For example, it referred to Alabama State College students singing "My Country, 'Tis of Thee" on the steps of the state capitol in Montgomery, when in fact the students sang "The Star-Spangled Banner." The ad said that school officials padlocked the dining hall on campus; in fact, though some students were barred from the cafeteria, there was no padlock. The ad claimed that King had been arrested seven times when, in fact, it had been four.

Claiming they had been defamed, six Alabama public officials sued the *New York Times* and a number of prominent Black ministers who were listed in the ad as supporters, seeking $500,000 each in damages. An all-white Montgomery jury was happy to oblige. The *Times* sought U.S. Supreme Court review, arguing that the judgment violated freedom of the press.

The problem with this defense was that it was well established at the time that the First Amendment didn't protect libelous publications. And whether the *Times* ad counted as libel was a factual question for the jury, not a legal question for the justices. More broadly, the First Amendment was generally understood to apply to laws passed by legislatures or the actions of executive officials such as licensors or police officers. If successful, the *Times* argument might invite federal judges to supervise state civil jury verdicts and state court rulings in the legions of ordinary tort or breach-of-contract cases that touched on someone's speech interests.

That said, a defamation suit can be a potent tool of harassment. Civil damages actions against unpopular defendants raise the specter of the jury being used as a tool of oppression, upsetting the Framers' expectations. The minister defendants in the *New York Times* case were prominent in the civil rights movement in Montgomery, but immediately after the verdict, the plaintiffs were able to ask the sheriff to seize their automobiles and property. Between the time of the plaintiffs' initial lawsuit and the Supreme Court's 1964 decision in *New York Times Co. v. Sullivan,* newspapers — many of which were from out of state — were on the hook for almost $300 million in libel damages before southern courts. The Supreme Court recognized this racial subtext when it ruled for the *Times,* holding that libel or defamation suits brought by public officials had to be premised on intentional or reckless disregard for the truth.

The Supreme Court was doing much the same work when it overturned disorderly conduct charges against comedian and activist Dick Gregory after he was arrested at an August 1965 march against school segregation in Chicago. *Gregory v. City of Chicago* is one of several cases that have come to stand for the idea that a speaker can't be punished just because his speaking inspires others — whether hostile critics or fellow travelers — to act unlawfully. Freedom of speech in the 1950s was primarily about sedition prosecutions and red-baiting. Within a decade, it would be about far more complex conflicts between expressive interests on the one hand and public order, community standards of decency, and local autonomy on the other.

Social and Economic Rights

The biggest challenge for rights recognition and enforcement in the past fifty years has been accounting for the role the government plays in our lives. The government pays us in the form of Social Security, unemployment compensation, and various federal, state, and local welfare programs. It funds our health care in the form of Medicare and Medicaid. It provides the professional and occupational licenses that we need to pursue a livelihood and the driver's licenses we need to get to and from work, the supermarket, the home of a relative, or places of worship. It doles out taxi medallions and broadcast licenses. It subsidizes our corn, sorts our mail, charters our businesses, protects us from criminals, educates our children, and employs tens of millions of us directly.

In 1964, legal scholar Charles Reich wrote a groundbreaking article titled "The New Property," in which he sought to wake Americans up to what the state's growing presence in our lives means for how we think about rights. Reich's core observation was this: our dependence on government isn't going away; indeed, it "is the inevitable outgrowth of an interdependent world." That reality upset many of the law's old assumptions about rights. For example, courts once tried valiantly to distinguish between "rights" and "privileges," the latter of which could be taken away without ado. Holmes himself famously said, in upholding the dismissal of a police officer for soliciting money for a political campaign, that the officer "may have a constitutional right to talk politics, but he has no constitutional right to be a policeman." That's cute, but for Reich it wouldn't do in a modern society. The fact that the state is not *required* to provide some good, service, or benefit doesn't mean that those things can't be understood as "rights" or that, once offered, they may be retracted on a whim.

In the decade following Estelle Griswold's day in front of the Supreme Court, the Court would decide cases in which plaintiffs argued for a public school teacher's right to publicly criticize the board of education, for a poor family's right to tie welfare benefits to family size, for a right to equal funding for public schools regardless of a neighborhood's property tax base, for a right not to be fired from a public university or kicked off the welfare rolls or have a driver's license suspended without a hearing. These were and remain the workaday questions of modern rights adjudication, but bromides about rights and privileges don't begin to provide answers. Reich understood that we were not in Topeka, Kansas, anymore, and he was right.

By the time the Court heard *Griswold v. Connecticut,* then, footnote 4 was starting to seem rather quaint. The footnote lived in a world of categories. In that world, the vast majority of laws didn't implicate anyone's constitutional rights. This judicial restraint was Frankfurter's work in cementing Holmes's legacy. Those laws that did implicate rights were tied to specific, readily identifiable, categorical problems: jailing one's political enemies, segregating public facilities by race, and the like. The Court that entered the 1960s reserved rights enforcement essentially for corrupt public officials who couldn't be trusted with state power. But the events of the 1960s would drag the Court into the very different world we live in today.

At the time of the 1938 filled milk case, less than 10 percent of the Supreme Court's docket comprised civil rights claims. That number jumped about 20 percent over the next two decades, then jumped another 20 percent just in the six years before *Griswold*. Since then, we've been living in a world in which claims for racial equality call not just for an end to intentional discrimination but also for structural changes in employment practices, school assignment, time-honored voting and districting procedures, and virtually every aspect of the criminal justice system. Indeed, in this world charges of intentional racial discrimination often reach courts as claims of white students or contractors chafing at race-based remedial measures. Equality isn't just about renouncing slavery and Jim Crow; it's also about upending traditional family roles and securing sexual autonomy and reproductive freedom, up to and including the freedom to abort a fetus. Challenges to discrimination aren't just about genes but also about a protected set of commitments, values, and preferences. The rights of criminal defendants extend beyond the bare formalism of a criminal trial and saddle the state with affirmative duties to provide competent defense lawyers, to share exculpatory evidence, and to inform suspects of their rights. Free speech norms have spread to unfamiliar spaces such as common-law courts and public universities, commercial airwaves and strip clubs. Courts now entertain not just claims of the right *against* government abuse but the right *to* government support in securing the conditions of citizenship.

We have been faced, for half a century and counting, with a rights explosion. Rights in this world are diverse and unruly; sometimes majoritarian and populist, other times protective of minorities or those on the margins of civil society; often supported by sophisticated lawyers or even government officials, just as often living outside the legal mainstream. Rights since the 1960s have been, perhaps above all, competitive. They cannot readily be hived off from other rights and interests with which they come into constant, at times adversarial, contact. The question for modern courts is not about which particular rights the government can't be trusted with. It's about how to reconcile a diverse, unpredictable array of conflicting, important, and deeply felt individual and group interests with the government's existential interest in governing.

Three Choices

The *Griswold* Court struck down the Connecticut birth control law, but the justices held very different views about how and why. With surprising clarity, the range of views expressed in the six opinions written in the case — four to overturn the law and two to retain it — reveal the three choices available to courts seeking to respond to the rights explosion: minimalism, discrimination, and mediation. The *Griswold* majority chose the middle course of discrimination between rights, and it is with us to this day.

The minimalist was Hugo Black, who dissented. Black, a former country lawyer and Alabama senator, had been Roosevelt's first appointee to the Supreme Court, but he had a race problem. He joined the Ku Klux Klan in the 1920s in order to win the Democratic nomination for the Senate, then resigned after he won. It's easy enough to describe Black's decision as a matter of sheer political calculation, but the Klan wasn't some Rotary club, even in 1920s Birmingham. Black's Klan ties dogged him the rest of his life and nearly derailed his Supreme Court appointment.

Perhaps it was to overcome this handicap that Black eventually developed a jurisprudence that enabled him to remain true to his populism while becoming one of the most progressive justices of his time on race issues. Today we would call that jurisprudence "originalism." On Black's view, it was the task of the Court to apply the text of the Constitution just as it was written. Where rights applied, they applied absolutely. Where they did not apply, the law should be upheld. The Constitution's text says nothing of birth control, and so that was the end of it for Black. "I like my privacy as well as the next one," he wrote, "but I am nevertheless compelled to admit that government has a right to invade it unless prohibited by some specific constitutional provision."

The nominal majority opinion belonged to William O. Douglas. Douglas was cantankerous and brilliant, too much of both for his own good. He circulated his first draft in ten days, scribbled on a yellow notepad, amounting to six typed, double-spaced pages. Like Black, Douglas believed that the constitutional text could guide the Court to the right answer. But Douglas was no minimalist. He just thought himself clever enough to stretch the text as he pleased.

His first draft would have struck down the Connecticut law as a breach of the constitutional freedom of association. The First Amendment does not mention this freedom expressly, but the Court had recently recognized it in a case in which Alabama had tried to obtain a list of the NAACP's members, so as better to harass them. What Douglas called "the association between husband and wife" — others call this "sex," among other things — seems not to fit in quite the same constitutional category as NAACP membership, but it was good enough for Douglas. Describing the right in First Amendment terms was awkward, but at least that got it into the text of the Constitution.

Douglas circulated the draft privately to Justice William Brennan, who was unimpressed. Brennan had his law clerk Paul Posner draft a memo to Douglas in which Posner suggested the opinion should rest instead on the right to "privacy," which Douglas had only hinted at. Just as the First Amendment contains a right to association on its periphery, Posner suggested, other Bill of Rights provisions, taken as a whole, "indicate a fundamental concern with the sanctity of the home and the right of the individual to be let alone." Douglas agreed, and within three days he sent a revised draft that would become the lead opinion in *Griswold*.

According to the Douglas opinion, the right to privacy lives in the shadows of the Bill of Rights. "Specific guarantees in the Bill of Rights have penumbras, formed by emanations from those guarantees that help give them life and substance." Thus the First Amendment contains within its "penumbra" a right of private association. The Third Amendment, prohibiting the quartering of troops without consent, also intersects with privacy interests, as does the Fourth Amendment's ban on unreasonable searches and seizures. Less obviously, the Fifth Amendment's protection of the right against self-incrimination allows a suspect to keep his inner thoughts private even if they implicate him in a crime. The right to privacy is *in* the Constitution, Douglas was suggesting, if not in so many words.

The Douglas opinion reflects a more creative iteration of Black's approach. In the face of a rights explosion, the Court could simply let the constitutional text be its guide. Douglas saw more there than Black did, and his opinion has been widely ridiculed for it. Penumbras and emanations are meet for Halloween, but they don't void democratically enacted laws.

The essential failure of Douglas's *Griswold* opinion reflects a deeper problem with a textualist-originalist response to the rights explosion. To reach most modern rights claims, the constitutional text must be read expansively or bent out of shape, thus undermining the very discipline that textualism and originalism are supposed to promote.

The alternative is Black's more skeptical version, but there's been no appetite either among the justices or among the American people for the kind of medicine Black's austerity would deliver: allowing states to ban birth control, to jail people for engaging in oral sex, to sterilize criminals or the intellectually disabled, or indeed to browse the membership lists of unpopular organizations, to name just a few of the many topics on which the constitutional text is silent. Americans have the shortest and oldest national constitution in the world. Which rights are important to us today bears little relationship to the Constitution's vague, sparse language. It touches modern rights only by happenstance. Pretending otherwise turns rights enforcement into a lawyer's game of textual manipulation and comma parsing rather than the sensitive process of moral or political deliberation that rights claims call for.

For non-originalists, though, the answer to Douglas has been just to try to discriminate *better,* to eschew the text as a guide to rightsism in favor of . . . something else. Arthur Goldberg, who had taken Frankfurter's seat, wrote a separate opinion in *Griswold,* joined by Brennan and Chief Justice Earl Warren, that emphasized a very different theory of what was wrong with the Connecticut law. For Goldberg, the rights protected by the Fourteenth Amendment were not "confined to the specific terms of the Bill of Rights." Noting that the Ninth Amendment says the Bill of Rights should not be construed to exclude unenumerated rights, Goldberg said that judges could extend the protections of the Constitution to "fundamental" rights. He defined fundamental rights, unhelpfully, as those rooted in "the traditions and (collective) conscience of our people." Goldberg was satisfied that the right to privacy, especially in relation to the marital bedroom, was so rooted.

This was footnote 4 with a twist. The footnote suggested that there were two categories of rights claims that could be recognized even if they were not mentioned in the specific text of the Constitution: rights to participate in the political process and rights claims by certain "discrete and insular minorities" facing prejudice. Douglas didn't have to consider these categories because he found the right to privacy in the Constitution's text. Goldberg simply leapfrogged the categories by adding another: privacy. Still more categories of rights might be added if a majority of the Court deemed them "fundamental."

This formulation of what have become known as "substantive due process" rights is the one law students learn to this day. They should ask themselves two questions in identifying a right: (1) Is the right in the specific constitutional text? (2) If not, is it "fundamental" in the sense that it is rooted in our traditions and collective conscience? If the answer to either question is yes, then the right is a "fundamental" one that is not to be infringed unless the government satisfies the highest level of scrutiny. If the answer to both questions is no, then the right is not fundamental and is subject to the lowest level of scrutiny.

Americans continue to debate constitutional rights in the parsimonious terms drawn by these *Griswold* opinions. On one side of the field are the textualist-originalists, typically conservatives such as Clarence Thomas and Neil Gorsuch, continuing in the tradition of Antonin Scalia. They claim to view strict adherence to the Constitution's text and history as necessary to judicial restraint. In practice, these justices have, like Justice Douglas, applied idiosyncratic glosses to the text and history in order to achieve desired outcomes, as, for example, in cases involving affirmative action, campaign finance, and gun regulation.

Across the pitch are the Goldberg and Brennan acolytes, who see the

Court's job in rights cases as determining which unspecified rights —
whether to abortion or assisted suicide or same-sex marriage — should be
deemed fundamental and therefore entirely outside the government's grasp.
The justices who view substantive due process as a living tradition incapa-
ble of precise definition are accused of a kind of lawlessness, conforming
the Constitution's meaning to the justices' own takes on what rights, interests, and commitments lie within the collective conscience of the American
people. Brennan himself famously would tell new law clerks that the most
important thing they needed to know to start working at the Supreme Court
was how to count to five. That's how many votes it took to change the Constitution.

Partisans on either side of this modern jurisprudential battle tend to miss
their common ground. Hugo Black and William Brennan, Antonin Scalia
and Ruth Bader Ginsburg, all agreed that the main question judges were
called upon to answer in rights cases was *whether* important rights were
involved or not. It remains a threshold question "originalists" and "living
constitutionalists" are constantly fighting about, but it's the wrong question.
The startling diversity of rights claims in the modern world ensures that
unless courts change their focus, the fight will never end.

But what *Griswold* takes away with one hand it gives back with the other.
Just as we see in the *Griswold* opinions the seeds of this seemingly existential
conflict in judicial method, we also see there, if faintly, a way out.

Mediation

Arthur Goldberg was Frankfurter's immediate successor, but he was not his
heir. Goldberg's *Griswold* opinion, the most expansive of the lot, shows how
very different philosophically the two men were. The man who took Frankfurter's seat in spirit was none other than John Marshall Harlan, grandson of
the Great Dissenter.

Harlan came to the Court in 1955, elevated by Dwight Eisenhower after
a long career at the white-shoe firm of Root, Clark, Buckner & Howland

and a brief stint on the court of appeals. He and Frankfurter knew each other well, having first met through Emory Buckner, a friend of Frankfurter's and a partner at Harlan's firm, who took Harlan along when he served as U.S. attorney in New York in the 1920s. When Harlan joined the Court, Frankfurter sensed an ally in his Republican, temperamentally conservative younger colleague. He immediately began an influence campaign that included seeking to spread his negative opinions of Black and Douglas, both of whom Frankfurter intensely disliked. (Harlan didn't bite.)

Harlan's reputation indeed lives in the same family as Frankfurter's. He is viewed as a conservative speed bump in the path of the Warren Court's activism, the role Frankfurter would have played had he lived through the 1960s. Nearly half of Harlan's 613 opinions were dissents, including a mind-boggling average of more than 62 dissents per term during the Warren Court's heyday of 1963 to 1967. But there was a crucial difference between Frankfurter and Harlan. Frankfurter had built his jurisprudential legacy around Holmes, and especially Holmes's pithy dissent in the *Lochner* case: absent extraordinary reasons later memorialized in footnote 4, judges should defer to legislatures whenever they act with minimum rationality. Harlan's view of due process wasn't Holmes's, though. It was Harlan's.

Harlan went along with the majority in *Griswold,* but he refused to join either the Douglas or the Goldberg opinion. In fact, Harlan's take on the Connecticut birth control statute echoed his grandfather's approach to the New York bakery law to a startling degree. He rejected the argument that the Fourteenth Amendment should apply only to government deprivations specified in the Bill of Rights. "Due process," Harlan wrote, "has not been reduced to any formula; its content cannot be determined by reference to any code." Rather, he said, "it has represented the balance which our Nation, built upon postulates of respect for the liberty of the individual, has struck between that liberty and the demands of organized society."

Just as the older Harlan accepted a right to contract that had to be balanced, with care, against the need for reasonable regulation, his grandson recognized a right to privacy that likewise called for a temperate balance against government interests. Indeed, far from demonizing *Lochner* as

Douglas and Black had, Harlan cited favorably the case (predating *Lochner*) in which the Court first recognized a right to contract. For Harlan, that right was one point on a continuum of liberty interests that must be adjudicated with sensitivity to their particular context and the government's reasons for limiting them. "No formula," Harlan wrote, "could serve as a substitute, in this area, for judgment and restraint." Restraint did not consist in refusing to recognize rights, but in *mediating* among them through careful attention to the particular facts of the case.

In the specific context of the Connecticut birth control law, Justice Harlan assumed that there was a constitutional right to privacy, but also that the government could regulate private spaces if it had a good enough reason. Here, it didn't. The space — the marital bedroom — was as private as any in our tradition. Moreover, the fact that the state didn't enforce the law showed that its police and prosecutors evidently didn't believe it was especially needed. The law's novelty also counted against it. Connecticut was the only state that banned the *use* of contraceptives (some states had, at various times, banned only their distribution). For Harlan, the case did not rise or fall on *whether* there was a specific right to privacy in the Constitution or on *whether* the law targeted minorities. What mattered was the law's justification and its operation on the ground. What mattered were the facts.

Our Loss

Harlan's views have not prevailed. The Court invalidated the Connecticut birth control law, but it did so by declaring that there was a "fundamental" right to privacy embedded in the Constitution. The "private" status of the relationship the government was targeting was what shielded it from regulation. Privacy was a new category, a new box, into which Americans could try to fit their conduct to exempt it from the state's reach. If a law intruded on privacy, it should usually be struck down. If it failed to get into the privacy box, or some other box of the justices' devising, it would be reviewed with great deference to the government.

Holmes had won. His binary view of constitutional rights persists to this day, bending awkwardly beneath the weight of facts it cannot accommodate. The limitations of the privacy category became apparent almost immediately, when the Court decided *Roe v. Wade*. Abortion opponents don't see terminating a pregnancy as a private decision. Isn't a fetus a person? What then? Unwilling to confront that question, the Court held that a fetus has no rights.

As the world has grown more complex, as Americans have come to understand themselves as a genuinely pluralistic political community, viewing rights as Holmes did has become an invitation to error — and to combat. We cannot lay our rights completely at the mercy of a state whose decisions affect all of us deeply but that represents the interests of only some of us. Neither, of course, can we give strong rights to everyone, trumping everyone else's. Most constitutional rights cases sit comfortably between these extremes, but American courts continue to treat them as exceptions. They are still trying to put rights into categories, still searching for the right box, the right formula. But both Justices Harlan were right all along. There is no formula. There is only judgment.

Part II

No Justice,

No Peace

AMERICAN COURTS TODAY FRAME RIGHTS as a zero-sum game. Faced with a rights conflict, they decide *who holds a right* instead of asking *what holding a right means.* Instead of accommodating the cacophony of rights that arise out of close contact between human beings of different backgrounds, circumstances, and values, they discriminate between us. This approach to rights isn't just wrong; it's dangerous.

It's wrong because it cuts rights off from justice. The rights Americans enjoy should depend on what the government has done to us and why it has done it: Is the government motivated by bigotry? Is it responding to evidence? Is the benefit the government is seeking proportionate to the burden placed on those affected by its actions? Instead, the rights Americans have depend on judges' morally arbitrary speculation about what Madison might have thought, what "test" an old court case laid out, or what values lie within the "collective conscience" of a deeply divided people. This is how we end up with a right to nunchucks but not to food.

The American approach is dangerous because it divides us into those who have rights and those who don't. It needlessly erases one side of rights disputes from the Constitution. This was the Supreme Court's biggest mistake in *Roe v. Wade,* in which it held that fetuses do not have constitutional rights. Denying that a fetus could be a subject of constitutional concern, the justices said, was the price of acknowledging that pregnant women have rights to reproductive autonomy. This erasure antagonized the anti-abortion movement, contributing to its radicalization. Contemporaneous events in German abortion politics suggest that a more accommodating judicial strategy might have brought the two sides closer together, and perhaps even better protected women, in this most divisive of political conflicts.

The American approach doesn't just force courts to choose which rights to care about and which ones to discard; it also causes us to view one another in the worst possible light. When our rights come into conflict, instead of seeking common ground, we see in the opposing position the worst version of our opponents. And so, for example, a Christian baker who refuses to bake cakes for same-sex weddings is compared, in court, to Jim Crow–era segregationists. The couple who want only to be served on equal terms are likened to a Babylonian king persecuting religious dissidents who refuse to prostrate themselves before him.

This attitude toward rights is madness. The Constitution doesn't require it. The Framers didn't intend it. Good sense doesn't recommend it. In a rapidly polarizing world, our courts are making things worse. Here's how.

4

"Too Much Justice"

The U.S. Constitution is not a code. Many of the rights Americans hold most dear, and nearly all of the rights we argue about, are absent from the text. Some of the Constitution's provisions are quite specific — a state can have neither three senators nor just one, and a thirty-four-year-old can't be president — but most of its rights provisions are surprisingly vague. The Constitution doesn't, in so many words, protect the right of citizens to vote. Its text contains no general right to freedom of speech. There's no specific ban on racial or sex discrimination. That's to say nothing of the right to birth control or abortion, the right to marry, or the right to remain silent. The Constitution is silent on all of these rights and many others Americans cherish.

Americans enjoy these rights because judges have read them into broad provisions offering "equal protection of the laws" and forbidding government deprivations of life, liberty, or property without "due process of law." These words are hardly self-explanatory — lifetimes have been spent unpacking them — and so a lot is at stake in working through how to apply them to our day-to-day lives. Even the rights that are more specific in the text, such as the right to bear arms or the right against self-incrimination, do not indicate how far they extend or what exceptions, if any, they might admit. Determining the scope and limit of constitutional rights requires judges to make difficult choices.

How should they choose? Should they focus more on what rights we have or on how far those rights extend?

A Right to Feed Pigeons?

A vignette from abroad can help clarify these options. In the late 1970s, in the West German city of Mönchengladbach in the state of North Rhine–Westphalia, a woman wanted to feed the pigeons in a public square. A local ordinance forbade anyone to feed pigeons "on the streets and in public facilities." The woman sued, claiming a violation of her constitutional rights. Her case eventually made its way to West Germany's constitutional court.

American courts would make quick work of this woman. For them, the key question would be whether the U.S. Constitution protects the right to feed pigeons. The answer U.S. courts would give is clearly no. Pigeon feeding goes unmentioned in the text of the U.S. Constitution (or any other constitution). There are no prior cases protecting the right to feed animals. The Framers would have found the idea of such a right completely mystifying. And for the vast majority of people, feeding birds is not an important part of a well-lived life. Because there is no right to feed pigeons, courts would cut off the woman's claim at the roots. After all, the courts would say, if there were a right to feed pigeons, then there'd be a right to do just about anything.

The West German constitutional court saw the pigeon-feeding case differently. For the judges of that court, the key question wasn't whether the constitution protects a right to feed pigeons. The answer to that question was clearly yes, and it required little discussion. Sure, most people don't care about feeding pigeons, but this woman did. Maybe she had no other hobbies. Maybe she found pigeons aesthetically pleasing or admired their unusual intelligence. Maybe she was lonely. If pigeon feeding was an important part of what made this woman's life meaningful, then she had a right to feed pigeons. That's what a right *is*.

But just because the woman had a right to feed pigeons didn't mean she should win her case. In this rights dispute, as in any other, the judges had to ask whether the government had good reasons for acting as it did. Here, although the woman's right to feed pigeons was indeed protected under the West German Constitution, called the Basic Law, the citizens of Mönchengladbach are part of a democratic community and therefore have to accept certain laws passed in the public interest. So long as a city ordinance is sufficiently proportional to the public interest, it can stand, even in the face of a right. In the pigeon-feeding case, the Court noted that flocks of feral pigeons can damage property, cause pollution, impede transportation, and spread disease. The ban on feeding them was an appropriate way to address these harms.

It may seem as though the difference between the American and German approaches is semantic or trivial. After all, the pigeon feeder would lose either way. But whether courts approach rights cases by, on the one hand, focusing on the existence of rights or, on the other hand, focusing on the government's reasons for acting is surprisingly consequential. The American rightsist approach severs the link between constitutional rights and constitutional justice. It turns rights conflicts into arid *interpretive* questions that are predetermined by the Constitution's text and structure, by the original intentions of the long-dead Founders, and by prior court cases. This is great news for lawyers and judges, whose professional training prepares them to mine these sources of wisdom and debate them among themselves. It's bad news for the rest of us, because it disrupts the law's contact with the imperatives of modern life.

Justice means we must confront the government's actual behavior, the legislators' or the executive's actual motives, the actual evidence available, and the degree to which individuals are actually burdened by government practices that restrict our liberty or favor one person's rights over another's. These questions are empirical, not interpretive, because justice isn't abstract or literary or historical, but rather depends on the facts in the here and now. But under the American approach, these factual questions take a back seat to "doctrinal tests," "tiers of scrutiny," and arcane inquiries into the placement of commas. Unsurprisingly, the rights judges declare us to have end up aligning with their own subjective sense of what is needed for a well-lived life. Rights stop being about justice and start being about the justices. We forget ourselves along the way.

The San Antonio Schools Case

The injustice the American approach produces is both arbitrary and staggering. On Thursday, May 16, 1968, about four hundred students staged a walkout at Edgewood High School in San Antonio. They had much to complain about. The school building was falling apart. Many of the windows were broken. Many of the teachers were uncertified and underpaid; a third of them had to be replaced every year. Temperatures in San Antonio reached the mid-80s that day, but the school had no air-conditioning. There was no toilet paper in the restrooms. A bat colony had nested on at least one floor of the school.

Edgewood was the poorest school district in the San Antonio area at the time. The district actually had the highest property tax rate in the area, but with only one in ten properties there valued at $10,000 or more, it was able to raise just $26 per student. The nearby Alamo Heights school district taxed its more-affluent residents and businesses at a much lower rate but raised more than twelve times as much money per student as Edgewood. Alamo Heights had newer school buildings, bigger classrooms, more library books, higher teacher pay, and fewer bats than Edgewood. Edgewood's dropout rate was four times that of Alamo Heights.

Demetrio Rodriguez, a Mexican-American sheet metal worker at Kelly Air Force Base and a parent to two Edgewood students, filed a class action lawsuit along with fifteen other parents. Rodriguez argued that the state's system of school financing, which relied heavily on local property taxes, infringed his children's constitutional right to an equal and adequate education. In 1973, the Supreme Court rejected Rodriguez's claims in a 5–4 decision.

The precise way in which the majority turned him away offers a startling case study in the Court's stilted approach to unfamiliar rights claims. For

Justice Lewis Powell, who wrote the majority opinion, the legal analysis had to begin with an all-important threshold question: "whether the Texas system of financing public education operates to the disadvantage of some suspect class or impinges upon a fundamental right explicitly or implicitly protected by the Constitution." In plain English, the question for Powell wasn't whether the San Antonio school system had any good reason to treat some of its students as second-class citizens. It was whether Rodriguez's children had a "right" to an equal and adequate public education. And the answer, the Court said, was no.

Footnote 4 of the filled milk case presaged this surprising framing and even more surprising answer. That footnote memorialized the American two-track approach, whereby courts give free rein to state laws unless they infringe on explicit constitutional rights, interfere with the political process, or disadvantage "discrete and insular minorities." Powell's talk of a "suspect class" is a reference to this last category. Not all laws that harm minorities are suspicious or call for special judicial scrutiny. Murderers, for example, are a minority group, but laws that burden them are treated as unremarkable. Rather, the Supreme Court gives high judicial attention, known as "strict scrutiny," only to laws that classify people along certain specific lines, most prominently race. For Justice Powell, discriminating between children in rich and poor neighborhoods didn't belong in this category and so didn't deserve any special scrutiny.

This conclusion cuts especially deep in a case like Rodriguez's. A funding arrangement of this sort is calculated to perpetuate disadvantage. People with fewer material resources are provided a lower-quality *public* service. That public service — education — is precisely the one citizens ordinarily call upon to facilitate their upward mobility. Denied opportunities for economic success, some residents turn to crime, further lowering property values. Those who manage to escape this unfortunate cycle and acquire more wealth can reliably be expected to leave the neighborhood on account of its poor schools and higher crime rates.

It gets worse. Texas's school financing scheme had predictable racial effects as well. Edgewood was 90 percent Mexican-American (Alamo Heights,

18 percent), a result of long-standing patterns of residential racial segregation. The concentration of poor-performing schools in racially identified
neighborhoods perpetuates racial stereotypes and race-based structural disadvantage. The San Antonio case was argued at the Supreme Court on the
same day as an important school desegregation case out of Denver, the first
such case to emerge from a northern school district. The Court was at the
time engaged in a pitched struggle over how to apply the lessons of *Brown
v. Board of Education* to school districts that were segregated in fact but had
not been subject to any official segregation policy. Indeed, Texas itself was in
this position with respect to Mexican-American students. Increasing school
funding was an important lever for advancing equality for minority students
stuck in under-resourced segregated schools.

Moreover, not only did Edgewood residents lack the means to fund their
public schools on a par with those in Alamo Heights or other wealthy neighborhoods, but the state actually forbade them to do so. Texas law placed
a cap of $1.50 per $100 of assessed property value on the amount a local
district could tax to contribute to the financing of its neighborhood schools.
In light of its property tax base, Edgewood could equal the highest local
contribution of any district in its county only by taxing at an impermissible
rate of $5.76 per $100. Alamo Heights could achieve that *same* contribution
with a tax of just $0.68 per $100 of property value. To say that this financing arrangement afforded Edgewood schoolchildren "the equal protection
of the laws" under the Fourteenth Amendment would require master-level
sophistry.

Justice Powell did not disappoint. He first declared, unbelievably, that the
case didn't even involve wealth discrimination because there wasn't any evidence that the people living in poor neighborhoods were themselves poor.
Maybe all those people living in dilapidated housing in an underperforming
school district were just being frugal. In any event, he said, the discrimination in this case couldn't be recognized by the Court because the Edgewood
schoolchildren weren't absolutely deprived of education. Since they still got
to go to school and those schools supplied them with "basic minimal skills,"
the equality argument had reached a dead end.

But all wasn't lost, perhaps, because Rodriguez didn't only make an equality argument. He also argued that education itself was so fundamental to the exercise of other rights, such as the right of free speech or the right to vote, that it could only be burdened under the most compelling circumstances. In *Brown v. Board of Education,* a unanimous Supreme Court had called education "perhaps the most important function of state and local governments." Moreover, the Supreme Court had recognized other "fundamental" constitutional rights that are not in the text of the Constitution, including the right to privacy that formed the basis for the *Roe v. Wade* abortion opinion that Powell had joined two months before the San Antonio school case. If abortion was a fundamental right, then certainly education must be, too, right?

Wrong. Justice Powell said he couldn't declare education a fundamental constitutional right. Not because it was unimportant. In fact, he conceded that education was of "grave significance" to both "the individual and to our society." Not because the right to education wasn't specified in the constitutional text. Again, textual specificity wasn't required in *Roe,* which Powell supported. No, the reason Justice Powell said education wasn't a constitutional right was because he saw no "logical limitations" on the theory. "How," he asked, "is education to be distinguished from the significant personal interests in the basics of decent food and shelter?" One might well ask why Powell seemed willing to hold that there is no constitutional right to food or shelter. The case wasn't about those deprivations, after all. But for him, it wasn't just that food and shelter weren't rights; it was that the very idea of seeing them as rights was so absurd that they could be trotted out as the final, climactic float in some grotesque parade of horribles. If we give them books, next thing you know they'll want food, too!

It takes a special failure of common sense, imagination, empathy, or all three to refuse to align rights with what individuals need in order to flourish, and yet American courts refuse. In understanding why, it helps to know a bit more about Lewis Powell. Nominated by President Nixon in 1971, Powell was a name partner at the white-shoe Virginia law firm of Hunton, Williams, Gay, Powell & Gibson. Patrician, well connected, and chivalrous, the son of a Richmond area box-company manager and a homemaker, Powell epito-mized white privilege. He had withdrawn his name from consideration for the Supreme Court two years earlier in part because he didn't want to take a pay cut.

Powell was also, like the man who appointed him, deeply paranoid and almost certainly a racist. Powell's public acts reveal an almost pathological commitment to maintaining the status quo. His law firm represented one of the segregated school districts in the *Brown* case, and as president of the Richmond School Board at the time of the decision, Powell said that he would "never" favor compulsory racial integration. Although Powell did not preach outright defiance of *Brown,* by the time his stint atop the school board ended in 1961, just *two* of Richmond's 23,000 African-American public school stu-dents attended a school with white children — Carol Irene Swann and Gloria Jean Mead, who enrolled at Chandler Junior High School in 1960. Powell believed that mass desegregation would encourage white flight and disrupt white community life, which he was committed above all to preserving. Of a piece with this commitment, in speech after speech in the 1960s and 1970s, Powell inveighed against "radical leftists," whom he believed were infiltrat-ing college campuses to try to brainwash "white middle-class Americans" to enlist them in the cause of a communist revolution.

American courts will always have judges like Lewis Powell — comfortable establishment men who reflexively defend the status quo and fear novelty. His vote in the San Antonio schools case was unsurprising. Rarely in his public life had Powell shown empathy for people like Demetrio Rodriguez. A degree of judicial bias was inevitable for Powell, as it is for all human judges. But when it comes to how deep that bias reaches into the justice sys-tem, Americans have choices. Justice Powell understood his task exclusively through the bloodless categories of American constitutional law rather than through the consequential facts of the real lives before the Court. We need not allow judges to deny, for all time, that startling, unjustified disparities in educational funding between rich and poor school districts are invisible to the Constitution. We need not tolerate judges declaring, in the Constitution's name, who gets to have rights and who doesn't. We can insist that the manifest injustice of the Texas funding scheme have some bearing on a judge's reasoning.

A court that believes it must decide the *category* a right is in before deciding whether the government is acting properly can cause much mischief. Loading the weight of constitutional analysis on this threshold definitional question rather than focusing on the government's actual behavior, motivations, and reasoning artificially separates the question of what rights we have from the question of what justice requires. This separation occurs not because of what the Constitution says — the document speaks of birth control or abortion or campaign spending no more or less than it speaks of food, shelter, or education. Instead, American judges ignore the demands of justice because they fear its consequences. A right to equal and adequate public schools could require courts to push the legislature to lay out funds. It might mean that courts are second-guessing educational policy decisions made by local administrators. Or it might mean that they feel compelled to recognize a bunch of other rights, such as Powell's dreaded rights to food and shelter, that are difficult to fully enforce through court decisions.

We need not fear these rights any more than the German court feared the right to feed pigeons. American judges can overcome their fear with a different frame of mind, one that focuses less on what rights we have and more on what it means to have a right. They can start by opening their eyes and having a look around.

The Indian Schools Cases

One hundred fifty countries around the world provide a right to free education in their national constitutions. Just about every one of those countries is poorer than the United States. India, for example, has more children than any country in the world. Two-thirds of the Indian population lives in rural areas, many of which lack basic infrastructure such as indoor plumbing. Hundreds of millions of Indians live on less than $2 a day. Fully one-third of the globe's illiterate people live in India.

If a constitutional right to education was a nonstarter in San Antonio, it seems absurd in India. Neither India's central government nor the governments of its individual states have the financial and material resources to provide a decent education to each of its more than 500 million children. Were Indians to treat the right to education the way Lewis Powell did, they would laugh it out of court. If the state utterly lacks the capacity to realize a right, they would say, it's pointless, even counterproductive, to declare the right in the first place. Wouldn't ordering India's governments to provide each of the country's school-age children with a decent education accomplish nothing except to reveal the Supreme Court of India's impotence?

This set of concerns moved India's constitutional framers. The Indian Constitution contains an extensive list of judicially enforceable rights, but it also includes what are called "Directive Principles of State Policy." Directive principles are not enforceable in court, but the state has a "duty" to apply those principles in the course of lawmaking. Much as how early American rights were understood, such principles are enforced through politics rather than courts, thereby ameliorating concerns that courts lack the wherewithal to make sensitive decisions in certain domains, including education policy.

The right to education originally appeared in the Indian Constitution as a directive principle. Article 41 of the constitution directs that "the State shall, within the limits of its economic capacity and development, make effective provision for securing the right . . . to education." A further directive principle of state policy (since amended) specified that the state "shall endeavour to provide, within a period to ten years from the commencement of this Constitution, for free and compulsory education for all children until they complete the age of fourteen years."

The right to education remained solely a directive principle until a 1992 Indian Supreme Court decision involving a woman, Mohini Jain, who had been denied admission to a private medical school in the south Indian city of Tumkur solely because she couldn't afford the 60,000-rupee annual fee. She challenged the state law permitting private medical colleges to charge prohibitive rates. Extending a series of earlier cases that had interpreted the constitutionally protected "right to life" broadly to include the right to live "with human dignity," the Supreme Court held that the right to education was encompassed within "life." Since the right to life was judicially enforceable, so, too, was the right to education.

The following year, the court further refined the right to education and held that every child in India has a judicially enforceable right to free education until the age of fourteen, but that, beyond that point, the right depended on the economic capacity of the state. In 2001, India amended its constitution to explicitly codify a judicially enforceable right to "free and compulsory education to all children of the age of 6 to 14 years in such manner as the State may, by law, determine."

Indian states lack the power and the political will to fully enroll every Indian child in a decent elementary or middle school. No court decision can change that. But the right to education is still meaningful. It is a hammer with more than one nail.

Consider, for example, a 2001 decision in which the High Court of Delhi said that the use of corporal punishment by school headmasters interfered with the right to live with dignity. A light caning on the hand in response to a student's violent or disruptive behavior might interfere only trivially with such a right in isolation. It seems a bit much to equate this traditional form of discipline with torture or other human rights abuses conventionally covered by the right to live with dignity. But the court emphasized that because corporal punishment could interfere with the educational process, it triggered additional constitutional guarantees beyond the bare right to a dignified life. The right to education, therefore, *amplified* other rights in the constitution.

Constitutionally enshrining a right to education has also enabled the Indian Supreme Court to pluck low-hanging fruit that bears directly on the lives of ordinary Indians. In 2004, a fire devastated a middle school in the city of Madras, killing ninety-three children. The fire was sparked by dry coconut leaves that the cooks were using for kindling as they prepared lunch for the children. The school's nine hundred students had to come and go through one entrance and exit, and there were no windows in the classrooms. Many of the children died instantly when the school's thatched roof, held aloft by bamboo poles, caught fire and collapsed on them.

Resolving a lawsuit over the fire, the Indian Supreme Court held that the constitutional right to education required states and the federal government to provide schools with safe infrastructure. Those requirements extended to fire-suppression equipment, adequate emergency exits, and secure construction materials capable of withstanding not just fire but also earthquakes and other natural disasters. The court even ordered that kitchens must be separate from main school buildings and that each of India's 750,000 primary schools had to observe Fire Safety Day on April 14. Some of what the court ordered was already required by national and local laws. But putting those requirements into a court judgment forced the government to triage its limited budget and enabled the court to set specific benchmarks that increased the leverage of political advocates.

A third example of the work the right to education does in India is more striking still. Recall that one of Lewis Powell's concerns in denying the right to education in the San Antonio case was that he could not see how to keep it from growing into other social and economic rights such as a right to food or shelter. A public interest group in India had the same thought but pushed it in a very different direction from Justice Powell. In 2001, the People's Union for Civil Liberties filed a lawsuit directly with the Indian Supreme Court arguing that the constitutional right to education required the government to provide schoolchildren with nutritious school lunches. With poverty endemic in India, providing food was a reliable way to get parents to send their children to school rather than have them work or stay at home. In November 2001, the Indian Supreme Court ordered the Indian state and federal governments to provide children at every school receiving state funding with a cooked, midday meal with at least 300 calories and between 8 and 12 grams of protein for at least two hundred days out of the year. The midday meal scheme has dramatically improved both student enrollment and children's health in India.

The right to education in India is, in effect, a partial rather than an absolute right. It is not enforced by requiring states to immediately enroll all children in high-performing schools, in the way Justice Powell seemed to assume. The Indian example shows that we can measure the effectiveness of the right to education not only in school enrollment or graduation outcomes but also in student safety and children's nutrition.

To be sure, Indian courts are very different from their American counterparts. The Indian Supreme Court, in particular, has developed a reputation for activism far outpacing anything conceivable in the United States. Yet the Indian example can inspire us. It isn't hard to imagine how a constitutional right to education could survive in the United States with just a little bit more imagination than we saw from the majority in the San Antonio case. Maybe it would push too hard on traditions of local control to require equal funding of all schools, at least right away. But would it be too much for a court to ask that poor schools have the same access as wealthy ones to air-conditioning, updated textbooks, and an exterminator? A court can, of course, try to impose these kinds of requirements directly, but the bare existence of a right to education would provide leverage to students, parents, teachers, school boards, and advocates to negotiate for these benefits themselves, through politics, so that the court's ultimate intervention would be needed less. Which is just as it should be.

The Death of Disparate Impact

It might seem as though there was a constitutional lever in the San Antonio case hiding in plain sight. Edgewood was (and remains) an overwhelmingly Mexican-American neighborhood sitting on San Antonio's impoverished West Side. The concentration of Mexican Americans in that part of the city wasn't accidental. It was the result, in part, of racially restrictive housing covenants that courts were all too willing to uphold, as well as discriminatory lending practices by a host of private and public actors, including the Federal Housing Administration.

In 1968, the same year those four hundred students walked out of Edgewood High, the U.S. Commission on Civil Rights published a report chronicling widespread discrimination against Mexican Americans in the Southwest, and in San Antonio in particular, from housing to employment, from voting to education. That was also the year the Mexican American Legal Defense and Educational Fund (MALDEF) was founded, with headquarters in San Antonio. MALDEF was created on the model of the NAACP's Legal Defense and Educational Fund (LDF), which had litigated the *Brown* case. Jack Greenberg, the LDF's legal director, had been instrumental in establishing a similar group focused on the civil rights of Mexican Americans. The plight of Edgewood High School was as much about race as it was about class.

Whatever we might think of a right to education or a right against wealth inequality, no one doubts that the Constitution has a lot to say about racial discrimination. The Fourteenth Amendment was a direct response to southern Black Codes, which restricted the rights of recently freed slaves to own property and to make and enforce contracts. Given the obvious racial effects of the Texas school financing scheme and the obvious racial causes of the residential segregation that created those effects, why was it necessary for the Supreme Court in the San Antonio case to go casting about for new rights to education or against wealth discrimination? Why wasn't the old right against racial discrimination potent enough for Demetrio Rodriguez to have a shot in his case?

There was some reason at the time to think it might be. In 1971, two years before the San Antonio case reached the Supreme Court, the justices held that the ban on race-based employment discrimination in the 1964 Civil Rights Act (Title VII) can sometimes be applied even to employers who did not specifically intend to discriminate. The case was brought by Black employees of a North Carolina energy company, Duke Power, that had a practice of openly segregating its Black workers into its low-wage labor department. After Title VII rendered this policy illegal, the company began to require transferees from the labor department to other departments within the company to pass two general intelligence tests on which Blacks generally scored lower than whites. The question for the Court was whether the plaintiff workers had to show that these tests were adopted specifically to discriminate on the basis of race or whether it might be enough to show that they had a negative "disparate impact" on Black employees.

The decision in the case that became *Griggs v. Duke Power Co.* was unanimous. Writing for the Court, Chief Justice Warren Burger said that even "neutral" acts by employers can be covered by Title VII if they "'freeze' the status quo of prior discriminatory employment practices." According to Burger, Congress in enacting the Civil Rights Act was concerned with "the consequences of employment practices, not simply the motivation." Duke Power was not a sympathetic defendant. Its aptitude tests reeked of pretext. Still, the *Griggs* opinion, written by Richard Nixon's first Supreme Court appointee, offered some hope that Chief Justice Burger's Court might adopt an approach to racial equality that took seriously the fact that white supremacy had been official state policy for the previous 350 years.

That hope turned out to be misplaced. In 1970, a group of African Americans who had failed an exam to become Washington, D.C., police officers sued District officials under the Fourteenth Amendment. Unlike the *Griggs* case, which was based on a federal statute, these plaintiffs argued that the Constitution itself recognized claims of racial discrimination based on "disparate impact." The exam, Test 21, wasn't exactly culturally neutral. The third question, for example, went as follows:

> Laws restricting hunting to certain regions and to a specific time of the year were passed *chiefly* to
>
> A) prevent people from endangering their lives by hunting
> B) keep our forests more beautiful
> C) raise funds from the sale of hunting licenses
> D) prevent complete destruction of certain kinds of animals
> E) preserve certain game for eating purposes

Other questions asked about the purposes of trademarks or whether applicants knew the meaning of words like "placidity" (question 59) or "promontory" (question 73). The plaintiffs argued that because the use of this test had the effect of excluding disproportionate numbers of Black applicants, it violated the Equal Protection Clause. The Supreme Court thought otherwise. The fact that a law or government practice has a "disparate impact" on members of a particular racial group may support a claim under the Civil Rights Act, but it was never sufficient, the Court said, to make out a *constitutional* claim against the law or practice.

In justifying the Court's decision, Justice Byron White made the same kind of "slippery slope" argument as Justice Powell made in the San Antonio schools case:

> A rule that a statute designed to serve neutral ends is nevertheless invalid, absent compelling justification, if in practice it benefits or burdens one race more than another would be far-reaching and would raise serious questions about, and perhaps invalidate, a whole range of tax, welfare, public service, regulatory, and licensing statutes that may be more burdensome to the poor and to the average black than to the more affluent white.

For the Supreme Court, the difficulty of distinguishing Test 21 from numerous other government practices that might have a disparate impact on Blacks meant that disparate racial impact must not involve *any rights at all.* It's yet another clear example of how American courts' absolutism leads them to restrict and not just expand rights.

In practical terms, the Court's ruling meant that the Constitution simply doesn't recognize claims of structural inequality. A government official is entitled to be entirely indifferent even to severe and predictable effects a law might have on historically disadvantaged groups, so long as the effect was not specifically intended. And so, for example, the Court in 1974 refused to say that a California disability insurance program that explicitly excluded pregnancy-related disabilities counted as sex discrimination. The discrimination wasn't against women as a class, the Court reasoned, but rather against *pregnant* women.

Five years later, a woman was rebuffed in her challenge to a Massachusetts policy that gave a lifetime preference in government jobs to military veterans, even though the military itself discriminated against women in a variety of ways. The state veterans preference was not *because* the law was biased against women, the Court said, even though the underlying military policy was itself intentionally discriminatory.

In a 1987 case, the justices held that they couldn't interfere with a death sentence even though the defendant, Warren McCleskey — a Black man convicted of killing a white police officer inside an Atlanta furniture store

— produced overwhelming statistical evidence, known as the Baldus study, showing that Black defendants with white victims were disproportionately likely to receive death sentences. The only way McCleskey could win, said Powell for the 5–4 majority, was if he was able to prove that the prosecutors, jury, or judge in his *individual* case sought the death penalty because of McCleskey's or his victim's race.

Most startling was Powell's worry, echoing his opinion in the San Antonio schools case, that "McCleskey's claim, taken to its logical conclusion, throws into serious question the principles that underlie our entire criminal justice system." Rather than being cause to take the claim all the more seriously, this was, for the Court, the reason to reject it. For if the Court accepted statistical evidence of the sort McCleskey put forward, as Powell worried in an internal memo to his law clerks, "no black defendant in Georgia may ever be given the death sentence." Moreover, he suggested anxiously in the majority opinion, other people prosecuted or sentenced based on arbitrary factors such as race or sex or physical appearance might also raise constitutional claims! As Justice Brennan wrote in dissent, McCleskey would be executed because the Court was afraid of "too much justice."

The Supreme Court's paralysis in the face of constitutional disparate impact claims follows directly from its all-or-nothing frame for rights disputes. The Court operates from a Holmesian baseline of complete deference to the government. It departs from that baseline only if the case triggers certain prefab categories of rights, which the Court then fetishizes and treats as presumptively absolute. The justices are appropriately anxious about this fetish. But rather than stop fetishizing, they instead define rights narrowly to limit the damage. And so, just as the right to education doesn't exist because it would (we are told) imply a limitless right to food or shelter, the right to have a racially disparate impact recognized as potential discrimination doesn't exist because it could jeopardize the tax laws or embarrass the criminal justice system.

Claims of disparate impact discrimination, also known as indirect discrimination, are common, indeed unremarkable, in courts around the world, where they somehow manage to coexist with tax codes and criminal laws. Consider South Africa, a country that, like the United States, promoted racism as official state policy through most of the twentieth century. Under apartheid, the City of Pretoria charged different electricity and water rates to the white residents of the old city versus the Black residents of the outlying townships, Atteridgeville and Mamelodi. Unlike old Pretoria, the neglected townships lacked the infrastructure for meters, and so their residents were charged a flat rate for the meager utilities they received. These fees often went unpaid. After the fall of the apartheid government, a white resident of the old city sued to end the differential treatment, claiming to be the victim of racial discrimination in violation of the new interim constitution. Rich, isn't it?

This claim would almost certainly fail in the United States, but for the wrong reason. The city would argue, correctly, that even though the rate discrepancy was perfectly correlated with race, the old Pretoria resident was not discriminated against because he was white. He was discriminated against because of where he lived. The U.S. Supreme Court doesn't care about discrimination on the basis of geography any more than it cares about discrimination on the basis of whether a defendant like McCleskey killed a cop. So long as the government had any conceivable rational reason for differentiation along these lines, the government wins. In a country with as storied a history of racial discrimination as the United States, many government policies are bound to produce stark racial effects. The Supreme Court's deliberate strategy for addressing those effects is to insist that they don't matter. A baby who is never fed eventually stops crying.

But, as everyone knows, the idea that the Pretoria case didn't involve racial discrimination is nonsense. Nearly everyone who benefited from the policy was Black. Nearly everyone burdened by it was white. Those effects were obvious, were known to the policy makers, and were avoidable. A constitution that cares about racial discrimination should care about a policy with those features. The Constitutional Court of South Africa had no difficulty understanding that. Justice Pius Langa, a Black jurist who came of age under apartheid, wrote the court's opinion: "It would be artificial to make a comparison between an area known to be overwhelmingly a 'black area' and another known to be overwhelmingly a 'white area,' on the grounds of geography alone," he wrote. "To ignore the racial impact of the differentiation is to place form above substance." Recognizing "indirect" discrimination of this sort is a common practice among the world's courts, from Canada to Israel, from Brazil to Germany, from the United Kingdom to Colombia.

Here's the thing, though: *just because the constitution cares doesn't mean the plaintiff has to win!* In the United States, concluding that the government intended to discriminate on the basis of race would have virtually ended the case. In South Africa, it didn't. It only meant that the court had to ask the further question of whether the discrimination was "unfair." That conclusion turns on a factually sensitive judgment. Under South African law, whether discrimination is unfair depends, among other things, on the place of the plaintiffs in society, whether they have suffered from past disadvantage, the importance of the benefit they are being denied, and the significance of the social goal the government is trying to advance. In other words, it depends on the facts. Here, the court said that while it was not unfair to charge different rates given the gap in metering infrastructure and service quality, it *was* unfair for the government to sue old Pretoria residents but not township residents for nonpayment.

South Africa is not a country whose judges are unaware of Justice Byron White's admonition that standard government policies can be more burdensome to one race than to another. Imagine, if you can, Pius Langa's life as a Black lawyer in 1970s Durban. He recognized that it was precisely because of — not in spite of — the persistence of racial disadvantage that the constitution could not remain blind to it. That means that some policies that are not intentionally discriminatory might on occasion be struck down. It also means that when government officials are designing policies, they need to *care* about the racial impact, even if for no other reason than to forestall litigation. The availability of a constitutional remedy opens doors to political negotiation and accommodation that would otherwise stay shut. It does not mean, contra Justice White, that every government policy must fall. Sometimes if you give a mouse a cookie, it just eats the cookie.

Proportionality

Most high courts around the world handle discrimination claims, along with other rights claims, through a process known as "proportionality." Under proportionality, the weight of analysis is less on whether a right has been identified — this inquiry is typically more generous than in the United States — and more on what the government's justification is for burdening the right.

Proportionality entails a stepwise series of increasingly more difficult tests for the government to meet. *First,* is there a basic congruence between the government's policy and some legitimate policy objective? A court hearing a challenge to the San Antonio schools case based on racial discrimination, for example, could spend less time musing about the right to shelter and more time on whether there's any good reason for Texas to tie school funding to local property taxes. *Second,* could the government achieve its ends in a way that restricts rights less? Given that poor neighborhoods in San Antonio are the outgrowth of discriminatory policies, the government would need to show that it cannot achieve the local control of schools (or whatever) it is seeking without this kind of property tax arrangement. *Third,* is the government's policy seriously out of proportion to the burdens it imposes on rights? Even if property taxes are the best way to achieve the autonomy the government says it wants to preserve, maybe the disproportionate effect on a school like Edgewood High is too much to bear. Maybe not.

Whatever the answers to these questions, they are the *right* questions: questions about *this* case, *this* policy, *this* school district, and *these* schoolchildren. These questions, and not hypothetical ones about rights that aren't part of the case, are the questions justice demands answers to.

U.S. courts rejected proportionality in favor of a more binary, categorical approach as an accident of history. Proportionality recalls the alleged sins of the *Lochner* case, which Frankfurter and his happy hot dogs exhumed Holmes to highlight and criticize. But Holmes's *Lochner* dissent is inadequate to the far more complex rights environment we have inhabited since the 1960s. The courts of other countries, most of which only came into being after World War II, are unburdened by the stigma of the *Lochner* era. These courts were born into the complexities of the postwar period and so have become more familiar with the technology—the *adjudicative* technology —needed to navigate it.

The alternative is to continue to sever rights from justice. Justice Antonin Scalia was more clear-eyed than most about this consequence. Warren Mc-Cleskey's case was one of Scalia's first as a Supreme Court justice. He joined Powell's abysmal opinion, but as he did so, he sent the following remarkable memo, which I quote nearly in full, to Powell's chambers:

> I plan to join Lewis's opinion in this case, with two reservations. I disagree with the argument that the inferences that can be drawn from the Baldus study are weakened by the fact that each jury and each trial is unique, or by the large number of variables at issue. And I do not share the view, implicit in the opinion, that an effect of racial factors upon sentencing, if it could only be shown by sufficiently strong statistical evidence, would require reversal. Since it is my view that the unconscious operation of irrational sympathies and antipathies, including racial, upon jury deliberations and (hence) prosecutorial decisions is real, acknowledged in the decisions of this court, and ineradicable, I cannot honestly say that all I need is more proof.

Scalia's view, that is, was that racism is inevitable within the criminal justice system. So long as it is unconscious, judges have no choice but simply to tolerate it, even if it results in an execution.

From Molehills to Mountains

The gap between rights and justice shows up most dramatically in the injustices courts tolerate when they look too hard for a right they can classify in binary terms. The result is Demetrio Rodriguez's children having to endure Edgewood's failing schools because Lewis Powell didn't know what box his claim fit into. It is the African-American applicants who couldn't get a job in the D.C. police department because they didn't know enough about hunting. It is the women in California denied disability insurance because their injuries resulted from pregnancy instead of flag football. It is the Massachusetts woman who aced numerous state civil service exams being repeatedly passed over because of a putatively gender-neutral preference for military veterans. It is Warren McCleskey being executed by the State of Georgia on a still September morning because the Supreme Court didn't want to give him "too much justice."

Injustice can also result from courts taking rights too literally. We are accustomed to heralding the role of rights in frustrating government power grabs. A more robust commitment to rights might have halted Hitler's abuse of the Weimar Constitution to acquire emergency powers and install himself as führer. Rights were unduly minimized under the apartheid constitutions of South Africa and in the United States under Jim Crow. But rights themselves are powerful tools of social control. Tying that power to a binary, prefab category can produce its own distortion of justice.

The Second Amendment is an obvious example. We need not deny that Americans have gun rights to say that guns are nonetheless subject to reasonable regulation in the name of public safety. And yet in 2008, when the Supreme Court affirmed the right of D.C. residents to keep loaded handguns in their homes, Justice Scalia said that a right subject to judicial balancing "is no constitutional guarantee at all." This view of gun rights renders invisible the right to personal security that the people of the District chose to protect through law, as the Framers intended.

Scalia compared gun rights to speech rights, which he correctly said U.S. courts viewed as nearly absolute. But this, too, is wrongheaded. Much as modern courts, and modern Americans in turn, are taken with speech rights, speech is not easily hived off from action. We perform many consequential acts by speaking. "You're fired." "Whites Only." "Fly heading zero-niner-zero." Surely some of those speech acts can and should be regulated. Free speech law has become a kind of game in which well-heeled litigants looking to evade regulation characterize their acts in purely expressive terms, and often get away with it.

There's *Citizens United*, of course, in which the Supreme Court threw out a law preventing corporations from using their treasury funds for election-eering. For the Court, the fact that the funds were being used for expressive acts made the law subject to just the same scrutiny as one that, say, targeted voters for engaging in political advocacy. In 2011, a group of data-mining and pharma concerns were able to persuade the Supreme Court to strike down a Vermont law forbidding pharmacies to sell doctors' prescription data to drug companies. Justice Anthony Kennedy acknowledged that the privacy and, indeed, the public health reasons for the law were "significant," but because the law seemed to target the marketing of drugs, he wrote for the majority that it impermissibly interfered with the *speech* rights of drug companies. More recently, the Court held that laws requiring municipal employees to contribute to the collective bargaining costs of the union that represented them in contract negotiations violated the employees' right to "speak" through their union dues.

To be sure, a judge who believes agency fees are coerced speech might find a way to hold against the union no matter what. But the American approach to rights lets the judge launder that decision by tying it to the lofty ideals of the First Amendment. The alternative approach used by courts around the world invites us instead to distinguish the kinds of acts that strike at the core of those lofty ideals — sedition laws, McCarthyism, targeted harassment of political opponents, and the like — from ordinary acts of workplace or con-sumer privacy regulation.

There are rights at stake in self-governance, too. Those rights might not be quite as amenable to the historical excavation, textual exegesis, and case analysis that we've come to associate with constitutional judging, but there is no reason to think that the rights we have are just whatever rights judges are comfortable explicating. When judges consistently celebrate the trivial and ignore the momentous, it's a sign that something has gone terribly wrong.

And it gets worse.

5

When Rights Collide

C onflict is a right's natural state. The right to pursue one's livelihood or to express oneself or to be admitted to a school on the basis of one's intrinsic qualities can conflict with the rights of others to be treated equally, or fairly, or with dignity. American rightsism is designed to avoid such conflicts by pretending that one right or another is not of constitutional significance. This attitude is both wrong and dangerous. Refusing to take all rights seriously, to meet all rights on their own terms, doesn't only debase our system of justice. It also fractures our politics just at the moment when politics is most needed.

There is no issue over which Americans are divided more starkly and passionately than abortion. Partisans in the debate over abortion rights seem to agree on nothing, indeed seem to hold views that are literally irreconcilable. They seem, moreover, to hate each other.

Opponents of abortion rights routinely liken the Supreme Court's decision in *Roe v. Wade* to its decision in the *Dred Scott* case, when it affirmed slaveholders' constitutionally protected property rights in their slaves and held that Black Americans could never become citizens of the United States. In 2019, Justice Clarence Thomas chose, in an otherwise uncontroversial and unanimous decision, to write separately to describe the decision to terminate a pregnancy because of fetal abnormalities as "modern-day eugenics." His opinion was issued two weeks after Alabama passed a law that made obtaining an abortion a criminal offense in nearly all cases. The preamble to the law, which the state called the Human Life Protection Act, compares abortion in the United States to the Holocaust, China's Cultural Revolution, Stalin's gulags, the Cambodian killing fields, and the Rwandan genocide. It says abortion is worse.

From a different perspective, *Roe v. Wade* is the single most emancipatory decision in the Supreme Court's history. A state forcing a woman to bear a fetus and beget an unwanted child is a form of involuntary servitude, which is literally forbidden by the Thirteenth Amendment. In one stroke, *Roe* made first- and second-trimester abortions legal in forty-six states, thirty of which had previously prohibited abortion in all circumstances. The decision has prevented many millions of women from being subjected to the physical, emotional, social, and financial toll of becoming mothers against their will. A prominent social media campaign launched in 2015 has accordingly encouraged women to "shout" their abortions — to share their abortion experiences without shame or apology — so as to make them seem more normal.

On the face of things, there can be no common ground between a woman who shouts her abortion and a protester who believes that the woman has murdered her child. The abortion issue presents a conflict of rights in its purest form. And yet deep-seated animosity around abortion politics is not universal. It is relatively absent, for example, in Canada or in much of Europe and Asia. Among the many reasons for this difference, American courts' insistence on choosing between rights — their systematic failure to account for and mediate rights conflicts — remains an important but largely untold story.

Allowing existentially competing rights to coexist requires a different approach that, again, looking abroad can help us better see. In the early 1970s, when *Roe v. Wade* was decided, abortion was a more divisive political issue in West Germany than in the United States. It is far less so today. The role of courts in each country, and in particular the West German Federal Constitutional Court's insistence on recognizing multiple and competing constitutional rights, is an important part of the reason why. By making both sides take all rights seriously, the West German court ensured that they were all engaged in the same conversations, the same politics. By giving all sides leverage in those conversations, the court allowed grievances to be aired and compromises brokered. And by insisting that abortion battles be waged in the political arena, the court gave each side reason to persuade others of their cause.

Today, even as German courts continue to insist on the value of fetal life, it is easier and cheaper to obtain an abortion in Germany than in most of the United States, and abortion politics has become ordinary rather than existential. Understanding how that's possible lights a path to a more constructive role for courts in other areas of intense political disagreement.

A Tale of Two Abortion Cases

Over a nineteen-day stretch in the late fall of 1975, John Paul Stevens was nominated to the Supreme Court, received a three-day hearing before the Senate Judiciary Committee, and was unanimously confirmed. Stevens had been selected by a Republican president, Gerald Ford, but Democrats controlled sixty-one seats in the Senate. Presidential primary season was in full swing. Barely a week before Stevens was picked, Ronald Reagan had announced that he would be challenging Ford for the Republican nomination. A month after Stevens was confirmed, a relatively unknown Georgia peanut farmer named Jimmy Carter won the Iowa Democratic Caucus. Had the Democrats held out against the badly weakened Ford, Carter might have gotten a chance to make what would have been his only Supreme Court appointment. And yet Stevens was confirmed that December, 98–0, after only five minutes of debate.

What makes the ease and swiftness of Stevens's confirmation all the more startling is that he was the first person to be nominated to the Supreme Court after its 1973 decision in *Roe*. And yet, at his confirmation hearing and in individual meetings with senators, Stevens was not asked a single question, by any senator, Democrat or Republican, about *Roe* or about abortion. It wasn't that senators didn't ask about sensitive or political issues — they asked freely about busing plans and free speech and government surveillance and the death penalty. It's just that abortion wasn't nearly as divisive or as urgent to judicial politics then as it is now.

Roe was a 7–2 decision. The majority included five Republican appointees, including three by Richard Nixon, as well as the only Catholic justice on the Court, William Brennan. *Roe* was assailed by many Roman Catholic leaders, but the decision preceded (and eventually helped to motivate) the deliberate fusion of Republican politics with the most conservative elements of the evangelical Protestant movement. Indeed, most Protestants in the early 1970s favored liberalized access to abortion. The Southern Baptist Convention in 1974 reaffirmed its position that it was necessary to seek "a middle ground between the extreme of abortion on demand and the opposite extreme of all abortion as murder."

The same year Justice Stevens was confirmed to the Supreme Court without fanfare, West Germany found itself in crisis over abortion rights. Abortion had been banned in most cases since the German Reich's founding in 1871. But in 1974, the left-leaning Social Democrats had teamed up with the Free Democrats to muscle an abortion liberalization bill through the Bundestag, West Germany's lower house. The vote, 247–233, was so tight that individual votes had to be counted for the first time in the country's history. Under the new law, a woman could obtain an abortion in the first twelve weeks of pregnancy following consultation with a physician and a social counselor. After twelve weeks, only medically necessary abortions were allowed. Had this law been passed in the United States, it would have been unconstitutional under *Roe* because it didn't sufficiently protect a woman's right to end a second-trimester pregnancy. The perspective of West Germany's Federal Constitutional Court was just the opposite: Did a law *permitting* a *first*-trimester abortion sufficiently protect the *fetus's* right to life? The court said no. Call it bizarre *Roe*.

Roe's author, Harry Blackmun, had entertained but quickly rejected the possibility that a fetus might hold constitutional rights. Blackmun's aim was to describe the abortion controversy in purely medical terms. The hope was that a medically oriented opinion could help depoliticize the issue, and the framing suited Blackmun to boot. He had once flirted with a career in medicine, and he kept a copy of Dorland's medical dictionary on a shelf behind his desk in chambers. In the 1950s, he had cut his teeth as general counsel for the Mayo Clinic, a job he was so fond of that he asked that his ashes be scattered on the clinic's grounds after his death. In the summer of 1972, just before *Roe* was argued, Blackmun spent ten days conducting research on abortion at the clinic's library in Rochester, Minnesota.

Blackmun's eventual opinion in *Roe* is nothing if not clinical. He described the decision whether to have an abortion as a medical judgment made by a doctor in consultation with his patient. The woman had a "privacy" interest in family planning. The state had an interest in ensuring the pregnant woman's health, which meant that it could, for example, require that abortions be performed by physicians. But as far as the Constitution was concerned, the fetus was not a person and was therefore irrelevant prior to the third trimester, the point at which viability became plausible under 1970s medical technology. If a fetus is a constitutional person, he wrote, then "[the woman's] case, of course, collapses."

The West German example shows that Blackmun was quite wrong about this consequence. The Federal Constitutional Court held not only that fetal life is a constitutional value but that the state has a *duty* to protect it. It had pretty good reasons, grounded in Germany's history, for saying so. A prohibition on abortion was part of the inaugural German penal code of 1871 and resisted numerous reform efforts over the subsequent century. Indeed, penalties for abortion were *enhanced* during the Third Reich, a concession to the eugenicist urge to repel perceived "attacks on race and heredity." But abortion liberalization faced its own dark resonances with the country's Nazi past. As the 6–2 majority wrote, the right to life was included in the West German Constitution (the Basic Law) "as a reaction to the 'destruction of life unworthy of life,' to the 'final solution' and 'liquidations,' which were carried out by the National Socialistic Regime as measures of state." Barely a generation removed from the end of World War II, the justices of West Germany's highest court were not comfortable endorsing the idea that certain lives were beneath the protection of the law. Because abortion involved the killing of a living being, the court said, West German law was obligated to condemn it.

But the fact that fetuses were protected under the West German Constitution didn't mean that women were not. In addition to safeguarding the right to life, the Basic Law also protected the "right to free development of [one's] personality" — the ability of individuals to pursue their life goals without undue interference from the state. For pregnant women, this meant that an abortion performed for legitimate reasons, though illegal, did not need to be criminally punished. Legitimate reasons did not mean *any* reason, as it does under *Roe*. Rather, the court specified that abortion could be decriminalized in the first trimester for reasons relating to significant threats to the woman's health or life, serious genetic irregularities of the fetus, severe emotional distress or unusual hardships associated with pregnancy or childbirth, and in cases of pregnancies resulting from rape or incest.

Two abortion decisions, in two different countries, two years apart, pointed in two opposite directions. In *Roe*, the U.S. Supreme Court struck down abortion restrictions for failing to respect women's autonomy. In the West German decision, the constitutional court struck down abortion liberalization for failing to respect fetal life. But court decisions on momentous constitutional issues are never fully separate from politics, and they can affect politics in surprising ways.

The Politics *Roe* Made

Relative to today, the U.S. anti-abortion movement in the years leading up to *Roe* was ecumenical, ideologically diverse, and bipartisan. By the start of the 1970s, its leaders were decreasingly framing their cause in terms of religious chastity, which the sexual revolution had neutered as a political appeal, and were instead emphasizing more broadly resonant messages: the human rights of the fetus as a beleaguered "minority" and the improvements in social welfare needed to make motherhood a real choice for poor women.

Two anti-abortion organizations enjoyed a nationwide profile before *Roe*. The earlier of the two, Americans United for Life (AUL), was headed by George Huntston Williams, a famously ecumenical Harvard Divinity School professor and Great Society liberal who had burned draft cards in front of

Boston's Arlington Street Church in 1967. The larger, the National Right to Life Committee (NRLC), was run by Marjory Mecklenburg, a women's rights advocate who strongly pushed birth control and social assistance for families. Mecklenburg's husband, Fred, also active in the movement, was a member of Planned Parenthood.

Building a big tent made political sense before *Roe*. Abortion politics at the time was primarily legislative rather than judicial. Sixteen states had liberalized their abortion laws between 1967 and 1970. But in 1971, with an increasingly mobilized anti-abortion political movement, all of the abortion legalization bills being debated in twenty-five states went down in defeat. The following year, abortion rights opponents successfully pushed the New York legislature to vote to repeal that state's own liberalization law before Republican governor Nelson Rockefeller vetoed the effort. It is also telling that among the first leaders to reach out to the NRLC to offer support after *Roe* were Black civil rights activists Jesse Jackson and Al Sampson. Americans' views on abortion rights did not align neatly along partisan lines.

But *Roe* tore the anti-abortion movement apart. In particular, the opinion's insistence that a fetus was not a constitutional person pushed the movement into a more radical, disruptive posture. Hard-liners pursued a "human life" amendment to the Constitution that would define a fetus as a human being entitled to constitutional rights from the moment of conception, with no exception even for an abortion necessary to save the life of the pregnant woman. In July 1973, six months after *Roe*, the NRLC explicitly condemned an alternative amendment that would simply reverse *Roe* and restore abortion regulation to state political processes. The organization did so over the objection of Mecklenburg and other "moderate" forces within the movement who believed, correctly, that a human life amendment was a political nonstarter. As one Kansas NRLC member described the anti-abortion movement in the summer of 1973, "There may be a few pragmatists, but by and large those who are committed to this cause are idealists who will refuse to compromise, who realize that our only defense is our moral position and if we abandon that position for even one exception, we have nothing left."

The Supreme Court's erasure of the fetus from the Constitution was, for many in the movement, a declaration of war. Anti-abortion forces had come to see the defense of fetal rights as their raison d'être. But in their zeal to define the movement through a futile constitutional amendment, anti-abortion conservatives knocked over several other dominoes. By the summer of 1974, moderate forces had been purged completely from the NRLC. Executive director Warren Schaller, an Episcopalian priest from St. Paul, Minnesota, who preached collaboration with abortion rights proponents on issues such as maternal health, was sidelined and eventually fired when a new slate of officers took over the organization at its 1974 convention. That convention saw Mecklenburg lose her bid for the NRLC presidency. She resigned two months later to form (along with Schaller and Judy Fink, another "moderate" who resigned from the NRLC board) American Citizens Concerned for Life (ACCL), which sought to emphasize abortion alternatives and try to build bridges to "antiwar pacifists, feminists, and blacks." It was, Mecklenburg said, an "organization concerned with finding solutions to social problems, not just banning abortion."

But the ACCL had a lower profile and much less funding than the NRLC. In 1976, the year of a crucial presidential election for the movement, the ACCL had fewer than seventeen thousand members compared with the NRLC's one million, which it owed in part to the support of the Catholic Church. The NRLC's purge of Mecklenburg and her allies had freed the organization to pursue a campaign during the 1974 midterm elections that defined being "pro-life" exclusively in terms of support for a constitutional amendment supported by a small minority of Americans.

Many pro-life Democrats with presidential aspirations — including Birch Bayh, Edward "Ted" Kennedy, Sargent Shriver, and Jimmy Carter — were willing to support a states' rights amendment or a social welfare law aimed at crisis pregnancies, but they were unwilling to support a human life amendment. Congressional bills were introduced to provide federal funds for state and local health agencies to offer health care and other social services to teenage mothers and to expand insurance coverage for pregnant women. These were legislative efforts aimed at providing abortion alternatives, which many centrist and Catholic Democrats insisted was the best way to respond to *Roe*. The NRLC turned on them. As the anti-abortion grass roots radicalized, they became increasingly toxic for Democratic politicians to affiliate with. And as the abortion issue's political middle hollowed out, even former moderates like Mecklenburg, forced to choose sides, became more conservative.

Meanwhile, Ronald Reagan, who had presidential ambitions of his own, embraced a human life amendment as a way to outflank President Ford to the right. Ford was nominally opposed to abortion rights, but his wife, Betty, and his vice president, Nelson Rockefeller, were among the country's most high-profile *Roe* supporters. With Ford becoming the first incumbent since Herbert Hoover to be voted out of office, a political crisis for the Republican Party became an opportunity for its activist fringe. The overt political strategy to help Republicans regain power heading into the 1980s was to use abortion and the human life amendment to create a permanent home in the Republican Party for Catholics and evangelical Protestants, aligning them with white southerners who associated Black civil rights with moral degradation. The Equal Rights Amendment (ERA) had been passed by Congress in 1972 and was being vigorously debated in the states, with thirty-five states passing it over the next five years. Phyllis Schlafly led the charge against the ERA by arguing that the word "choice" was code for both abortion and homosexual lifestyles. Many feminist supporters of the ERA also supported abortion rights, and ERA opponents actively touted liberalized abortion access as emblematic of what the amendment portended.

The so-called New Right already had its national figurehead in the charismatic Reagan. On the ground, Richard Viguerie, the George Wallace acolyte and founder of *Conservative Digest*, was using his unparalleled direct mail skills to raise money for archconservatives. Heritage Foundation cofounder Paul Weyrich conducted trainings for conservative activists and, with Howard Phillips, pushed Jerry Falwell to join with him in cofounding the Moral Majority in 1979. That became a fundraising, lobbying, and messaging juggernaut leading up to the 1980 presidential election. Fiscally conservative Goldwater Republicans wary of the party's courtship of evangelicals could

find political cover in the 1976 Hyde Amendment, which prohibited Medicaid from being used to fund abortions.

By 1981, six years after Justice Stevens's uneventful Supreme Court nomination, abortion was the central issue in Sandra Day O'Connor's confirmation hearing before a *Republican* Senate. In 1970, while serving as a state
senator in Arizona, O'Connor had cast a committee vote in favor of a law
that would have decriminalized abortion. Senator Strom Thurmond, who
was chairing the Judiciary Committee, pressed her on that vote in his first
set of questions at the hearing. "My own knowledge and awareness of the issues and concerns that many people have about the question of abortion has
increased since those days," O'Connor responded, channeling the American
people more generally. "It was not the subject of a great deal of public attention or concern at the time." Senators Thurmond, Kennedy, Hatch, Dole,
DeConcini, East, and Denton all asked O'Connor about her abortion views
during her hearing. Denton, from Alabama, threatened to withhold his yea
out of concern over O'Connor's abortion views even though she said on the
record that she was opposed to abortion and that it was repugnant and personally offensive to her. Like many Americans before *Roe*, O'Connor the
legislator had treated abortion as a difficult and complex question that nonetheless could be resolved through political deliberation and negotiation. At
her hearing a decade later, senators were pushing O'Connor the judge to
reveal a "stance" on the issue, to show what side she was on, to the exclusion
of the other side.

And there we remain, as far apart politically as possible. In 2020, Congress had just seven pro-life Democrats and three pro-choice Republicans.
The runner-up for the Democratic presidential nomination, Bernie Sanders,
said pro-life Democrats were not welcome in the party. The year before, Alabama, Georgia, Kentucky, Louisiana, Mississippi, Missouri, and Ohio all
passed laws that would ban abortion at eight weeks and sometimes earlier
— times when many women do not yet even know they are pregnant. Americans can and do disagree about *Roe*'s moral consequences, but in one sense
Roe eerily mimicked the *Dred Scott* decision: by choosing sides in a vexing

rights conflict, the Supreme Court eroded the political center, making compromise more difficult. And the war has come.

The "Group Bill"

It's tempting to take the disastrous history of abortion politics in the United States to mean that the justices should have kept their powder dry in *Roe*. According to the standard account — offered by no less an authority than Ruth Bader Ginsburg — *Roe* prompted a conservative backlash that might have been averted had the Supreme Court waited for the nation's politics to catch up to its elite self-assurance. Whether or not waiting would have served as some kind of political panacea, which is far from clear, too many Americans assume that complete forbearance was the sole alternative to *Roe* at the time of the decision. This attitude reflects American rightsism at its most pernicious: we must either accept *Roe*'s schismatic political consequences or leave tens of millions of women to the mercy of their state legislatures.

The German experience reveals another option, one in which the constitutional court did not simply choose between rights but instead forced the state to take both the rights of the fetus and the rights of women seriously. What has resulted is the kind of consensus politics around maternal health and social services for women and families that *Roe* helped eradicate.

Let's return, then, to February 25, 1975, the day the West German abortion decision came down. For all its attempts at Solomonic wisdom, the Federal Constitutional Court's abortion decision managed to make no one happy. Not at first, anyway.

To opponents of abortion rights, the decision meant that too many first-trimester abortions would be permitted. Under the new law implemented in 1976 after the court's decision, there was no prohibition against abortions before implantation, a period during which the zygote is alive within Catholic theology. More significantly, a woman could terminate her pregnancy in the first trimester if she could find two doctors willing to certify that carrying the fetus to term would cause severe emotional or financial distress and if she went through social counseling. This exception, called a "social indication," became the main way for a woman to obtain an abortion in West Germany. In 1977, a year after the new abortion law went into effect, 37 percent of legal abortions were medically indicated (based on threats to the woman's health or life), while 57 percent were socially indicated. Within five years, those numbers were 19 percent and 77 percent, respectively. By 1990, just before reunification, 85 percent of legal abortions were socially indicated. In part because of the relative ease of obtaining a social indication, the West German legal regime didn't seem to reduce the overall number of abortions. The number was more or less the same as in East Germany, where first-trimester abortions were not only permitted after 1972 but were free. For the Catholic Church and many conservative West Germans, the constitutional court had done little to protect the life of the unborn.

But proponents of abortion rights had much to complain about as well. West German feminists in the 1960s and 1970s had sought total repeal of the abortion prohibition in the penal code. What they got instead was an arbitrary patchwork that still declared women who obtained abortions to be criminals. Like the United States, West Germany was a federal republic, and — again like the United States today — how easily a woman could obtain an abortion depended on which state, or *Land*, she lived in. Although (unlike in the United States) abortion was primarily legislated at the national level, the counseling agencies whose approval was required to obtain a first-trimester abortion had to be authorized by the various *Länder*. More-Catholic, more-conservative *Länder*, such as Bavaria and Baden-Württemberg, could put women through their paces by, for example, segregating social and medical counselors into different offices or requiring that women be counseled in a directive or confessional, rather than a neutral, way. As in the United States, moreover, some of these *Länder* simply lacked an adequate number of medical facilities licensed to perform abortions. The disparities among *Länder* made it common for women seeking abortions to have to travel from the more-conservative West German south to northern *Länder* or to the Netherlands. A practice even emerged of forcing gynecological exams on women crossing the Dutch–West German border in order to smoke out "abortion tourism."

And so in the same year John Paul Stevens was breezing through a Senate controlled by the opposition party without being asked a single question about abortion, West Germany was in turmoil. The constitutional court's decision leaked a month in advance. By the time of its official release, a thousand protesters had gathered in the center of Karlsruhe, where the constitutional court sits, and mass demonstrations had been planned in all of the major West German cities. Judges were burned in effigy, and protesters hurled stones at the court, which the police barricaded, before eventually resorting to tear gas and billy clubs. In Berlin, Frankfurt, and Munich, protesters demonstrated at Catholic churches, whose influence was (not unreasonably) blamed for the decision.

But the political and social climate changed, and quickly. The framing of abortion rights in the court decisions in the United States and West Germany seems to have made a difference in how newspapers covered abortion and how advocates on both sides talked about it.

Prior to the decision, West German abortion rights supporters freely emphasized themes of choice and autonomy, with feminists deploying popular slogans such as *"Mein Bauch gehort mir"* (roughly equivalent to "My body, myself") and *"Was in der Vagina versteckt, wird von uns jetzt selbst entdeckt"* ("What is hidden in the vagina will now be discovered by ourselves," meant to rhyme in German). Sociologist Myra Marx Ferree has shown that in the 1970s, American women were in fact more likely than their West German counterparts to emphasize the need for the state, via legalized abortion, to protect women from the psychological and social burdens of unwanted pregnancy and from the health and safety risks posed by illegal abortions. But *Roe* and subsequent U.S. cases emphasized the autonomy of women in making abortion decisions, and the accompanying lack of a state duty to support that decision in any way other than through legalization. By contrast, the West German "indications model" expressly tied the decriminalization of abortion to women's social and emotional needs. And so, by 1977, West

German women were using protectionist (as opposed to choice) arguments in support of abortion rights much more than American women. These arguments rose sharply among both men and women in West Germany after the constitutional court decision.

West German abortion politics was tested quickly. The United Nations proclaimed the International Year of the Child in 1979, providing an opportunity for the Catholic Church to push its opposition to the social and genetic indications in the revised abortion law. Abortions had risen by some 30 percent since the new law was passed, prompting Joseph Cardinal Höffner, head of the Roman Catholic Church in West Germany, to condemn the Social Democratic Party (SDP) for promoting a "right to abortion." Although the SDP had sponsored the original 1974 revision, they did not respond to Höffner's provocations in the language of choice that prevails in U.S. abortion discourse. Instead, West German progressives echoed the constitutional court's framing. Johannes Rau, chair of the SDP in North Rhine–Westphalia, answered Höffner by refuting what Rau called "this ethically and legally untenable and false" phrasing. "There is no 'right to abortion,'" he wrote in a letter to the cardinal. "According to the law, an induced termination of pregnancy is fundamentally illegal. That is not the case only if certain legal conditions are given, specifically the existence of an indication." Still, Rau continued, "it is completely indisputable and must remain indisputable that pregnant women who find themselves in an economic crisis should and must be economically and financially supported in order to remedy this financial emergency."

The court's requirement of an indications model had influenced the SDP's political strategy. The distress of an unwanted pregnancy wasn't just something the state might have an interest in; it was something the state had an affirmative duty to mitigate, both through making abortion available and in other ways. Rau ended his letter not by suggesting that the cardinal was insensitive to women's individual freedom to choose to end their pregnancies, but instead by arguing that Höffner was improperly politicizing pregnant women who were experiencing social and emotional distress. He wrote,

"Surely the individual needs of pregnant women are not an appropriate topic for controversy or polemical debates in the public sphere."

It wasn't just abortion rights proponents who seemed to soften their position. Heading into the 1980 elections, Christian Democrats were showing signs of fissures in their alliance with the Church on abortion issues. In July 1979, Cardinal Höffner appeared to approve of a Christian Social Union official's likening of abortion rights proponents to Nazis, a charge that traversed the brightest red line of West German politics. Höffner's comments alienated liberal, younger, and female Catholics who might otherwise have been sympathetic to the Church's position. A 1980 survey indicated that 70 percent of West German Catholics rejected the Church's negative stance on the 1976 abortion law, and that a majority of those who parted ways with the Church believed that the law should be made even more liberal. Likewise, by the 1980s the Evangelical Church in Germany (EKD), a federation of the major West German Protestant denominations, emerged as a supporter of the social and medical indications model, after having opposed abortion in all circumstances prior to the constitutional court decision.

When the Christian Democratic Union (CDU) returned to power in 1982, the party's leadership tried and failed to pass laws that would abolish federal funding and require dissuasive rather than neutral counseling for socially indicated abortions. Much of the opposition to the CDU's anti-abortion agenda came from women *within* the party. The Women's Union of the CDU (CDU-FU) had played essentially no role in the 1970s debates over abortion law reform, but by the 1980s it was a major player in preventing conservative reform. The CDU-FU emphasized the need to support women by making the law more family-friendly. Again, this was consistent with the constitutional court's emphasis on the social needs of pregnant women contemplating abortion. The Catholic Women's Association of Germany (KFD) also moved from its prior opposition to the 1976 law to support for decriminalization in the 1980s. These efforts paved the way for broader cooperation between the KFD and the leftist Green Party on a 1990 law banning embryological research, egg donation, and surrogacy. The 1975 abortion decision had forced political compromise over abortion, which in turn enabled cooperation on related issues.

The constitutional court thus shifted the Overton window around abortion in West Germany. By recognizing fetal life as constitutionally protected, it made impossible a *Roe*-style approach that implied an absolute right to a first-trimester abortion. By characterizing abortion rights as nonetheless encompassed within the Basic Law — and by emphasizing the rights dimension of the social indication — the court forced those seeking to reduce the number of abortions to do so by making women's reproductive choices more meaningful, just what Marjory Mecklenburg and some moderate Democrats were punished politically for trying to promote after *Roe*.

Abortion rights proponents in West Germany (and later reunited Germany) argued less that women had absolute freedom of choice over their bodies and more that any anti-abortion law had to provide women with real alternatives in light of the social and emotional burdens of pregnancy, birth, and motherhood to which the court gave constitutional notice. And abortion rights opponents argued less that abortion is murder and therefore must be criminalized and more that the alternatives to abortion were in fact sufficient to reduce the justification for social indications. As Green Party politician Margarethe Nimsch wrote in the early 1990s, "Unlike twenty years ago, all relevant groups in society today concentrate on the protection of unborn life."

So when the abortion debate roared back into the spotlight at that time, its frame within German constitutional law and politics was relatively narrow. Abortion had almost derailed German reunification, which became official in October of 1990. In East Germany, abortion had been widely available and paid for by the national health service since 1972. Because that regime was inconsistent with the West German constitutional court's interpretation of the Basic Law, negotiators sought to craft a single law that would both be politically acceptable and survive the likely court challenge. The various political parties held a range of positions on what the law should look like, ranging from the Green Party's call for abortion on request to the most conservative Christian Democrats' support for an indications model that excluded social indications.

Still, very few Germans supported complete repeal of abortion restrictions, and there was likewise a general consensus that counseling and financial assistance to pregnant women and families protected fetal life far better than a prohibition on abortion. And so the liberal Free Democratic Party and the Christian Democrats agreed to a suite of services that had to be made available to women and families as part of any law regulating abortion: financial assistance for stay-at-home parents; a guaranteed return to a parent's prior job if he or she took off *up to three years* to care for a child; extended day care and extensive tax credits for day care costs; increased rates for child support payments; extended paid leave to care for sick children; reemployment guarantees for empty nesters; sex education services; and a host of other measures relating to adoption, housing, and taxation.

Those service improvements for parents were negotiated politically by parties that held very different views on core questions of abortion rights but that were forced by the constitutional court to see points of common ground. The law passed in 1992, which resulted from many months of intense bargaining, was dubbed the *Gruppenantrag,* or "group bill," a reference to the fact that it resulted from a diverse cross-party coalition. The basic political compromise that emerged was that an abortion obtained during the first twelve weeks of pregnancy, after dissuasive counseling and a three-day waiting period, was declared not to be illegal. After that period, however, abortion was permitted only when necessary to avoid a serious threat to the woman's life or to her physical or mental health. Abortions could be funded through the national health service, and there would be the already mentioned financial support and other guarantees for people who chose to have and care for children.

The new law was immediately challenged by Christian Democrats, and eventually, after nearly a year of deliberation, the constitutional court struck parts of it down. The court objected to the notion that a "non-indicated abortion" could be declared legal, but it allowed that the state could choose not to *punish* a woman for having such an abortion or her physician for performing one. Rather, the government could protect life by offering more supportive counseling and social benefits to women contemplating an abortion. Although job security and financial benefits for caregivers were already part of the 1992 law, the court suggested that such benefits might need to be strengthened in light of the constitutional mandate to protect life. At the same time, the court held that neither public nor private insurance could cover non-indicated abortions except for women receiving welfare.

The Bundestag responded with a revision in 1994 that defined abortion as a crime but permitted a woman to choose an abortion in the first trimester without fear of prosecution, even if she did not let her counselor in on her reasons. The law followed the court decision in permitting public funding of abortions for women receiving welfare and allowing funding for other women only if their abortions were the result of health issues, genetic issues, or rape or incest. The law also strengthened childcare support and job security guarantees for parents who took time off to care for their children.

Unlike in the 1970s, abortion today is a far less politically polarizing issue in Germany than it is in the United States. To take one measure, the March for Life protest organized by Germany's largest pro-life group, the Bundesverband Lebensrecht (BVL), typically draws fewer than ten thousand marchers. By contrast, the annual March for Life in Washington, D.C., regularly draws crowds in the hundreds of thousands. The two leading German political parties — the Christian Democrats and the Social Democrats — were once bitter rivals in abortion politics but now take moderate stances that more or less hew to the 1994 compromise law. The parties whose rhetoric best approximates the U.S. pro-choice/pro-life dichotomy are the leftist Die Linke and the right-wing populist Alternative für Deutschland, both of which remain at the margins of political power.

It's not that Germany has a perfect regime of abortion regulation, but rather that a complex and divisive political issue has become a subject of genuine politics — within the bounds set by the Federal Constitutional Court. Partisans on both sides can find much to criticize. The court insists that abortion is and must remain a criminal act that often can't be paid for even by private insurance, and there are significant legal constraints on abortions after the first trimester. A controversial ban on doctors' advertising of abortions remains in place. The language of "choice" that many American women find empowering and affirming is frowned upon in Germany, forcing many feminists to the margins of mainstream abortion politics. At the same time, abortion on request is available in the first trimester. It is easier and cheaper for many German women to obtain an abortion than for many American women, and there is universal recognition in Germany that limits on abortion are inseparable from serious financial, childcare, and professional support for parents.

"Choice"

A "group bill" on abortion of the sort that followed German reunification is simply inconceivable in the United States today. Abortion is a subject of political power, but it is not a subject of political negotiation. It isn't just that abortion legislation tends to fall along party lines, though it does. It's that abortion legislation is almost never the result of compromise between legislators who hold fundamentally different views on the issue and must weaken their demands in order to win votes. Abortion politics countenances no "grand bargain," no "comprehensive reform," no bipartisan "gang" of legislators.

The result is that in many states, American women, unlike their German counterparts, have no realistic legal options when it comes to abortion. The politics of abortion in the United States primarily involves red state attempts to push the constitutional envelope with laws banning abortions as soon as a fetal heartbeat can be detected, requiring women to view ultrasounds, requiring abortion doctors to obtain onerous hospital admitting privileges, or banning abortions when the fetus is alleged to be able to feel pain. These efforts are provocations meant to prompt test cases before a Supreme Court thought to be hostile to *Roe*.

At the federal level, the politics of abortion is simply the politics of judicial appointments. When the Court makes political compromise impossible, the losing side sees changing the Court as its only legal option. The Republican Party has used that message to structure its political appeal even to voters who reject much of the rest of the party's platform.

Perhaps the single most significant legislative obstacle to women obtaining abortions in the United States is the Hyde Amendment. Attached each year to the appropriations bill for the Department of Health and Human Services, this provision prevents Medicaid funds from being spent on abortions, even those that are necessary to preserve the woman's health. *Roe's* absolutist rhetoric around privacy rights and medical autonomy made it easier to mobilize forces against public funding for abortions. Illinois congressman Henry Hyde, cosponsor of the 1976 provision, explained his reason for supporting the amendment using a quote from Robert Bork when he was solicitor general. "The privacy right vindicated in Roe v. Wade . . . is not the right affirmatively to obtain an abortion, but rather the lesser right to be free to seek abortion services without Government obstruction or interference," Bork said. "The government has no constitutional obligation financially to facilitate the exercise of privacy rights."

The grand bargain that lowered the temperature of German abortion discourse was a constitutional recognition of the value of fetal life in exchange for a holistic approach to protecting that life. This holistic approach meant that women needed support from the state in order to make meaningful reproductive choices. Because indicated abortions were understood as urgent and not "just" a choice, they could and should be paid for out of public insurance like any other medical necessity. *Roe* did not distinguish "chosen" from "indicated" abortions except in the third trimester, and so it was easy to rally people against public money being spent on them. In other words, your body, *your* choice.

Of course, Germany has become a social welfare state; public assistance for abortions and for parents caring for young children was always going to be an easier sell there than in the United States. Reagan's neoliberal agenda made the language of "choice" an especially appealing message for the abortion rights movement, and it made a grand bargain centered on financial security for families and the provision of childcare seem all the more remote. Still, it is worth noting that the terms of the German abortion détente were not part of the conversation in West Germany until the constitutional court forced both sides to give something up. The abortion rights movement in the United States has continued to emphasize the language of "choice" not only because of the resonance the idea has with many supporters but also because movement leaders have not perceived a viable alternative frame. Emphasis on the need for public funding to support the "choice" of poor women is simply not politically saleable.

Abortion rights opponents have leapt into the void. The ascendant trope of "post-abortion syndrome," for example, emphasizes women who develop regrets about having had abortions. As Myra Marx Ferree notes, organizations such as American Victims of Abortion, Birthright, and Feminists for Life argue that the degradation of fetal life leads women to abort too easily and without the support needed to make good decisions. In a 2007 Supreme Court case about the federal ban on so-called partial-birth abortions, Justice Kennedy wrote in his majority opinion, "While we find no reliable data to measure the phenomenon, it seems unexceptionable to conclude some women come to regret their choice to abort the infant life they once created and sustained." Kennedy cited a brief that had been submitted in the case by Sandra Cano, the "Doe" in *Roe*'s companion case, *Doe v. Bolton,* who became an anti-abortion activist after the decision. The Cano brief was on behalf of herself and "180 women injured by abortion." It described depression, suicidal thoughts, substance abuse, promiscuity, and other ills resulting from, in the brief's words, "the 'choice' [of these women] to abort their baby." The women "have regretted their 'choices,'" the brief added, putting the words "choice" and "choices" in quotation marks for emphasis.

Much of the reaction on the left to Justice Kennedy's reliance on the Cano brief and argument was to criticize him for echoing anti-abortion tropes rather than to acknowledge the presence of abortion regret as a powerful argument for social welfare and—in its absence—the availability of abortion. The urge instead has been to destigmatize abortion, thereby alienating women who want but cannot have children (including some who had abortions solely because of financial distress). Because the pro-choice movement has strategically abandoned the discourse of support, with its implication that some women may in fact regret having made the termination decision, it has opened a space for the anti-abortion community to build ties to such women.

To be fair, the court's approach to abortion has changed in important ways since *Roe*. Like their German counterparts, U.S. justices had an opportunity to reconsider abortion rights in the early 1990s. The occasion was not a grand political compromise, as in Germany. Rather, and tellingly, it was the dawn of a new Supreme Court.

With Clarence Thomas's replacement of Thurgood Marshall, the last five justices to join the Court were assumed abortion opponents, and each of the justices they replaced had been members of the *Roe* majority. With *Roe* dissenters William Rehnquist and Byron White still on the Court, the overruling of *Roe* seemed less a question of *if* than *when*. So in October 1991, when a court of appeals judge by the name of Samuel Alito wrote an opinion upholding a Pennsylvania law that, among other things, imposed a twenty-four-hour waiting period and required women to notify their spouses before obtaining an abortion, the stage was set for *Roe*'s final act.

The American Civil Liberties Union (ACLU) and Planned Parenthood's southeastern Pennsylvania affiliate took the unusual step of petitioning the Supreme Court just three weeks after the decision. If the Court was going to overturn *Roe*, as many expected, advocates were eager for the case to be decided in time to make the 1992 presidential election into a referendum on the issue. The petition urged the justices to answer a single question: "Has the Supreme Court overruled *Roe v. Wade*, holding that a woman's right to choose abortion is a fundamental right protected by the United States Constitution?" The fashioning of abortion rights as a zero-sum battle between the rights of women and the lives of their fetuses had positioned the Supreme Court justices as the ultimate referees in that battle. The Court's composition took on an existential cast for the anti-abortion movement.

When the ultimate decision in *Planned Parenthood of Southeastern Pennsylvania v. Casey* came down in June 1992, the Court did not overrule *Roe* but instead modified it. A surprise opinion by the Court's most centrist justices — O'Connor, Kennedy, and David Souter — recognized and sought to correct two problems with *Roe.* In doing so, they neglected and in some ways exacerbated a third problem. First, the justices emphasized that the state had interests in potential fetal life prior to viability. This meant that the state could pass informed consent, parental consent, and waiting period laws in order to encourage a woman's choice to be more deliberate. This was meant as a corrective to the *Roe* Court's thin understanding of the state's interest. Second, the *Casey* trio described the woman's interest not in terms of the medical judgment of her (likely male) doctor, as the *Roe* Court had, but instead as among "the most intimate and personal choices a person may make in a lifetime." They wrote, "At the heart of liberty is the right to define one's own concept of existence, of meaning, of the universe, and of the mystery of human life." In reconciling the state's interest with the woman's rights, the Court held that the state may not impose an "undue burden" on a woman's right to have an abortion prior to viability.

Casey proceeded from noble instincts. Certainly it seems more sensitive to say that a state has some interest in potential fetal life than to deny that possibility entirely. And certainly it seems more respectful to assign the right to terminate a pregnancy to the woman and not to her doctor. The *Casey* Court's progress along both these dimensions was commendable.

But the *Casey* Court believed that its job was to depoliticize abortion rights, when in fact its job was just the opposite. Indeed, the three justices said that Americans' "belief in themselves as [a people who aspire to live according to the rule of law] is not readily separable from their understanding of the Court invested with the authority to decide their constitutional cases and speak before all others for their constitutional ideals." This is quite wrong. The job of the Court is not to speak "before all others" for our constitutional ideals, but to speak *with* all others. It is not to eliminate political conversation around difficult issues, but to facilitate it.

The state had already spoken for a constitutional ideal, on *its* understanding, namely by passing a law designed to protect fetal life. The *Casey* Court saw this constitutional ideal as simply a state "interest," no different, say, from its interest in tax revenue. But a court that takes fetal life seriously as a constitutional value need not — indeed cannot — simply give carte blanche to the Alabamas of the world. An abortion ban in the absence of meaningful alternatives doesn't, in fact, protect fetal life, and it risks the lives of women. A right to fetal life might require, then, that pregnant women be given a certain degree of prenatal care, paid work leave, and meaningful options if they choose to have a child. Americans United for Life lists U.S. states in order of how protective of "life" they are. Of the top ten "life-protective" states, only one requires that businesses offer pregnancy leave (beyond the federal minimum) to enable women who become pregnant to keep their jobs. In Germany, by contrast, expectant mothers are *required* to receive paid leave. When courts prevent each side of a conflict from digging in and retreating to their corners, when recognizing the rights on one side does not mean denying them on the other, it opens space for political dialogue and enables us better to see each other and find shared ground.

Leaning into the language of women's autonomy was laudable in rejecting the paternalism of Justice Blackmun's purely medical frame in *Roe,* but it doubled down on the notion that abortion is a decision women make *alone.* Support for women struggling with their choice or in need of better options, though not inconsistent with abortion rights and choice, has tended to drop out of the political conversation. What has taken its place are measures like Alabama's virtual total ban on abortion. The ascension of a Supreme Court justice, Brett Kavanaugh, believed to be favorable to the state's position, encouraged it to press its advantage to the maximum possible extent.

The point here is not to laud the German abortion law, which many may object to, but to laud the way in which it came about. Abortion is a subject of German politics not because Germans agree about abortion any more than Americans do, but, in significant part, because Germany's highest court sought to put abortion into politics instead of trying to take it out. That is just what courts should be doing in a divided society.

The way for courts to do that is to recognize *more* rights, and thereby give more people voice and leverage within high-stakes politics. Back in 2009, when Scott Roeder thought he had no leverage, he took politics into his own hands and killed Dr. George Tiller. We shouldn't make constitutional law to appease murderers, but the prevalence of people holding Roeder's

views should give us serious pause. Like Americans, Germans disagree ve-
hemently about abortion. But unlike Americans, Germans have not resolved
conflicts over abortion by passing laws like Alabama's, much less by killing
and maiming each other. Rights on both sides of this intense moral conflict
have been governed by and enforced through impassioned but ordinary law
and politics, not by the trolling of women seeking abortions, and certainly
not by people like Roeder.

The Problem of Sex Selection

The fetal right to life and a woman's right to reproductive autonomy and social equality are not the only rights conflicts that can complicate the abortion
debate. A number of countries and nine U.S. states have enacted bans on
obtaining an abortion for the purpose of rejecting a disfavored sex, typically
a girl.

It is anathema within the U.S. "choice" paradigm to restrict the *reasons*
for which a woman may obtain an abortion at any stage prior to viability.
Under *Roe,* the only justification for a state regulating abortion before the
third trimester was to protect the woman's health. Under the modern *Casey*
regime, the state may additionally pass laws prior to viability that are "aimed
at ensuring that a woman's choice contemplates the consequences for the fetus," but the state may not ultimately interfere with that choice. The Supreme
Court has not to date upheld a state's effort to confine abortion to certain
reasons along the lines of the German indications model.

Many abortion rights proponents in the United States defend the legality
of sex-selective abortion as encompassed within a woman's nearly unquali-
fied right to control her own reproduction. A ban on sex selection opens the
door to doctors or police probing a woman's reasons for abortion in ways
that can be patronizing. The probe itself is an interference with her autonomy. Permitting sex-selective abortion might also in some circumstances
help to prevent female infanticide.

But to view sex selection as simply one among many other reasons a
woman might choose an abortion seems insensitive to the equality dimen-

sions of this practice. Selective abortion of female fetuses is widespread in eastern Europe and in parts of East and South Asia where abortion is not itself highly stigmatized and cultural norms favor male children. There is little evidence of widespread sex-selective abortion in the United States, but the practice is difficult to defend on its own terms.

The U.S. model of abortion rights denies us the resources to think this problem through. The slightest concession that society is permitted to deem some abortion choices to be poor ones endangers the rest of the choice defense. And so to preserve the absolute supremacy of choice requires one to deny any rights dimension to sex selection, just as it requires a denial of any fetal rights at all. With more than three out of four Americans in favor of a sex-selection ban, abortion rights proponents are forced simply to cede ground to opponents who can accuse them, rightly, of having no answer to a genuine human rights problem. It is not surprising that the emerging sex-selection bans in the United States do not typically distinguish first- and second-trimester abortions and do not, for example, contain exceptions for inherited sex-linked diseases such as hemophilia or Duchenne muscular dystrophy. The kind of political negotiation that could temper the reach of the law is absent from U.S. abortion politics. Courts could do much to change that.

The Supreme Court's willful blindness to conflicts of rights is not just a problem for abortion rights. In cases ranging from affirmative action to campaign finance to gun regulation, the justices almost never acknowledge the presence of constitutional rights on both sides of the cases they hear. As with abortion, doing so leaves the law erratic and disrupts the possibility of political compromise. Worse, it makes us hate each other a little bit more, to tragic effect.

6

When Rights Divide

If there's a ground zero in the culture wars, you might find it somewhere along the roughly one-hundred-mile drive from Colorado Springs to Boulder, just east of the Front Range of the Rockies. The route takes you due north on I-25 through Denver before veering northwest along the Denver–Boulder Turnpike. Your journey begins with views of Pikes Peak to the west before passing through the low hills of the Greenland Open Space and ending with a big sky over the Flatirons as you cruise into Boulder. There's beauty at each end of the drive, but you can't see it from the other side.

Colorado Springs is one of the most conservative cities in America. Nicknamed "the Evangelical Vatican," the city is home to more than one hundred evangelical Christian churches and organizations, including Focus on the Family and the ten-thousand-member New Life Church, Ted Haggard's former ministry. The fortresslike Planned Parenthood clinic in Colorado Springs is the target of constant protests. In 2015, an anti-abortion vigilante shot and killed three people and injured nine others at the clinic. Colorado Springs is also a military bastion. The Fort Carson army base is the city's largest employer, and accounting for the three other bases in town, the military remains the city's dominant industry. Donald Trump lost the state of Colorado by five points in 2016, but he took El Paso County, where Colorado Springs sits, by 22 points.

So in March 1975, when Dave McCord and Dave Zamora tried to get a marriage license from the El Paso County clerk, it was no surprise that the clerk refused. "Go to Boulder," she told the two men. "They do that type of thing there." Boulder enjoys a well-cultivated reputation as the most liberal city in Colorado. The city is home to the notoriously left-leaning flagship campus of the University of Colorado, and, while its reputation as a haven for hippies has largely succumbed to a tech boom, the Boulderites most likely to be in the closet are there because they're Republicans. Jared Polis, the first openly gay male governor in the country, decided to live with his husband in Boulder rather than in the governor's mansion in Denver. Hillary Clinton won Boulder County by 48 points in 2016.

Still, the El Paso County clerk wasn't quite right. As of March 1975, Boulder County had never issued a marriage license to a same-sex couple. When McCord and Zamora made that drive north from Colorado Springs to Boulder, they encountered a young clerk named Clela Rorex, who had been on the job for just three months. When they asked Rorex for a marriage license, she said she wasn't sure whether Colorado's marriage code allowed her to grant their request. Rorex turned to the county district attorney, who told her that state law didn't say anything about whether marriage had to be between a man and a woman. It was up to her, the DA said, and so she granted the license.

It was the first valid marriage license ever to be issued to a same-sex couple in the United States. Rorex became a minor, if not quite willing, celebrity, especially after an old Boulder rabble-rouser named Ros Howard rode up on his horse, Dolly, and asked for a license to marry the mare. (Rorex denied him, deadpanning that the eight-year-old horse needed to get her parents' written consent.) Rorex went on to issue licenses to six same-sex couples before the Colorado attorney general shut her down. The last of those couples, Anthony Sullivan and Richard Adams, married on April 21, 1975, then requested a spousal visa for Sullivan, an Australian citizen, from the Immigration and Naturalization Service. They were denied. The government laid out its reasoning in its official response: "You have failed to establish that a bona fide marital relationship can exist between two faggots."

The tale of these two Colorado cities, the Zax to Denver's south and the Zax to its north, exemplifies a broader tug-of-war in Colorado's politics, and in America's. We are a polarized people. According to the most widely used measure of congressional polarization, the parties have been growing apart rapidly since the 1970s and have now reached levels of polarization last seen 150 years ago during the Reconstruction Era. Anecdotes about Tip O'Neill and Ronald Reagan sharing a drink together at the end of the day seem quaint, and not just anecdotally. Party conflicts increasingly fall along rather than across ideologically liberal and conservative lines. Extremely conservative and extremely liberal members of Congress are more common than they once were; the parties are increasingly homogeneous ideologically and, on average, further apart; and there is far less ideological overlap. Conservative Democrats are increasingly to the left of the most liberal Republicans. This polarization has been accompanied by sharp increases in animosity between partisans of each side, who increasingly believe those in the other party actively threaten the country's well-being.

The reasons for polarization are many. The parties, and especially the Republican Party, have become more monolithic. LBJ's shepherding of the Civil Rights Act of 1964 and the Voting Rights Act of 1965 helped shatter the New Deal coalition of southern white populists and city-dwelling African Americans. The flight of southern whites from the Democratic Party made the GOP much more culturally conservative, a shift that Reagan exploited to win the presidency in 1980. The parties themselves have also been weakened by changes in the structure of campaign finance facilitated by various Supreme Court decisions refusing to allow limits on outside spending while at the same time permitting limits on contributions to individuals and parties. Parties' diminished power yields messaging authority to demagogic or well-resourced outsiders.

That trend is amplified by broader, and independently challenging, changes to the media environment. Even as technology has made it easier for us to get around and to connect with others, our lives have become

Balkanized. We are segregated, both residentially, subdivided into "communities" and "developments," and socially, hived off into online networks whose members share our background and values. Trusted intermediaries, the Walter Cronkites of old, are increasingly hard to come by, leaving us with personalized Facebook and Twitter feeds and citizenship in either a Fox News America or an MSNBC America. They are easy to mistake for two different countries.

Colorado helps us to see a reason for polarization that's easy to miss: *rights.* It's not just abortion. It's guns and campus speech; it's race and religion; it's terrorism and surveillance; it's health insurance and the coronavirus pandemic response. Our political conversation stubbornly, reflexively, adopts the language of rights. How judges, politicians, the media, and ordinary citizens view their rights and the rights of others matters immensely. And yet we disagree passionately — *and often reasonably* — about who holds them and what they mean. Our judges resolve these conflicts in ways that are morally arbitrary, homing in on arid precedents, logical fallacies, or anachronisms. Too often judges believe they must award total victory to one party's rights or else the other's.

Politics then becomes a battle between those the judges think the Constitution sees and those they think it leaves out, between those whose claims have paramount legal value and those whose claims have none. It makes sense, under these trying circumstances, for us to trumpet our own rights and deny that others have them. By fetishizing their rights at the expense of ours, our political opponents are literally out to destroy us.

Judges aren't the reason we hate each other. American polarization has deeper roots. But judges, more than most, have the power to make it better, and instead they are making it worse. Rights conflicts can offer a teachable moment, one in which judges mediate, in which they tell a divided people what they share and where they can find common ground. The Supreme Court tends instead to view our most sensitive rights conflicts as an opportunity to scold the side the judges decide is wrong, often by reminding them of the repugnance of their bedfellows. Constitutional law has high enough stakes, but our courts keep making them higher.

Amendment 2

On the same day in 1992 when Colorado voters helped Bill Clinton take the presidency — Republicans had won the state in the last six presidential elections — they also voted for Amendment 2, a state constitutional revision prohibiting gays and lesbians from benefiting from antidiscrimination legislation. It targeted ordinances passed in Boulder, Aspen, and Denver that outlawed sexual orientation discrimination in housing, employment, education, public accommodations, and a number of other areas. The amendment's supporters argued that it was designed to prevent gays and lesbians from obtaining "special rights," but its language was broader. On a plain reading of the law, even businesses that were open to the public, such as hotels and restaurants, could exclude gay and lesbian customers with impunity.

The amendment's chief architect, a folksy Colorado Springs car dealer named Will Perkins, argued that the ordinances in Boulder and other cities would lead to teachers recruiting Colorado schoolchildren into a gay lifestyle. Pro–Amendment 2 ads featured suggestive images of flamboyant revelers at a gay pride parade in San Francisco. In the wake of the law's passage, antigay hate crimes spiked in the state. Four gay men were murdered near the state capitol in Denver. A Colorado Springs psychotherapist was knocked unconscious and had crosses cut into her hands for driving with a "Celebrate Diversity" bumper sticker. Neo-Nazi gangs roamed the Denver streets. Some gay rights groups, allies, and local businesses called for a selective boycott of the state. "Buy in Aspen or Boulder," a prominent social club owner in Aspen put it, "but not in Colorado Springs or Pueblo or Grand Junction or Canyon City." The state was at war with itself.

Rights fetishism acted as an enabler. For opponents of the local antidiscrimination ordinances, rights were not simply a marker of citizenship, a declaration of equal membership in the political community. They were unable to see rights for gays and lesbians as anything other than "quotas" or "special rights." For them, the only alternative to "special treatment" was to deny rights entirely. In arguments promoting the measure, Perkins specifically brought up the Supreme Court's criteria for making a group a "suspect class," reducing a political conflict over the dignity of his fellow citizens to the Supreme Court's abstruse legalisms. Identifying a group as a "suspect class" historically means that courts will view a law burdening that group with deep suspicion. To Perkins and other supporters of Amendment 2, the fact that gays and lesbians were not "politically powerless" and did not "possess a clearly identifiable, immutable physical [characteristic]" meant they couldn't be a suspect class and therefore could not be protected by antidiscrimination laws. As Perkins told CNN, "They're wanting some special protection because of the way they have sex at home."

In 1996, the Supreme Court struck down Amendment 2 as unconstitutional. It was the first time the Court had ever ruled in favor of gay and lesbian rights. Justice Kennedy began his majority opinion in the case, known as *Romer v. Evans,* with a quote from the first Justice Harlan's dissent in the *Plessy* railway car case: the Constitution "neither knows nor tolerates classes among citizens." For Kennedy, the law defined a class of persons by a single trait — sexual orientation — and subjected that class to a wide array of burdens unrelated to that trait. Amendment 2 bore no rational relationship to any objective a state is permitted to pursue. The only way to understand the law was as the product of "animus," and, Kennedy said, "it is not within our constitutional tradition to enact laws of this sort."

As Kennedy well knew, and as his *Plessy* quote amplifies, this statement was not true. This country has a long, disgusting history of passing just these kinds of laws — against Blacks, Catholics, Jews, Chinese and Japanese immigrants, women, and many other classes of Americans. Indeed, at the time *Romer* was decided, it remained permissible for states to ban sodomy, and even to do so selectively for same-sex partners. The law likewise imposes wide-ranging, at times severe, burdens on convicted criminals, on undocumented immigrants, on smokers, on the poor, on the young, and on people with mental and physical disabilities. Within the court's rights tradition, a law like Amendment 2 could easily be struck down if gays and lesbians constituted a "suspect class," but Kennedy conspicuously refused to concede that they were. If the state could make a felony of gay sex, why couldn't it impose the seemingly lesser burden of Amendment 2?

It's for that reason that Justice Scalia's searing dissent accused the majority of being "long on emotive utterance" and "short on relevant legal citation." Existing jurisprudence was focused on classes that could easily be compared to Black victims of Jim Crow. Gays and lesbians were not a "discrete and insular" minority but rather an anonymous and diffuse one. And opprobrium for gays and lesbians was at least notionally grounded not in their superficial physical characteristics but in their behavior. Behavior that, at the time of *Romer,* could be criminalized. For Justice Scalia, the battle between Colorado Springs and Boulder that found expression in Amendment 2 was not about "animus" but simply about the cultural norms that are so often the subject of ordinary political conflict. The majority, Justice Scalia said, had "mistaken a Kulturkampf for a fit of spite."

Romer models a deep problem in the Supreme Court's rights jurisprudence. The Court's existing categories are crude and premodern, but the justices haven't repudiated them. They stick to them except, as in *Romer,* when they don't. The way to argue against Amendment 2 was to suggest, as Kennedy did, that a law passed by an electorate that voted for Bill Clinton was just like the white supremacist Separate Car Act. This position makes no sense either of the presence (at the time) of legal sodomy bans or of the evident political power of gays and lesbians in places like Boulder, Aspen, and Denver.

On the other side, the way to argue in favor of Amendment 2 was to suggest, as Perkins and Scalia did, that gays and lesbians may be treated just like drug addicts or felons, a position that makes no sense of the changing social meaning of queer identity. And the idea that groups defined in terms of their behavior are categorically beneath the Constitution makes no sense of the constitutional protection of religious freedom. Scalia wasn't quite right about Kulturkampfs — they can be plenty spiteful — but there was no doubt that the Court was taking sides in the culture wars. Indeed, it was fanning them.

A Masterpiece de Résistance

Colorado's cultural politics has vacillated impressively since Amendment 2. A decade after the Supreme Court struck the amendment down, Colorado voters approved, by a margin of 56 to 44 percent, a new state constitutional amendment banning same-sex marriage. But the very next year, with a new Democratic governor in office, the state added sexual orientation (and religion) to the list of statuses protected against employment discrimination. The fact that Bill Ritter cruised to victory in the governor's race on the same day the electorate voted to ban same-sex marriage is telling of Colorado's political diversity. In 2008, Ritter signed into law a bill banning sexual orientation discrimination in housing and in places of public accommodation such as hotels, restaurants, and, yes, bakeries.

Such was the state of the law in 2012 when Charlie Craig and David Mullins walked into Masterpiece Cakeshop in Lakewood, Colorado, in search of a cake for their wedding. Lakewood sits a hair to Denver's west, just a few minutes' detour off the drive from Colorado Springs to Boulder. With its green open spaces, many miles of hiking trails, and pristine views of the Rockies, Lakewood boasts the best of what makes Colorado famous.

And the worst.

Masterpiece Cakeshop's owner, Jack Phillips, refused to bake a wedding cake for Craig and Mullins. Phillips's high regard for his pastries is evident in the name he chose for his shop. For him, preparing a cake for a couple's wedding is not just about arranging eggs and flour and sugar in the proper proportions, popping it in the oven, and slapping a price tag on it. Rather, as an artisan, Phillips sends a message through his wedding cakes, one that celebrates each couple's love and commitment. When he bakes a wedding cake, Phillips said, he is *performing* in the wedding no less than if he turned up to sing a ballad during the first dance.

As a devout Christian, Phillips claimed that participating in a same-sex wedding in this way contravened his religious beliefs. Craig and Mullins sued, claiming sexual orientation discrimination in violation of the 2008 state law, and they won before Colorado's Civil Rights Commission. Phillips's challenge to the commission's decision argued that his First Amendment rights to freedom of religion and speech had been violated. It reached the Supreme Court in 2017.

When word of the case got out, it became an enticing target for the culture warriors who shape so much of American public opinion. Unflattering comparisons came from both directions. Phillips was said to be just like Piggie Park, a South Carolina barbecue chain whose owner claimed in the 1960s that serving Black customers violated his religious freedom. Or Bob Jones University when it argued that its religiously inspired ban on interracial dating shouldn't jeopardize its tax-exempt status. Some of the more than one hundred groups that submitted briefs in the case said that a win for Phillips would mean that landlords could henceforward refuse to rent to interracial couples, or that employers could refuse to hire women. A racist baker could refuse to sell cakes to Black customers. A portrait studio could refuse to photograph Mexican families. A hairstylist opposed to immigration could refuse to help a teenage girl prepare for her quinceañera. A win for Phillips would mean no less than "a constitutional right to discriminate."

To hear the other side tell it, the gay couple's demands were even more outrageous. What they were asking was like forcing someone whose child was killed in a school shooting to design NRA T-shirts. Or like a KKK grand wizard asking a Black tailor to take up the hem of his robe. A win for the couple would amount to a violation of the Thirteenth Amendment's ban on involuntary servitude. It would mean the government could choose to disbar Christian lawyers or take licenses away from Christian doctors. Making Phillips bake a wedding cake for a same-sex couple, one brief offered, was like forcing Christians to bow before Roman gods or making Jews submit to the golden statue of the Babylonian king Nebuchadnezzar. Nay, forcing a baker to prostrate himself before the public accommodation laws of the state of Colorado was little different than beheading Sir Thomas More for refusing to affirm the annulment of Henry VIII's marriage to Catherine of Aragon. These were all actual arguments made by real lawyers and ostensibly serious commentators. Kulturkampfs, again, can be plenty spiteful.

The justices played right along. At the oral argument, Justice Neil Gorsuch asked the ACLU lawyer representing the couple whether the Colorado law would require a baker to sell a cake with a cross on it to a Klansman. Justice Samuel Alito asked the lawyer for Colorado whether its public accommodation law could force the baker to provide a cake honoring the anniversary of Kristallnacht. On the other side, Justices Stephen Breyer and Elena Kagan both likened Masterpiece Cakeshop to Ollie's Barbecue, the "whites only" Alabama joint that challenged the public accommodation provisions of the Civil Rights Act of 1964.

This madness makes it easy to miss — indeed, makes it impossible to *see* — just how narrow the dispute between Phillips and the same-sex couple actually was. Phillips didn't argue that he could refuse to serve gay customers, or even that he could discriminate against them in any way. He conceded that Colorado law prohibits him from sexual orientation discrimination, and in fact he said he would readily sell to gay customers any cakes or other items that he would sell to straight ones. His argument was that a customized wedding cake for a same-sex ceremony was not something he would sell to *anyone,* gay or straight, just as he wouldn't sell anyone a cake glorifying divorce or, indeed, a cake with a message *disparaging* gays.

For their part, Craig and Mullins agreed with Phillips that, in general, he could refuse to bake cakes for customers for religious or even purely ideological reasons. Both sides agreed that the mere fact that Masterpiece Cakeshop was a business did not in itself mean Phillips had a duty to serve all comers. Phillips could refuse to bake a cake simply because he didn't like the cut of the customer's jib. And both sides agreed that refusing to sell a cake to a gay or lesbian customer was an exception to that general license. The couple's argument was that if they had been an opposite-sex couple, the case would never have arisen, and Phillips's argument was that the issue was not the customer but the ceremony. The main question that divided the two sides was simply whether Phillips's refusal to bake this cake, under these special circumstances, in fact constituted discrimination on the basis of sexual orientation.

You probably have feelings about how this case should have come out.

Bracket those feelings for the moment and notice that the parties, the amici, the media, and the judges ratcheted the stakes of the case *up* rather than *down*. This case was not the same as Ollie's Barbecue. It was not the same because that restaurant refused service entirely to Black customers. It was not the same because its refusal wasn't grounded in religious freedom, which the Constitution specifically protects. And it was not the same because blanket refusal of service to Black customers in the Jim Crow South was pervasive, had been pervasive for centuries, and had the implicit sanction of the state. There was no epidemic of gay customers in Colorado being refused artisanal wedding cakes. Quite the opposite, in fact. Before Craig and Mullins even filed suit, dozens of bakeries both locally and from around the world offered them free custom cakes in response to their complaints about Phillips on Facebook.

Needless to say — and yet I need to say it — this case was also not the same as a Nazi or a Klansman asking Phillips for a cake to celebrate racial genocide. Never mind that even many devout evangelicals would concede that there's nothing *malevolent* about marrying someone of the same sex — and most of us think malevolence is morally relevant. Let it suffice that both sides agreed that a customer's racism, unlike their sexual orientation, is not a protected status under Colorado's public accommodations law. Moreover, Craig and Mullins did not request that Phillips put any particular message on their wedding cake. And so even if Masterpiece cakes are so expertly crafted that they make a statement without saying a word, a court could easily decide that an across-the-board refusal to bake any same-sex wedding cake regardless of the cake's particular content strikes closer to the heart of discrimination on the basis of sexual orientation — *which both sides agreed is forbidden* — rather than discrimination on the basis of a message or viewpoint.

Masterpiece Cakeshop was a hard case. It disserves us to pretend otherwise. It was a hard case because homosexuality is, in large part, a lifestyle and not simply a status. That lifestyle is bound to come into conflict with religious freedom in a country that protects both. It is indeed unsurprising that same-sex wedding ceremonies have been the sites of numerous objections from religious service providers. A Portland custom cakeshop that wouldn't host a wedding cake tasting for a lesbian couple based on the bakers' religious conviction. A florist in southeastern Washington who would provide uncut flowers but not a floral arrangement for the wedding of a gay couple who had long been customers of hers. An Albuquerque photographer who wouldn't shoot a lesbian commitment ceremony as a matter of conscience.

These conflicts can only be resolved at retail, based on their facts. It should matter to a court whether service providers are consistent in which kinds of ceremonies they are willing to serve and why; the inherent expressiveness of the service provided; whether they in fact sell other, less expressive products to gay and lesbian clients; what was said to the customer in the moment as compared to what was written by lawyers in response to litigation; the size of the shop and the degree of the religious objector's personal involvement in performing the service; what alternatives are available to the couple; relevant legal judgments made by state courts and enforcement agencies; and the sensitivity of each to the range and depth of the interests at stake. Wholesale sloganeering about "Whites Only" signs from the 1960s or the made-up scourge of customers demanding Nazi cakes disable courts from treating the many layers of this kind of conflict with care.

We instead retreat to our battle lines. This is not just a legal problem but a social problem as well. Courts should be reminding litigants of what they have in common, not encouraging them to view their opponents in the worst conceivable light. We could see Phillips or Craig and Mullins — and they could see each other — as fellow citizens, compatriots who see value in each other's commitments and accept each other's basic rights but hold eminently reasonable disagreements about how to apply those values in the novel context of wedding ceremonies for same-sex couples. Instead, the way courts frame rights leads us to characterize the baker and the couple — and them to characterize each other — as in league with segregationists and Nazis. You don't negotiate with such people; you destroy them.

Succumbing to this polarizing posture goes beyond one gay couple and a Christian baker. The case went viral because so many of us see ourselves in these parties. What if a store refused to serve *me*? What if *I* were made to serve someone whose ends I found repugnant? When the courts make it appear as though what is at stake is *who* holds rights rather than *what holding a right enables,* it becomes too easy to characterize the stakes of the case in existential rather than contingent terms: *Is there a constitutional right to discriminate?* Someone who believes that the bare assertion of a religious objection gives rise to such a right is the enemy not just of gays and lesbians but also of African Americans, of women, of people with disabilities, and of progressives more generally. To hold that belief *categorically* is no less than to deny the basic citizenship of persistently disadvantaged groups. On the other side, it makes some sense to see tyranny in the belief that *any* service provider may be required to ignore the commitments or ends of their customers. Masterpiece Cakeshop sits between Boulder and Colorado Springs in more ways than one. The case became a fight for America's soul. We're bound to hate each other a little more after a case like this.

Some of us are bound to hate the Constitution, too. How else should you respond when a case is framed as being about whether you have rights or not? A Constitution that gives blanket rights to discriminate against gays and lesbians doesn't deserve their allegiance or anyone else's. A Constitution that would force a Black clothing designer to make a Klan robe isn't one a Black person, or anyone else, should reasonably be expected to support or defend. Every loss under this frame chips away at the basis for political solidarity. It becomes too easy to believe that the Constitution has no underlying integrity or purpose. The game is simply to staff the courts with one's own partisans. If it's not us, it's them, right?

On Having One's Cake and Eating It, Too

Courts can do better than this, and many do.

The United Kingdom's highest court navigated its own cake case in 2018. Daniel and Amy McArthur run a thriving bakery, Ashers, in Belfast. The McArthurs are devout Christians, hence the name of the bakery, which derives from Genesis: "Bread from Asher shall be rich, And he shall yield royal dainties." Gareth Lee, a volunteer for an LGBTQ rights organization called

QueerSpace, decided in May 2014 to bring a cake to a party marking the end of Northern Ireland's Anti–Homophobia and Transphobia Week. You can guess the rest. Using the company's "Build-a-Cake" service, Lee placed an order for an Ashers cake to be iced with a picture of *Sesame Street*'s Bert and Ernie, the QueerSpace logo, and the words "Support Gay Marriage." Amy McArthur took his order, but after some deliberation over the weekend, the McArthurs determined that making this cake would violate their religious conscience, and they refunded Lee's money.

Lee sued, claiming that the McArthurs' conduct violated his rights to freedom from discrimination on the basis of sexual orientation, political expression, and religion, guaranteed under various Northern Ireland laws and regulations. The bakers countered that if the legislation covered this transaction, it violated their own rights to freedom of expression and religion, guaranteed under the European Convention on Human Rights. It was, in other words, a conflict of rights. But instead of ratcheting up the case, deciding it based on the existential question of whether gays and lesbians should best Christendom, the UK high court looked to the facts.

Baroness Brenda Hale's lead opinion for the Supreme Court of the United Kingdom contained no talk of Nazis or Babylonians or quinceañeras. Instead, Lady Hale carefully noted that the McArthurs' objection was not to Lee "the man" but rather to what he wished to put on the cake. Lee's own sexual orientation was not what doomed his cake, and there was no evidence that the bakery had ever discriminated against gay customers as such. The McArthurs' refusal, Lady Hale said, was over "the message, not the messenger."

To be sure, the case wasn't quite as simple as this slogan suggests. Had a straight man asked for a cake with the message "Support Heterosexual Marriage," the McArthurs would have baked it without incident. Was that the right comparison? The lower court judge thought it was. Sometimes the message is inseparable from the messenger, as may indeed have been the case in *Masterpiece Cakeshop*. Someone in the business of making wedding cakes who refuses to do so for same-sex weddings edges awfully close to simply refusing to serve customers who wish to marry someone of the same sex. Lady Hale discussed *Masterpiece Cakeshop* at some length and glommed on to just this difference:

> The important message from the Masterpiece Bakery case is that there is a clear distinction between refusing to produce a cake conveying a particular message, for any customer who wants such a cake, and refusing to produce a cake for the particular customer who wants it because of that customer's characteristics. One can debate which side of the line particular factual scenarios fall. But in our case there can be no doubt. The bakery would have refused to supply this particular cake to anyone, whatever their personal characteristics. So there was no discrimination on grounds of sexual orientation.

In other words, *Masterpiece Cakeshop* was a close case precisely because it involved a difficult, contextual question of whether Phillips was, in fact, discriminating on the basis of sexual orientation. Only gay people have same-sex weddings. But same-sex marriage is *supported* by many people, gay, straight, and in between. Recruiting hypotheticals about Nazis into the Ashers bakery case would have distracted from delicate factual nuances.

Importantly, the court's resolution of the case did not require Lady Hale to deny that important rights were at stake on both sides of the issue. She devoted a long paragraph of her opinion to "the very real problem of discrimination against gay people," emphasizing that under the Universal Declaration of Human Rights, everyone is "born free and equal in dignity and rights." Her opinion acknowledged that "providers of employment, education, accommodation, goods, facilities and services do not always treat people with equal dignity and respect," and that "it is deeply humiliating, and an affront to human dignity, to deny someone a service because of that person's race, gender, disability, sexual orientation or any of the other protected personal characteristics." Lady Hale lingered on the fact that discrimination against gays and lesbians denies their rights to equality and dignity in order to make the point that this case was different on its facts. "It does the project of equal treatment no favours," she wrote, "to seek to extend it beyond its proper scope." Whatever we think of the UK Supreme Court's outcome in the Ashers case, no one can say it exaggerated the stakes or failed to confront the complexity of the case.

Just the Facts

The justices of the UK Supreme Court also did not resolve or purport to resolve inapposite cases. Barely mentioned, for example, was the most famous of the UK cases involving claims for religious exemption from the accoutrements of same-sex unions. That case, even more than the Ashers case, shows what *Masterpiece Cakeshop* could have been but wasn't.

Lillian Ladele was the registrar of births, marriages, and deaths in the London borough of Islington. At the time she took the position, in 2002, the UK afforded no means by which same-sex couples could formalize their relationship and obtain the suite of benefits associated with marriage. Two years later, Parliament provided for civil unions by passing the Civil Partnership Act. Ladele, a Christian who believed same-sex unions to be "contrary to God's instructions," told her superiors that she was unwilling to officiate such unions. For a time, she was able to work out an informal "swap" with her colleagues whenever a same-sex union case arose, but after two of her coworkers complained, Ladele was eventually told she either had to officiate civil partnerships or risk losing her job. She sued.

A clear difference between Ladele's case and many others bounds from the page. Ladele was a government employee. This seems consequential, though just how is less obvious than it may appear. On the one hand, a secular government cannot adjust the services it offers its citizens based on the idiosyncratic religious scruples of its employees. Ladele's position at first blush bears a resemblance to that taken by Kim Davis, the former Rowan County, Kentucky, clerk who refused to issue marriage licenses to same-sex couples following the U.S. Supreme Court's decision in *Obergefell v. Hodges*, which requires states to make such marriages available. Davis's personal faith couldn't excuse the lawless acts of Rowan County.

On the other hand, it wasn't obvious that any adjustment was needed in Ladele's case. Unlike in Rowan County, where Davis was the only official with the authority to issue marriage licenses, Ladele was one of several Is- lington registrars able to officiate same-sex unions. We might also think it relevant that at the time Ladele took her position, officiating partnerships in a way she thought contrary to her religion wasn't part of the job. This differ- ence in factual posture converts the case from one about the government's equal treatment of the citizens it regulates, which Kim Davis denied, to the government's treatment of the religious claims of its own employees, consci- entious objectors such as Ladele.

Ladele lost both at the Court of Appeal in London and in her follow-up appeal to the European Court of Human Rights, but every court took seri- ously her claims of religious discrimination in a way that U.S. courts would not have. Religious freedom offers an especially stark example of the U.S. Supreme Court's all-or-nothing approach to rights. According to the Court, a "neutral" government practice, one that is not intended to burden reli- gion, simply cannot be challenged on First Amendment religious freedom grounds. A 1990 opinion by Justice Antonin Scalia said that were the Court to recognize such claims, it would require the strictest of scrutiny to apply, resulting in much mischief: "the prospect of constitutionally required reli- gious exemptions from civic obligations of almost every conceivable kind." This included, he offered, exemptions from military service, tax payments, child neglect laws, drug laws, traffic laws, animal cruelty laws, and so forth. Never mind that the actual claim before Justice Scalia's Court involved Na- tive Americans who had been fired for smoking peyote as part of a religious ritual. To allow this claim, Scalia insisted, would be to commit to allowing all other hypothetical claims for exemptions. This, he said, would be "courting anarchy."

The courts that rejected Ladele's arguments managed to avert anarchy, but they didn't think that in order to do so they needed to deny that her re- ligious freedom was of any constitutional significance. The Court of Appeal acknowledged that this was a case of "indirect discrimination," what Amer- icans would call "disparate impact." Unlike in the United States, this meant that the government had indeed interfered with Ladele's rights by putting her "at a disadvantage when compared with other persons," and so the government's actions needed to be justified. Did Islington's policy choices represent "a proportionate means of achieving a legitimate aim"? The question wasn't whether Ladele had rights — of course she did. The question was, on these particular facts, what did her rights enable her to do?

For the Court of Appeal, the borough's motivation in refusing to accommodate Ladele, a *factual* question, was hugely significant. If Islington's aim was merely to ensure that it efficiently and effectively officiated civil partnerships, then Ladele's claim had some real force. She was the only registrar with a religious objection. If all it took to enable her to keep her job consistent with her religious conscience was a bit of internal bureaucratic shuffling, then a constitutional commitment to religious freedom might well require the government to endure this inconvenience.

As it turns out, though, Islington had an established policy of "Dignity for All," which required equal treatment not just of its citizens but of government employees as well. The borough's policy was staff focused and required all employees to promote values of equality and diversity. Reasonable people can disagree about whether accommodating Ladele would contravene the "Dignity for All" policy or instead would implement it. The key for the Court of Appeal was that the policy was a bona fide one that the borough itself reasonably believed an exemption for Ladele would violate: "Islington wished to ensure that all their registrars were designated to conduct, and did conduct, civil partnerships as they regarded this as consistent with their strong commitment to fighting discrimination, both externally, for the benefit of the residents of the borough, and internally in the sense of relations with and between their employees."

The European Court of Human Rights, the Strasbourg court that adjudicates disputes over the application of the European Convention on Human Rights within signatory states such as the UK, likewise didn't trivialize the burden on Ladele. The consequences of the Islington policy, the court said, were "serious" in light of "the strength of her religious conviction." The court also took note that officiating same-sex partnerships was not part of her job description when she first took the job, and so there was some unfairness in forcing her now to choose between her religion and continued employment.

The justices agreed that forcing Ladele to officiate civil partnerships "had a particularly detrimental impact on her because of her religious beliefs" and therefore triggered the religious freedom and equality protections of the convention.

The question, then, was "whether the policy pursued a legitimate aim and was proportionate," and what was decisive for the European court here was the fact that the borough's policy was designed to protect the rights of others. Under the jurisprudence of the European Court of Human Rights, local authorities trying to balance competing rights protected under the European convention receive substantial deference, and here that deference was exercised reasonably and with care.

The court's decision shows a way of bringing political actors into the constitutional conversation about rights. The American approach, by contrast, preserves little role for politics once a right is identified. If policy makers know that the deference they receive from courts will depend not on comma placement or on the Federalist Papers but on the actual policies they pursue and the care they take in articulating and implementing those policies, they have incentives to actually take such care and to demonstrate that they are doing so. When court decisions depend, in part, on how responsive the government is to affected parties, the government has reason to speak to those parties and to negotiate with them. Lillian Ladele's case is ultimately about how a court allows a people to *democratize* the rights of others, much in the way the American Framers contemplated it. The Revolution lives on in the British courts.

The Forgotten Middle

I've been hard on *Masterpiece Cakeshop*. It is indeed frustrating that the case was framed to elide the important contextual features the courts in the Ashers case and *Ladele* were determined to highlight and confront: the obvious presence of rights on both sides; the significance of an inscription or not on a wedding cake; the recency of the state imposition in relation to the voluntary choices made by the service provider; the state's motives and its own accountable decision-making; and the availability and quality of alternative service providers. The British courts seemed less interested in the question of who, categorically, must win these battles than on which facts the answer turned on. They made clear that what the cases were *about* were these facts, not whether the Constitution of the United Kingdom prefers gays or Christians. The decisions in these cases preserved the possibility that another gay cake customer (in the Ashers case) or another devout service provider (in *Ladele*) could win on different facts. The courts gave all sides reason to remain invested in the constitutional project.

Justice Anthony Kennedy, who wrote the eventual opinion in *Masterpiece Cakeshop*, did seem to glimpse the problem. At the start of the opinion, he lamented some disagreement in the record over what exactly Phillips was willing or unwilling to provide the couple, suggesting some sensitivity to the importance of factual context. Kennedy also took some care to emphasize both that "gay persons and gay couples cannot be treated as social outcasts or as inferior in dignity and worth" and that "religious and philosophical objections to gay marriage are protected views and in some instances protected forms of expression." There is good reason to believe that Justice Kennedy was sincere in his regard for both sets of rights. Before his retirement in 2018, he was the author of every one of the Court's opinions endorsing the rights of gays and lesbians, including *Obergefell*, affirming the right of same-sex couples to marry. Kennedy is also the justice most protective of freedom of expression of any in the history of the Court.

Confronted with this conflict of rights and the manifest need for balancing and proportionality, Justice Kennedy found a categorical way out. Even though U.S. courts do not recognize religious freedom claims when the law or government practice only incidentally infringes faith, *intentional* burdening of religion receives the strictest review and is nearly certain to be invalidated by the Supreme Court. In hearing Craig and Mullins's complaint, a member of Colorado's Civil Rights Commission said that Phillips's religious objections amounted to "despicable pieces of rhetoric" and noted that religious arguments had been used in the past to justify atrocities such as slavery and the Holocaust. What's more, the commission had ruled in favor of bakers in prior cases involving objections to the messages on cakes. Justice Kennedy treated this constellation of facts as akin to intentional religious discrimination against Phillips. The idea was that the commission was treating religious refusals to serve customers differently from secular ones. And so Phillips won his case without the Court resolving the basic conflict between Phillips and the couple.

There's nothing wrong, of course, with avoiding difficult constitutional questions by relying on easier ones. If the commission indeed showed special hostility to religious service providers, its decision should have been invalidated. But Justice Kennedy's opinion deferred guidance on how American courts should handle the many cases that bear some resemblance to *Masterpiece Cakeshop*. His dodge won't work for long. Most cases involving a conflict between religious freedom and the rights of gays and lesbians will not result from laws or practices that intentionally harm religious observers. Forced to choose, conservative justices will reliably side with religious objectors, and progressive justices will reliably side against them. Who wins will depend predictably on which political party "controls" the Court, just as surely, we'll say, as the sun rises in the east.

There was middle ground in the Colorado bakery case, but it lay hidden behind the sparkle of the lawyers' sequins. Socialized into American rights absolutism, judges and lawyers don't even pause to consider what a negotiated outcome would look like in a case like *Masterpiece Cakeshop*. We have come to see negotiation as the governing logic of politics (if that), not of litigation, which requires clear rules that denominate clear winners and losers. But modern rights conflicts will not submit to clear rules whether we wish them to or not. We need a different logic.

I offer two possibilities, one of which both Lillian Ladele's case and common experience help us better to see. A few years back, my wife and I took a trip to Istanbul. We had a lovely dinner at a café in a little Kumkapi cul-de-sac lined with several other restaurants. After finishing our entrée, we decided we were in the mood for baklava, and we asked the server if it was available. "Yes, yes, of course," he assured us, nodding vigorously as he left. Seconds later, I glimpsed a flash out of the corner of my eye. It was the waiter, sprinting out of the café and into another restaurant across the square. He emerged a few minutes later with a plate of sweet, golden baklava. It was delicious.

If we assume they weren't under common ownership (which they might well have been), the second restaurant was, in effect, a subcontractor. Services can be subcontracted even, perhaps especially, when they impose particular duties on the service provider. Indeed, this is a fair description of what happened in Lillian Ladele's case before her coworkers complained. Ladele wasn't seeking to prevent same-sex couples from obtaining civil partnerships; she was just objecting to her personal involvement. The Court of Appeal felt that Islington's "Dignity for All" policy prevented it from requiring an accommodation that would permit Ladele to substitute an equivalent registrar to officiate such partnerships.

Still, accommodations of this sort are common in cases involving religious freedom. Conscientious objection to military service, of course, has a long history. Most states include "conscience clauses" in their abortion laws that permit religious objectors to refuse to perform the procedure, and many states permit pharmacists to refuse to fill prescriptions for birth control or abortifacient drugs.

Federal laws in the United States are indeed required to exempt people whose religious practices the law substantially burdens, even if that burden is unintentional. Twenty-one states impose similar religious accommodation requirements on their own state and local laws. The federal accommodation law, the Religious Freedom Restoration Act (RFRA), was at the heart of the Supreme Court's 2014 decision requiring that the arts-and-crafts chain Hobby Lobby be exempted from an Affordable Care Act rule that employers provide their female workers with a health insurance plan that includes birth control coverage. As interpreted by the Court, RFRA requires courts to foreground two questions: (1) How big is the burden on religious exercise? (2) Is there an alternative that works just as well without imposing such a burden?

This framing is perfectly workable, so long as courts resist the urge to fetishize the rights RFRA creates. In the Hobby Lobby case, for example, the Court determined that the Department of Health and Human Services

(HHS) could exempt religious objectors from the contraceptive requirement without any prejudice to employees. This is because, under the Affordable Care Act, insurers could still be required to provide contraception coverage for the employees of objecting employers, just as they are required to do for the employees of churches or other organizations that HHS regarded as exempt even prior to Hobby Lobby's lawsuit. Appropriately, whether the Court was willing to supply an exemption appeared to depend on whether the legal duty could be delegated to someone else—in this case, insurers—without affecting the availability or quality of the service.

How could an analogous accommodation have worked in *Masterpiece Cakeshop*? A court could have imposed a duty on Phillips to provide a custom cake—*or its equivalent*—to Craig and Mullins. He could have fulfilled this duty by hiring a sous chef who was willing to service same-sex weddings. Alternatively, like my Istanbul café, he could have contracted with another cakeshop to prepare a cake whenever a same-sex couple made a request. Craig and Mullins would have gotten their cake, and Phillips wouldn't have needed to bake it. This solution wouldn't be perfect. A baker whose conscience doesn't allow him to facilitate a same-sex wedding would still experience some coercion. And subcontracting a cake, even behind the scenes, would mean that same-sex couples would be receiving a different product from what other customers receive. The dignitary harm this substitution might confer may be more tolerable in relation to a cake than, say, a photographer. The degree of harm, like other facts, should matter to a court.

A second possible resolution of some of the conflicts that have sprung up between religious freedom and LGBTQ rights would be to hive off wedding ceremonies from other activities. Weddings are inherently expressive in a way that eating in a restaurant, staying in a hotel, or getting one's car fixed just isn't. A food order, a hotel reservation, or auto body work is typically functional and doesn't call for substantial creativity or art from the service provider. Weddings are different, which is why wedding planning is a billion-dollar industry in the United States—and that's before we even get to the cost of the wedding itself. Again, this solution carries with it some dignitary and logistical harm to same-sex couples, who would need to further grow the "Green Book" for same-sex weddings. Depending on the numbers, this might not be such a bad thing. There is, after all, something to be said for knowing which service providers will be hostile to one's wedding.

Some Americans, maybe even most, wouldn't like these solutions. They aren't perfect, and many, on both sides, might think no compromise is called for here. But the job of the courts in a pluralistic democracy isn't to please their base. It's to work to resolve conflicts, to ratchet them down rather than up. Courts should be reminding us of what we have in common. They should be granting just enough constitutional leverage on each side that we have no choice but to sit across from each other at the table, to look each other in the eye, and to speak to and hear each other. Too often, U.S. courts instead see their job in constitutional cases as declaring who's right. The answer, so often, is neither side — or both.

Judicial Partisanship

Justice Kennedy's opinion in *Masterpiece Cakeshop* was one of his last majority opinions as a Supreme Court justice. Known as a swing justice par excellence, he was himself something of a compromise, nominated and quickly confirmed after the spectacular failure of Robert Bork's polarizing nomination and Douglas Ginsburg's withdrawal of his nomination over his prior marijuana use.

Kennedy's replacement, Brett Kavanaugh, was chosen because of his sterling partisan credentials. Kavanaugh was Ken Starr's deputy in the Whitewater investigation into President Bill Clinton. He was part of the legal team for the Cuban boy Elián González's Florida family members, who sought to keep him in the United States against his father's wishes in 1999 and 2000, and for George W. Bush during the contested Florida electoral recount in the 2000 presidential election. He served in Bush's White House counsel's office and as the White House staff secretary, where his main job was policy coordination across the executive branch. Those who advised President Trump on whom to nominate to replace Kennedy were looking for a reliable GOP vote on the Court. With those metrics, it's hard to conceive of a better choice than Brett Kavanaugh.

We should fully expect partisan concerns to dominate judicial selection in a system that takes the American approach to rights. If rights conflicts are existential battles, presidents will try to win. What else would they do? But nominations of this sort further erode the perception, if not the reality, of courts as fair dealers. Wielding neither sword nor purse, U.S. courts must ground their authority in the public's confidence in their integrity.

One day, the jig will be up. If courts don't have our confidence, we will stop listening to them. And when the day comes when it really is time to take a stand against tyranny, we will turn to our courts, and they won't be there to help us.

Part III

Rehabilitating
Rights

WE HAVE GIVEN OUR CONSTITUTION TO THE COURTS. The binding of rights to judges runs so deep that most Americans don't see it as a choice that we make. Any suggestion of alternatives is met with blank stares at best and horror at worst. We have come to see deciding what rights we have and what rights we don't have as simply the thing that courts do. The rest of us are meant to obey.

Judicial supremacy of this sort wasn't the Framers' vision. It isn't the norm outside the United States today. And it has consequences. Judges tend to reduce conflicts over rights to the abstract, idealized questions their legal training prepares them to resolve. Disputes involving human experiences and emotions, state violence and government spoils, are reduced to "text" and "precedent" and "original meaning." Courts cast about for the right rule to apply, the most familiar box in which to cram the dispute, limbs and all. This isn't judiciousness or restraint. It is what philosophers call a "category mistake." Conflicts over rights are not *about* texts and precedents and original meanings. They are about pain.

Courts are not the only institutions that have something to say about rights. Politicians, agency officials, police officers, jurors, teachers, and school administrators all have the capacity to identify rights and to accommodate rights to the other imperatives of our collective lives. Americans once understood that. But overreliance on courts has reduced that capacity. The muscle has atrophied.

It's one thing to diagnose a condition but quite another to figure out how to treat it. Turning rights back in the right direction will require judges to help the rest of us rebuild our constitutional muscle. Rehabilitation will require reengaging many of the same political actors the Framers sought to empower, but doing so in ways more sensitive than the Founding generation was to the rights of the disempowered. Courts have a part to play in setting the bounds for political reconciliation, but they should usually be supporting actors. Placing the rest of us in a lead role frees us to approach rights conflicts through our collective experience and not just through logic.

In cases involving people with disabilities, U.S. courts have declared that demands for accommodation are almost per se beneath constitutional concern. Rights need to be consistently applied, they say, and the burdens on people with disabilities have too much in common with the burdens on those who are elderly or mentally ill or simply overweight. This posture writes people with disabilities out of the Constitution, for no reason other than the perceived incompetence of judges to make fine-grained distinctions. A rights conflict in the disability context shouldn't be resolved based on the abstract question of whether there is a "right to accommodation," but on the very real question of how much accommodation is needed and what the reasons were for it being denied.

U.S. courts have gone to the opposite extreme in race-based affirmative action cases. They have flattened complex conflicts between rights holders — the rejected and the accepted applicant — into a trumping "right" against racial discrimination, one that can be overcome only by "state interests" that judges recognize as compelling and fastidiously applied. The mismatch between the messiness of real-life racial conflict and the strict lines courts try to draw around affirmative action has led to a maelstrom of subterfuge, deception, and recrimination. We need a reset that allows school administrators to forthrightly identify structural racial inequality as their reason for acting and to be transparent about how their admissions officers use race. A different approach to rights can get us there.

Elsewhere on campus, though often supported by outside agitators, students engage in ritual clashes over freedom of speech. Conservative groups invite charlatans onto campuses to make a show of their speech rights, and progressive opponents shout them down and petition for the canceling of unwelcome ideas. American rightsism enables this sordid dance. It treats campus speakers at public universities in just the same way as it would treat a political prisoner. As quintessential curators of speech, universities should be granted the freedom to decide whom to invite or disinvite into their educational spaces and whether and how to expose their students to intense discomfort.

Sacrificing justice to legal formalisms both denies justice and distorts the law. All of us, judges included, must contribute in order for the rights of our fellow citizens to be recognized, protected, and reconciled with what else we value. Doing so requires supplementing the logic of the common law with the logic of common sense. It's not that we need to think outside the box. It's that we need to recognize when there is no box.

7

Disability

As a novel and deadly coronavirus surged across the world in the early months of 2020, state health officials found themselves contemplating a tragic choice: if they wound up short on the ventilators needed to provide oxygen to the most distressed victims of the virus, whose lives were the most worth saving?

Deciding whom to treat first when hospitals are low on supplies — whether of hospital beds, organs, blood, medications, or the attention of surgeons — is routine in emergency medicine. Detailed triage protocols for access to critical care resources routinely take account of a patient's likelihood of survival, directing the most urgent attention to those for whom care is most likely to make the difference between life and death. Patients who won't live without immediate intervention but who might survive with it are first in line.

But in the early days of the coronavirus outbreak, Alabama's initial ventilator triage plan contained a curious additional factor: "persons with severe mental retardation, advanced dementia or severe traumatic brain injury may be poor candidates for ventilator support." The state appeared to be contemplating allocating ventilators based not just on the likelihood of survival but also on the state's assessment of the value of a patient's life. And the lives of those with severe intellectual impairments would be found wanting.

Three states over, two elderly inmates at a geriatric prison near College

Station, Texas, sued the state for not implementing appropriate virus protocols. Laddy Valentine, a sixty-nine-year-old with a heart condition, and Richard King, a seventy-three-year-old diabetic, argued that the state's failure to provide adequate access to soap and hand sanitizer, its lax approach to physical distancing, and its lack of attention to disinfecting common areas and door handles posed a particular threat to older inmates and those with underlying medical conditions. The state, they said, was violating the Americans with Disabilities Act (ADA), which requires that state and local governments not discriminate against people with disabilities. The state's response? The ADA "doesn't apply in exigent circumstances."

Had the State of Alabama chosen to prioritize white patients over African Americans in allocating ventilators, reasoning that whites live higher-quality lives, it would have violated the Constitution in the most flagrant way possible. Putting such a preference into an official policy document would have been unthinkable. Had Texas prison officials chosen to violate the rights of inmates of Mexican origin, concluding that state and federal civil rights laws protecting against race or national origin discrimination simply don't apply in emergencies, they would have been excoriated across the political spectrum, and justly so.

And yet discrimination against people with disabilities is not just common but is ignored by American constitutional law. Public officials and private employers alike routinely treat people with disabilities as less fully human than others, their lives less fulfilling and more expendable. Most states forbid people with developmental disabilities to get married. Federal law allows employers to pay people with disabilities significantly less than minimum wage. The accommodations needed for many people with disabilities to live dignified lives routinely go missing, whether it's subway stations with elevators or polling places with audio ballots for visually impaired voters. The Supreme Court sees none of these issues as a constitutional problem.

Whether governments, businesses, and other institutions take seriously the equality demands of people with disabilities will depend, in part, on constitutional law. But there is no area of American law in which the gap between the rights we have and the rights justice requires is wider or less justified than disability law. The Court's failure here isn't because unequal treatment of people with disabilities is just or reasonable, or even because judges believe it is. It's rather because, we are told, it's hard to define the bounds of the disability category with precision. Rights must be all or nothing, and rights for people with disabilities can't possibly be all, so they are left with nothing.

The Supreme Court's casual disregard of the rights of people with disabilities would be intolerable for others viewed as less expendable. Progress in this area will require careful thinking — not about the Framers, but about the facts.

Is Disability Different?

Disability isn't quite like other grounds for antidiscrimination laws. Many cases of disability discrimination don't involve "negative" treatment of people with disabilities relative to those without them. Rather, such cases often involve a "positive" demand for the accommodation of individuals' physical or mental impairments. Advocacy for the rights of people with disabilities don't just target laws, policies, or practices that treat similar people as if they were different, as in the classic case of racial or sex discrimination. They also, indeed paradigmatically, insist that the government and other power-wielding institutions *not* treat people who are different as if they were the same, a distinct but no less important kind of inequality.

Ensuring equality for people with disabilities requires both the government and private actors to change their behavior and to spend money. Business owners might have to install ramps or lifts or shift work responsibilities. Cities and counties might have to create curb cuts, audible pedestrian signals, or brighter streetlights. Courts might have to provide hearing devices for litigants or witnesses. A person with schizophrenia might need a special advocate or assistant to receive government services. Landlords might have to allow service animals notwithstanding policies banning pets.

More broadly, standards of merit that we take for granted — in the workplace, in the classroom, on the soccer pitch — often assume the justice of discriminating against those who are less able. Disability rights chip away at that assumption in ways that are difficult to control or confine. Rather than asking if employers must provide ramps or interpreters, we may one day be asking a more radical set of questions. Well-paying and high-prestige jobs within our culture privilege those with logical-mathematical and verbal-linguistic intelligence who are able to engage in abstract or symbolic thinking; who can pursue systematic, stepwise inquiry; and who can read, write, and memorize at a high level. These capacities can be sharpened with practice, but they are not choices we make, and privileging them underwrites deep social and economic inequality.

These features of disability discrimination claims mark this area as uncomfortable terrain for a court committed to the American approach to rights. The Supreme Court has been reluctant to extend strict scrutiny to disability discrimination, for little reason other than that it would be too complicated.

The leading case involved discriminatory zoning against a home for mildly "mentally retarded" people in the small city of Cleburne, Texas. A woman, Jan Hannah, bought a four-bedroom stucco-and-frame house on Featherston Street in 1980, intending to use it as a group home for people with special needs. Shortly after Hannah bought the house, a local dentist whose office was close by got twenty-nine families to sign a petition opposing the home. The city told Hannah that it would be characterized as a "hospital for the feeble-minded" and as such needed a special-use permit of the sort required for prisons, halfway houses, and addiction treatment facilities. Hannah applied for the permit, but it was denied after neighbors expressed opposition at a public hearing.

The Supreme Court eventually struck down the zoning law, saying it was motivated by irrational prejudice, but the justices pointedly refused to say that discrimination against people with disabilities should be singled out as special in the way of racial or sex discrimination. Writing for the majority, Justice Byron White noted the wide variety of ways in which someone described as disabled might be impaired, and he bemoaned the lack of any "principled way" to distinguish people with disabilities from those who are elderly, sick, or mentally ill. The Court's inability to define the category with precision meant, for White, that laws impairing the rights of people with disabilities couldn't receive any special scrutiny. Laws burdening people with disabilities had to be treated in the same maximally deferential way as a law regulating milk substitutes or one forbidding opticians to fit lenses to glasses.

Hannah still managed to win the case, but this was essentially an accident. Justice White had initially intended only to hold that courts should review policies that impair the rights of the intellectually disabled with maximal deference to the government, sending the case back to the lower court to apply this lax standard to the facts of the Cleburne case. He only decided to perform the analysis himself, and to strike down the ordinance, because — owing to a quirk in how the various justices lined up in the case — he might have lost his majority had he done otherwise.

Conflicts over the rights of people with disabilities check every box that breeds anxiety among courts adopting the American rights approach. Slippery slopes are all around the rights of people with disabilities. The category itself has famously soft edges. The ADA defines a disability as "a physical or mental impairment that substantially limits one or more major life activities." As Justice White implied in the Cleburne case, impairments on a par with a disability also afflict the elderly and people with physical and mental illnesses. One could add to that list people who are obese, who are pregnant, who are drug addicts, or who are very tall or very short. People with severe intellectual disabilities are exempt from the death penalty; courts have struggled to figure out how to assess those disabilities for this purpose. Those with other mental impairments are unable to stand trial, a precursor to conviction and sentencing. But people who commit heinous crimes are usually not well. If we maintain that the rights of people with disabilities deserve special constitutional treatment only if the category can be defined so as to avoid slippery slopes, then we will never give the rights of people with disabilities special constitutional treatment.

Equal opportunity for these people also can readily conflict with the rights of others. Recall the conflict over whether the South African runner and double amputee Oscar Pistorius could, using specially fitted artificial limbs, compete against able-bodied runners in international track events. Or whether Casey Martin, a professional golfer with a congenital disorder in his right leg, could compete on the PGA Tour using a golf cart while able-bodied golfers had to walk. Service animals can inconvenience others by creating waste or noise or allergic reactions in neighbors, coworkers, or seatmates. An approach to rights that places the weight of the analysis on whether the rights holder is special and can fit into a certain box, rather than focusing on the balance of interests in particular cases, lacks the analytical resources to confront these kinds of multilateral disputes honestly.

And those are the easy cases. Others are harder. As prenatal genetic screening becomes more sophisticated, it will increasingly be possible to selectively abort disabled fetuses. This practice is already widespread for fetuses with Down syndrome or Huntington's disease, an incurable brain disorder that reliably kills people in middle age. These acts are controversial, but they usually are not illegal. Selective abortion on the basis of disability, like sex-selective abortion, is outlawed in some countries, but not in most of the United States. In fact, it is constitutionally protected under the Supreme Court's abortion cases.

Should the law care about a disability-selective abortion based on a prediction that the child will have hemophilia or autism or cancer? What about impaired hearing or vision, or below-average intelligence? The rights at stake include those of women, men, and others planning for parenthood and of fetuses whose lives many Americans view as having inherent value. But they also include the rights of people with disabilities whose dignity hangs in the balance of how the law views discrimination on the basis of ability. The Supreme Court lacks any language in which it can discuss these conflicting rights with transparency and sensitivity.

Indignity

Three examples reveal the depth of the problem. All involve the kind of callousness people with disabilities suffer daily. They show varying degrees of intolerance, neglect, and garden-variety discrimination. Constitutional law in the hands of the Supreme Court sees none of this as problematic. The Court lacks any instruments for distinguishing these examples either from each other or from government decisions as banal as renaming a local highway or raising the gasoline tax.

The Screaming Bucket

Barbara Keske's seven-year-old son, Steven, was autistic and hyperactive. One of the ways the boy's conditions manifested was that he occasionally let out a high-pitched scream for no apparent reason. One day Keske, who lived in Toulon, a small town outside of Peoria, Illinois, was told that her son had been suspended from riding the school bus for punching a bus aide in the face the day before. Keske disciplined her child, but a few days later another student approached her at a gas station and told her why Steven had hit the aide: "He was trying to get the bucket off his head." The school bus aide had developed a regular practice of physically restraining Steven so that she could place a five-gallon pail over his head, extending down over his arms and torso, in order to mute his shrieks. The other kids on the bus called it "the screaming bucket."

The driver and the aide were subsequently dismissed, but Keske sued them along with the school district. Keske alleged a number of state and common-law torts, as well as a violation of the Fourth Amendment ban on unreasonable search and seizure and of multiple federal laws, including the ADA. Keske's complaint did not allege that the school district or the bus aide had violated Steven's right to *equal* treatment under the Constitution.

If a school bus aide had put a large bucket over the head and shoulders of the only Black student on the bus in order to keep him quiet, his lawyer in any subsequent lawsuit would surely have brought a constitutional equality claim. I don't fault Steven's lawyers for not doing so in his case. The Cleburne decision was calculated to make that equality claim a loser. Steven's screams were in fact annoying to others on the bus and to the driver, perhaps even in a way that affected the safety of his driving. Putting a bucket over his head was an effective and therefore perfectly rational way to shut him up. The problem with this remedy isn't that it was irrational but that it was excessive and an affront to his dignity.

Antidiscrimination law isn't about what is irrational; it is about what is wrong. Believing in rights for people with disabilities means that sometimes others must suffer greater inconvenience, or cost, to accommodate the needs of their fellow citizens. The only way to balance these various rights and interests is to . . . balance these various rights and interests. The difficulty of this task — its inconvenience, if you will — is no reason to treat people with disabilities as if they are of no constitutional concern.

The End of Care's Life

People living with severe life impairments often rely on family members to care for them. The aging, disability, or death of a caretaker can have devastating, often unseen consequences for a person with special needs who has come to rely on the caretaker's constant attention and intimate know-how.

Vernon Gray, an adult, was living with his mother in the small house he grew up in, on Martin Luther King Jr. Way in Seattle's Central District. Gray had a severe mental disability and an IQ of 60. His mother was his full-time caretaker. She fed him, clothed him, groomed him, and paid the bills. Then, in 2000, she died.

Gray lived for several days with his mother's dead body in the house before authorities showed up to remove it. The house had been paid off years earlier, but the utility bills required constant attention that Gray wasn't equipped to offer. A few months later, the water and electricity were cut off. Concerned neighbors regularly dropped off plates of food at his doorstep, but he lived a decade in the house with no electricity or plumbing. Gray's parents had left tens of thousands of dollars stashed in the house, but because Gray didn't know how to pay property taxes, the house eventually went into foreclosure and, in 2013, was sold at auction. By then, Gray was living in a house filled with garbage, feces, and hundreds of rats that had chewed their way in and could be seen scurrying in waves across the lawn or hanging from the drapes at all hours of the day. The stench was unbearable. Suddenly homeless, Gray began living on the streets, eating out of garbage cans. He developed glaucoma and went nearly blind before, finally, after police discovered him wandering in traffic, he was placed in a group home for adults.

Twice during Gray's time living in his house, at neighbors' behest, social workers had been assigned to investigate whether he had cognitive disabilities that prevented him from being able to care for himself. Both times, the case was closed after a brief investigation. Many states impose duties on their social welfare agencies to offer assistance in cases like Gray's, and their negligence is actionable in court. In Gray's case, a lawsuit filed on his behalf was eventually settled for $8 million.

Gray had to bring his claims under state law, not the U.S. Constitution. This is because the Supreme Court has held that under the Constitution, a state owes no duty of care to its citizens. The state isn't required to educate children. It isn't required to protect its residents from homicide, rape, or other crimes. It isn't required to protect vulnerable people from abuse or neglect. In 1989, the Supreme Court said that a four-year-old Wisconsin boy named Joshua DeShaney, who had been beaten into a coma by his father, had no constitutional claim against the government caseworkers who had negligently ignored complaints of prior abuse. Sixteen years later, the Court said that the town of Castle Rock, Colorado, couldn't be held liable after its police ignored Jessica Gonzales's reports that her estranged husband had kidnapped their three daughters in violation of a restraining order. The husband subsequently murdered the girls. For the Court, even the existence of the restraining order gave Gonzales no enforceable rights against the town under the federal Constitution.

Any constitutional claims by Gray would have fared no better than those of DeShaney or Gonzales. As far as the Supreme Court is concerned, the State of Washington was perfectly entitled under the Constitution to let Gray rot among the rats. But let the state try to prevent pharmacies from selling prescription data to drug companies, and suddenly it becomes a matter of high constitutional principle. This is not morally defensible. It shouldn't be legally defensible either. But it is consistent with the Supreme Court's hands-off approach to affirmative constitutional rights. Gray's treatment shows how a constitution that never recognizes state duties of care simply cannot protect the core rights of people with disabilities.

The Subminimum Wage

The federal minimum wage has been $7.25 since 2009. In 2010, employees at an Applebee's in Westbury, New York, were paid between $3.97 and $5.96 per hour. In 2017, Chris Wilson, a thirty-three-year-old employee of Kandu Industries in Janesville, Wisconsin, was paid less than $3 per hour to pack brackets used in playground equipment or to package food. In 2009, some workers for the Goodwill Industries charity worked for as little as 22 cents per hour. These businesses were able to pay their employees below the minimum wage solely because the workers had disabilities. The Fair Labor Standards Act (FLSA), which instituted the federal minimum wage in 1938, has since its inception permitted employers to pay a subminimum wage to people with mental or physical disabilities.

This practice is controversial. At the time the FLSA was passed, the best that people with disabilities could hope for was charity, not equal rights. The statute was barely a decade removed from an 8–1 Supreme Court decision affirming Virginia's sterilization of a woman the state believed to be intellectually impaired. Of course, workers who are blind or have Down syndrome or are paraplegic might work less quickly or less well than other employees. Enabling them to be hired for subminimum wages, primarily at so-called "sheltered" workplaces — segregated sites that ostensibly prepare them to transition to integrated employment — might be the only way to provide gainful employment to many workers with disabilities.

Still, the very idea behind a minimum wage is that the state should, as a matter of human dignity, ensure a subsistence salary regardless of a worker's productivity. Paying someone 22 cents an hour recalls the sweatshops of the Gilded Age. Moreover, the track record of sheltered workplaces in helping disabled employees into integrated settings has been poor.

The controversy over the subminimum wage exposes a challenge that sits deep within the core of disability law. As a society, we are accustomed to believing that employees should be paid in line with their marginal productivity. It's economically inefficient to hire workers who are producing less for the company than they are earning in wages. Neoclassical economic theory predicts that in a competitive labor market, companies simply won't hire workers whose marginal productivity sits below the minimum. Encouraging private employers to hire disabled employees and to pay them adequately and equally would require either the carrot of taxpayer-funded financial incentives or the stick of a coercive legal regime that treats disability as similar to more familiar anchors for antidiscrimination law, such as race, sex, and religion. In either case, equal treatment in the employment space would require us to relax or overcome standard assumptions about the relationship between labor productivity and pay.

To put the issue more plainly, equality for people with disabilities ultimately requires society at least sometimes to choose fairness over efficiency. Doing so challenges deep-seated intuitions about merit and costs real money. We often defer this choice in the case of race or sex. We tell ourselves that racial profiling is bad policing or that refusing to hire or promote working mothers is economically irrational. Both are surely true, sometimes. Other times, both are surely false. Sometimes racial profiling will catch more criminals, and sometimes discriminating against women will lead to a more productive workforce, but such instances are sufficiently exceptional, or the potential inefficiencies sufficiently small, that we often persist in using market logic to make the case against racial or sex discrimination. Disability strains that logic to its breaking point.

More broadly, forbidding discrimination against people with disabilities presents a challenge to prevailing definitions of merit. What it typically means within our culture to "deserve" a particular job or wage or opportunity is to outperform others on the exam, to sail through the interview, to make the sale, to reel in the client, to score more points on the court. People who lack the physical or mental capacities to compete along these dimensions do not, within this culture, deserve to succeed. The American approach to rights seems to require courts either to reject this model of merit in favor of one that is more openly egalitarian or to reject the very idea of disability rights. They have chosen the latter option. But a third choice is available, if courts are willing to look past the American approach to rights.

Congress and the Constitution

When resolving rights conflicts depends less on an evaluation of which category a right falls into and more on mediation among competing rights in light of the facts, courts necessarily must cede some power to recognize and enforce rights to political actors. The qualitative, incremental distinctions that many rights rely on and the difficult fiscal tradeoffs that they require are best made, in the first instance, by legislatures and agencies rather than by judges. Those institutions have the resources to conduct complex empirical analyses, have the oversight and subpoena power to hold wide-ranging hearings and solicit information from a variety of sources, and have the luxury of approaching problem-solving under a prevailing assumption that compromise will be necessary. The enforcement of positive rights in particular — rights to receive a benefit or support, as opposed to rights against being burdened — invites the political branches into a *conversation* about rights that has become too rare in our modern age of judicial supremacy.

The American approach bears significant responsibility for that rarity. This approach turns rights conflicts into interpretive questions about precedents, textual exegesis, and original intent that judges are uniquely comfortable exploring. It also quite specifically *disempowers* Congress from making the complex judgments that modern rights enforcement requires.

Prior to the Civil War, Congress had very limited power to pass laws protecting civil rights. During Reconstruction, the Republican Congress passed the Civil Rights Act of 1866, which forbade racial discrimination in the making and enforcement of contracts and in property transactions. The Fourteenth Amendment was enacted two years later in order to resolve the controversy over whether Congress had the constitutional power to pass this act. That is why, in addition to providing its famous protections for state violations of due process and equal protection of the laws, the Fourteenth

Amendment also specifically empowers Congress to enforce its provisions "by appropriate legislation."

But the structure of the Fourteenth Amendment leaves an important question unanswered: Who gets to decide which rights Congress may enforce? Is it the Supreme Court or Congress? On the one hand, if Congress can decide on its own which rights the Fourteenth Amendment protects, the amendment could dramatically expand its legislative powers. On the other hand, it would be odd for the same Congress that passed the Fourteenth Amendment to declare that rights recognition was the exclusive domain of federal courts. That Congress had asserted extraordinary and aggressive political power. Its members were substantially the same as those who had passed the Civil Rights Act of 1866, had excluded southern members from the chamber until the Fourteenth Amendment was passed, and had impeached and very nearly removed President Andrew Johnson. They had lived through and condemned the Supreme Court's denial of the rights of Black citizens in *Dred Scott*, a case the Fourteenth Amendment specifically overruled. Preserving an important role for Congress in rights recognition and enforcement would be consistent with a rights tradition that had assumed a significant political dimension since before the Founding Era.

The Supreme Court provided an initial answer to the question of who gets to recognize Fourteenth Amendment rights in an 1883 decision invalidating the Civil Rights Act of 1875. That act had sought to ban racial discrimination in public accommodations (theaters, inns, amusement parks, and the like), but the Supreme Court struck it down because it directly regulated private institutions rather than states. According to the Court, Congress was not free to deem any discrimination by private actors as triggering the protections of the Fourteenth Amendment.

Congress labored under the influence of that 1883 decision when it passed the Civil Rights Act of 1964, which also banned racial discrimination in public accommodations. To get around the "state action" issue, Congress eschewed the Fourteenth Amendment and instead relied on its expansive power to regulate interstate commerce. As interpreted by the Supreme Court at the time, Congress's power under the Commerce Clause enabled it to regulate activities of private actors so long as those activities had a substantial effect on interstate commerce.

This meant that the way for Congress to prohibit a Birmingham barbecue joint or an Atlanta motel from putting up "Whites Only" signs wasn't through Congress's power to enforce the Equal Protection Clause but instead through its power to regulate commerce between the states. The idea was that Jim Crow inconvenienced African-American interstate travelers, artificially limited the supplies purchased by restaurants, and affected the market for business offices, plants, and conventions. In the 1960s, the Warren Court quickly and unanimously affirmed Congress's power to restrict private discrimination using its authority over the national economy.

Armed with a Court-consecrated constitutional "hook," Congress went on to justify many major civil rights bills as an exercise of its Commerce Clause power rather than its power to enforce the Fourteenth Amendment, including the Age Discrimination in Employment Act (1967), the Pregnancy Discrimination Act (1978), the ADA (1990), and the Violence Against Women Act (1994).

For years, using the Commerce Clause was just fine. It got Congress just about the same kind of law it would have gotten had it relied on a constitutional provision that had something to do with civil rights. But as the Supreme Court became more conservative, particularly during the tenure of Chief Justice William Rehnquist (1986–2005), it began to tamp down on what kinds of activities Congress could regulate using the Commerce Clause. For example, in 1996 the Court held that the Commerce Clause couldn't be used to authorize a lawsuit seeking damages from state governments. In 1995, the Court struck down a law regulating gun possession near schools, and in 2001 it invalidated a provision of the Violence Against Women Act that supplied a federal court civil remedy for victims of gender-motivated violence. Over the course of those decisions, the majority made clear that the Commerce Clause could only reach "economic" activities. Then, in 2013, in its first Affordable Care Act decision, the John Roberts Court said that the clause was limited to "activity" rather than "inactivity." This holding seems to suggest that Congress can prevent private citizens from discriminating but can't force them to act in particular ways.

The ADA is vulnerable under these precedents. The act doesn't just ban classic "negative" discrimination against people with disabilities. It also compels employers to provide "reasonable accommodations" to qualified applicants or employees and requires that a wide range of businesses — hotels, restaurants, retailers, movie theaters, private schools, and so forth — meet minimum accessibility standards and make "reasonable modifications" to their usual practices in order to accommodate people with disabilities. *Neglecting* to install a lift, widen an entryway, modify a work schedule, or provide closed-captioning is not an "activity."

To be sure, the argument goes a step beyond the Affordable Care Act decision. Unlike individuals subject to the health care mandate at issue in that case, businesses subject to the ADA have already made the voluntary decision to enter an economic market. Still, the tone and trajectory of the Rehnquist and Roberts Courts' cases on Congress's Commerce Clause power cannot be reassuring to advocates for the rights of people with disabilities.

The Supreme Court has already weakened the ADA through its narrow definition of disability discrimination. In 1997, two Alabama state employees, Patricia Garrett and Milton Ash, sued under the ADA, arguing that state agencies had failed to accommodate their disabilities. Garrett had been demoted from her nursing position at the University of Alabama at Birmingham Hospital after her radiation and chemotherapy treatments for breast cancer forced her to take a leave from work. Ash, an asthmatic who worked as a security officer for the Alabama Department of Youth Services, was denied a request to modify his duties so as to reduce his exposure to cigarette smoke and carbon monoxide. Because Garrett and Ash sought damages from state entities, they could proceed with their suit only if the ADA provisions they relied upon could be justified under the Fourteenth Amendment rather than the Commerce Clause.

The Cleburne case stood in the way of that argument. "The result of *Cleburne* is that States are not required by the Fourteenth Amendment to make special accommodations for the disabled, so long as their actions toward such individuals are rational," Rehnquist wrote for the 5–4 majority in the Alabama cases. "They could quite hardheadedly — and perhaps hardheartedly — hold to job-qualification requirements which do not make allowance for the disabled."

In practical terms, this means that a refusal to accommodate — the bread and butter of disability discrimination — is almost per se rational. As such, Congress has no Fourteenth Amendment enforcement power to require accommodation by states. The Supreme Court has adopted a narrow view of disability rights because of the supposed inability of courts to make contextual distinctions and avoid slippery slopes, but then it has used that narrow definition to constrain the power of the *political* branches as well.

The Court's enforced limitation of disability rights under the Constitution to cases involving commercial activities carries deeper meaning. We condemn discrimination because it is wrong, not because it is economically irrational. Internment of U.S. citizens of Japanese descent would have been wrong even if there had been a fifth column loyal to the emperor of Japan operating on the West Coast during World War II. Extra TSA screening of Arab-looking men at airports would be wrong regardless of its efficacy relative to random or universal screening. Failing to accommodate people with disabilities is likewise an infringement of their rights regardless of whether doing so is costly or inefficient. The difficult law and policy question is not the threshold one of whether there has been an infringement, but rather the incremental question of just how much cost is too much for society to bear.

This point would be easier to see if the courts took constitutional disability rights seriously. To characterize those rights in terms of rationality or economic logic is simply to erase people with disabilities as subjects of moral concern. Taking disability rights seriously means recognizing that lack of accommodation is, prima facie, a denial of equal treatment and therefore a constitutional injury. It means allowing Congress the leeway to use its civil rights powers under the Fourteenth Amendment to enforce the rights of people with disabilities through accommodation mandates, which is the only way in which such enforcement can mean anything.

Solutions

Of course, no formula can tell a court how to sort out disability rights claims. Justice White's concern in the Cleburne case wasn't facetious. There are indeed a great variety of ways in which a person can be impaired, from severe physical or mental disabilities to cognitive limitations that fall at various points along a spectrum, sometimes in ways that change over time. Moreover, it is conceivable that the availability of accommodation itself affects the prevalence of disability diagnoses. For example, the College Board, which administers the SAT and other standardized tests, relaxes time limits for students with documented learning disorders. The College Board approves such requests so long as they are consistent with a student's existing IEP, or individualized education program. From 2010–11 to 2015–16, the number of requests for SAT accommodations doubled from 80,000 to 160,000. We can assume that learning disabilities weren't contagious during this period. The regulatory regime affects the behavior of the regulated.

American courts need not start from a blank slate, though. The ADA itself is a fine prototype for how to protect the rights of people with disabilities. It needs a stronger constitutional foundation, one actually grounded in civil rights, and one that is invulnerable to the numerous Republican efforts to weaken the law since its inception. Moreover, while protections against disability discrimination are exotic under U.S. federal constitutional law, they are quite normal elsewhere. One in four countries specifically protects the rights of people with disabilities in their national constitutions.

Canada offers an especially instructive example of how two different disability rights cases, each decided under constitutional standards, can come out differently depending on factual distinctions that judges are more than capable of recognizing.

The first is an education case. Emily Eaton was a twelve-year-old girl with cerebral palsy. She could not speak. She could not use sign language. She was partially blind and mostly confined to a wheelchair. At her parents' request, Emily started kindergarten at her neighborhood school, with a full-time educational assistant in the classroom to work with her. After three years of this arrangement, Emily's teachers and assistants determined that a fully integrated setting was not in her best interest. Her need for individualized educational attention was substantial, she was unable to communicate with teachers or interact socially with classmates, she regularly mouthed objects, and she had increasingly been crying and falling asleep in class. Emily's parents objected to a segregated placement, and after several rounds of internal administrative appeals went against them, they took their case to the courts, and eventually to the Supreme Court of Canada.

The constitutional aspects of Emily's case would be straightforward in the United States. She has no right to a particular primary educational placement, or indeed to any education at all. In Canada, however, freedom from disability discrimination is among the rights recognized in the Canadian Charter of Rights and Freedoms, Canada's equivalent of the Bill of Rights. In this case, the decision to place Emily in a specialized class (albeit one in a regular school with some interaction with the rest of the student body) was clearly a distinction made on the basis of her disability. That meant it was necessary to determine whether the burden on Emily, if any, was reasonable.

That question doesn't lend itself to grand theory or glib answers. The Canadian Supreme Court largely relied on the detailed assessment of Emily's case made by the Ontario Special Education Tribunal, whose decision had been appealed to the courts. The court noted the attention the tribunal paid to the benefits of integration. Empirical data suggest that in many circumstances, integration is in the best interest even of children who need significant support, and segregating students with disabilities can be just as stigmatizing as segregating students based on race. The court was careful to entertain the logic of integration, which understands disability in terms of normal human variation rather than as a status to be marginalized or pitied. But the court rejected the appeals court's position that there should be a *presumption* in favor of integrated education. The Supreme Court's worry was that "the operation of a presumption tends to render proceedings more technical and adversarial" and risks decisions being "made by default rather than on the merits." This worry is precisely what has materialized under the various presumptions that characterize the American approach to rights.

Instead, consistent with its general support for proportionality, the Canadian Supreme Court assessed how the tribunal had handled each of the particular needs that contributed to Emily's best interest: her intellectual and academic needs, which the tribunal thought were better served in an environment in which her inability to communicate would be less of a hindrance; her social and emotional needs, which didn't seem to be met in a classroom in which she wasn't interacting with classmates; and her safety needs, which were difficult to accommodate without major alterations to the physical environment. The court also noted the tribunal's focus on the need for ongoing assessment of Emily's needs so that her placement could be evaluated dynamically. The tribunal itself had emphasized that Emily's case required sensitivity that "can only be realized through cooperation, and most important compromise." It was clearly a message to her parents, but it could well have been a message to U.S. courts in how to handle disability cases.

Some may disagree with how the Supreme Court of Canada came out in Emily's case. Its rejection of a presumption in favor of integrated education has come in for some criticism. Perhaps it gave the tribunal too much credit. Perhaps it should have required more detail about the benefits of a segregated setting rather than just what is lacking in an integrated one. The point here isn't to praise the *outcome* but rather the *method*. The court's mode of decision-making reflects attention to evidence, careful consideration of the interests on all sides (including Emily's, which the court took care to emphasize were distinct from her parents' but unfortunately unknowable), and humility about its ability to offer an evergreen answer to the problem. The opinion invites debate — not over period dictionaries or the writings of long-dead judges but, appropriately, over Emily's well-being.

The proportionality approach the Canadian Supreme Court employs enables it to reach different conclusions on very different facts. Take a second case, this one involving accommodations for hearing-impaired hospital patients. In 1990, British Columbia hospitals discontinued sign language services for deaf patients after the private organization that had been providing interpreters ran out of funds. A group of deaf hospital patients sued, arguing that the province's refusal to fund these services, and the hospitals' refusal to offer them, violated the equality provisions of the Charter of Rights and Freedoms.

Like Emily's case, this one would be very easy to resolve under the U.S. Constitution as courts read it today. Hospitals have no constitutional duty to provide sign language services, even if neglecting to do so impairs doctor-patient communication, and—no matter its reasons—the state certainly has no duty to fund sign language interpreters (or much of anything else).

But the province and the hospitals lost. The Canadian Supreme Court held, first, that ostensibly private hospitals may be considered to be bound by the charter when providing medical services that are funded through the national health insurance law and that the law requires hospitals to provide. This degree of public-private partnership would likely be insufficient to subject a private business in the United States to constitutional scrutiny, but it was sufficient in Canada. Justice Gérard La Forest, who delivered the judgment for the court, then recounted the historical marginalization of people with disabilities and related that treatment to the structural inequality they face: "Statistics indicate that persons with disabilities, in comparison to non-disabled persons, have less education, are more likely to be outside the labour force, face much higher unemployment rates, and are concentrated at the lower end of the pay scale when employed."

The court next noted that the policy of declining to provide sign language services does not intentionally discriminate against deaf persons. This fact alone would be fatal to a U.S. constitutional equality claim, but it was no matter to the Canadian court, which has held that "identical treatment may frequently produce serious inequality," and therefore that even unintentional discrimination may, depending on the context, violate the charter. In the disability context, recognizing "adverse effects discrimination" is especially important because policies that incidentally favor more-able people are more common than those that actively single out people with disabilities for disfavored treatment. And in the case of health care delivery, the consequences of the adverse effect of not providing sign language services for deaf people could be catastrophic.

It was also not enough to say, as the hospitals and the province tried, that the government is, categorically, under no obligation "to implement programs to alleviate disadvantages that exist independent of state action." Recall from chapter 4 that Justice Lewis Powell invoked what he thought was the obvious absence of any such positive state obligation in order to reject Demetrio Rodriguez's plea for fair funding of San Antonio public schools. Here, the Canadian court said, it was enough to note that once the government undertakes an obligation, it must do so equally. A government that provides free medical services but does not offer deaf people the means to communicate with doctors can be in violation of the charter.

Significantly, the judgment that the government was interfering with the rights of deaf hospital patients was far from the end of the court's analysis. It still had to determine whether that interference was reasonably justified. Under the prevailing Canadian framework, that meant the court had to ask (1) whether the failure to provide interpreters was meant to serve a substantial objective; (2) whether the impairment of rights that failure occasioned was in fact "rationally connected" to that objective; (3) whether the province's interference with rights was avoidable; and (4) whether the burden on the rights of deaf patients outweighed its social benefit. According to Justice La Forest, the failure to provide sign language interpreters failed the third test. Because the government could achieve substantially the same fiscal objective without denying sign language services, its denial of those services was unnecessary. The annual cost of those services for all of British Columbia was estimated to be $150,000, a rounding error for the health care budget of Canada's third-largest province.

The hospitals didn't contest this cost, but they advanced an American-style "slippery slope" argument. If they provided sign language services, they said, they would also have to provide translators for patients who didn't speak English or French. So even if the cost of sign language services was trivial, the costs of various hypothetical other services they would need to provide would add up. It would require, to paraphrase, too much justice.

The court responded to this concern by noting that abstract cases not before the court, involving different constitutional provisions and with no actual cost estimates offered, were "purely speculative." Although the burden on patients who could not speak English or French *might* be similar to the burden on deaf patients, the cases also might be very different, "from the perspective of the state's obligations." In other words, the important questions in comparing different constitutional cases in Canada turn on facts and evidence related to the government's actual costs, motives, and duties, not simply on an abstract flattening of rights into categories of burden.

In any event, Justice La Forest astutely observed, the communication burden on those who are hearing impaired is different from the burden on people who can hear but cannot communicate in a foreign language. Many deaf people cannot develop strong proficiency in oral communication and must make special arrangements to locate someone capable of interpretation. It might be that those who don't speak English or French have similar difficulties, but it might not be. "*There is no evidentiary basis* from which to assess whether non-official language speakers stand in a similar position" (emphasis added).

The court rejected, and with like dispatch, a further, even more outré hypothetical about the consequences of responding to a demand for sign language services. The hospitals argued that "virtually everyone" in the health care system who was denied a service would claim that the denial of that service would exacerbate some disadvantage, thereby creating an untenable strain on the resources of the hospitals and the province. To accept this kind of hypothetical as a basis for denying an accommodation would be to slide down the other side of the slippery slope, just as U.S. courts have done. Justice La Forest recognized this. "To deny the appellants' claim on such conjectural grounds would denude [the charter's equality provision] of its egalitarian promise and render the disabled's goal of a barrier-free society distressingly remote." The court was unanimous in its decision.

The difference between this analysis and the American approach is bracing. The Canadian Supreme Court took seriously a claim for positive rights. It did so because the rights of people with disabilities could not otherwise

be meaningful. It also took seriously the fact that rights impose social burdens and therefore must submit to genuine, reasonable, and proportionate
government policy decisions. The justices refused to ignore manifest, factually supported injustice they saw in front of their faces based on data-free
conjecture about how other, more egregious cases that were not in front of
them might come out. They took rights seriously, but they also took rights
reasonably. The court came out with a different decision than it did in Emily
Eaton's case not because of political changes in its composition, as we might
expect in the United States, but because the facts were different. Just as justice requires.

The remedy the Canadian Supreme Court ordered is also noteworthy. It
did not order the government or the hospitals to implement any particular
program. It identified the inability of deaf patients to communicate about
their medical needs as a constitutional problem with no adequate justification. It declared that the government had to solve this problem. But it recognized at the same time that "it is not this Court's role to dictate how this
is to be accomplished." The court gave the government six months to come
up with its own fix, reserving judgment on any more-coercive court-ordered
remedies until the political branches got to take their own shot at a solution. The Canadian Supreme Court justices understood, as the U.S. constitutional Framers did, that rights recognition and enforcement is not just the
province of courts. Courts can nudge political institutions when they fail us,
but judge-made law is no substitute for politics. Modern rights adjudication
can't work without the compromises politics is calculated to produce.

But that's Canada, you might be saying to yourself, before cracking a joke
about the legendary civility of the Canucks. While it is undoubtedly true
that the United States has a more individualistic, classically liberal political
culture than its neighbor to the north, the U.S. legal culture isn't somehow
irredeemably obtuse. The United States does have a well-established legal
framework, the ADA, that requires accommodations for people with disabilities. And for a country that rarely amends its Constitution, landmark
statutes like the ADA are a better gauge of a political culture's temperature,
its innate sense of justice, than the Constitution's vague language.

Even so, constitutionalizing disability rights could go beyond the ADA framework. The ADA, for example, has been read to extend its protections solely to people whose disabilities cannot be controlled with medication or other adjustments, which excludes, for example, many people living with epilepsy or diabetes. This limitation reflects the Supreme Court's insistence, abetted by its narrow understanding of disability rights, that the ADA is best understood as a law about economics rather than a law about civil rights. At the same time, the Court has interpreted the disabilities that "count" as those that significantly impair one's daily life, and not merely those needed to do one's job. Work-related disabilities are, therefore, necessary to trigger the ADA's protections but they are not sufficient.

A constitutional foundation for disability rights would also inform other cases currently adjudicated wholly under other provisions, including, for example, the rights of people with intellectual disabilities within the criminal justice system or the due process right of people with mental illness to refuse medication. The right of an intellectually impaired criminal defendant not to be executed shouldn't simply be a matter of the cruelty of the punishment — a measure that harks back to the treatment of disability through a lens of charity or pity — but it should be informed by consideration of the right of the condemned to equality and human dignity.

Until the Supreme Court decides that impairing the rights of people with disabilities requires something more than a minimally rational law, there can be no constitutional justice for such people. Employers can pay them pennies on the dollar. State welfare officers can ignore their needs. School administrators can segregate and demean them. Prison guards can put their lives at risk. Doctors can let them die. If and when American courts start getting rights right, Americans with disabilities should be first in line.

8

Affirmative Action

U ntil America gets rights right, it won't get race right either. Unlike in the case of disability, U.S. courts understand full well that overt racial discrimination by the government requires their attention. But they understand it too well. The right against racial discrimination has become one of the most precious in the American constitutional firmament. It is indeed so precious that, to paraphrase Lenin, it must be rationed.

In 2014, an organization opposed to race-based affirmative action accused Harvard of discriminating against Asian-American undergraduate applicants. Although Harvard is a private university, its receipt of federal funds binds it to a set of antidiscrimination norms that mimic the constitutional standards that attach to public schools. The group, called Students for Fair Admissions (SFFA), claimed in a lawsuit that Harvard's ostensibly "holistic" admissions process concealed a preference for non-Asian students.

SFFA seemed to be onto something. From 2014 to 2019, Asian-American students were admitted to Harvard at about the same rate as whites even though they had better grades, did better on standardized tests such as the SAT and ACT, and participated in relevant extracurricular activities at a higher rate. Comparing Asian-American to African-American and Hispanic applicants revealed even greater disparities in academic and extracurricular performance. In fact, the trial court that heard SFFA's case found that race was a determinative factor in admission for nearly half of all African-American and Hispanic students admitted to Harvard. Race appeared to be a "plus" for applicants of some races but a "minus" for Asian Americans.

This conflict is a powder keg teetering on the edge of a tinderbox. Access to America's most reliable gatekeeper to elite status and financial success seems, at a glance, to have been a zero-sum game based in part on crude racial preferences, with judges tapped as referees. It's not too much to say that the future of our multiracial constitutional democracy hinges on the judges' performance. Under the standard American approach, they must assign a winner and a loser in this dispute. That assignment, like Harvard's, will appear to be based on race. But unlike Harvard's, the judges' determination will purport to measure the Constitution's favor and not just a school's. Does the Constitution care more about the African-American and Hispanic applicants who got in or the Asian Americans who didn't?

My description of the Harvard case conceals enormous complexity that the Supreme Court makes it impossible for other courts to engage with. American rightsism reduces disputes over race-conscious college admissions into contests of *us* versus *them.* Harvard's open use of race in admissions subjects it to maximum skepticism from courts. The same is true of the many public colleges and universities that have modeled their use of race on Harvard's celebrated admissions plan from the 1970s. The skepticism is the same whether the program intends to boost or to harm underrepresented minorities. It requires the same level of review as would apply to a state that decided to ban interracial marriage, a more stringent standard than would apply to a state prohibiting women from attending college or to a federal ban on Muslims entering the country. Racial discrimination of any kind can only be overcome by the most compelling of government "interests."

The flattening of conflicts like the one at Harvard into a bare case of racial discrimination on one side and a government "interest" on the other trivializes the presence of injustice on all sides. Relative to whites, the Asian-American students who apply to Harvard are not wealthy in economic terms. They are not aristocrats or the scions of billionaires. Many are the children of first- or second-generation immigrants from China or India or South Korea. For many, admission to an elite college is the only available ladder to social and economic mobility. Society tells them that the surest way to get into top schools is to earn top grades and test scores, and for them anyway, this is true. These students studied, they worked hard, and they aced the test. They sought admission on the basis of "merit," in just the way we typically understand the meaning of that fraught term.

But eliminating any consideration of race in its admissions decisions would cause a rupture in the demographics of Harvard's student body. In particular, it would drop Hispanic admissions by more than a third and would cut African-American admissions in half.

Should we care? The fact that some group lacks access to an elite college does not in itself raise a serious question of constitutional law or distributive justice. We would not and should not spend much time worrying about a sharp reduction in the admission of students who are good soccer players, who are of above-average height, or whose last name starts with the letter P. If race is just like these other categories, then Harvard has no good rights-related reason to adjust its racial makeup.

But race is not like these categories. Black and Hispanic disadvantage is not simply a matter of bad luck or random variation, but is rather produced by a panoply of interrelated, mutually reinforcing processes that extend well beyond SAT scores. The median income of white households is more than 50 percent greater than that of Black households; the median white household also has roughly fifteen times the wealth of the median Black household. Those African-American and Hispanic families living outside of poverty live in poorer neighborhoods with higher crime rates, worse pollution, and weaker infrastructure than those of whites with similar incomes. One important study found that Black households making more than $100,000 per year live in more-disadvantaged neighborhoods and are more likely to be surrounded by other severely disadvantaged neighborhoods than white households making less than $30,000 per year. African Americans are incarcerated at nearly six times the rate of white Americans, and Black men have a harder time getting a job upon release than non-Blacks with similar criminal records. Police respond more quickly to white crime victims. Doctors are less likely to give pain medication to Black patients. Black babies are twice as likely to die at childbirth as white babies, twice as likely to be born with a low birth weight, and 1.5 times as likely to be delivered prematurely.

When group disadvantage metastasizes across myriad areas, it indicates a problem of *structural* inequality. For example, housing discrimination can produce residential segregation, which reduces property values and access to municipal services, which can lead to crime and health problems, which affects household stability and education. In chapter 4, I described the Supreme Court's rejection of Black police officer applicants' challenge to a civil service exam in Washington, D.C. Many of the failed applicants had been educated in the same D.C. public schools whose intentional racial segregation policy had been struck down by the Court barely two decades earlier for producing inadequate education for Black students.

Structural inequality of this sort is a serious problem for distributive justice. If the same group consistently comes up short in wealth, criminal justice, access to social services, educational outcomes, public health, and so on, then policy makers have good reason to treat that group differently than they treat others not stuck in the same web of disadvantages. Indeed, to treat members of such groups in just the same way as members of groups that don't suffer from structural inequality is to treat them *unequally,* recalling the French novelist Anatole France's faint praise of "the majestic equality of the law which prohibits the wealthy as well as the poor from sleeping under the bridges, from begging in the streets, and from stealing bread."

Reconciling efforts to address structural inequality with individual acts of racial discrimination doesn't lend itself to rightsism or to neat line drawing. It calls for substantial deference to those political and administrative decision-makers struggling to accommodate the various competing interests in good faith and with sensitivity. That deference shouldn't be infinite, and, importantly, it should depend on a degree of transparency that the Supreme Court, spooked by race, has clearly discouraged.

Race dug the hole American rights have fallen into. If we can't see where the light's coming from, we'll just keep digging.

Color Blindness and the Constitution

The persistence of structural inequality makes up the irreducible core of race-conscious college admissions. But because of the American approach to rights, our courts have nothing to say about structural inequality and indeed forbid public and private institutions alike to openly acknowledge it as the basis for their decisions.

The Supreme Court insists that the fact of a law's or a government practice's "disparate impact" on members of a particular racial group is *never* sufficient to support a constitutional claim against that law or practice. A government official is entitled to be entirely indifferent to even severe and predictable effects a law might have on historically disadvantaged racial and ethnic groups, so long as the racial effect was not the specific intent of the law. And so according to the Supreme Court, the Fourteenth Amendment, which rose from the ashes of the Civil War, does not distinguish between a law that reinforces structural racial inequality and one that ameliorates it. Under the Court's reasoning, the problem Harvard and other schools with race-conscious admissions plans are trying to address is of no moment to the Constitution.

It's worse than that. For the Supreme Court, not only does the Constitution not see structural inequality as a problem, but that very same Constitution takes a maximally dim view of affirmative action plans motivated by that inequality. This is because such remedies result from a conscious, intentional desire to change the racial makeup of institutions. The Supreme Court automatically codes structural inequality as being of no constitutional significance, but it automatically codes intentional use of race in policy making as being a matter of urgent constitutional concern, even when the use of race is intended as a remedy for structural inequality.

The Supreme Court arrived at its skepticism of race-based affirmative action via a series of cases beginning in the 1970s and running into the 1990s. The first affirmative action case the Court decided on its merits, in 1978, involved a UC Davis medical school plan that reserved sixteen seats in the one-hundred-member entering class for minority students, a designation that included "Blacks," "Chicanos," "Asians," and "American Indians." Justice Lewis Powell wrote the controlling opinion in the case, holding that race-based affirmative action plans should be reviewed with exactly the same level of suspicion as Jim Crow laws.

According to Powell, a rule that took context into account would mean that judges would have to make a constantly shifting assessment of which racial groups should receive "preferred" status. "The 'white' majority itself is composed of various minority groups, most of which can lay claim to a history of prior discrimination at the hands of the State and private individuals," Powell wrote. "Not all of these groups can receive preferential treatment and corresponding judicial tolerance of distinctions drawn in terms of race and nationality, for then the only 'majority' left would be a new minority of white Angle-Saxon Protestants." For Powell, the difficulty of articulating a principle that could resolve hypothetical cases in advance left the Court with no choice but to ignore the context in which racial classification was occurring in the case that was actually before it: a severe underrepresentation of Black and Hispanic students at one of the top medical schools in the country's most populous state.

In 1995, a majority of the Court formally endorsed Justice Powell's rule and extended it to all government policies. Whenever any federal, state, or local government conditions a policy or practice on the race of those affected, no matter the government's motive and no matter which groups benefit or are burdened, the policy is subjected to "strict scrutiny," the most stringent, least forgiving test known to constitutional law. At the same time, the Court continues to adhere to the rule announced in the D.C. police officer case: policies that disproportionately burden disadvantaged minority groups without specifically intending to harm those groups because of their race receive "rational basis review," the least stringent, most deferential test known to constitutional law. All or nothing.

Hiding the Ball

The Supreme Court's distaste for overt race-conscious admissions plans doesn't, of course, mean that those plans don't exist. It just means that instead of forthrightly acknowledging structural racial inequality and tailoring their programs to the metes and bounds of that special social problem, schools — with the Court's blessing — pursue racial justice in the shadows.

They do so in at least three ways. First, they recite that their overriding interest is not in overcoming structural race-based disadvantage but rather in attaining the educational benefits of a racially diverse student body. Second, they conceal the magnitude of the race-based bump they give to African-American and Hispanic students. Third, they value methods of increasing the representation of disadvantaged minority students that appear to be — but in fact are not — race neutral. Each of these practices is deceptive, each is encouraged by U.S. courts, and each contributes to the impression that schools aren't fair dealers. Schools' chronic, legally compelled lack of transparency in turn makes it harder to trust them when they say, for example, that they don't discriminate against Asian-American students.

The Diversity Rationale

All American schools that take race into consideration claim to do so because it's crucial to their "diversity" efforts. This isn't quite hogwash, but it's close. Few would deny, of course, that some diversity in the student body is better than none, and I don't doubt the sincerity of those college faculty or administrators who claim to value diversity of a sort. But the more one thinks about diversity, the less plausible it seems that diversity *as such* is the main driver of typical race-based affirmative action plans. For one thing, the disproportionate focus of recruitment efforts on Black and Hispanic students, in particular, at many top schools makes it likely that "diversity" is standing in for some other value. Members of these racial and ethnic groups may have an interesting perspective to bring to a seminar room or a lunch table, but so do Maoris and albinos and Alaskan fishing boat deckhands and diabetics. One senses less urgency in attracting critical masses of such people to Ivy League classrooms.

Even within the category of race and ethnicity, many top schools have no trouble filling their class with "Asians," but fewer seem to devote much effort to swelling the ranks of Laotians or Bangladeshis to supplement the Han Chinese and upper-caste Indians who are in abundance in a typical elite undergraduate class. The high-profile litigation over the affirmative action plan at the University of Texas at Austin, which the Supreme Court allowed in 2016, showed that the university appeared to tie the number of Black and Hispanic students it wished to admit to the proportion of each group within the state's population. A state's flagship university might well have good reasons to seek to enroll students in rough proportion to the racial and ethnic mix of the state, but those reasons necessarily go well beyond "diversity." The amount of diversity present within a classroom surely doesn't depend on the racial demographics of the state in which the school is located.

Schools' insistence that student body diversity drives their race-conscious admissions is less an educational imperative than a litigation strategy. In the 1978 UC Davis medical school case, Justice Powell suggested that student body diversity was the only permissible motivation for a race-based affirmative action plan at a public university. In the years and then decades that followed, countless schools modeled their programs and their stated justifications on Powell's opinion. When the Supreme Court upheld the affirmative action plan at the University of Michigan Law School in 2003, Justice Sandra Day O'Connor's majority opinion reiterated that student body diversity is a "compelling" goal that a school may use to justify its affirmative action plan. The Court has never accepted any other goal. "Diversity" is, therefore, a school's one and only safe harbor.

An interest in diversity is an empty vessel, though, without a theory of why diversity is valuable. The Supreme Court's understanding of diversity and what its benefits might be is thoroughly undercooked. Without acknowledging any daylight, O'Connor's opinion differed in significant ways from Powell's. In the UC Davis case, Powell tied diversity in student admissions to the academic freedom of the university to "select those students who will contribute the most to the 'robust exchange of ideas.'" Minority students might, on the whole, offer different "ideas and mores" to the school's vital "atmosphere of 'speculation, experiment and creation,'" which in turn improves the training of the nation's future leaders. This conception of the role diversity plays is focused on the school's internal educational process. Racial diversity improves the service, as it were, that schools provide to their students.

In the Michigan case, by contrast, O'Connor embraced a much broader vision of the benefits of racial diversity. The Court accepted the school's submission that racial diversity "promotes cross-racial understanding, helps to break down racial stereotypes, and enables students to better understand persons of different races." But the Court also relied, in part, on amicus briefs submitted by various Fortune 500 companies and retired military leaders. The corporate briefs emphasized that well-prepared workers in a global economy needed to have "exposure to widely diverse people, cultures, ideas, and viewpoints." The military brief suggested that a diverse and well-qualified officer corps was essential to an effective fighting force.

These pleas bolstered Justice O'Connor's claim that racial diversity at elite colleges was needed "in order to cultivate a set of leaders with legitimacy in the eyes of the citizenry." Citizens' faith in the openness of a society required "that the path to leadership be visibly open to talented and qualified individuals of every race and ethnicity." Whatever one thinks of this set of reasons for pursuing a diverse student body — Justice Clarence Thomas, in dissent, derisively labeled it an "aesthetic" interest — the reasons go significantly beyond lively classroom discussion. O'Connor all but says that racial diversity in elite educational institutions is necessary for both the success and the basic legitimacy of the Republic.

Elite schools' attention to populating their classes with critical masses of Black and Hispanic students, but not necessarily other groups, makes some sense on Justice O'Connor's view in a way that it doesn't on Justice Powell's. Any variety in talents and life experiences can make a classroom discussion deeper and more interesting, but a lack of, say, Chechens or synchronized swimmers at elite U.S. colleges confers no crisis of public legitimacy. By contrast, Texas's African-American and Hispanic population is just south of 50 percent. If the state's top school admits and sends into the professions only trivial numbers of students from these groups, group members (and perhaps others) may view the education system as an essentially corrupt enterprise. The desire to avoid this outcome is less an interest in educational "diversity" than it is a much broader project in social reengineering, and one that makes real sense under conditions of structural inequality. Diversity is most valuable not for its own sake, but to the degree that it both mitigates and makes less palpable existing structural inequality.

"Individualized Assessment"

But there's a problem here, and it illuminates the second way in which school admissions programs lack needed transparency. Elite schools generally assess the merits of candidates for admission in ways that sit in serious tension with the schools' apparent recognition of structural inequality. On the internal logic of elite schools' admissions policies, they place significant weight on College Board entrance exams that systematically discriminate against qualified applicants on the basis of race. But rather than scrap the exams, they give them much more weight in evaluating candidates of some races than of others.

Understanding how and why this peculiar ecosystem operates as it does requires a toe dip into the history of elite education in the United States. Affirmative action was once limited to aristocrats. Until the turn of the twentieth century, elite schools like Harvard, Yale, and Princeton admitted students on the basis of school-created entrance exams in particular subjects. Those subjects included Greek and Latin, which were generally taught only by private tutors or in the crusty New England and mid-Atlantic private schools that educated upper-class WASPs. Lest the proportion of high-status and wealthy admits be too small, exemptions from the entrance exams were freely offered to low-performing children of the well-heeled.

Much of the story of twentieth-century elite college admissions revolves around the tension between this more traditional model and the dramatic growth of public secondary school education. As education became more freely available, especially in America's rapidly expanding cities, there was an upsurge in the number of students able to get into Ivy League schools and their competitors. In the early 1900s, those high-performing students included large numbers of Jewish immigrants from central and eastern Europe. Jewish enrollment at Harvard, for example, rose from 9.8 percent in 1909 to 27.6 percent in 1925.

In an era of rampant anti-Semitism, top schools responded by imposing discriminatory restrictions. Columbia implemented a 22 percent Jewish quota in 1921; before, it had regularly admitted classes that were more than 40 percent Jewish. In 1923, Yale capped its freshman enrollment at 850, increasing the competition for spots, and weighted its admissions process toward subjective assessments of "personality and character." Its Jewish enrollment wouldn't again reach the 13.3 percent it hit in 1923 for another four decades. Harvard was led in this period by the anti-Semitic reactionary Abbott Lawrence Lowell, who was able to persuade the faculty to adopt a more discretionary selection policy that, like Yale's, took greater account of "character" as a backdoor way to exclude Jewish students.

The trajectory that Harvard admissions has taken from the 1920s to the present deserves special attention. Harvard has been a trendsetter in elite college admissions, not just because of its academic reputation but also because Justice Powell, in the UC Davis case, specifically designated the Harvard College admissions plan as a legal safe harbor for schools seeking to implement race-based affirmative action policies. Under that plan as Powell understood it, there were no separate "tracks" of students, and race was used as one "plus" factor among many others in an "individualized assessment" of each candidate. Many readers will recognize this "individualized assessment" model in the college admissions process they went through themselves or that they find themselves navigating with their children: the accumulation of extracurriculars, the personal essay, the reference letters and interview that are said to provide a more holistic sense of the applicant than grades and test scores alone can offer.

In Harvard's case, as with many of its peers, the advent of individualized assessment was crafted in large part to facilitate the exclusion of Jewish students. This happened through two avenues. First, the focus on subjective measures of "character" allowed both conscious and unconscious bias against less "desirable" students to infest the evaluation process. Second, the lack of any transparency about the process enabled the school to pursue its demographic goals without accountability. The discriminatory origin of the Harvard plan doesn't necessarily mean that subjective, individualized assessment is tainted today. But when race-based decision-making is involved, opaque admissions processes should be disfavored, especially when their opacity is intentional.

Unfortunately, the Supreme Court has encouraged, indeed required, this opacity. Not only has it refused to allow schools to align their admissions policies with their genuine reasons for seeking to enroll Black and Hispanic students, but it also has forbidden schools to adopt safeguards to prevent just the kind of invidious discrimination Harvard and its peers were guilty of in the 1920s. The Supreme Court took up the Michigan Law School case at the same time as it heard an affirmative action case involving Michigan's undergraduate college. Whereas the law school modeled its admissions plan on the Harvard plan, the college instead used a numerical system. Applicants received "points" based on standard academic variables such as GPA, standardized test scores, and the quality and rigor of their high school, along with other variables such as in-state residency, legacy status, essay quality, athletic recruitment, and leadership skills. Among the variables receiving an especially large number of points was a student's membership in an underrepresented minority group. Students whose cumulative score exceeded a set amount were automatically admitted.

The Supreme Court upheld the Michigan Law School plan and invalidated the undergraduate plan. Justice O'Connor and Justice Stephen Breyer, the only two members of the Court who agreed with both outcomes, argued that the law school plan was better because it emphasized individualized consideration, whereas the undergraduate plan was a "nonindividualized, mechanical one." This distinction might make some sense if the goal is to assess what each student's particular contribution to classroom discussion might be, but it makes little sense if the purpose of an affirmative action policy is to combat structural inequality. The reason structural inequality is so difficult to root out is that it does not manifest in easily identified, individualized acts of discrimination. A school committed to the belief that Black and Hispanic students face structural disadvantage should be able to name that disadvantage, identify it as *group based,* and pursue transparent admissions policies that respond to it. By contrast, a plan similar to the Michigan Law School's black box process should give much more pause to a Court concerned about the possibility of admissions officers abusing their discretion or punishing academic highfliers based on their ethnicity. Such a plan raises the specter of race being used in just the way SFFA accused Harvard of using it: not just as a "plus" but in some cases as a "minus."

Race "Neutrality"

The third way in which modern race-conscious admissions plans hide the ball is in even assessing what counts as an impermissible racial preference. In 2019, Stuyvesant High School in Manhattan's Tribeca neighborhood was ranked by *U.S. News and World Report* as the twenty-fifth-best public high school in the country. The school's average SAT score of 1510 exceeded the average score of admits to Harvard, Yale, and Princeton. Prominent Stuyvesant alums include Nobel laureates in economics, chemistry, and physiology (twice over); politicians Eric Holder and Jerry Nadler; actors James Cagney, Tim Robbins, and Ron Silver; political consultants David Axelrod and Dick Morris; and the virtuoso jazz pianist Thelonious Monk.

Admission to Stuyvesant, the most elite of New York City's eight specialized public high schools, is determined by an entrance exam. In recent decades, Asian-American admissions to these specialized schools have skyrocketed, and African-American and Hispanic admissions have plummeted. In 1976, Stuyvesant was 16 percent Asian and 14 percent Black. In 2019, nearly three-quarters of the school's students were Asian and less than 1 percent — twenty-nine out of 3,300 — were Black. Only seven of the 895 newly admitted students that spring were Black. To put these numbers in perspective, 70 percent of the students in New York City public schools are Black or Hispanic.

In 2018, in response to concerns about the polarized racial and ethnic makeup of Stuyvesant and the other New York specialized high schools, Mayor Bill de Blasio proposed changing the admissions process. Under de Blasio's plan, eighth graders would be admitted based on a variety of criteria, including both grades and test scores. Rather than simply admitting the highest-scoring students in the city as a whole, the new formula would have the effect of distributing seats across the city's diverse neighborhoods. The plan was expected to cut in half the number of Asian students admitted to the schools. Black admissions would increase by a factor of five.

Mayor de Blasio's proposal relied on a model most famously used in the University of Texas system. In 1997, in response to a court decision striking down UT Austin's affirmative action policy, the Texas legislature authorized the school to implement a so-called 10 percent plan. Under the plan, students in the upper 10 percent of GPAs at every high school in the state would gain automatic admission to UT Austin, the state's flagship public university. Given high levels of residential racial and ethnic segregation in the state, a 10 percent plan would have the effect of increasing racial and ethnic diversity without needing to ask about the race of applicants. The de Blasio plan likewise would cleverly exploit the presence of intense residential segregation to automatically add diversity to New York City's specialized high schools.

As the swing vote on the Supreme Court before he retired in 2018, Justice Anthony Kennedy seemed to endorse this kind of plan as one that should be subject to only minimal scrutiny, but it's no less racially motivated than a conventional affirmative action plan. Indeed, the origins of the 10 percent plan show that it can be susceptible to just the kind of abuse that a higher degree of judicial scrutiny is designed to smoke out. During the anti-Jewish hysteria of the 1920s, Harvard implemented a "top-seventh" plan that would automatically admit the top seventh of students from schools in the South and the Midwest. That plan, like the Texas 10 percent plan and the de Blasio plan in New York, was motivated by concern over the racial and ethnic demographics that the status quo admissions policy was producing. To say that such a plan should receive far less scrutiny than a conventional affirmative action plan encourages schools to hide their racial motivations.

Worse, a superficially race-neutral plan is a blunt instrument for achieving racially motivated outcomes. The Supreme Court requires individualized consideration of applicants when race appears on the face of an admissions plan, while at the same time encouraging schools to adopt racially motivated but superficially neutral admissions plans in which individualized consideration is impossible.

This confusion follows from the assumption that there is a right against any governmental recognition of race. Rights in the American sense — that is, presumptively absolute — simply lack the sensitivity to address racial conflict. A thermometer without a tenths digit can't measure thousandths. The law has come to treat a school's bare recognition of race as a proxy for using race poorly. The admissions system school administrators then build around the proxy (with the help of their lawyers) come to overshadow their genuine motives. We're telling schools they can't use vowels and then squabbling over their diction.

The Baseline Problem

Lack of transparency undermines trust all by itself, but the danger in schools' opacity about their motives and methods is compounded by Americans' deep ambivalence about the schools' missions. The idea that students are ideally admitted to elite universities on the basis of their grades and test scores is a myth and always has been. Schools have multiple, competing objectives, only some of which are consistent with admitting students who are the highest fliers numerically. Indeed, some of the benefit of admitting these students manifests purely in reputational terms. The numerical lift high-SAT and high-GPA admits offer a school confers its own kind of "aesthetic" benefit, raising the question of who, exactly, is receiving affirmative action and who is simply serving the school's core purposes.

Still, it's reasonable for high school students to expect academic performance to determine admission to competitive schools. Elite college education plays a different role in American social and economic life than it did at the turn of the twentieth century. Then, the New England and mid-Atlantic colleges that dominated higher education were, by and large, finishing schools for America's aristocracy. There was no pretense that the vast majority of students attending elite colleges got there on the basis of intellectual candlepower. Most Americans, even successful ones, did not attend college. Only 2 percent of eighteen- to twenty-four-year-old Americans attended college in 1899–1900. It was 7 percent thirty years later. It's 41 percent today.

Sharp rises in income inequality mean that the returns on an elite college degree are higher than ever. The U-shaped trend in the share of income going to the top 1 percent of U.S. families from the prewar period to today — bottoming out in the 1970s — has been well documented by Thomas Piketty and others. A startling percentage of the GDP growth in recent decades has been captured by the wealthiest Americans. From 1993 to 2012, average real income growth was 6.6 percent for the bottom 99 percent and 86.1 percent for the top 1 percent. The top 1 percent captured more than two-thirds of economic growth over that period. That income gap is tied quite directly to an academic achievement gap. The gap in average achievement between the 90th percentile and the 10th percentile of the family income distribution was about 30 to 40 percent higher for children born in 2001 than it was for those born in 1976.

A number of simultaneous developments after World War II conspired to change both the economic value of an elite college degree and the social meaning of elite college admissions. The GI Bill brought a surge in student demand that forced schools to take a hard look at the balance in their classes between top performers and the privileged. Reputational concerns and increased competition among elite schools led to high demand for academic achievement in terms of grades and standardized tests such as the SAT. Geopolitics also played a role, as the Soviet Union's Sputnik coup and the recent success of the Manhattan Project increased the demand for capable scientific researchers. As significantly, in 1958 the College Board for the first time began to release SAT scores to students and not just to their schools and the colleges they applied to. This development imposed a measure of accountability on schools claiming to prize academic excellence. The next year, on cue, the median SAT score of Harvard's admitted class rose by 50 points, the school's second-highest increase ever.

Unsurprisingly, students admitted strictly on the basis of their academic records tend to outperform those admitted on the basis of their prep school pedigree, their familial wealth, their legacy status, or their athletic skill. Indeed, a Harvard admissions office study conducted in 1959 found stark differences in collegiate academic achievement between students who had attended top public schools in New York and Philadelphia and those who had gone to elite prep schools.

And yet relationships with alums, connections with wealthy donors and the boarding schools their children attend, and success on the football field or the basketball court are cash cows for top colleges. Schools perceive continuing to admit students who help along these dimensions to be a matter of urgent institutional need. As Harvard told the U.S. Department of Education during a federal investigation into the school's treatment of Asian-American students in the 1980s, alumni not only "support the college by devoting immense amounts of time in recruiting and other volunteer activities, by contributing financially, and by informing other people . . . about the College," but they also "provide the bulk of scholarship funds provided to all students."

This, then, is the rub. Elite colleges and universities formulated race-based affirmative action programs (and in some cases enhanced existing programs) in the late 1960s in the wake of violent race riots in Los Angeles, Newark, Washington, D.C., and other cities and in response to agitation by Black students. (In fact, Harvard's plan was set in motion after Black students confronted administrators who were on their way out of a memorial service for Martin Luther King Jr. following his assassination.) Yet African-American students tend to score worse than other students on standardized tests. This is unsurprising, of course, in light of structural disadvantages such students face. But introducing significant numbers of additional students who score lower on these exams forces schools into a choice: (1) they can keep standardized tests but tolerate lower average test scores in the class; (2) they can eliminate or dramatically reduce reliance on the tests; (3) they can reduce the number of legacy students, athletes, and other lower-performing students; or (4) they can raise the bar on exam performance for students who don't fall into any of these categories.

The first two options are sensible in the abstract. The internal logic of elite schools' admissions practices condemns standardized tests as systematically biased against qualified students. But eliminating those tests or at least sharply reducing their importance would create problems for schools that are not at all abstract. In 1983, *U.S. News and World Report* began to issue its college rankings, which have since become enormously influential. For schools, improving and retaining their ranking is not just a matter of vanity, though it is that, too. A school's ranking influences which students apply to the school, which students decide to attend once accepted, whether donors give to the school and how much they give, and even the school's access to credit. These factors are self-reinforcing. The applicant pool and yield affect a school's average test scores and average GPA; alumni giving and yield are themselves factors in the rankings; and donations affect other ranking factors such as financial resources, faculty-to-student ratio, faculty salaries, and library holdings. Scrapping standardized tests would trigger a cascade that would be disastrous for a school's prestige, an existential asset for elite colleges.

The lawsuit against Harvard did not, of course, ask the school to de-emphasize the SAT. Instead, SFFA argued that the school should choose a version of the third option — reduce admissions of low-performing African-American and Hispanic students — but it has instead chosen the fourth option: it has impermissibly raised the bar on exam performance for Asian-American students.

This is a plausible factual claim. Race-based affirmative action continues apace. And although aristocratic affirmative action has declined significantly since its heyday, elite colleges continue to fill their classes with large numbers of wealthy students, athletes, and children of alums whose grades and scores are below average. These forms of affirmative action do not typically benefit Asian-American applicants as much as others. If average test scores haven't declined — and they haven't — it means that many Asian-American applicants necessarily need very high test scores to be admitted. The math is unforgiving.

The dramatic rise in Asian-American applicants to top colleges has followed from demographic changes enabled by the Immigration and Nationality Act of 1965, which took effect in 1968. That act lifted ethnic quotas that banned most Asian migration to the country and opened America's gates to a flood of immigrants from India, mainland China, Taiwan, and the Philippines. The Asian-American population hovered around one million at the time of the act. That number now exceeds twenty million. A substantial portion of those immigrants, especially those from India and China, are highly educated professionals in technically oriented fields, such as physicians, engineers, and scientists. No region of the world sends more high-skilled immigrants to the United States, and that's been the case continuously since the late 1960s. The children of high-skilled immigrants tend to be high performers, especially in math and science.

There is an additional cultural element at work that bears mention. Throughout much of Asia, and certainly in India and China, admission to competitive high schools and universities relies strictly on testing rather than on a holistic model like the Harvard plan. You don't get into Tsinghua University in Beijing or one of the Indian Institutes of Technology (IITs) by setting your high school's touchdown record or charming an alumnus/ alumna interviewer. In both countries, rather, what matters is performance on a national entrance exam not unlike the test that determines admission to New York City's specialized high schools. (India does have a well-developed affirmative action system, but there it takes the form of explicit, aboveboard quotas that serve to calibrate expectations about how the system operates.) As a result, the parents of many Asian-American students who are rejected from their elite school of choice here were able to attend their own school of choice in their birth country simply by passing a competitive exam. Holistic admissions can, therefore, feel foreign in multiple ways.

The stakes here are high. The social and economic meaning of a university education has changed. Witness the outrage over the 2019 bribery scandal that took down actors Felicity Huffman and Lori Loughlin. There's a deep tradition in the United States of paying a school to admit one's child, and yet many Americans experienced the scandal as breaching a fundamental promise of the education system. Most of the students at top schools, including wealthy students, received excellent grades, studied hard, and did well on their exams in high school. As Daniel Markovits points out, their ability to do so is, indeed, the form that modern inheritance takes. From preschool arts programs to music lessons to sports leagues to extra tutoring and science camps and chess club and trips abroad and, of course, high-end test prep and excellent private schools or public schools in expensive neighborhoods like Alamo Heights, wealthy parents pour enormous financial resources into the academic success of their children. By one estimate, the excess amount wealthy families invest in education beyond what middle-class families are able to afford amounts to an inheritance of roughly $10 million per child.

This wasn't always so. It used to be that wealthy parents just gave their kids money or property, and with it the ability to live a life of relative leisure. That's what someone like Felicity Huffman would likely have gifted her child a century ago. The wealthy still give their kids cash, but increasingly their most significant bequest is the capacity to succeed in a world that handsomely rewards admission into elite schools. What this means is that the vast majority of elite college students, including those admitted under various preference regimes, subjectively experience their success as resulting from their own hard work.

Elite schools, of course, benefit from this perception and seek to perpetuate it. One of the most significant inputs into the *U.S. News and World Report* ranking algorithm is an academic reputation score that's based on the assessments of peer faculty. Through their emphasis on GPA and standardized tests, elite schools have helped to endow "merit" with a particular kind of social meaning. It's hard to say whether a holistic admissions process that gives significant boosts to athletes, legacies, and Black and Hispanic students constitutes a departure from admission based on "merit" or simply an alternative definition of it.

The schools will tell you it's the latter. In the 1950s, Harvard accepted more than two-thirds of its applicants. By the late 1960s, this number had fallen to under 20 percent. In 2019, Harvard admitted 4.5 percent of its 43,330 applicants. It's not as if students who got in during the 1950s didn't deserve to go to Harvard. It's that merit meant something different than getting high test scores. The same may be true today, but at the same time, elite schools want to be able to show off their test scores.

Under the circumstances, there is unfairness in every direction. Asian-American students who work hard and play by the rules are rejected without explanation. Black and Hispanic high schoolers are evaluated on the basis of standardized tests that are biased against students whose intelligence and character are not in doubt. Dramatically reducing legacy admissions or wealthy student enrollment would come at a substantial cost to the school — and therefore to its students — in terms of the resources it is able to provide to those in need of financial aid. The reputation of a school also forms an intimate part of what it is selling to its students and its graduates. That reputation bears a complex, at times uncomfortable, relationship to donor support and athletic success. A Harvard that admitted only the top test takers would be a very different institution, and not just racially.

The complexity of it all has been too much for the Supreme Court to bear. Racial identification is bad, we are told, and so it must be smuggled in through the back door. But the cloak-and-dagger use of race undermines the trust needed for race to be used at all. And the important — indeed *obviously* important — questions of what kind of institution is wielding race, to what ends, and with what care go missing from public conversation.

We are left with an almost surgically inadequate response to the challenges of confronting the legacy of white supremacy in a cosmopolitan and conflict-ridden society. The Court permits the use of race, but only in the furtherance of diversity goals that fail to make sense of why race is prioritized over other measures of diversity. It requires schools that use race to do so in ways that are maximally discretionary, subjective, and hidden from scrutiny by both applicants and members of the public. And it openly encourages schools to adopt measures, such as the 10 percent plan, that hide the role race plays in their decisions. The Supreme Court isn't (yet) completely unreceptive to the use of race, but it has been implacably hostile to schools being honest about it.

Solutions

This is a perverse, unsustainable outcome. Government use of race triggers discomfort among courts, as it should. This country has been legally white supremacist for the vast majority of its history. But the magnitude of the burden that history places on its victims is reason for sensitivity of a very different sort from the Supreme Court's. The degree to which courts are skeptical of a government's recognition of race should be attentive to the nature of the problem the government is trying to address, not simply to whether the government uses race to address it. Race-based structural inequality calls for racially attentive structural remedies. And so when public institutions put race-based affirmative action programs or other forms of in-kind reparations in place, courts should place significant weight on the fact that the state is seeking to advance the equality rights of people suffering from stubborn forms of disadvantage.

Thus, when a public school district with a long history of de facto segregation chooses voluntarily to take race into account in its student placements — as a Seattle school district did in a case the Supreme Court decided in 2007 — the Court's review should give some deference to the fact that public officials are addressing a genuine, complex social problem, one that implicates the rights of the students who benefit from the policy as much as of those burdened by it.

John Roberts wrote for four members of the Court in that case that the policy should be struck down as "pure racial balancing," which, he said, is "patently" unconstitutional. "The way to stop discrimination on the basis of race," Roberts wrote, glibly, "is to stop discriminating on the basis of race." That's certainly one theory of how to address chronic racial discrimination, but it's far from the only one. Democratically accountable local officials might have different ideas from Roberts as to how to address trenchant racial inequality in their public schools. Unlike during the Jim Crow era, there is little reason to doubt those officials' sincerity or good faith. Courts should give their ideas some room to breathe.

That breathing room shouldn't be infinite, of course. In fact, the approach the Seattle school district used wasn't very thoughtful on at least one score. In deciding how it would take race into account in desegregating its schools, the district coded all students as either "white" or "nonwhite." Then, as now, Seattle had substantial Asian-American and Latino student populations. The crude use of a "white/nonwhite" binary made it difficult to match the problem of school segregation to the texture of the district's racial makeup. As Roberts pointed out, under the district formula, a school that was 50 percent Asian-American and 50 percent white would be coded as integrated, whereas a school that was 30 percent Asian-American, 25 percent African-American, 25 percent Latino, and 20 percent white would be seen as segregated. The school district's clumsy racial categories were enough for Justice Kennedy to provide a fifth vote to strike down the plan, but he acknowledged the importance of the government's interest in "ensuring all people have equal opportunity regardless of their race."

Instead of using the Seattle school district's clumsiness as a reason to invalidate entirely its effort to adopt race-conscious means of integrating, the Court should have alerted the district to the problem and given it a chance to address it within a reasonable amount of time. That's how courts work with rather than against the democratic institutions that — as the Framers anticipated — should form the front line in protecting our rights. Judges should attend less to what abstract "right" is being interfered with than to the actual behavior of public actors and to the problems they are trying to solve. Public institutions should be given leeway to respond reasonably to complex social problems. The leeway they receive should be significant when they seek to advance the rights of their citizens, as in the case of race-based affirmative action.

The Constitution should permit colleges and high schools, whether public or private, to adjust their admissions standards to the reality of racial inequality in America. The reality is that such inequality is group based, stubborn, and imperfectly sensitive to differences in income, geography, and social class. But when schools use race in their admissions process, they should be required to do so in ways that are reasonably related to their goals, that are data-driven, and that, above all, are transparent. Their honesty speaks to their good faith, which should matter much more than incantations of the word "race." Public officials should get less deference when their actions are shrouded in mystery or intentionally mislead the public. It's hard to hold someone accountable if you don't know what they're doing.

Transparency is especially important in cases involving race-based affirmative action. There's good reason to trust politics to work reasonably well in this area. Both history and common sense tell us that suspicion of the government should run especially deep when self-dealing is involved. If rights protection happens to come at the expense of less powerful minority groups, judges should take special care in scrutinizing the government's motivations and instrumental rationality. When, however, the rights being advanced are those of political minorities, there is less reason to be concerned about so-called tyranny of the majority. But the argument that race-based affirmative action programs that benefit minorities call for less judicial vigilance surely depends on a community having a basic awareness that they or the institutions under their political control are in fact trying to benefit minorities. State and local actors should be able to minimize suspicion of self-dealing when — and only when — they help minorities in the broadest of daylight.

Transparency also touches on constitutional values of due process and equal treatment. Imagine an extreme scenario in which a state institution announces publicly that admissions decisions are to be based on test performance. A group of students take prep courses, they study intensely for the exam, and they get high test scores. If the school then instead admits students with lower scores, the school has breached a promise to prospective students. Even if that breach isn't legally actionable — and I don't think it would be — when the state makes representations to its citizens, those citizens should be entitled to rely on those representations in structuring their affairs. The Due Process Clause bans arbitrary deprivations of life, liberty, or property. The spirit of that clause, if not the letter, likewise frowns on the state cajoling people to invest time, energy, and money based on a false promise.

This hypothetical is, as noted, extreme. Elite schools don't typically make public promises of admission. Still, the magnitude of the boost given at many top schools to the children of alums and donors, to athletes, and to African-American and Hispanic students is hardly common knowledge. The University of Michigan's college admissions program tried to make it common knowledge, and the Supreme Court forbade the school to do so. The college's openness should instead be a model. It would promote honesty, enable accountability, and make it more difficult for schools to give a "minus" to particular applicants on the basis of their race, ethnicity, or religion. The lawsuit against Harvard would have been a nonstarter under the Michigan plan, which confined its use of race as a "plus" explicitly to "underrepresented minorities" and didn't conceal its magnitude or effect.

The Harvard suit wasn't looking for transparency. It argued instead that Harvard and other schools should "outright prohibit" racial preferences. This would be a profound mistake. Whether or not you or I believe race-based affirmative action is a necessary response to structural racial inequality, schools should be entitled to use it as a remedy. Democracies solve difficult problems through publicly accountable forms of policy experimentation, not by willing those problems away. Schools shouldn't mislead their applicants or the public, but they don't need to adopt a particular conception of "merit." It is hardly obvious that schools should only want the top academic performers, as in China or India — or France, for that matter. Many of the most distinguished graduates of elite universities were not its top academicians. The law school at which I teach includes not one but two President Roosevelts among its dropouts.

Indeed, schools shouldn't be required to admit students on the basis of "merit" at all. If a public college wishes to prioritize substantive equality over merit, it should be able to do so. When a state is doling out economic opportunity and social capital, accounting for the fact that standardized tests are one of many sites of disadvantage for certain racial and ethnic minority groups is simply what equality demands.

I am not naïve. It might seem too much to ask that a public school pursue racial equality transparently. Race-based affirmative action consistently polls poorly, especially among white Americans. The publicity around the Michigan Law School's 2003 Supreme Court win led to an overwhelmingly successful ballot initiative banning all affirmative action in the state. The reality of racial politics in America might mean that the only way to sustain race-based affirmative action is either to hide its use or to hide its scope.

This is a problem for progressive politics, but it is not in itself a problem for constitutional law. The Constitution does not require that schools explicitly take race into account in filling their classes. That said, were a state's educational system set up in such a way that members of structurally disadvantaged minority groups had little to no access to lucrative opportunities or leadership positions, it would be important to ask what the state is doing in response to this problem. A state shouldn't be entitled to view the perpetuation of race-based subordination with complete indifference. That would deny rights every bit as much as even the clumsiest affirmative action plan.

The Supreme Court should empower itself to see that rights are on both sides. How exactly to respond should, in the first instance, be the school's decision to make. Rather than trying, quixotically, to discriminate between the rights at stake in college admissions, courts should recognize that higher education is too complex for glib slogans.

And what's true when students are admitted remains true when they arrive on campus.

9

Campus Speech

Freedom of speech is the most famous right in the Constitution. The heart of its protection is obvious: the government cannot silence its political opponents.

But speech is everywhere. Much conduct, in both personal and commercial life, is accomplished by talking, writing, or otherwise communicating information. Taken literally, restricting the government from abridging the freedom of speech could swallow all regulation. Individuals speak through the plans, reflections, and promises they relate to each other; through the e-mails, tweets, and text messages they send; through the letters they pen, the art they design, the glances they exchange. Companies speak through advertisements, marketing materials, and contracts. To view the First Amendment as protecting all of these activities absolutely, or nearly so, is to court chaos.

We've gone too far in that direction.

In 2009, the Texas Division of the Sons of Confederate Veterans (SCV) proposed that the state department of motor vehicles (DMV) make available to drivers a license plate with the Confederate flag on it. The DMV said no. The SCV sued, claiming a violation of its freedom of speech, and the case made it all the way to the Supreme Court. This case should have been easy. Texas was once part of the Confederacy, a traitorous pseudo nation founded to preserve and extend race-based chattel slavery. More than 600,000 Americans died in the Civil War, nearly as many as in all other U.S. wars put together. The SCV has every right to embrace the Stars and Bars, but the people of Texas should have every right to ban a symbol of treason and white supremacy from state-issued license plates. It was a clash of rights, to be sure, but good sense dictated that Texas should win.

A majority of the justices seemed to agree, but the case put them in a bind. The Supreme Court has long maintained that the government is almost never allowed to burden speech because of the speech's content or the speaker's identity or viewpoint. This absolutist posture is what protected the *New York Times* and the *Washington Post* when they published the Pentagon Papers in 1972 over the Nixon administration's fierce objections. But it is also what brought us *Citizens United* and its blessing of unlimited corporate spending on elections. Texas drivers express themselves through their specialty license plates no less than corporations through their political spending.

By a 5–4 vote, the Court's solution was to declare that Texas license plates express the opinions of *the State of Texas.* Because the government needs to be able to promote its favored policies, its own speech need not be neutral between different viewpoints. In fact, there is no constitutional restriction at all on government speech. And so a state act that restricts expression but fits into the box of "government speech" gets no First Amendment scrutiny by a court. A state act that restricts expression but falls outside the "government speech" box receives *maximal* scrutiny. It's all or nothing.

In the Texas case, this solution, though handy, was absurd. As Justice Samuel Alito's dissent gleefully observed, among the specialty license plates that the state made available were those that said "Rather Be Golfing," that promoted NASCAR driver Jeff Gordon, and that bore the names of public universities from outside the state, including the Texas Longhorns' hated rivals, the Oklahoma Sooners. The idea that these messages were those of the state rather than of its individual drivers was preposterous. But the dissenters' solution was no better. They would have had the Court require Texas to put the Confederate flag on some of its state-issued plates. By Alito's logic, it would have had to permit a swastika as well.

This all-or-nothing approach to speech is the reason the Supreme Court said that Vermont data miners had absolute rights to prescription data. It is the reason the Court said that the State of Maryland could not permit a lawsuit against a group that showed up at the funeral of a marine killed in Iraq holding signs saying "Thank God for Dead Soldiers." It is the reason the justices treated burning a cross in front of the house of an African-American family that just moved into the neighborhood the same as they would treat an op-ed on neighborhood gentrification. The problem with this approach isn't that these practices shouldn't be protected. It's that they should be evaluated based on their own benefits and burdens, their own factual context. We must stop pretending that protecting grieving families from political agitators or letting a state keep hate symbols off its license plates threatens the Republic.

These cases just scratch the surface of the free speech problems the next generation of Americans are going to have to confront. For example, rights to reproductive autonomy and to fetal life were not the only rights bound up with the George Tiller case. Prior to his murder, Dr. Tiller was one of several doctors whose photograph and clinic address had appeared on "Wanted" posters produced by anti-abortion activists. His name had also appeared on the Nuremberg Files, a website that listed abortion doctors — "abortionists," it called them — and accused them of crimes against humanity. Doctors who had been murdered were listed with strikes through their names. Those merely wounded were shaded in gray.

The anti-abortion activists who produce such lists believe their free speech rights extend to provocations of this sort. Doctors targeted by these efforts believe they have a right to be protected by the state against those who incite their murders. It's one of many examples of opportunists using technology and the umbrella of the First Amendment to invade privacy. Think about sex videos of ex-girlfriends posted on porn sites as revenge. First Amendment absolutists defend these practices as no different than an author writing a memoir about his sexual experiences. Smartphones have dramatically increased the amount of data available for potential public consumption. No pat formula can draw the line between free expression and privacy in the modern world.

Or consider this: The Constitution protects arms, and it protects protest. Does it protect armed protest? In August 2017, a group of white nationalists held a rally in Charlottesville, Virginia. A man who had driven from Ohio to attend the rally drove his Dodge Challenger into a group of counterprotesters, killing a thirty-two-year-old woman named Heather Heyer. Videos circulated at the time of the rally and after showed that many of the white nationalist marchers were armed with assault rifles and other firearms. The First Amendment protects the right of peaceful assembly. The Second Amendment protects the right of individuals to possess loaded weapons, at a minimum in their homes. Virginia is an open-carry state, meaning that it is legal to openly carry a handgun, and anyone with a concealed-carry permit can openly carry a rifle with a large-capacity magazine.

On the one hand, there is a certain arithmetic logic to the idea that the Constitution protects the right to protest while armed. One plus two equals three, not zero. On the other hand, the presence of firearms can disturb the peaceful nature of a protest even if the guns remain holstered. It can intimidate counterprotesters, thereby reducing rather than increasing the overall volume of speech. Gun rights and speech rights are both on the march through much of the country. Whether they march together or apart will be a vital civil liberties question of our time. The question will stump a Supreme Court — and a people — paralyzed in the face of competing rights.

Here's another example. Social media has come to shape our political culture and public discourse in ways unimaginable a generation ago. Most U.S. adults get their news from social media sites such as Facebook, Twitter, and Reddit. All of these companies censor their users in various ways, relying on a combination of algorithmic and human monitors. Important as they are to freedom of speech in the United States, and indeed around the world, these are private companies, and so their policies do not fit into any of the

Supreme Court's boxes: they can do whatever they want when it comes to speech restrictions.

But the line between public and private actions is not nearly as bright as the Court pretends. Were a Twitter user whose post was deleted to sue the company for breach of contract, a court deciding the issue would be an arm of the state. Likewise, a private university that receives millions of dollars in research funding from the National Institutes of Health might be as reliant on the government as a public college that receives much less, but private schools are not held to the same strict freedom of speech standards as public schools.

Speech restrictions are ubiquitous. Courts must exercise discipline — of some kind — in deciding which ones to allow and which to strike down. Enter rightsism, which demands a choice between "right" or "no right," a choice that, in a complex world, too often rests on a fiction. Constitutional law in this area thus has come to turn on crude categories of the Court's choosing — government versus individual, speech versus conduct, public versus private — rather than the on-the-ground facts of individual cases and the weight of the interests involved. This approach is increasingly arbitrary, nowhere more obviously than on America's college campuses.

Academic Freedom

If eleven o'clock on Sunday morning remains the most segregated hour in America, the college green has become the most polarized place. It is polarized precisely because it is *not* segregated, but instead forces teenagers, whose capacities for nuanced thinking, independent living, and tolerance remain raw, into close intellectual, social, physical, and sexual contact with each other. The stakes of these interactions are high. For college students, speaking on campus, assembling with others of like mind, and hearing from those who inspire and challenge them is an essential part of their self-discovery and their evolution into adulthood.

But the debate over campus speech suffers from serious, debilitating confusion over the proper relationship of colleges and universities to the First Amendment. These institutions enjoy robust academic freedom that the Constitution protects, and they should. Public school students and speakers invited to their campuses also enjoy robust academic freedom under the Constitution, but they shouldn't. Indeed, the academic freedom of the university *requires* that students not have the same degree of freedom as the institution itself. In their role as educators, a university's faculty and administrators quite properly control what speech their students are exposed to. Good teachers do not shoot information at students from a fire hose. They edit, they curate, they discriminate.

Auburn University is a public school. In April 2017, a Georgia State University graduate student named Cameron Padgett rented out the auditorium at Foy Hall, a building on Auburn's campus. Padgett, a segregationist who described himself as a white "identitarian," was booking the space for a speech by Richard Spencer, the neo-Nazi propagandist and fellow "identitarian" who coined the term "alt-right." The university initially agreed to allow Spencer to speak but then canceled the event following protests. The school claimed that it was doing so in response to a security threat. Padgett sued and won.

The Supreme Court interprets the First Amendment to require government neutrality regarding different speech content and especially different viewpoints. The judge in Padgett's case dutifully recited the case law and noted, correctly, that the reaction of a hostile audience is not a content-neutral reason to regulate speech. Surely, Auburn would not have canceled a speech promoting racial equality based on the objections of racists. According to the judge, then, the school had impermissibly discriminated against Spencer on the basis of his speech, and it would need to let the talk proceed.

There are many problems with the judge's approach. Begin with the judge's failure to find even minimally interesting Auburn's status as a university structuring its own on-campus affairs. Perhaps the least defensible aspect of the Supreme Court's approach to freedom of speech is its general insensitivity to the nature of the government actor or the action it is performing. Had Auburn been the police, arresting Spencer in anticipation of his racist speech, the court would have been right to prevent that from happening. But more nuance is called for when the actor is an educational institution, and one that didn't arrest Spencer but merely denied him a live audience in a four-hundred-seat assembly hall within its community.

The same blindness to obvious contextual differences hamstrung the Supreme Court in the Texas license plate case. The dissent analyzed the case in just the same way it would have if Texas had been criminally prosecuting the Sons of Confederate Veterans. The majority felt bound to do the same unless it said, indefensibly, that the State of Texas itself was speaking. But Texas was no more speaking for its drivers than Alabama was speaking for Richard Spencer.

What's more, it's not just that Auburn is not the police, who have little legitimate reason to discriminate on the basis of speech content, but a university, which has a very specific right and obligation to do so. Courts once understood that.

The seminal case in this regard is the Supreme Court's 1957 decision in *Sweezy v. New Hampshire*. Paul Sweezy was a University of New Hampshire economics professor who refused to answer certain questions about his associations before a McCarthy-era subversive activities inquiry led by the New Hampshire attorney general. He was held in contempt and jailed. In reversing Sweezy's contempt conviction, Chief Justice Earl Warren penned a tribute to the academic freedom of universities:

> The essentiality of freedom in the community of American universities is almost self-evident. No one should underestimate the vital role in a democracy that is played by those who guide and train our youth. To impose any strait jacket upon the intellectual leaders in our colleges and universities would imperil the future of our Nation . . . Teachers and students must always remain free to inquire, to study and to evaluate, to gain new maturity and understanding; otherwise our civilization will stagnate and die.

Note that the "regulators" in *Sweezy* were the attorney general who subpoenaed and questioned Sweezy and the state court that held him in contempt. The "regulated party," the one who Warren said shouldn't be put in a "strait jacket," wasn't a student or an outside speaker but rather a faculty member, and through him the university itself. Justice Felix Frankfurter amplified this point in a separate concurring opinion. "It is the business of a university to provide an atmosphere which is most conducive to speculation, experiment and creation," he wrote, quoting a statement by South African scholars opposed to the dictates of the apartheid government. "It is an atmosphere in which there prevail 'the four essential freedoms' of a university—to determine for itself on academic grounds who may teach, what may be taught, how it shall be taught, and who may be admitted to study."

A decade later, the Supreme Court invalidated a New York law that required public school teachers, in this case professors at the State University of New York at Buffalo, to sign a pledge stating that they were not communists. Justice Brennan, who wrote the majority opinion, stressed the "transcendent value" of academic freedom, which he called "a special concern of the First Amendment." Again, the improperly regulated parties were professors, not students. It is true that Justice Brennan called the classroom "peculiarly the 'marketplace of ideas'" and said that "the Nation's future depends on leaders trained through wide exposure to that robust exchange of ideas which discovers truth 'out of a multitude of tongues, (rather) than through any kind of authoritative selection.'" But he did not, of course, mean that students have a First Amendment right to require public university faculty and administrators to teach them however and whatever they want. Instead, he meant that the educational needs of students are an important reason why *faculty* need to be free from state compulsion.

The Court placed particular emphasis on the university's autonomy to pursue its academic mission in the UC Davis affirmative action case, discussed in chapter 8. Justice Powell declared that universities had a "compelling" interest in the educational benefits of student body diversity and therefore should be given some leeway to consider the race of applicants in constructing a class. Powell referred both to Frankfurter's "four essential freedoms" opinion in the *Sweezy* case and to Justice Brennan's emphasis on "the robust exchange of ideas" in the SUNY Buffalo case.

None of this is to say that students don't themselves have some measure of academic freedom. Justice Abe Fortas famously wrote for seven justices at the height of the Vietnam War protests that "it can hardly be argued that either students or teachers shed their constitutional rights to freedom of expression at the schoolhouse gate." The case he was referring to, *Tinker v. Des Moines Independent Community School District,* involved two high schools and a junior high school suspending students for wearing black armbands in silent protest of the war, which the Court said violated the students' free speech rights. The school district argued that the armbands could lead to disruptions that the principals preferred to avoid in a school setting, but the Court said there was no evidence that the armbands caused or were likely to cause any disruption.

There are plenty of reasons to think of a school prohibiting armbands differently than a school declining to give a platform to a neo-Nazi. Neither Spencer nor Padgett were Auburn students or affiliates, but many of the objections came from members of the university community. Spencer and Padgett were not, moreover, facing suspension but rather disinvitation. For a court to order an academic institution to allow Spencer to speak over its objection and in its own auditorium *in the name of academic freedom* takes that concept to a strange and dangerous place.

And yet our courts cannot see these distinctions. Speech is speech, they say, and censorship is censorship, though the heavens may fall. This attitude is not just uniquely American; it is uniquely modern. The idea of a court intervening to prevent a public university from disinviting a provocateur bent on dividing its students would have mortified the Framers. Our courts' bizarre pivot from associating academic freedom with universities being regulated by the state to associating that freedom with students and others being regulated by the university reflects the confluence of two relatively recent historical episodes: the Berkeley-led Free Speech Movement of the 1960s and the speech code movement of the 1980s.

The Free Speech Movement

University campuses have not always been obvious sites for unfettered expression or protest. Apart from a few bursts of socialist energy that Joseph McCarthy helped spook students away from, student protest had until the 1960s largely been around bad food, dilapidated housing, and other personal grievances. Movements against perceived hegemony or oppression are, of course, often led by young people. Younger generations not only tend to be more energetic and less risk-averse than their parents but also have relatively little personal investment in the established order. Prior to the 1960s, however, the vast majority of college-age people in the United States didn't go to college. Those who received a college education tended overwhelmingly to be wealthy, with much to lose in upsetting the status quo.

Many students before the 1960s got to college not by being social justice advocates or even by scrapping their way to good grades, but rather by entering into and remaining within the good graces of elite prep school admissions officers. "He wants very little because he has so much and is unwilling to risk what he has," a 1950s Gallup report remarked of a typical college student. "He is old before his time; almost middle-aged in his teens." Universities themselves have long been highly regimented and hierarchical institutions. Classroom curricula and decorum are controlled by largely unaccountable faculty who have the power to reward students who abide by their rules and to punish students who don't.

The University of California, Berkeley, has become notorious for campus activism, but prior to the 1960s its student body generally played by the rules. An 1893 piece in the *Occident*, the on-campus student literary journal, needled that the "most prominent feature" of the school's typical student was his "sleepy, absent-minded manner, devoid of purpose or enthusiasm," and "his utter inability to keep a deep interest in anything." The "wishy-washyness" of Berkeley students made them "a hopeless task for the reformer." Little had changed by the 1950s. Berkeley's student government, the Associated Students of the University of California (ASUC), was generally more partner than antagonist of the administration.

That ended in 1959, when a group of progressive students won the majority of the officer positions in the government. The university responded by barring graduate students from membership and by issuing a set of directives that, among other things, forbade all political action on campus and barred student organizations from taking positions on off-campus issues. That meant no electoral politics, no protests, no political advocacy of any kind. At Berkeley.

Notably, the students didn't respond by suing. As draconian as Berkeley's actions were — for example, President Clark Kerr threatened to defund ASUC for publicly objecting to the firing of a University of Illinois biology professor for his condoning of premarital scx — they were legally uncontroversial. *Tinker,* the armband case, had not yet been decided. *West Virginia State Board of Education v. Barnette,* which said students couldn't be suspended for not saluting the flag, involved elementary school children who were subject to compulsory education laws. It also involved a mixture of compelled speech and religious freedom that wasn't present in Berkeley's case. The idea that student organizations voluntarily enrolled at a university had a constitutional right to on-campus political activism, though pushed by a handful of students, simply wasn't a mainstream legal position.

It was indeed the subsequent actions of Berkeley's own students that helped reshape the legal culture's view of freedom of speech. In the 1950s and 1960s, Berkeley students became involved in the civil rights movement, including the sit-ins and boycotts that swept the Deep South in the early 1960s. A number of students participated in Freedom Summer in 1964, which also happened to be the year the Republican National Convention was held at the Cow Palace in Daly City, just south of San Francisco. The top two contenders for the Republican nomination were the libertarian conservative Barry Goldwater and the more moderate Pennsylvania governor William Scranton. Electoral politics was banned on Berkeley's main campus, but the busy intersection along the campus's southern edge, at the corner of Bancroft Way and Telegraph Avenue, had become a popular site for student activists to make speeches and hand out literature.

It turned out, though, that that stretch of sidewalk was technically owned by the university, not the city. The *Oakland Tribune,* which supported Gold-water, made sure to remind the university that the use of Bancroft Way vio-lated the school's rules. That fall, when a group that included many Berkeley students protested the newspaper's lack of diversity in hiring, the paper's publisher, Bill Knowland, objected, and the school responded by closing the Bancroft strip to political activity without warning or consulting with stu-dents.

It would be difficult for a move to backfire more spectacularly. A number of student groups banded together to form the United Front, whose mem-bers not only retook the Bancroft strip but also set up tables directly outside Sproul Hall, which housed the main campus administrative offices. On Oc-tober 1, 1964, two Berkeley deans had a police lieutenant drive his squad car onto campus to arrest Jack Weinberg, who had set up a table in front of Sproul in violation of university rules. But after Weinberg was placed in the police car, hundreds of students surrounded the vehicle and sat down, hold-ing it hostage. The crowd soon swelled to thousands. Mario Savio, a philos-ophy major who had spent the summer registering Black voters in Missis-sippi, was the first of several students to climb on top of the police car and use it as a podium for the two-day sit-in. The demonstration didn't end until the next evening, when Kerr agreed not to press charges against Weinberg.

Two months later, though, the school announced that the leaders of the protests, including Weinberg and Savio, would be facing administrative dis-cipline. That move launched a full-scale student takeover of Sproul that was broken up in a predawn police raid resulting in the arrests of 773 people. A three-day strike against the university followed. It concluded with a large majority of faculty members endorsing an Academic Senate resolution in support of the demands of the Free Speech Movement and the principle of free speech on campus. By the spring semester, student political activity was routine throughout Berkeley's campus.

More significantly, the Free Speech Movement became the model for col-lege student activism later in the decade, especially as U.S. involvement in Vietnam intensified. The origins of the Free Speech Movement in Berkeley's fascistic student speech rules makes it difficult to translate the movement's lessons to other, less extreme but more typical contexts. A school at war with its students, having denied them altogether the right to participate meaningfully in political discussion, has some explaining to do. Berkeley was using its academic freedom as cover to protect its own administrators from criticism. A school trying to shield its students from being harassed by their classmates is different. Speech may be speech, but Richard Spencer isn't Mario Savio.

Speech Codes

The Berkeley example underscores that the history of freedom of speech in the United States is inseparable from the struggle for racial equality. An inordinate number of the speakers whose words the Supreme Court protected from punishment in the landmark First Amendment cases of the 1950s and 1960s were advocates for racial justice. This includes the defendants whose defamation convictions were overturned in *New York Times Co. v. Sullivan*. It includes the Alabama NAACP chapter whose membership list the Court protected from investigation by the state in *NAACP v. Alabama*. It includes Dick Gregory, whose disorderly conduct conviction the Court overturned in 1969.

The march at which Gregory was arrested preceded a better-known Congress of Racial Equality (CORE) demonstration in the city of Cicero, Illinois, where a Black teenager looking for a job had recently been beaten to death by white gang members. Several hundred hecklers threw bottles and rocks at the marchers. What saved CORE members from themselves risking prosecution for incitement was the strong First Amendment presumption against the "heckler's veto." The First Amendment requires the government to punish lawless audience members, not the speakers who arouse their ire. Not for nothing, when Jack Weinberg was arrested in front of Sproul Hall, he had been tabling for CORE.

Understanding this history helps clarify why the United States takes an extreme position on the regulation of hate speech. In much of the world, including throughout Europe and in Canada, speech that calls particular racial groups into disrepute may lawfully be punished by the state. As late as the 1950s, the same was true in the United States. In 1950, a Chicago man named Joseph Beauharnais, president of a militant segregationist group called the White Circle League of America, was convicted under an Illinois law prohibiting "group libel," the publication of any picture or performance that "portrays depravity, criminality, unchastity, or lack of virtue of a class of citizens, of any race, color, creed or religion," and that exposes those citizens to "contempt, derision, or obloquy." Beauharnais had gotten into trouble by distributing leaflets calling for Chicago's white population to rise up to prevent their "[mongrelization] by the negro" and asking Chicago mayor Martin Kennelly to "halt the further encroachment, harassment and invasion of white people, their property, neighborhoods and persons, by the Negro." The Supreme Court upheld Beauharnais's conviction in 1952, a result that would be inconceivable today.

The *Beauharnais* case was less than a decade removed from a devastating war that had begun as part of a genocidal project, with charismatic speech as its engine. There was little reason to assume at the time that the post–World War II human rights revolution that resulted in so much anti–hate speech legislation abroad would pass over the United States. The year before *Beauharnais,* the Supreme Court had upheld the criminal convictions of eleven members of the Communist Party for espousing a revolutionary ideology. A few years earlier, the Court had explicitly exempted "fighting words" from First Amendment protection. The most famous heckler's veto case at the time of *Beauharnais* arose out of the arrest of a Syracuse man named Irving Feiner for breach of the peace after his soapbox appeals for racial equality had attracted a hostile crowd. Feiner lost at the Supreme Court.

It's not hard to appreciate a civil rights advocate's general wariness of the kinds of laws that led to Feiner's arrest. Restrictions of this sort can easily miss their mark. Given the tactics of the civil rights movement, laws punishing inciting speech were at least as likely to be used against people of color as on their behalf. The NAACP successfully opposed a congressional bill introduced in 1943 that would have prohibited the mailing of writings expressing racial or religious hatred. Great Britain's 1965 Race Relations Act, which prohibits the incitement of hatred based on race or national origin, was used early on to prosecute a Black Power leader named Michael X (né Michael de Freitas) for advocating the killing of any white man caught "laying hands" on a Black woman. A member of the Universal Coloured People's Association was prosecuted under the act for, among other things, encouraging Black nurses to give patients the wrong injections and urging Indian restaurant owners to "put something in the curry" they made for white people.

If the NAACP didn't push the passage of anti–hate speech laws in the United States, they weren't going to happen, and for a while, they didn't. Meanwhile, a series of decisions in the 1960s and 1970s strengthened the idea that the First Amendment tolerates a great deal of expressive activity that most people would rather not see or hear. Not only wearing armbands in high schools but wearing "Fuck the Draft" on a jacket in a courthouse; advocating violent or illegal acts; carrying a Nazi flag and marching in SS uniforms in a town known for its population of Holocaust survivors; and all manner of pornography and performative exploitation of women.

So when some public universities began experimenting with speech-restrictive policies designed to address racist campus incidents in the 1980s, many courts and advocates reflexively treated the schools just as they would any other government regulator. The speech code movement was quite ordinary from a certain perspective. Even as increasing numbers of minority students were admitted onto America's college campuses, they were not always welcome.

At the University of Michigan in January 1987, someone anonymously distributed a flyer in a residence hall in which Black female students were meeting that declared "open season" on "saucer lips, porch monkeys, and jigaboos." A few days later, a student DJ at an on-campus radio station aired a program that included racist jokes. "Who are the two most famous black women in history? Aunt Jemima and motherfucker," one joke went. "Why do black people smell? So blind people can hate them too," went another. When demonstrators protested at the radio station, some of their fellow students decided to greet them by hanging a KKK outfit from a dorm window. In 1989, at the University of Mississippi, Beta Theta Pi fraternity brothers thought it might be fun to write "KKK" and "we hate niggers" on the naked bodies of two white pledges and drop them off on the campus of the historically black Rust College, in nearby Holly Springs. At Emory University in 1990, a Black female freshman arrived at her dorm room one night to find her teddy bear slashed, her clothing doused in bleach, and "NIGGER HANG" written in lipstick on the wall. She later found "DIE NIGGER DIE" written in nail polish on the floor of her room, under her rug.

Between 1986 and 1990, more than 250 colleges and universities reported similar racist incidents on campus, from swastikas to death threats and physical violence. A 1989 survey found that nearly two-thirds of research university presidents indicated that sexual harassment was a moderate or major problem on their campuses, and nearly half said the same about racial intimidation.

The freedom of students to express themselves is, of course, important in a university setting, but so, too, is an environment in which all members of the community are welcome on equal terms. Both are human values, both are educational values, and, at a public university, both are *constitutional* values. Courts and others within the debates over campus speech have acted as if free expression is a trump, as threatened when a student doesn't get to stump for a political candidate on the college green as when she doesn't get to call her classmate a nigger.

The University of Michigan responded to the incidents on its campus by putting in place a code of conduct that targeted stigmatization, harassment, and intimidation along various protected grounds, including race, religion, sex, and sexual orientation, in "educational and academic centers." The policy varied liability and sanction based on the nature and location of the violation, and it excluded school-sponsored publications from coverage.

A psychology grad student sued the school and won. He claimed that his discussion of scientific theories suggesting racial and sex differences might fall under the code of conduct, or at least that the presence of the code might "chill" his academic speech. The court said a public university is simply forbidden to put in place "an anti-discrimination policy which had the effect of prohibiting certain speech because it disagreed with ideas or messages sought to be conveyed." The court did not acknowledge that a university might have different rights or immunities based on its status as an educational institution. To the contrary, citing the *Sweezy* case, the judge indicated that a university had a greater *obligation* than other public institutions to permit "the free and unfettered interplay of competing views," which the judge said "is essential to the institution's educational mission."

A different court invalidated a similar policy at the University of Wisconsin. That school had also endured a rash of overt racism directed at its students, including a fraternity "slave auction" in which pledges performed minstrel shows in blackface. The school implemented a new rule forbidding discriminatory expression that was directed at an individual; was demeaning on the grounds of race, sex, or religion (among other grounds); or created an intimidating or hostile environment for education or university-related work or activities. The policy did not apply to faculty, and it did not apply to comments made about racial groups in general in, for example, a classroom setting.

By the time the case reached a trial court, students had been disciplined under the policy for barging into a Black student's room and calling him "Shakazulu"; for calling a student a "fucking bitch" and a "fucking cunt" because she had criticized the athletic department; for telling an Asian-American student that "some day the Whites will take over" and that "people like you" who "don't belong here" are the reason for the country's problems; for needling a Turkish-American student by pretending to be an immigration officer asking for documents; for calling a residence hall staff member a "piece of shit nigger"; for sending an electronic message saying "Death to all Arabs!! Die Islamic scumbags" to an Iranian faculty member; for stealing a roommate's ATM card and withdrawing money from the student's bank account out of resentment that the roommate was Japanese and didn't speak English well; for calling a Black student a "fat-ass nigger"; and for yelling at a female student in public, "You've got nice tits." In none of these incidents was the offending student expelled from school, and in only one was the student even suspended. Typically, students were placed on probation and/or made to engage in sensitivity training or counseling for substance abuse or psychological issues.

In striking down Wisconsin's code, the judge spent most of the opinion rejecting the notion that the racist and harassing speech the school targeted was subject to an exception from the general rule that the government may not regulate speech on the basis of its content. In response to the school's argument that the speech it was targeting damaged the educational environment, the judge offered his own opinion that, to the contrary, "by establishing content-based restrictions on speech, the rule limits the diversity of ideas by students and thereby prevents the 'robust exchange of ideas' which intellectually diverse campuses provide." The school argued further that it was protecting the constitutional equality rights of its students, an argument the court rejected on the ground that because the offending students were not state actors, their victims' constitutional rights were not threatened. Like the Michigan court, the Wisconsin court treated the university in just the same way as it would have treated the state legislature passing a criminal ban on racist speech.

The Michigan and Wisconsin decisions are profoundly, dangerously wrong. "Nice tits" is not an "idea" whose free traffic the Constitution requires a public educational institution to tolerate. Indeed, if academic freedom means anything, it's that it isn't for an agent of the state, including a judge, to dictate *to a university* what is or is not essential to its educational mission. That, not a university's regulation *of its own students,* was what the *Sweezy* decision was about.

The Michigan and Wisconsin courts were indifferent not just to the fact that the schools were in the business of education but also to the fact that the sanction in most cases was probation and sensitivity training. These responses to incivility are precisely what one would expect at an educational institution whose job is, in part, to teach students to express themselves not just with honesty but with care. Further, the courts' narrow focus on the perpetrators' speech privileges made them unable to see that the state wasn't just interfering with rights but protecting them, too. Women and minority students have a right to attend state schools free of discrimination and harassment. At a minimum, a state school has a right to protect the students it is trying to teach from verbal abuse and threats, as an exercise of its own academic freedom. That academic freedom also implicates the victims' rights to freedom of speech.

These cases are tragic. We anxiously mourn the death of civility in public life. Meanwhile, our courts say the Constitution requires a public school to grin and bear the incivility of the students it is charged with educating. Courts' unwillingness to assess the serious contextual differences between university codes of conduct and criminal statutes follows directly from the American approach. That approach prioritizes the threshold question of the nature of the right — speech in both cases — and flattens factual differences — the nature of the regulatory institution, its motives, and the severity of the sanction — that speak to whether interference with the right is justified. The code of conduct at Berkeley banning all political advocacy and the code at Wisconsin banning racist barbs and harassment both dealt with speech, and so they were deemed to be constitutionally indistinguishable.

The Michigan and Wisconsin courts are not alone in this regard. Public university codes of conduct (and even the private university code at Stanford) have consistently been deemed violations of the Constitution when they seek to regulate racist or harassing student speech. Such codes have also been struck down at Central Michigan and Northern Kentucky, at Shippensburg and Texas Tech, at Temple, Tarrant County College, and the University of the Virgin Islands. A 2007 court case out of San Francisco seems especially poignant. The College Republicans at San Francisco State University held a rally at which they stomped on Hezbollah and Hamas flags. Some Muslim students objected, as the flags being trounced contained the word "Allah" on them. The administration put the students' case before a hearing panel, which cleared them of any violation of the school's code of conduct. The College Republicans sued anyway, challenging the bare existence of the rule they had been charged with violating. That rule said that students "are expected to be good citizens and to engage in responsible behaviors that reflect well upon their university, to be civil to one another and to others in the campus community, and to contribute positively to student and university life."

As in the Michigan and Wisconsin cases, the judge noted, correctly, that the school's policy reached speech that is not itself exempt from the First Amendment's scope. The judge also noted, again correctly, that prior court cases have held public universities to the same obligation that other state institutions have to respect the First Amendment rights of those it regulates, in this case students. The school's requirement that students be "civil to one another" therefore couldn't stand. "A regulation that mandates civility easily could be understood as permitting only those forms of interaction that produce as little friction as possible, forms that are thoroughly lubricated by restraint, moderation, respect, social convention, and reason," the judge wrote. "The First Amendment difficulty with this kind of mandate should be obvious."

In other words, a school requiring students to be restrained, moderate, civil, and reasonable is inconsistent with our Constitution. We're doomed.

Solutions

Outside the shadow of absolute rights, colleges can carry out their missions based on the wisdom of regulating campus speech rather than out of fear that they will be sued by students or off-campus agitators. Rigorous speech codes are often unwise; most university administrators don't need to be persuaded of that. All regulation may, of course, be abused, and courts might well have a role to play should university speech regulation outpace its justification, as at Berkeley in the 1960s. But given the competing demands on educators, none of us should be so immodest as to declare campus bans on harassing or hateful speech categorically unwise. Precluding public educators from deciding that regulating racist or sexist speech, based directly on its content, is important to a school's educational mission is a recipe for incivility to grow in just the place where it should most obviously be extirpated.

We have come to see the university green as the quintessential public square. It is not. The purpose of a university is not to provide a forum for free speech. It is to prepare students for democratic citizenship. Universities do so not by permitting speech but by curating it. Universities discriminate, pervasively, based on the content and viewpoint of the speech to which students are exposed, consistent with the pedagogical judgments of faculty and administrators. Schools hire faculty based on the content of their written work. They do so in part to ensure that the information conveyed to students is of high quality. Universities, both private and public, have every right to deny appointments or tenure to faculty who hold racist, sexist, or other views that the school judges to be of low quality. Indeed, a faculty member who directs racist or sexist invective at colleagues or students can and should face discipline, including at a public school. Curating the faculty in this way is an exercise of academic freedom. It's imperfect, of course, but freedom always is.

The same is true of racist or sexist students. We seem to understand that when it comes to admissions. Schools discriminate in deciding whom they admit into their communities. Apart from race-based decision-making, the admissions processes of public colleges are largely left to each school's unaccountable discretion. Colleges do not typically admit students at random. Rather, they make a judgment not just about whether applicants are likely to be well prepared academically, whether they are gifted athletes, whether their parents are supportive alums, and so forth, but also whether they are likely to enhance the overall intellectual and social life of the school. Justice Powell seemed to recognize the constitutional significance of this discretion in the UC Davis affirmative action case, which emphasized that admissions decisions include an evaluation of the perspective students will bring to class discussion.

And yet once students arrive on campus, we are told, the school must relinquish any subsequent interest in their views, socialization, or style of argument. This posture bypasses a critical moment of intervention in a student's intellectual and social development by people whose professional training equips them better than most to intervene. Worse, by styling student speech controversies as matters of fundamental constitutional rights, courts distort the educational process.

Recent events on the campus at which I teach are instructive. In the fall of 2017, the Columbia University College Republicans held a "free speech month" in which, in the span of three weeks, they hosted speeches by Tommy

Robinson and Mike Cernovich. Robinson, a cofounder of the English Defence League, is an Islamophobic football hooligan who has been banned from Facebook, Twitter, Instagram, and Snapchat for violating the platforms' policies on hate speech, including by calling for "war" against Muslims. Cernovich is a notorious peddler of fake news, including "Pizzagate," a conspiracy theory whose spread led to a man opening fire on a Washington, D.C., pizzeria falsely implicated in a nonexistent child sex trafficking ring. Robinson had been invited to discuss immigration, a subject on which he has no expertise. Cernovich is most famous for saying things that are not true.

The College Republicans did not invite Robinson and Cernovich to speak in order to promote the robust exchange of ideas. Rather, they invited them in order to make a point about freedom of speech. Time and resources that could have been spent engaging a conservative with actual knowledge of immigration law and policy, or one who is known for saying things that are true, were instead spent on professional agitators and carnival barkers. Predictably, the speeches drew large protests; Robinson's talk had to be cut short due to loud interruptions. The invitations prompted the university's Black Students' Organization to call for the College Republicans to be defunded by the university.

In other words, what "free speech month" accomplished wasn't the exchange of ideas at all, but rather recriminations, increased security costs, and animosity among students and between students and university administrators. Had the university determined in advance that this costly exercise in rights fetishism by its students served little educational purpose, it would have been dead right. Would it not have been in the spirit of academic freedom for faculty or administrators to determine, just as they are paid to do in the classroom, that the invitations to Robinson and Cernovich would not meaningfully contribute to the education of Columbia's students? Is there not pedagogical value in requiring students to make a case, on the merits, for a speaker's contribution to the intellectual life of the school?

The conspicuous constitutionalization of these conflicts makes the bare exercise of rights something worth fighting for—and about. And so students are encouraged to make a spectacle in the name of rights rather than actually needing to convince, or have their guests convince, their colleagues and teachers of anything.

Of course, part of preparing students for democratic citizenship might include letting them make the mistakes we all make as we learn to be autonomous moral agents and to express ourselves. It might also include teaching students to tolerate views that are different from, even repugnant to, their own. But there are ways to teach these lessons that don't involve inviting bigots onto campus and passing the popcorn. As law professor Paul Horwitz writes, universities "are laboratories *for* democracy, not laboratories *of* democracy: they contribute to democratic discourse, but not by following its rules."

What's more, universities are not just offering lessons in tolerance. They are also helping students to develop empathy, to live in a community governed by social norms, and to learn how to *persuade* others through evidence and reason rather than simply to "own" them. A college's curating of the speakers invited to campus based on the speakers' demonstrated views and methods isn't just about making some students in the school's care feel better or preventing emotional harm (though it's that, too). It's just what schools do.

The world needs curators, now more than ever. It isn't hard for students either to hear a wide range of ideas or to themselves disseminate ideas to a wide audience. From social media, the World Wide Web, books, and other sources, they have a startling amount of information at their fingertips. The hard part is learning to separate the wheat from the chaff. This is an existential challenge for the future of global democracy. We are surrounded constantly by information that isn't just false or ill-informed but that is calculated to distract or mislead us. Colleges and universities are better suited than most institutions to help students learn how to navigate a rich but challenging informational ecosystem.

A constitutional law that respects both freedom of speech and the demands of governance in a complex world should be able to distinguish a ban on all political discourse from a ban on racial insults and sexual harassment. It should be attentive to codes of conduct that use sanctions as a mode of education rather than merely to censor. It should care if the institution regulating speech is a school to which students have entrusted their education or a police officer submitting all comers involuntarily to the state's orthodoxy. Rights live in courts, but as the Framers well knew, they also live in local democratic institutions like public colleges and universities. Courts should give far greater deference to those institutions to exercise the very academic freedom they have previously recognized as constitutionally meaningful.

This is not to say that rigorous speech codes or micromanagement of student organizations' entreaties to outside speakers make good sense. But schools' decisions about how to structure the information environment should generally be made based on the pedagogical judgments of educators rather than the political theories of judges. A school would, of course, have the professional discretion to determine that it should prioritize tolerance rather than hierarchical management of student speech. To live in a pluralistic society is to be surrounded by and forced to engage with people of opposing views. Students need to learn how to speak to such people, understand their claims, compromise with them, and accept their right to ground policy in divergent beliefs. To the extent college students remain in filter bubbles in which they engage only with like-minded friends and colleagues, there is much to be said for a school deciding to puncture that bubble for learning's sake.

Moreover, even if school administrators believe in good faith that they should shield their students from racist or sexist speech, converting that belief into a code of conduct is challenging. The line-drawing problems are legion. Racist or sexist theories can be couched in misleading or pseudoscientific terms, and well-supported research can have disturbing implications for racial or gender equality. The administrators making these judgments can be ill-informed or biased. Provocateurs can use censorship to generate publicity for themselves, which is just what they seek. And as we've seen, ham-handed application of speech codes can make martyrs out of drunken frat boys.

These very good reasons to approach campus speech restrictions with caution don't state the full case, however. As noted, a school's role isn't just to support student expression and facilitate ideas, as it is sometimes caricatured by courts and critics. It is also to develop students' capacities for civility, critical reasoning, and persuasion. Democracy needs those capacities every bit as much as it needs informational freedom. The practical and strategic justifications for permitting unfettered free expression on campus also cut both ways. A college platform can legitimate a conspiratorial or racist speaker and draw a crowd as much as being turned away can generate headlines.

Finally, we should not lose sight of the actual harm of racist or sexist speech. Too often, the fact that such speech is constitutionally protected leads us to assume that it is, for that reason, not harmful. But we protect hateful speech not because of its innocence but rather in spite of its harm. Racial and sexual harassment and intimidation are threatening and traumatic to those it targets. Minority students also spend an enormous and disproportionate amount of time and energy defending against and protesting speech that demeans them. It is reasonable for a university to protect the students in its care from harm and to alleviate the burdens they bear just for being minorities. They have that right.

The costs and benefits of curating speech point in different directions on different campuses with different histories and in different contexts. This doesn't call for bright-line rules policed by judges. It calls for the exercise of judgment by educators, who are trained and motivated to think carefully about how to construct ideal environments for teaching and learning. Reasonable people who believe deeply in the liberal values underlying freedom of speech, and who also believe deeply in judicial review and limits on government, can disagree about whether and how university administrators should deplatform speakers they believe to be racist or sexist or discipline students who violate norms of civility.

We can expect colleges and universities given the discretion to craft their own regulations of campus expressive activity to arrive at a wide range of policies. Schools would cover different specific acts; they would reach different judgments about which acts cross the line; they would develop different suites of exemptions from regulation; they would impose a different range of punishments and other remedies; they would structure their hearing processes differently; they would put in place different screening and approval processes for speakers; and they would implement different policies around funding and insurance arrangements. We tend to celebrate policy experimentation of this sort as one of the main benefits of a federal system of government. The fifty states can act as "laboratories of democracy" that serve as testing grounds for a range of ideas and can motivate best practices amid the uncertainty typical of a complex regulatory environment. There is no reason to see experimentation in speech regulation among America's five thousand colleges as less valuable.

The suggestion here isn't for the abdication of judicial review. Courts could still play a role in this space, not by deciding whether they agree with the balance public universities have struck, but by assessing whether a particular school has been reasonable in its own striking of that balance. It's not clear, for example, what values Berkeley was protecting when it banned political advocacy on campus. It is eminently clear, by contrast, that the University of Wisconsin was protecting the rights of its minority and female students, as the university reasonably understood those rights. The school's attempt to exempt academic discussion from its speech restrictions indicated serious attention to minimizing the burden on academic freedom. Once the school's degree of care became obvious, the court's interest in Wisconsin's code of conduct should have been at an end.

There's every reason to expect this level of care to be common. Campus speech codes went away not primarily because of court cases but because of self-regulation by schools. Despite much of the rhetoric around campus speech, academics are in fact unusually predisposed to value freedom of expression. Scholars are well accustomed to the exchange of controversial ideas, and schools have a politics of their own, with a range of constituencies within faculties, among administrators, and across the student body. They also face pressure from politicians, ordinary citizens, and competitors. Students and faculty can be expected to self-select into or out of schools that censor student speech. Outside the shadow of rights, folks usually just kind of work things out.

Conclusion

There is such a thing as society, Lady Thatcher. We are not merely individuals and families; the body politic is more than the sum of its parts. That's obvious in an emergency — during a global pandemic, say, or a war — but it is no less true in ordinary times. The world is irretrievably interconnected. Speakers have listeners who must hear them and other speakers who can't be heard over them. Conscientious objectors send others to kill and die in their place. Public defenders cost taxpayers money. Higher wages and better working conditions raise prices for consumers. Every voter reduces the weight of everyone else's vote. We can't quit one another.

There is also such a thing as rights. Those individual people and families have hopes and fears that matter but that conflict with the fears and hopes of their fellow human beings. Their aspirations and worries don't depend on what the Framers believed, or how Madison phrased the Bill of Rights, or whether some judicial opinion says "strict scrutiny" applies to a case. They depend on what people's expectations are, how they are treated by others, and why. We are bound to experience the rights we have differently than anyone else does — this is what makes them ours. The central challenge for any system of justice has always been that we dream alone but we live together.

The Framers wrote the U.S. Constitution for an agrarian society far less interdependent than the one we were born into. Yet even then they under-

stood that rights will always be too contested for pat formulas or neat resolution by courts. For them, there was no better guardian of rights than the
people themselves, banded together in jury boxes and meetinghouses, in
posse comitatus and over dinner. Rights are lofty and aspirational, and they
cannot speak for themselves. We don't get far without knowing their limits,
and those limits need to be worked out through deliberation and negotiation
— that is, through politics.

White supremacists can't be trusted, alas, to resolve rights disputes
through politics. This racial context yields the true lesson of *Brown v. Board
of Education,* but we have instead styled that great decision as a case about
the importance of rights in the abstract. Ever since America's notional rejection of white supremacy in the middle of the twentieth century, we've been
treating distrust as inherent in rights conflicts instead of as merely inherent
in white supremacy. Identifying a right has become a reason to ignore context — the magnitude, scope, and permanence of the burden; the government's reasons; available alternatives — rather than all the more reason to
fixate on the facts.

This is a grave mistake. Absolute rights cannot be, as rights are, ubiquitous, so courts artificially limit what counts. Worse, those limits track a
judge's capacity to isolate and discipline a right rather than tracking the rea-
sonableness of the state's actual behavior. This is how we get rock-ribbed
rights to guns and data scraping and corporate election spending, but no
rights to food and shelter and education. Rights conflicts, again ubiquitous,
are treated as unilateral, sending a message to the losers that they don't matter to the Constitution. State efforts to protect rights through law escape
judicial identification because they are incremental, qualitative, implicit, and
measured, avoiding the wooden abstractions of court decisions. We come to
distrust the law, and each other, because the law doesn't trust us either.

The Framers' insights here are worth recovering, not for history's sake
but for the sake of we the living people of the United States. A diverse people
who disagree intensely about the law will stay invested in the constitutional
project only if their biggest losses are not permanent. Each of us inhabits
an imagined universe — a "nomos," in the words of the legal scholar Robert

Cover — in which our most intimate vision of the law is preserved as right and true. When judges treat rights conflicts as a choice between absolute entitlements, they raze those alternative visions, never to be rebuilt. We are left either to control the courts or to stop respecting what they pronounce.

America's had a good run, all told. But we should not mistake its endurance for rigidity. Its constitutional longevity has been underwritten less by its Founders, and much less by its judges, than by those who have dared, in the face of the law, to dream. This is how Frederick Douglass was able to tell a Scottish crowd in 1860 that the U.S. Constitution was an antislavery document. It is how Susan B. Anthony was able to see the Fourteenth Amendment as guaranteeing her right to cast a ballot in a Rochester election in 1872. It is how the Reverend Dr. Martin Luther King Jr. could preach "the highest respect for law" over violence from his cell in a Birmingham jail. The heroes of our constitutional order have been those who have held out hope that, one day, the Constitution will recognize their pain, and so make their dreams flesh.

Sometimes it doesn't take much to change history. In the summer of 1991, four years after he retired, Lewis Powell sat down with his biographer John Jeffries. Jeffries, a University of Virginia law professor and a former law clerk of Powell's, asked him whether, with the benefit of hindsight, he would have changed his vote in any case. Powell's immediate response was *McCleskey v. Kemp,* which held that statistical evidence of severe racial bias in capital sentencing wasn't enough to reverse a death sentence. *McCleskey* came down only two months before Powell left the bench. It was a 5–4 decision.

A different vote in *McCleskey* would have opened the pernicious interaction between race and the criminal justice system to far greater judicial scrutiny. A different vote in the San Antonio schools case, in which Powell's vote was also decisive, would have forced state officials to address massive disparities in public educational financing, and therefore outcomes for students. A single vote in the UC Davis affirmative action case — Powell's — would have radically changed the college admissions process for minority students and for others.

Americans can, do, and should disagree about the outcomes in these kinds of cases. They are difficult. They require judges to confront value judgments that we perform differently simply by virtue of being different from one another. We all have different backgrounds, different influences, different genes. But when constitutional law approaches these conflicts in binary terms, as if the winner has a right and the loser does not, it magnifies those differences. It makes us believe that we win constitutional cases not by being right about the facts but rather by finding judges who are more like us. Rights, understood in this way anyway, keep us divided.

This book has offered a better way to think about rights. Embraced and practiced successfully the world over, it's an approach that, by encouraging decision-makers to mediate rather than discriminate among rights, by emphasizing mutual respect for multiple and competing values and commitments, brings rights closer to justice and aspires to bring us closer to each other. The suggestions offered for how courts should address three trenchant conflicts in particular — over disability rights, affirmative action, and campus speech — are invitations, not manifestos, in the spirit of humility to which we all should aspire. I don't have all the answers to these challenges, and neither do judges. There's no shame in that.

In a chaotic, dynamic, dangerous, conflicted, and yet profoundly connected world, constitutional law can never have just one right and true answer, just one solution for all time. We're stuck with one another, caught, as King said, "in an inescapable network of mutuality, tied in a single garment of destiny." We need one another, and we all have a part to play in figuring out how to live together.

Constitutional law can help — but only when it stops being about judges peering at law books and dictionaries, and starts being about the rest of us. For "we must never forget," as Chief Justice John Marshall wrote in 1819, "that it is a *constitution* we are expounding." Its high calling is to bring us together, into more perfect union. It's about time it lived up to its name.

Acknowledgments

I started writing this book before I knew I was writing it. *How Rights Went Wrong* brings into close conversation insights I have developed over at least fifteen years of thinking about constitutional law. Early in my academic career, I found myself wanting to understand better the peculiarly American preoccupation with invoking the Framers in legal argument. The work of two scholars in particular have been indispensable to what progress I have made on the question: Philip Bobbitt, who has so well understood that a method of constitutional interpretation can't justify *itself*, and the late Robert Cover, who saw law in places judges don't want us to look. I owe thanks to the teachers and scholars who introduced me to and have built upon that work, in particular Akhil Reed Amar, Jack Balkin, Owen Fiss, Robert Post, and Reva Siegel.

The distinctive problem of rights fetishism is too central to American life to have gone unnoticed by other scholars. Of those who have addressed aspects of the problem, it is worth singling out Mary Ann Glendon and Jeremy Waldron for their especially searing, though quite distinct, critiques of contemporary American rights practice, and Duncan Kennedy, Samuel Moyn, Mark Tushnet, and Robin West, who stand out among those who have noticed and named some of the ways in which rights talk can distract from questions of justice. My diagnoses and prescriptions differ significantly from theirs, and theirs from one another's, but the diversity in our ideological and methodological perspectives speaks to the urgency of the preoccupation we share. The problem of American rights cuts deep and wide.

Law beyond our borders plays a central role in this book. For cultivating my interest in comparative public law, which has brought into focus many of the objects in my own backyard, I owe a world of thanks to Vicki Jackson, who has also illuminated, with greater care than most, both the possibilities and the limits of proportionality analysis. I owe a conceptual debt as well to Robert Alexy, whose understanding of legal principles as "optimization" requirements has lingered with me since I first read *A Theory of Constitutional Rights* many years ago.

The community of comparative constitutional law scholars has grown immensely in recent years, but it has managed to retain both an intimacy and a freshness that I value more than I thought I could. I have learned from too many comparativists to single them all out, but on the particular themes of the book, I offer gratitude to Richard Albert, David Beatty, Moshe Cohen-Eliya, Rosalind Dixon, David Fontana, Sudhir Krishnaswamy, Susanna Mancini, Jud Mathews, Iddo Porat, and Michel Rosenfeld. Menaka Guruswamy deserves particular mention for heroic work at Incheon Airport, and Yvonne Tew deserves special thanks not just for enabling me to manage the Incheon fallout but — more important — for her generous engagement with early drafts and her enduring friendship.

For helpful comments and challenges on the specific chapters of this book and related arguments, I offer additional thanks to Jessie Allen, Nicholas Bagley, Randy Barnett, Seyla Benhabib, Benjamin Berger, Carlos Bernal Pulido, Evan Bernick, Deborah Brake, Jedediah Britton-Purdy, Jud Campbell, Jane Cohen, Aaron Dhir, Kellen Funk, Maeve Glass, David Golove, Michael Grevė, Stephen Griffin, Rick Hills, Samuel Issacharoff, Isabel Jaramillo, Jeremy Kessler, Suzanne Kim, Jill Lepore, Gillian Lester, Daryl Levinson, Daniel Markovits, Michael McConnell, John McGinnis, Gillian Metzger, Henry Monaghan, Abigail Moncrief, Trevor Morrison, Francisca Pou Giménez, David Pozen, Richard Primus, Jack Rakove, Gonçalo Almeida Ribeiro, Russell Robinson, Adam Samaha, Frederick Schauer, Sarah Seo, Geoffrey Sigalet, Lawrence Solum, Karen Tani, Francisco Urbina, Matthew Waxman,

John Fabian Witt, and workshop participants at UC Berkeley School of Law, Columbia Law School, Georgetown University Law Center, the University of Iowa College of Law, the University of Michigan Law School, New York University School of Law, Osgoode Hall Law School, the Seminario en Latinoamérica de Teoría Constitucional y Política in Buenos Aires, the annual conference of the International Society of Public Law in Santiago, and the Originalism Works-in-Progress Conference at the University of San Diego School of Law.

For excellent research assistance, my gratitude goes to Joshua Bean, Molly Brachfeld, Nicholas Campbell, Katherine Yon Ebright, Nico Galván, Gregory Graham, Michael Lemanski, Jordan Lieberman, Rohan Mishra, Omobolaji Ogunsola, Stephen Piotrkowski, Gregory Smith, and Aden Tedla. My administrative assistant, Khamla Pradaxay, is world-class.

For thoughtful conversations about the business of writing a book, thanks to Michelle Au, Alex Carter, Elizabeth Emens, and Michael Heller. My agent, Andrew Stuart, has offered perceptive guidance at every stage of turning this seed into a meal. And for expert shepherding of this project into print, I thank my wonderful editor, Alexander Littlefield; Olivia Bartz and the team at HMH Books and Media; and copyeditor Barbara Jatkola.

For shepherding of a more personal sort, thank you to Brenda Greene, Perry Greene, Talib Kweli Greene, Beverly and Lloyd Moorehead, Javotte and Stanley Greene Sr., Lori Moorehead, Joann and Dennis Adams, Abena Edwards, Taiwo Gaynor, Kehinde Gaynor, Lloyd Mebane, Linda Pierce, Portia Rose, Fred Johnson, Nita and Arun Mukherjee, Angela Mukherjee, Nirav Lad, and others far too numerous to mention.

To Guido and JPS, thank you for showing me that judging is, above all, about judgment.

To Elora, Riya, Ayan, and Kian, your love and support sustain me. Thank you for making things right.

Jamal Greene
June 2020

Notes

FOREWORD

page

x   *"discourse about rights"*: Mary Ann Glendon, *Rights Talk: The Impoverishment of Political Discourse* (New York: Free Press, 1991), x–xi.
"has virtually declared": Michael J. Klarman, *From Jim Crow to Civil Rights: The Supreme Court and the Struggle for Racial Equality* (New York: Oxford University Press, 2004), 58.

INTRODUCTION

xiii   *A performance artist:* NEA v. Finley, 524 U.S. 569 (1998).
Citizens United: Citizens United v. Federal Election Commission, 558 U.S. 310 (2010).
Two Orthodox Jewish merchants: Braunfeld v. Brown, 366 U.S. 599 (1961).
a Colorado baker: Masterpiece Cakeshop, Ltd. v. Colo. Civil Rights Comm'n, 138 S. Ct. 1719 (2018).
Two Missouri women: Niang v. Carroll, 879 F.3d 870 (8th Cir. 2018).
A group of neo-Nazis: Kessler v. City of Charlottesville, No. 3:17CV00056, 2017 WL 3474071 (W.D. Va. Aug. 11, 2017).

xiv   *A Louisiana man:* Sibley v. United States, No. 03-3540 (E.D. La. dismissed June 9, 2004).
his homemade nunchucks: Maloney v. Singas, 351 F. Supp. 3d 222 (E.D. N.Y. 2018); Meagan Flynn, "Right to Bear . . . Nunchucks? Federal Judge Strikes Down Ban on Weapon as Violation of Second Amendment," *Washington Post,* December 18, 2018, https://www.washingtonpost.com/nation/2018/12/18/right-bear-nunchucks-federal-judge-strikes-down-ban-weapon-violation-second-amendment/.
"scarcely any political question": Alexis de Tocqueville, *Democracy in America,* trans. Henry Reeve (New York: Adlard & Saunders, 1838), 1:261. Others who have lingered on this point more recently include Robert Bellah, Mary Ann Glendon, and — from a global perspective — Samuel Moyn. Robert N. Bellah, "Civil Religion in America," in *Beyond Belief: Essays on Religion in a Post-traditionalist World* (Berkeley: University of California Press, 1991), 168–89;

Mary Ann Glendon, *Rights Talk: The Impoverishment of Political Discourse* (New York: Free Press, 1991); Samuel Moyn, *Not Enough: Human Rights in an Unequal World* (Cambridge, MA: Belknap Press, 2018).

Scott Roeder: Devin Friedman, "Savior v. Savior," Culture (newsletter), *GQ,* January 8, 2010, https://www.gq.com/story/abortion-debate-george-tiller-scott-roeder; Reynolds Holding, "Abortion Doctor Killer Allowed to Use 'Necessity Defense,'" ABC News, January 12, 2010, https://abcnews.go.com/WN/abortion-doctor-killer-allowed-necessity-defense/story?id=9546849.

xv   Roe v. Wade: Roe v. Wade, 410 U.S. 113 (1973). Notably, some anti-abortion activists since *Roe* have even used the term "guerrilla" to describe legal and nonviolent strategies. See, for example, Mark Crutcher's *Firestorm: A Guerrilla Strategy for a Pro-life America,* a manual referenced in Carol Mason, "From Protest to Retribution," in *Killing for Life: The Apocalyptic Narrative of Pro-life Politics* (Ithaca, NY: Cornell University Press, 2002), 53.

take rights seriously: The late Ronald Dworkin popularized the term "taking rights seriously," and he remains the canonical expositor of the idea that rights should be understood as "trumps" over competing government interests. Ronald Dworkin, *Taking Rights Seriously* (Cambridge, MA: Harvard University Press, 1977), xi.

xvi   *"the problem of the color-line":* W. E. B. DuBois, "Of the Dawn of Freedom," in *The Souls of Black Folk,* ed. Jonathan Scott Holloway (New Haven, CT: Yale University Press, 2015), 12.

"will be lynched": Jason Morgan Ward, *Hanging Bridge: Racial Violence and America's Civil Rights Century* (New York: Oxford University Press, 2016), 63.

Jackson Giles: Giles v. Harris, 189 U.S. 475, 478 (1903); State of Alabama, *Journal of the Proceedings of the Constitutional Convention* (Montgomery: Brown Printing, 1901), 9.

Brown v. Board of Education: Brown v. Board of Education of Topeka, 347 U.S. 483 (1954).

Loving v. Virginia: Loving v. Virginia, 388 U.S. 1 (1967).

erode the solidarity: Glendon, *Rights Talk,* 14–15.

xix   *access to politicians:* Buckley v. Valeo, 424 U.S. 1 (1976).

to pornography: Stanley v. Georgia, 394 U.S. 557 (1969).

open-shop workplaces: Coppage v. Kansas, 236 U.S. 1 (1915); Janus v. AFSCME, 138 S. Ct. 2448 (2018).

moral reflection: Jeremy Waldron offers one of the most cogent modern defenses of the quality of political versus judicial deliberation as it pertains to American courts. Jeremy Waldron, "The Core of the Case Against Judicial Review," *Yale Law Journal* 115, no. 6 (April 2006): 1382–85.

know what other people do not: "My name is Sherlock Holmes. It is my business to know what other people do not know." Sir Arthur Conan Doyle, *The Adventure of the Blue Carbuncle,* ed. Christopher Morley (New York: Baker Street Irregulars, 1948), 46.

xxii   *"foreign moods, fads, or fashions":* Foster v. Florida, 537 U.S. 990, n.* (2002) (Thomas, J., concurring). Justice Antonin Scalia repeated this line in his dissenting opinion in Lawrence v. Texas, 539 U.S. 558, 598 (2003) (Scalia, J., dissenting).

in the streets: For a comprehensive account of how early American constitutional law lived through "the people out-of-doors," see Larry D. Kramer, *The People Themselves: Constitutionalism and Judicial Review* (New York: Oxford University Press, 2004).

what it protected against: It is worth noting that James Madison's particular views on the threat to individual rights from state legislatures were more modern — at least as they pertained to white men — but those views aren't reflected in the Bill of Rights the states ratified. Jack N. Rakove, *Original Meanings: Politics and Ideas in the Making of the Constitution* (New York: Vintage, 1997), 288–338.

xxiii Lochner v. New York: Lochner v. New York, 198 U.S. 45 (1905). The Supreme Court effectively overruled the *Lochner* case in West Coast Hotel Co. v. Parrish, 300 U.S. 379 (1937), where it upheld the constitutionality of minimum wage legislation enacted by Washington State.

xxvi   *IMS Health:* Sorrell v. IMS Health Inc., 564 U.S. 552 (2011).
       Warren McCleskey: McCleskey v. Kemp, 481 U.S. 279 (1987); "Warren McCleskey Is Dead,"
       New York Times, opinion, September 29, 1991.

xxvii *a wealthy partisan: Citizens United,* 558 U.S. 310.
       A schoolteacher: Janus, 138 S. Ct. 2448.
       Nazis clad in SS uniforms: Village of Skokie v. Nat'l Socialist Party of Am., 373 N.E.2d 21 (Ill.
       1978).
       worried about *"too much justice": McCleskey,* 481 U.S. at 339 (Brennan, J., dissenting).

xxviii *"may be more burdensome":* Washington v. Davis, 426 U.S. 229, 248 (1976).
       right to education: San Antonio Indep. Sch. Dist. v. Rodriguez, 411 U.S. 1, 54 (1973).
       Rights for people with disabilities: City of Cleburne v. Cleburne Living Ctr., Inc., 473 U.S. 432
       (1985).
       the constitutional project: I have been influenced by Robert Cover's emphasis on the impor-
       tance, in a pluralistic society, of preserving a vision of law as fundamentally ecumenical in
       character. Robert M. Cover, "Foreword — Nomos and Narrative," *Harvard Law Review* 97, no.
       1 (November 1983): 42–43. "To state the problem as one of unclear law or difference of opin-
       ion about *the* law seems to presuppose that there is a hermeneutic that is methodologically
       superior to those employed by the communities that offer their own law . . . The position that
       only the state creates law thus confuses the status of interpretation with the status of political
       domination."

xxx   *West Germany's constitutional court:* Donald P. Kommers, "Abortion and Constitution: United
       States and West Germany," *American Journal of Comparative Law* 25, no. 2 (Spring 1977): 255.

xxxii *a school's interest in "diversity":* Grutter v. Bollinger, 539 U.S. 306 (2003) (upholding the con-
       stitutionality of the University of Michigan Law School's admissions program).
       Party polarization in Congress: Nolan McCarty, *Polarization: What Everyone Needs to Know*
       (New York: Oxford University Press, 2019), 25, 31, 61–67.

xxxiii *A case about a wedding cake: Masterpiece Cakeshop,* 138 S. Ct. 1719; Jamal Greene, "Foreword:
       Rights as Trumps?," *Harvard Law Review* 132, no. 1 (November 2018): 31–32, 80–81. For pop-
       ular commentary on the case, see, for example, Tisa Wenger, "Discriminating in the Name of
       Religion? Segregationists and Slaveholders Did It, Too," *Washington Post,* December 5, 2017,
       https://www.washingtonpost.com/news/made-by-history/wp/2017/12/05/discriminating-in
       -the-name-of-religion-segregationists-and-slaveholders-did-it-too/; Montel Williams, "Mas-
       terpiece Cakeshop Reminds Me of Jim Crow. We Can't Create New 2nd-Class Citizens," *USA
       Today,* December 5, 2017, https://www.usatoday.com/story/opinion/2017/12/05/masterpiece
       -cakeshop-reminds-me-jim-crow-no-new-second-class-citizens-montel-williams-column/
       923122001/; Michael Farris, "Why Masterpiece Cakeshop Case Could Bring a Major Su-
       preme Court Ruling on Free Expression," Fox News, December 4, 2017, https://www.foxnews
       .com/opinion/why-masterpiece-cakeshop-case-could-bring-a-major-supreme-court-ruling
       -on-free-expression. For digital access to the various amicus curiae briefs submitted to the
       Supreme Court in the lead-up to its 2018 decision, see "Masterpiece Cakeshop, Ltd. v. Colo-
       rado Civil Rights Commission," SCOTUSblog, n.d., https://www.scotusblog.com/case-files/
       cases/masterpiece-cakeshop-ltd-v-colorado-civil-rights-commn/.

xxxiv *Sophocles's* Antigone: Sophocles, *Antigone,* ed. Martin L. D'Ooge (Boston: Ginn & Company,
       1890).

xxxv   *"essence of tragedy":* G. W. F. Hegel, *Hegel's Aesthetics: Lectures on Fine Art,* trans. T. M. Knox
       (Oxford: Oxford University Press, 2015), 2:1196, 1213, 1217.

xxxvi *everyone but the angels:* "If men were angels, no government would be necessary. If angels
       were to govern men, neither external nor internal controls on government would be neces-
       sary." James Madison, "No. 51: The Structure of the Government Must Furnish the Proper
       Checks and Balances Between the Different Departments," in *The Federalist Papers,* ed. Clin-
       ton Rossiter (New York: Penguin Group, 1961).

1. GETTING THE BILL OF RIGHTS RIGHT

8   *delivered a sermon:* Jim Schmidt, "The Reverend John Joachim Zubly's 'The Law of Liberty' Sermon: Calvinist Opposition to the American Revolution," *Georgia Historical Quarterly* 82, no. 2 (July 1998): 350–68; Joel A. Nichols, "A Man True to His Principles: John Joachim Zubly and Calvinism," *Journal of Church and State* 43, no. 2 (Spring 2001): 297, 301; M. C. Tyler, *The Literary History of the American Revolution,* 2nd ed. (New York: G. P. Putnam's Sons, 1897), 483, 486.

"There was a time": John J. Zubly, *The Law of Liberty: A Sermon on American Affairs, Preached at the Opening of the Provincial Congress of Georgia* (Philadelphia: Henry Miller, 1775): 1, 6–7, 19.

9   *"Let the Americans enjoy":* Zubly, *The Law of Liberty,* xix.

10   *Many prominent Framers:* Alexander Hamilton, "No. 84: Certain General and Miscellaneous Objections to the Constitution Considered and Answered," in *The Federalist Papers,* ed. Clinton Rossiter (New York: Penguin Group, 1961); James Wilson, "The Debates in the Convention of the State of Pennsylvania on the Adoption of the Federal Constitution," in *The Debates in the Several State Conventions on the Adoption of the Federal Constitution,* ed. Jonathan Elliot, 2nd ed. (Philadelphia: J. B. Lippincott, 1836), 2:435–38 (hereafter cited as *Elliot's Debates*).

Several states: Akhil Reed Amar, *The Bill of Rights: Creation and Reconstruction* (New Haven, CT: Yale University Press, 1998), 14.

Writing to Madison: Thomas Jefferson to James Madison, December 20, 1787, in *The Papers of Thomas Jefferson,* ed. Julian P. Boyd (Princeton, NJ: Princeton University Press, 1955), 12:440.

11   *ultimatums of that era:* Leonard W. Levy, *Origins of the Bill of Rights* (New Haven, CT: Yale University Press, 2001), 10–11.

we should not ascribe: Jud Campbell, "Republicanism and Natural Rights at the Founding," *Constitutional Commentary* 32, no. 1 (2017): 85; Levy, *Origins,* 10, 40 (killing off state limits).

it wasn't until Massachusetts: Levy, *Origins,* 10.

equally "self-evident": Declaration of Independence, para. 2 (1776).

George Mason: "Objections of the Hon. George Mason, One of the Delegates from Virginia in the Late Continental Convention, to the Proposed Federal Constitution," in *Elliot's Debates,* 1:494; "A Letter of the Excellency, Edmund Randolph, Esq., on the Federal Convention," in *Elliot's Debates,* 1:482.

12   *Henry had been born:* John A. Ragosta, *Patrick Henry: Proclaiming a Revolution* (New York: Routledge, 2017), 10–11.

The men sent as delegates: Levy, *Origins,* 14, 39–40, 104.

Every one of the twelve: Levy, *Origins,* 23.

The legislature and jury together: Jack N. Rakove, *Original Meanings: Politics and Ideas in the Making of the Constitution* (New York: Vintage, 1997), 294–95; Geoffrey Stone, *Perilous Times: Free Speech in Wartime from the Sedition Act of 1798 to the War on Terrorism* (New York: W. W. Norton, 2004), 43; Levy, *Origins,* 23; John Adams, "The Earl of Clarendon to William Pym," *Boston Gazette and Country Journal,* January 27, 1766, quoted in *The Political Writings of John Adams,* ed. George W. Carey (Washington, D.C.: Regnery, 2000), 650.

"The great security": James Madison, "No. 51: The Structure of the Government Must Furnish the Proper Checks and Balances Between the Different Departments," in *The Federalist Papers,* ed. Clinton Rossiter (New York: Penguin Group, 1961), 318–19.

13   *formation of the democratic culture:* Jack M. Balkin, "Cultural Democracy and the First Amendment," *Northwestern University Law Review* 110, no. 5 (2016): 1054.

14   *"write, print, utter or publish"*: An Act for the Punishment of Certain Crimes Against the
       United States (Sedition Act of 1798), ch. 74, § 2, 5 Stat. 596, 596–97 (1798) (lapsed 1801).
       The first indictment brought: Stone, *Perilous Times*, 20.
       debates over the Sedition Act: Stone, *Perilous Times*, 40.
       meant "nothing more than": William Blackstone, *Commentaries on the Laws of England* (Phil-
       adelphia: William Young Birch & Abraham Small, 1803), 4:151–52 (emphasis added).
15   *undeclared war with France*: Stone, *Perilous Times*, 34.
       Samuel Dana put it: 8 Annals of Cong. 2112 (1798) (statement of Rep. Dana).
       famously resisted: James Madison, "Virginia Resolutions of 1798, Pronouncing the Alien and
       Sedition Laws to Be Unconstitutional, and Defining the Rights of the States," in *Elliot's De-
       bates*, 4:528–29; Thomas Jefferson, "Kentucky Resolutions of 1798 and 1799," in *Elliot's De-
       bates*, 540–45.
       "the states or the people": Jefferson, "Kentucky Resolutions of 1798 and 1799," 4:545 (emphasis
       added).
       Virginia Declaration of Rights: Va. Declaration of Rights of 1776, §12. "That the freedom of
       the press is one of the great bulwarks of liberty and can never be restrained but by despotic
       governments."
       Kentucky Constitution: Ky. Const. of 1792, art. XII, cl. 7. "That the printing-press shall be
       free to every person who undertakes to examine the proceedings of the Legislature or any
       branch of Government, and no law shall ever be made to restrain the right thereof. The free
       communications of thoughts and opinions is one of the invaluable rights of man, and every
       citizen may freely speak, write, and print on any subject, being responsible for the abuse of
       that liberty."
       seditious libel continued: Levy, *Origins*, 111.
       In December 1792: 8 Annals of Cong. 2149 (1798) (statement of Rep. Otis).
16   *John Peter Zenger*: Levy, *Origins*, 105; Vincent Buranelli, ed., *The Trial of Peter Zenger* (New
       York: New York University Press, 1957), 28–40. For a detailed description of Zenger's trial, see
       Jill Lepore, *New York Burning: Liberty, Slavery, and Conspiracy in Eighteenth-Century Man-
       hattan* (New York: Vintage, 2005), 72–77.
       Prior restraints: Levy, *Origins*, 122, 127; John H. Langbein, Renée Lettow Lerner, and Bruce P.
       Smith, *History of the Common Law*, 2nd ed. (New York: Aspen, 2009), 478–79.
       Punishing speech after the fact: Levy, *Origins*, 122.
       libel prosecutions were rare: Langbein, Lerner, and Smith, *History of the Common Law*, 478–79.
       viewed the religion provisions: Amar, *The Bill of Rights*, 32–33.
       Churches in colonial America: Patricia U. Bonomi, *Under the Cope of Heaven: Religion, Society,
       and Politics in Colonial America* (Oxford: Oxford University Press, 2003), 3, 6, 88, 212, 218,
       222; Jon Butler, *Awash in a Sea of Faith: Christianizing the American People* (Cambridge, MA:
       Harvard University Press, 1990), 105–6, 166–67, 171, 201–2.
17   *Selectmen would canvass*: Bonomi, *Under the Cope of Heaven*, 5–6.
       "assumed responsibility for propagating": Butler, *Awash in a Sea of Faith*, 166.
       Local parishes were permitted: Michael Zuckerman, *Peaceable Kingdoms: New England Towns
       in the Eighteenth Century* (New York: Knopf, 1970), 38–40.
18   *This history makes plain*: Amar, *The Bill of Rights*, 32–33.
       State churches were: Butler, *Awash in a Sea of Faith*, 202, 258–59, 267–68; Joseph Story, *Com-
       mentaries on the Constitution of the United States*, ed. Thomas Cooley (Boston: Little, Brown,
       1873), § 1868; Kellen Funk, "Church Corporations and the Conflict of Laws in Antebellum
       America," *Journal of Law and Religion* 32, no. 2 (July 17): 263.
       "Probably at the time": Story, *Commentaries on the Constitution*, § 1868.
       the runt piglet: William S. Fields and David T. Hardy, "The Third Amendment and the Issue
       of the Maintenance of Standing Armies: A Legal History," *American Journal of Legal History*
       35, no. 4 (October 1991): 395.

"this amendment seems": Samuel F. Miller, *Lectures on the Constitution of the United States* (New York: Banks & Brothers, 1893), 646.

19   *opposes a United Nations treaty*: Colum Lynch, "U.N. Approves Global Arms Treaty," *Washington Post,* April 2, 2013.

Wayne LaPierre said: Christopher Ingraham, "What Arms Looked Like When the 2nd Amendment Was Written," *Washington Post,* June 13, 2016.

At the time the Second Amendment: Adam Winkler, *Gunfight: The Battle over the Right to Bear Arms in America* (New York: W. W. Norton, 2011), 115–17; Pa. Const. of 1776, art. XIII; N.C. Const. of 1776, Declaration of Rights, art. XVII; Vt. Const. of 1777, §18; Mass. Const. of 1780, ch. 1, art. XVII.

Less than two years: Pa. Const. of 1776, art. XIII; Act of Apr. 1, 1778, ch. 61, § 5, 1777–1778 Pa. Statutes at Large 238, 242.

Massachusetts included: Mass. Const. of 1780, ch. 1, art. XVII.

forbid Boston residents: An Act in Addition to the Several Acts Already Made for the Prudent Storage of Gun-Powder Within the Town of Boston, ch. 13, 1783 Mass. Acts 218–219.

20   *transporting of gunpowder*: Act of June 26, 1792, ch. 7, 1792 Mass. Acts 21.

1796 constitution: Tenn. Const. of 1796, § 26; Act of October 19, 1821, ch. 13, 1821 Tenn. Pub. Acts 15; Saul Cornell and Nathan DeDino, "A Well Regulated Right: The Early American Origins of Gun Control," *Fordham Law Review* 73 (2004): 513.

Saul Cornell has noted: Saul Cornell, *A Well-Regulated Militia: The Founding Fathers and the Origins of Gun Control in America* (New York: Oxford University Press, 2006), 141–43.

An inheritance: Bill of Rights, 1688, 1 W. & M. c. 2 (Eng.). "That the subjects which are Protestants may have arms for their defence suitable to their conditions and as allowed by law."

Apprehension of fugitives: Levy, *Origins,* 136.

A white man had: Cornell and DeDino, "A Well Regulated Right," 493, 505.

21   *Akhil Reed Amar notes*: Amar, *The Bill of Rights,* 51.

"boldness, enterprise": Levy, *Origins,* 141–42.

this forgotten amendment: Engblom v. Carey, 677 F.2d 957 (2d Cir. 1982).

a standing federal army: Fields and Hardy, "The Third Amendment," 395; Amar, *The Bill of Rights,* 62.

22   *"A man's house"*: Levy, *Origins,* 151.

Consider some of the complaints: Oliver Morton Dickerson, comp., *Boston Under Military Rule <1768–1769> as Revealed in a Journal of the Times* (Boston: Chapman & Grimes, 1936), 71–75, 90, 93, 99, 108, 114.

23   *about five thousand slaves*: Lorenzo Johnston Greene, *The Negro in Colonial New England* (New York: Columbia University Press, 1942), 79–82.

Adams's October 29, 1768: Dickerson, *Boston Under Military Rule,* 16, 18, 21.

"[travel] over your estates": Tom W. Bell, "The Third Amendment: Forgotten but Not Gone," *William & Mary Bill of Rights* 2, no. 1 (1993): 127.

24   *For a range of crimes*: Robert Bartlett, *Trial by Fire and Water: The Medieval Judicial Order* (New York: Oxford University Press, 1986), 1, 2, 25.

Trial by battle: Theodore F. T. Plucknett, *A Concise History of the Common Law,* 5th ed. (Boston: Little, Brown, 1956), 116–18.

King Henry II: Levy, *Origins,* 210–13; Langbein, Lerner, and Smith, *History of the Common Law,* 97.

The jury took on: John W. Baldwin, "The Intellectual Preparation for the Canon of 1215 Against Ordeals," *Speculum* 36 (October 1961): 613–14.

With priests no longer: Levy, *Origins,* 210–13.

25   *Medieval juries*: Langbein, Lerner, and Smith, *History of the Common Law,* 208, 224–27, 479; James Bradley Thayer, *A Preliminary Treatise on Evidence at the Common Law* (Boston: Little, Brown, 1898), 90–91.

brim with jury protections: Amar, *The Bill of Rights,* 88–95; Levy, *Origins,* 227; Leonard W. Levy, "Bill of Rights," in *Essays on the Making of the Constitution,* ed. Leonard W. Levy, 2nd ed. (Oxford: Oxford University Press, 1987), 258, 269; Albert W. Alschuler and Andrew G. Deiss, "A Brief History of the Criminal Jury in the United States," *Chicago Law Review* 61, no. 3 (1994): 867, 869–70.

William Grayson: "Convention of Virginia," in *Elliot's Debates,* 3:569.

An act allowing: John Phillip Reid, *Constitutional History of the American Revolution* (Madison: University of Wisconsin Press, 1995), 54–55.

The other rights: Amar, *The Bill of Rights,* 112–14; Story, *Commentaries on the Constitution,* § 1787.

26   *The importance of juries:* Amar, *The Bill of Rights,* 84–85.

The right was first recognized: Levy, *Origins,* 196–97, 204, 222.

27   *The amendment contains:* Amar, *The Bill of Rights,* 68.

best protected by legislatures: Amar, *The Bill of Rights,* 69–71.

28   *In 1765, when Blackstone's:* Levy, *Origins,* 234–38.

Titus Oates: Levy, *Origins,* 236–37; Anthony F. Granucci, "'Nor Cruel and Unusual Punishments Inflicted': The Original Meaning," *California Law Review* 57 (October 1969): 856, 858.

traitors could be burned alive: John F. Stinneford, "The Original Meaning of 'Unusual': The Eighth Amendment as a Bar to Cruel Innovation," *Northwestern University Law Review* 102 (2008): 1742.

That fate was reserved: Lepore, *New York Burning,* xii.

30   *"One object":* Hamilton, "No. 84," 515.

typically involves negotiation: Jeremy Waldron, "The Core of the Case Against Judicial Review," *Yale Law Journal* 115, no. 6 (April 2006): 1349.

31   *Reverend Zubly's fame:* Marjorie Daniel, "John Joachim Zubly — Georgia Pamphleteer of the Revolution," *Georgia Historical Quarterly* 19 (March 1935): 6; Nichols, "A Man True to His Principles," 302; William E. Pauley Jr., "Tragic Hero: Loyalist John J. Zubly," *Journal of Presbyterian History* 54 (Spring 1976): 61, 69.

2. RIGHTS MEET RACE

32   *"had no rights":* Dred Scott v. Sandford, 60 U.S. 393, 407 (1857).

33   *reinforce the tyranny:* Ronald Dworkin, *Taking Rights Seriously* (Cambridge, MA: Harvard University Press, 1977), 191–92, 239–40.

the tale of Phineas Gage: Antonio Damasio, *Descartes' Error: Emotion, Reason, and the Human Brain* (New York: Putnam, 1994), 3–8.

34   Marbury: Marbury v. Madison, 5 U.S. 137 (1803).

American legal canon: J. M. Balkin and Sanford Levinson, "The Canons of Constitutional Law," *Harvard Law Review* 111, no. 4 (February 1998): 963–1024.

decisions are famously wrong: Jamal Greene, "The Anticanon," *Harvard Law Review* 125, no. 2 (December 2011): 392n66.

earliest of the cases: Don E. Fehrenbacher, *The Dred Scott Case: Its Significance in American Law and Politics* (New York: Oxford University Press, 1978), 243–47.

35   *"blacks were either":* Leon F. Litwack, *North of Slavery: The Negro in the Free States* (Chicago: University of Chicago Press, 1961), 97. The term "Jim Crow" was used to describe Massachusetts railcars as early as 1841. Gilbert Thomas Stephenson, "The Separation of the Races in Public Conveyances," *American Political Science Review* 3, no. 2 (May 1909): 181.

36   *Black voting rights:* Roger D. Bridges, "Antebellum Struggle for Citizenship," *Journal of the Illinois State Historical Society* 108, no. 3 (Fall 2015): 296–97; Phyllis F. Field, *The Politics of Race in New York: The Struggle for Black Suffrage in the Civil War Era* (Ithaca, NY: Cornell

University Press, 1982), 19; C. Vann Woodward, *The Strange Career of Jim Crow,* 2nd rev. ed. (New York: Oxford University Press, 1966), 19–20.

No African American: Albert W. Alschuler and Andrew G. Deiss, "A Brief History of the Criminal Jury in the United States," *University of Chicago Law Review* 61, no. 3 (Summer 1994): 884.

In Indiana: Litwack, *North of Slavery,* 70. The 1851 Indiana Constitution outright banned any "negro or mulatto" from entering the state. Ind. Const. of 1851, art. XIII, § 1 (repealed 1881). The 1848 Illinois Constitution obligated the state legislature immediately to pass a law prohibiting Black immigration and settlement. Ill. Const. of 1848, art. XIV. The general assembly obliged in 1853. Elmer Gertz, "The Black Laws of Illinois," *Journal of the Illinois State Historical Society* 56, no. 3 (Autumn 1963): 466. Oregon excluded free Blacks by statute in 1844, then added an exclusion provision to its 1857 constitution. Quintard Taylor, "Slaves and Free Men: Blacks in the Oregon Country, 1840–1860," *Oregon Historical Quarterly* 83, no. 2 (Summer 1982): 155; Ore. Const. of 1857, art. I, § 35 (repealed 1926).

an 1842 Supreme Court decision: Prigg v. Pennsylvania, 41 U.S. 539 (1842).

"it is too clear": Dred Scott, 60 U.S. at 410.

38   *It was a test case:* Cheryl I. Harris, "The Story of Plessy v. Ferguson: The Death and Resurrection of Racial Formalism," in *Constitutional Law Stories,* ed. Michael C. Dorf (New York: Foundation Press, 2004), 209–12; Sheldon Novick, "Homer Plessy's Forgotten Plea for Inclusion: Seeing Color, Erasing Color-Lines," *West Virginia Law Review* 118, no. 3 (2016): 1193.

a tsunami of segregation laws: Eric Foner, *Reconstruction: America's Unfinished Revolution, 1863–1877* (New York: HarperCollins, 2005), 567–81.

39   *"I think the policy":* Foner, *Reconstruction,* 581.

"is at liberty": Plessy v. Ferguson, 163 U.S. 537, 550–51 (1896).

"The curves of callousness": Charles L. Black Jr., "The Lawfulness of Segregation Decisions," *Yale Law Journal* 69, no. 3 (January 1960): 422n8.

40   *"promissory note":* Martin Luther King Jr., "I Have a Dream" (speech, March on Washington for Jobs and Freedom, Washington, D.C., August 28, 1963), available at http://avalon.law.yale .edu/20th_century/mlk01.asp.

"right to make a contract": Lochner v. New York, 198 U.S. 45, 53 (1905).

41   *"a society of island communities":* Robert H. Wiebe, *The Search for Order, 1877–1920* (New York: Hill & Wang, 1967), xiii–xiv.

More than three times: Sean Dennis Cashman, *America in the Gilded Age: From the Death of Lincoln to the Rise of Theodore Roosevelt* (New York: New York University Press, 1993), 100.

"Lawmakers by the score": Wiebe, *The Search for Order,* 13–28.

Among those attracted: Richard Hofstadter, *The Age of Reform: From Bryan to F.D.R.* (New York: Knopf, 1955), 8–9, 23.

42   *"Crazy old buildings":* Jacob A. Riis, *How the Other Half Lives* (New York: Trow's Printing & Bookbinding, 1890), 12–14.

43   *Nearly every member:* Planned Parenthood of Southeastern Pennsylvania v. Casey, 505 U.S. 833, 861–62 (1992) (O'Connor, Souter, and Kennedy, JJ., issuing the opinion of the Court); Casey, 505 U.S. at 959–62 (Rehnquist, CJ., with White, Scalia, and Thomas, JJ., concurring in the judgment in part and dissenting in part); McDonald v. City of Chicago, 561 U.S. 742, 878 (2010) (Stevens, J., dissenting).

"line of authority": Nomination of Judge Ruth Bader Ginsburg to Be an Associate Justice of the Supreme Court of the United States: Hearings Before the Senate Committee on the Judiciary, 103d Cong. 270, 288 (1993) (statements of Judge Ruth Bader Ginsburg). Justice Thomas affirmed at his confirmation hearing that "it [is] the role of the legislature to make . . . complex decisions about health and safety and work standards." *Nomination of Judge Clarence Thomas to Be an Associate Justice of the Supreme Court of the United States: Hearings Before the Senate Committee on the Judiciary, Part 1,* 102d Cong. 173, 241 (1991) (statements of Judge Clarence Thomas).

44   *Every American law student:* Sheldon M. Novick, *Honorable Justice: The Life of Oliver Wendell Holmes* (Boston: Little, Brown, 1989), 8–18, 95; Oliver Wendell Holmes Sr., "The Contagiousness of Puerperal Fever," *New England Quarterly Journal of Medicine and Surgery,* no. 1 (March 1843): 503–29; Oliver Wendell Holmes Sr., "The Professor's Story," *Atlantic Monthly,* January 1860, 91 (referring to the "Brahmin Caste of New England," from his 1861 novel, *Elsie Venner*).

45   *"three generations of imbeciles":* Buck v. Bell, 274 U.S. 200, 207 (1927).
       Holmes was always: M. A. De Wolfe Howe, *Holmes of the Breakfast-Table* (New York: Oxford University Press, 1939), 64; Novick, *Honorable Justice,* 202; Charles Henry Pearson, *National Life and Character: A Forecast* (New York: Macmillan, 1893), 30, 64.
       startling derring-do: Novick, *Honorable Justice,* 34–37, 46–52, 66, 77–78, 81.

46   *so much as a word:* G. Edward White, *Oliver Wendell Holmes, Jr.* (Oxford: Oxford University Press, 2006), 11.
       Holmes's injuries: Novick, *Honorable Justice,* 61, 71, 77–89.
       Many of his friends: Novick, *Honorable Justice,* 15, 80; Howe, *Holmes of the Breakfast-Table,* 24, 66–67.

47   *During the war:* Novick, *Honorable Justice,* 34, 54, 74, 80.
       Thomas Malthus believed: Edwin W. James, "The Malthusian Doctrine and War," *Scientific Monthly* 2, no. 3 (March 1916): 263; Thomas Robert Malthus, *An Essay on the Principle of Population* (London: J. Johnson, 1798), 31.
       "naïve idea": Novick, *Honorable Justice,* 34–39.

48   *never liked southerners:* Novick, *Honorable Justice,* 22, 60, 72–73; Howe, *Holmes of the Breakfast-Table,* 70–71.
       "a bad man": Oliver Wendell Holmes Jr., "The Path of the Law," *Harvard Law Review* 10, no. 8 (March 1897): 459–62.
       In 1902, Jackson Giles: Giles v. Harris, 189 U.S. 475 (1903); Greene, "The Anticanon," 429–30; Richard H. Pildes, "Democracy, Anti-democracy, and the Canon," *Constitutional Commentary* 17, no. 2 (Spring 2000): 299–317.

49   *Between Reconstruction:* J. Morgan Kousser, *The Shaping of Southern Politics: Suffrage Restriction and the Establishment of the One-Party South, 1880–1910* (New Haven, CT: Yale University Press, 1974), 42, 61, 197, 241.
       "The [complaint] imports": Giles, 189 U.S. at 488.

50   *"The importance of things":* Novick, *Honorable Justice,* 259.
       protects the right to contract: Lochner, 198 U.S. at 53.
       "It is settled": Lochner, 198 U.S. at 74–76 (Holmes, J., dissenting).

51   *a favorite of social Darwinists:* Robert C. Bannister, *Social Darwinism: Science and Myth in Anglo-American Social Thought* (Philadelphia: Temple University Press, 1979), 34–38. Herbert Spencer originated the phrase "survival of the fittest." George Claeys, "The 'Survival of the Fittest' and the Origins of Social Darwinism," *Journal of the History of Ideas* 61, no. 2 (April 2000): 227.
       "The word 'liberty'": Lochner, 198 U.S. at 76.
       more celebrated than Holmes's: Novick, *Honorable Justice,* 282.

52   *The Harlans were ambivalent:* Tinsley E. Yarbrough, *Judicial Enigma: The First Justice Harlan* (New York: Oxford University Press, 1995), 8–9, 38–56.
       Harlan didn't mourn: Yarbrough, *Judicial Enigma,* 57–61.

53   *And yet something changed:* Yarbrough, *Judicial Enigma,* 60–66.
       a Louisville law practice: Yarbrough, *Judicial Enigma,* 67.
       Harlan's half brother: Yarbrough, *Judicial Enigma,* 10.
       "tobacco-spittin' judges": Loren P. Beth, *John Marshall Harlan: The Last Whig Justice* (Lexington: University Press of Kentucky, 1992), 174.
       "my lion-hearted friend": Beth, *John Marshall Harlan,* 174; Novick, *Honorable Justice,* 254.

54   *"It is true fellow-citizens":* Yarbrough, *Judicial Enigma,* 77.

"public accommodations": The Civil Rights Cases, 109 U.S. 3, 26–62 (1883) (Harlan, J., dissenting); Civil Rights Act of 1875, 18 Stat. 335–337 (1875) (overturned 1883).
prosecute a private school: Berea College v. Kentucky, 211 U.S. 45, 58–70 (1908) (Harlan, J., dissenting).
"our Constitution is color-blind": Plessy, 163 U.S. 537, 552–64 (Harlan, J., dissenting).
Jackson Giles's effort: Giles, 189 U.S. at 493–504 (Harlan, J., dissenting).
New York bakery case: Lochner, 198 U.S. at 65–68 (Harlan, J., dissenting).
"Speaking generally": Lochner, 198 U.S. at 65–68 (Harlan, J., dissenting).
55   *"pure and healthful"*: Lochner, 198 U.S. at 70 (Harlan, J., dissenting).

3. RIGHTSISM

58   *"of laws, and not of men"*: Mass. Const. of 1780, art. XXX.
59   *Holmes's disciples and friends*: For an illuminating discussion of the appropriation of Holmes by young Progressives, see G. Edward White, *Justice Oliver Wendell Holmes: Law and the Inner Self* (New York: Oxford University Press, 1993), 354–411.
more famous than Holmes: Sheldon M. Novick, *Honorable Justice: The Life of Oliver Wendell Holmes* (Boston: Little, Brown, 1989), 282.
lived the American dream: H. N. Hirsch, *The Enigma of Felix Frankfurter* (New York: Basic Books, 1981), 13, 17, 20, 24.
60   *When Stimson became*: Noah Feldman, *Scorpions: The Battles and Triumphs of FDR's Great Supreme Court Justices* (New York: Twelve, 2010), 9.
child of working-class Jewish immigrants: Hirsch, *The Enigma*, 23–24.
Dupont Circle boardinghouse: Brad Snyder, *The House of Truth: A Washington Political Salon and the Foundations of American Liberalism* (New York: Oxford University Press, 2017), 1–3.
roommates hosted dinners: Snyder, *The House of Truth*.
"the gay soldier": Novick, *Honorable Justice*, 319.
five feet, five inches tall: Feldman, *Scorpions*, 5.
grab firm hold: Feldman, *Scorpions*, 3.
Holmes's Northwest D.C. home: G. Edward White, *Oliver Wendell Holmes, Jr.* (Oxford: Oxford University Press, 2006), 101.
"the King": Hirsch, *The Enigma*, 42.
"To know you": Hirsch, *The Enigma*, 87.
61   *"It will be many years"*: Hirsch, *The Enigma*, 33.
"conception of the Constitution": Felix Frankfurter, *Mr. Justice Holmes and the Supreme Court*, 2nd ed. (Cambridge, MA: Belknap Press, 1961), 59.
first Jewish professor: Feldman, *Scorpions*, 11.
"Much of our labor": Hirsch, *The Enigma*, 42.
62   *a glowing study*: Felix Frankfurter, "The Constitutional Opinions of Justice Holmes," *Harvard Law Review* 29, no. 6 (April 1916): 683.
"the philosophy behind": Felix Frankfurter and James Landis, *The Business of the Supreme Court: A Study in the Federal Judicial System* (New York: Macmillan, 1928), 192.
struck down a D.C. law: Adkins v. Children's Hospital, 261 U.S. 525 (1923).
"Holmes' classic dissent": Frankfurter, *Mr. Justice Holmes*, 64.
returned to Washington in 1917: Hirsch, *The Enigma*, 52–53; Feldman, *Scorpions*, 11.
rekindled the relationship: Michael E. Parrish, *Felix Frankfurter and His Times: The Reform Years* (New York: Free Press, 1982), 199–200.
tended to be circumspect: Parrish, *Felix Frankfurter and His Times*, 220–21.
63   *Some newspapers offered*: Parrish, *Felix Frankfurter and His Times*, 221.

coined the term: Raymond Moley, *After Seven Years* (New York: Harper & Brothers, 1939), 23.

"patriarchal sorcerer": Moley, *After Seven Years,* 285.

"the most influential single individual": Feldman, *Scorpions,* 39; Matthew Josephson, "Profiles: Jurist-I," *The New Yorker,* November 30, 1940, 26.

"plague" of young Washington lawyers: Melvin I. Urofsky, *Felix Frankfurter: Judicial Restraint and Individual Liberties* (Boston: Twayne, 1991), 36.

These disciples: Hirsch, *The Enigma,* 103–17.

His fingerprints were everywhere: Jamal Greene, "The Anticanon," *Harvard Law Review* 125, no. 2 (December 2011): 451; Feldman, *Scorpions,* 69, 78, 83, 84, 127, 165–66, 383; Urofsky, *Felix Frankfurter: Judicial Restraint,* 37.

64 *declining Roosevelt's offer:* Feldman, *Scorpions,* 39.

"for men concerned with": Joseph P. Lash, *From the Diaries of Felix Frankfurter* (New York: W. W. Norton, 1975), 50.

leading constitutional law scholars: James Vorenberg, "In Memoriam: Paul A. Freund," *Harvard Law Review* 106, no. 1 (November 1992): 13.

65 *Erwin Griswold:* Parrish, *Felix Frankfurter and His Times,* 224; Feldman, *Scorpions,* 476n17.

Charles Fairman: Richard L. Aynes, "Charles Fairman, Felix Frankfurter, and the Fourteenth Amendment," *Chicago-Kent Law Review* 170, no. 3 (1995): 1199–204; Feldman, *Scorpions,* 315.

"An entire philosophy": Charles Fairman, *American Constitutional Decisions,* rev. ed. (New York: Henry Holt, 1950), 335.

Some would go on: Greene, "The Anticanon," 451.

These men: And they were men. Frankfurter never hired a female law clerk, even resisting Albert Sacks's entreaties to hire Ruth Bader Ginsburg in 1961. This even though Ginsburg was Jewish and, in accord with Frankfurter's preferences in women, never wore pants. Jane Sherron de Hart, *Ruth Bader Ginsburg: A Life* (New York: Vintage, 2018), 84–85.

66 *Filled Milk Act of 1923:* United States v. Carolene Products, 304 U.S. 144, 152 (1938).

"a reasonable man might think": Lochner v. New York, 198 U.S. 45, 76 (1905) (Holmes, J., dissenting).

the fourth footnote: Carolene Products, 304 U.S. at 152 n.4.

John Hart Ely's: John Hart Ely, *Democracy and Distrust* (Cambridge, MA: Harvard University Press, 1980), 75–88.

67 *"natural outcome":* Lochner, 198 U.S. at 76.

an Oklahoma optician challenged: Williamson v. Lee Optical, 348 U.S. 483 (1955).

all the justices save Frankfurter: West Virginia State Board of Education v. Barnette, 319 U.S. 624 (1943).

68 *Connecticut had banned:* David J. Garrow, *Liberty and Sexuality: The Right to Privacy and the Making of Roe v. Wade* (New York: Macmillan, 1994), 15–16.

The plaintiffs in the case: Poe v. Ullman, 367 U.S. 497, 498–501 (1961).

Frankfurter decided to punt: Poe, 367 U.S. at 507–9.

69 *initiated a prosecution:* Poe, 367 U.S. at 501; State v. Nelson, 11 A.2d 856 (Conn. 1940).

The Planned Parenthood League of Connecticut: Garrow, *Liberty and Sexuality,* 196–207.

70 *The sit-in movement:* C. Vann Woodward, *The Strange Career of Jim Crow,* 2nd rev. ed. (New York: Oxford University Press, 1966), 170–71; Garner v. State of La., 368 U.S. 157 (1961); Griffin v. State of Md., 378 U.S. 130 (1964); Bell v. State of Md., 378 U.S. 226, 241 (1964).

71 *Supreme Court's blessing:* Heart of Atlanta Motel v. United States, 379 U.S. 241 (1964); Katzenbach v. McClung, 379 U.S. 294 (1964); Daniel v. Paul, 395 U.S. 298 (1969).

passage of the Civil Rights Act: Helen B. Shaffer, "School Desegregation: 1954–1964," in *Editorial Research Reports* (Washington D.C.: CQ Press, 1964), 1:301, 305–6.

shut down its public school system: Jill Ogline Titus, *Brown's Battleground: Students, Segrega-*

tionists, and the Struggle for Justice in Prince Edward County, Virginia (Chapel Hill: University of North Carolina Press, 2011), 10.

"freedom of choice" plans: Green v. County Sch. Board of New Kent County, Va., 391 U.S. 430 (1968).

women consistently lost: Bradwell v. Illinois, 83 U.S. 130 (1873); Goesaert v. Cleary, 335 U.S. 464 (1948); Hoyt v. Florida, 368 U.S. 57, 62 (1961).

72   *"fact of life":* Cary Franklin, "Inventing the 'Traditional Concept' of Sex Discrimination," *Harvard Law Review* 125, no. 6 (April 2012): 1321–22; *Report of the Committee on Home and Community to the President's Commission on the Status of Women* (President's Commission on the Status of Women, Washington, D.C., October 1963), 9.

added to the bill: Franklin, "Inventing the 'Traditional Concept,'" 1320.

Equal Employment Opportunity Commission: Franklin, "Inventing the 'Traditional Concept,'" 1340.

73   The Feminine Mystique: Betty Friedan, *The Feminine Mystique* (New York: W. W. Norton, 1963); Franklin, "Inventing the 'Traditional Concept,'" 1339; Louis Menand, "Books as Bombs," *The New Yorker,* January 24, 2011, 76.

The government's shoddy enforcement: Franklin, "Inventing the 'Traditional Concept,'" 1342.

At the time of the Civil Rights Act: Jo Freeman, "How 'Sex' Got into Title VII: Persistent Opportunism as a Maker of Public Policy," *Law and Inequality* 9, no. 2 (March 1991): 163–64.

cases running from the 1920s: Nixon v. Herndon, 273 U.S. 536 (1927); Smith v. Allwright, 321 U.S. 649 (1944); Terry v. Adams, 345 U.S. 461 (1953).

Voting Rights Act (VRA): Voting Rights Act of 1965, Pub. L. No. 89-110, § 5, 79 Stat. 437–46 (1965).

74   *couldn't collect poll taxes:* Harper v. Va. Bd. of Elec., 383 U.S. 663 (1966).

"one man, one vote": Wesberry v. Sanders, 376 U.S. 1, 7–8 (1964); Reynolds v. Sims, 377 U.S. 533, 562–63 (1964).

Frankfurter's last significant opinion: Urofsky, *Felix Frankfurter: Judicial Restraint,* 171–72; Baker v. Carr, 369 U.S. 186, 266 (1962) (Frankfurter, J., dissenting). In that case, Frankfurter called the Court's intervention into redistricting "a massive repudiation of the experience of our whole past" (at 267).

illegally seized evidence: Mapp v. Ohio, 367 U.S. 643 (1961).

too poor to afford a lawyer: Gideon v. Wainwright, 372 U.S. 335 (1963).

present during their interrogation: Escobedo v. Illinois, 378 U.S. 478 (1964).

"right to remain silent": Miranda v. Arizona, 384 U.S. 436 (1966).

mass use of automobiles: Sarah A. Seo, *Policing the Open Road* (Cambridge, MA: Harvard University Press, 2019), 15–20, 136–42.

75   *a group headed by A. Philip Randolph:* Mary-Rose Papandrea, "The Story of *New York Times Co. v. Sullivan*," in *First Amendment Stories,* ed. Richard W. Garnett and Andrew Koppelman (New York: Thomson Reuters/Foundation Press, 2012), 230–33.

trivial factual errors: New York Times Co. v. Sullivan, 376 U.S. 254, 258–59 (1964).

Claiming they had been defamed: Papandrea, "The Story of *New York Times Co. v. Sullivan*," 236–37, 241–42.

Civil damages actions: Sullivan, 376 U.S. at 294–95 (J. Black, concurring); Papandrea, "The Story of *New York Times Co. v. Sullivan*," 237, 242.

76   *The Supreme Court recognized:* Sullivan, 376 U.S. at 279–80.

overturned disorderly conduct charges: Gregory v. City of Chicago, 394 U.S. 111 (1969).

one of several cases: Terminiello v. City of Chicago, 337 U.S. 1 (1949); Edwards v. South Carolina, 372 U.S. 229 (1963); Cox v. Louisiana, 379 U.S. 536 (1965).

77   *a groundbreaking article:* Charles A. Reich, "The New Property," *Yale Law Journal* 73, no. 5 (April 1965): 733.

"the inevitable outgrowth": Reich, "The New Property," 778.

"constitutional right to talk politics": McAuliffe v. City of New Bedford, 29 N.E. 517, 517 (Mass. 1892).

public school teacher's right: Pickering v. Board of Education, 391 U.S. 563 (1968).

poor family's right: Dandridge v. Williams, 397 U.S. 471 (1970).

right to equal funding: San Antonio Indep. Sch. Dist. v. Rodriguez, 411 U.S. 1 (1973).

right not to be fired: Board of Regents v. Roth, 408 U.S. 564 (1972); Perry v. Sindermann, 408 U.S. 593 (1972).

kicked off the welfare rolls: Goldberg v. Kelly, 397 U.S. 254 (1970).

driver's license suspended: Bell v. Burson, 402 U.S. 535 (1971).

78   *At the time of*: Charles R. Epps, *The Rights Revolution: Lawyers, Activists, and Supreme Courts in Comparative Perspective* (Chicago: University of Chicago Press, 1998), 2; Richard L. Pacelle Jr., *The Transformation of the Supreme Court's Agenda* (Boulder, CO: Westview Press, 1991), 138.

protected set of commitments: Kenji Yoshino, "The New Equal Protection," *Harvard Law Review* 124, no. 3 (January 2011): 747.

79   *joined the Ku Klux Klan*: Feldman, *Scorpions*, 57–59.

On Black's view: Hugo L. Black, "The Bill of Rights," *New York University Law Review* 35, no. 4 (April 1960): 865–81.

"I like my privacy as well": Griswold v. Connecticut, 381 U.S. 479, 510 (1965) (Black, J., dissenting).

80   *He circulated his first draft*: Garrow, *Liberty and Sexuality*, 245.

had recently recognized it: Natl. Ass'n for Advancement of Colored People v. State of Ala. ex rel. Patterson, 357 U.S. 449 (1958).

"the association between husband and wife": Garrow, *Liberty and Sexuality*, 245.

circulated the draft privately: Garrow, *Liberty and Sexuality*, 246–48.

"Specific guarantees": Griswold, 381 U.S. at 484–86.

81   *game of textual manipulation*: Jeremy Waldron, "The Core of the Case Against Judicial Review," *Yale Law Journal* 115, no. 6 (April 2006): 1380–85.

"confined to the specific terms": Griswold, 381 U.S. at 486 (Goldberg, J., concurring).

82   *"the traditions and (collective) conscience"*: Griswold, 381 U.S. at 493.

Goldberg was satisfied: Griswold, 381 U.S. at 495.

83   *Brennan himself famously*: Seth Stern and Stephen Wermiel, *Justice Brennan: Liberal Champion* (Boston: Houghton Mifflin Harcourt, 2010), 196.

Harlan came to the Court: Tinsley Yarbrough, *John Marshall Harlan: Great Dissenter of the Warren Court* (New York: Oxford University Press, 1992), 13, 82, 119.

84   *He and Frankfurter knew*: Yarbrough, *John Marshall Harlan*, 16.

Frankfurter sensed an ally: Yarbrough, *John Marshall Harlan*, 119–33.

Harlan's 613 opinions: Yarbrough, *John Marshall Harlan*, viii.

"has not been reduced": Poe, 367 U.S. at 542 (Harlan, J., dissenting).

far from demonizing Lochner: Poe, 367 U.S. at 543; Allgeyer v. Louisiana, 165 U.S. 578 (1897).

85   *"No formula"*: Poe, 367 U.S. at 542.

In the specific context: Poe, 367 U.S. at 448–555.

a "fundamental" right to privacy: Griswold, 381 U.S. at 485–86.

4. "TOO MUCH JUSTICE"

92   *wanted to feed the pigeons*: Bundesverfassungsgericht [BVerfG] [Federal Constitutional Court], May 23, 1980, 54 Entscheidungen des Bundesverfassungsgerichts [BVerfG] 143, 1980 (Ger.), http://www.servat.unibe.ch/dfr/bv054143.html.

93   *protected under the West German Constitution*: Grundgesetz für die Bundesrepublik Deutsch-

land [GG] [Basic Law for the Federal Republic of Germany], May 23, 1949, art. II, § 1, translation at http://www.gesetze-im-internet.de/englisch_gg/index.html.

address these harms: 54 BVerfG 143 (Ger.).

94   *walkout at Edgewood High School:* Paul A. Sracic, *San Antonio v. Rodriguez and the Pursuit of Equal Education* (Lawrence: University Press of Kansas, 2006), 19–20.

poorest school district: San Antonio Indep. Sch. Dist. v. Rodriguez, 411 U.S. 1, 11–13 (1973).

Demetrio Rodriguez: Sracic, *San Antonio,* 20.

rejected Rodriguez's claims: Rodriguez, 411 U.S. at 1.

95   *"financing public education": Rodriguez,* 411 U.S. at 17.

Texas's school financing scheme: Rodriguez, 411 U.S. at 12.

96   *residential racial segregation:* Sracic, *San Antonio,* 10–12.

important school desegregation case: Keyes v. Sch. Dist. No. 1, Denver, 413 U.S. 189, 191 (1973).

Texas law placed a cap: Rodriguez, 411 U.S. at 64–67 (White, J., dissenting).

didn't even involve wealth discrimination: Rodriguez, 411 U.S. at 19–25.

97   *"perhaps the most important function":* Brown v. Board of Education of Topeka, 347 U.S. 483, 493 (1954).

"grave significance": Rodriguez, 411 U.S. at 30.

"logical limitations": Rodriguez, 411 U.S. at 37.

son of a Richmond area: John C. Jeffries Jr., *Justice Lewis F. Powell, Jr.: A Biography* (New York: Charles Scribner's Sons, 1994), 14–17; Earl M. Maltz, "The Triumph of the Southern Man: *Dowell, Shelby County,* and the Jurisprudence of Justice Lewis F. Powell, Jr.," *Duke Journal of Constitutional Law and Public Policy* 14, no. 1 (June 2019): 171.

98   *withdrawn his name:* Jeffries, *Justice Lewis F. Powell,* 1–6.

compulsory racial integration: Jeffries, *Justice Lewis F. Powell,* 140.

attended a school with white children: Tina Eshleman, "An Incomplete Legacy," *Richmond Magazine,* November 4, 2018, https://richmondmagazine.com/news/sunday-story/an-incomplete -legacy/.

"radical leftists": Asad Rahim, "Diversity to Deradicalize," October 14, 2019, accessed August 25, 2020, https://ssrn.com/abstract−3469365.

99   *One hundred fifty countries:* This number was obtained via a search on the Constitute website, June 17, 2020, https://www.constituteproject.org/.

India, for example: "Population Ages 0–14, Total," World Bank, accessed December 1, 2019, https://data.worldbank.org/indicator/SP.POP.0014.TO; "Rural Population (% of Total Population)," World Bank, accessed December 1, 2019, https://data.worldbank.org/indicator/ SP.RUR.TOTL.ZS; "Poverty Headcount Ratio at $1.90 a Day (2011 PPP) (% of Population) —India," World Bank, accessed June 17, 2020, https://data.worldbank.org/indicator/SI.POV .DDAY?locations=IN; Mansa Pande and Sonia Relia, "Educating Adolescents in India: Challenges and a Proposed Roadmap," in *Educating Adolescents Around the Globe,* ed. Meike Watzlawik and Alina Burkholder (Cham, Switzerland: Springer, 2020), 32.

100   *"Directive Principles of State Policy":* Constitution of India, 1950, art. XXXVII.

right to education originally appeared: Constitution of India, 1950, art. XLI.

"shall endeavour to provide": Constitution of India, 1950, art. XLV, amended by Constitution (Forty-Second Amendment) Act, 1976.

challenged the state law: Mohini Jain v. Karnataka, (1992) 3 SCR 658, 659 (India).

101   *court further refined:* Unni Krishnan v. Andhra Pradesh, (1993) 1 SCR 594, 596–97 (India); Jai S. Singh, "Expanding Horizons of Human Right to Education: Perspective on Indian and International Vision," *Journal of the Indian Law Institute* 52, no. 1 (January–March 2010): 45.

"free and compulsory education": Constitution of India, 1950, art. XXI-A, amended by Constitution (Eighty-Sixth Amendment) Act, 2002.

A *light caning on the hand:* Parents Forum for Meaningful Educ. v. Union of India, (2001) AIR, paras. 12–15, 21–25 (India).

devastated a middle school: Avinash Mehrotra v. Union of India, (2009) 6 SCC 398 (India).

102   *Indian Supreme Court ordered:* People's Union for Civil Liberties v. Union of India, Writ Petition [Civil] 196 of 2001.

    The midday meal scheme: Rajshri Jayaraman, Dora Simroth, and Francis de Véricourt, "The Impact of School Lunches on Primary School Enrollment: Evidence from India's Midday Meal Scheme," *Scandinavian Journal of Economics* 117, no. 4 (2015): 1176; Abhijeet Singh, Albert Park, and Stefan Dercon, "School Meals as a Safety Net: An Evaluation of the Midday Meal Scheme in India," *Economic Development and Cultural Change* 62, no. 2 (2014): 275–76.

103   *chronicling widespread discrimination:* Helen Rowan, "The Mexican American" (paper prepared for the U.S. Civil Rights Commission, Washington, D.C., 1968).

104   *The plight of Edgewood High School:* Matt Worthington and Bekah McNeel, "ICYMI: This Was All About Racism," Folo Media, December 6, 2017, https://www.folomedia.org/icymi -this-was-all-about-racism/.

    Griggs v. Duke Power Co.: Griggs v. Duke Power Co., 401 U.S. 424 (1971).

105   *"'freeze' the status quo":* Griggs, 401 U.S. at 430–32.

    Test 21: Davis v. Washington, 512 F.2d 956, 967 (D.C. Cir. 1975) (reproducing Test 21 in an appendix), reversed, Washington v. Davis, 426 U.S. 229 (1976).

    it was never sufficient: Washington, 426 U.S. at 229.

106   *"A rule that a statute":* Washington, 426 U.S. at 248.

    the Court in 1974 refused: Geduldig v. Aiello, 417 U.S. 484 (1974).

    a woman was rebuffed: Personnel Administrator of Mass. v. Feeney, 442 U.S. 256 (1979).

    interfere with a death sentence: McCleskey v. Kemp, 481 U.S. 279, 314–19, 339 (1987).

107   *in an internal memo:* Memorandum of Lewis F. Powell, Jr., to Leslie (Gielow) and Ronald (Mann), November 1, 1986, in *McCleskey v. Kemp* Basic File, 110, 113, http://law.wlu.edu/ deptimages/powell%20archives/McCleskeyKempBasic.pdf.

    "too much justice": McCleskey, 481 U.S. at 239 (Brennan, J., dissenting).

108   *the City of Pretoria:* City Council of Pretoria v. Walker, 1998 SA 1 (CC) (S. Afr.).

    Black jurist who came of age: Chris Barron, "Obituary: Pius Langa: Former Chief Justice," *Sunday Times* (South Africa), July 28, 2013, https://www.timeslive.co.za/sunday-times/lifestyle/ 2013-07-28-obituary-pius-langa-former-chief-justice/.

    "artificial to make a comparison": Walker, 1998 SA, para. 32.

109   *discrimination was "unfair":* Walker, 1998 SA, paras. 36–38.

110   *Most high courts:* Niels Petersen, *Proportionality and Judicial Activism* (Cambridge, UK: Cambridge University Press, 2017), 6; Alec Stone Sweet and Jud Mathews, *Proportionality Balancing and Constitutional Governance* (Oxford: Oxford University Press, 2018), 1; Kai Möller, *The Global Model of Constitutional Rights* (Oxford: Oxford University Press, 2012), 15.

111   *"I plan to join Lewis's opinion":* Memorandum of Justice Antonin Scalia to the Conference, January 6, 1987, in *McCleskey v. Kemp* Basic File, 147.

112   *"is no constitutional guarantee at all":* District of Columbia v. Heller, 554 U.S. 570, 634 (2008).

    threw out a law: Citizens United v. Federal Election Commission, 558 U.S. 310 (2010).

113   *data-mining and pharma concerns:* Sorrell v. IMS Health Inc., 564 U.S. 552 (2011).

    laws requiring municipal employees: Janus v. AFSCME, 138 S. Ct. 2448 (2018).

5. WHEN RIGHTS COLLIDE

114   *"modern-day eugenics":* Box v. Planned Parenthood of Ind. & Ky., Inc., 139 S. Ct. 1780, 1783 (2019) (Thomas, J., concurring).

115   *Human Life Protection Act: Alabama Human Life Protection Act,* Ala. Code § 26-23H-2(i) (2019).

forbidden by the Thirteenth Amendment: Professor Andrew Koppelman has argued that "the Thirteenth Amendment provides a textual basis for a right to abortion." Andrew Koppelman, "Forced Labor: A Thirteenth Amendment Defense of Abortion," *Northwestern University Law Review* 84, no. 2 (January 1990): 480; Andrew Koppelman, "Originalism, Abortion, and the Thirteenth Amendment," *Columbia Law Review* 112, no. 7 (November 2012): 1917–45.

social media campaign: Shout Your Abortion, website, accessed May 27, 2020, https://shoutyourabortion.com/; Caitlin Gibson, "How #ShoutYourAbortion Is Transforming the Reproductive Rights Conversation," *Washington Post,* November 15, 2015, https://www.washingtonpost.com/lifestyle/style/how-shoutyourabortion-is-transforming-the-reproductive-rights-conversation/2015/11/13/aa64e68a-895f-11e5-9a07-453018f9a0ec_story.html.

largely untold story: Mary Ann Glendon has usefully remarked on the contrast between the German and U.S. approaches to legal regulation of abortion and how they reflect different understandings of rights. Mary Ann Glendon, *Rights Talk: The Impoverishment of Political Discourse* (New York: Free Press, 1991), 63–66. Glendon attends less to how this contrast is also reflected in broader legislative politics around abortion. Donald Kommers has discussed political effects, but with less attention than Glendon to the overall poverty of U.S. rights discourse. Donald P. Kommers, "The Constitutional Law of Abortion in Germany: Should Americans Pay Attention?," *Journal of Contemporary Health Law and Policy* 10, no. 1 (Spring 1994). The discussion in this chapter has benefited from the sociological work of Myra Marx Ferree, who has extensively studied the rhetoric of abortion rights in the United States and Germany. Myra Marx Ferree, William Anthony Gamson, Jürgen Gerhards, and Dieter Rucht, *Shaping Abortion Discourse: Democracy and the Public Sphere in Germany and the United States* (Cambridge, UK: Cambridge University Press, 2002).

116   *Stevens was confirmed:* Lesley Oelsner, "Senate Confirms Stevens, 98 to 0," *New York Times,* December 18, 1975; Adam Liptak, "John Paul Stevens: Canny Strategist and the 'Finest Legal Mind' Ford Could Find," *New York Times,* July 16, 2019, https://www.nytimes.com/2019/07/16/us/politics/john-paul-stevens-dies-supreme-court.html.

117   *Southern Baptist Convention:* Robert C. Post and Reva B. Siegel, "*Roe* Rage: Democratic Constitutionalism and Backlash," *Harvard Civil Rights–Civil Liberties Law Review* 42, no. 2 (Summer 2007): 412–15; Fred Barnes, "Abortion: A Two-Sided Crusade," *Washington Star-News,* March 22, 1974; Mary Ziegler, *After Roe: The Lost History of the Abortion Debate* (Cambridge, MA: Harvard University Press, 2015), 14; "Resolution on Abortion and Sanctity of Human Life," Southern Baptist Convention, 1974, accessed May 27, 2020, http://www.sbc.net/resolutions/14/resolution-on-abortion-and-sanctity-of-human-life.

banned in most cases: Kommers, "The Constitutional Law of Abortion in Germany," 4.

abortion liberalization bill: Kommers, "Abortion and Constitution," 262–63; Kommers, "The Constitutional Law of Abortion in Germany," 4; Kimba Allie Tichenor, "Protecting Unborn Life in the Secular Age: The Catholic Church and the West German Abortion Debate, 1969–1989," *Central European History* 47, no. 3 (September 2014): 622.

individual votes had to be counted: Tichenor, "Protecting Unborn Life," 622. For a concise summary of the provisions of the Abortion Reform Act of 1974, see Kommers, "The Constitutional Law of Abortion in Germany," 5.

flirted with a career in medicine: Harry A. Blackmun, interview by Harold Hongju Koh, July 6, 1994, transcript, Harry A. Blackmun Papers, Library of Congress, Washington, D.C., 4, https://memory.loc.gov/diglib/blackmun-public/page.html?FOLDERID=D0901&SERIESID=D09; Tinsley Yarbrough, *Harry A. Blackmun: The Outsider Justice* (New York: Oxford University Press, 2008), 23; Nan D. Hunter, "Justice Blackmun, Abortion, and the Myth of Medical Independence," *Brooklyn Law Review* 72, no. 1 (Fall 2006): 147, 162, 173; Linda Greenhouse, *Becoming Justice Blackmun: Harry Blackmun's Supreme Court Journey* (New York: Times Books, 2005), 27, 90–93, 99, 248–49.

118   *opinion in Roe:* Roe v. Wade, 410 U.S. 113 (1973).

the fetus was not a person: Roe, 410 U.S. at 156–58.

a duty to protect it: Robert E. Jonas and John D. Gorby, "West German Abortion Decision: A Contrast to Roe v. Wade," *John Marshall Journal of Practice and Procedure* 9, no. 3 (Spring 1976): 642. This article includes a full English translation of the decision (605–84).

"attacks on race and heredity": Jonas and Gorby, "West German Abortion Decision," 613–15.

"'destruction of life unworthy of life'": Jonas and Gorby, "West German Abortion Decision," 637.

119   *"free development of [one's] personality":* Jonas and Gorby, "West German Abortion Decision," 643.

abortion could be decriminalized: Jonas and Gorby, "West German Abortion Decision," 647–48.

more broadly resonant messages: Daniel K. Williams, *Defenders of the Unborn: The Pro-life Movement Before Roe v. Wade* (New York: Oxford University Press, 2016), 4–7.

had burned draft cards: Ziegler, *After Roe,* 35; Forrest Church, "Williams, George Huntston (1914–2000)," Harvard Square Library, accessed May 27, 2020, https://www.harvardsqu arelibrary.org/biographies/george-huntston-williams/https://www.harvardsquarelibrary.org/biographies/george-huntston-williams/.

120   *strongly pushed birth control:* Williams, *Defenders of the Unborn,* 157–58.

debated in twenty-five states: Williams, *Defenders of the Unborn,* 2.

Jesse Jackson and Al Sampson: Shortly after the Supreme Court's *Roe* decision, right-to-life leaders associated with the National Right to Life Committee held a meeting to discuss various strategies for continuing their pro-life advocacy. According to the meeting minutes, "Dr. [Herbert] Ratner [shared with meeting attendees] that Marcie Sneed got a call from Rev. Sampson and he advised her that he and Jesse Jackson wanted to be counted in this Right to Life group." "National Right to Life Board Members Meeting Minutes," February 11, 1973, box 4, folder 1, American Citizens Concerned for Life (ACCL) Records, Gerald R. Ford Library, Ann Arbor, MI (hereafter cited as ACCL Records).

condemned an alternative amendment: Williams, *Defenders of the Unborn,* 215; Ziegler, *After Roe,* 43.

objection of Mecklenburg: Williams, *Defenders of the Unborn,* 216; "Balance Improves in National Right to Life Committee," *The Wanderer,* June 20, 1974; Susan Fogg, "Abortion Opponents Part Ways," *Newark Star-Ledger,* September 29, 1974.

one Kansas NRLC member: Patricia Goodson, "In Defense of NRLC," letter to the editor, *The Wanderer,* July 16, 1973, box 3, folder 3, ACCL Records.

121   *had been purged completely:* Fogg, "Abortion Opponents."

saw Mecklenburg lose her bid: "Balance Improves in National Right to Life Committee."

Schaller and Judy Fink: Fogg, "Abortion Opponents."

"antiwar pacifists, feminists, and blacks": Fogg, "Abortion Opponents."

"finding solutions to social problems": Williams, *Defenders of the Unborn,* 217.

fewer than seventeen thousand members: Williams, *Defenders of the Unborn,* 217.

pro-life Democrats with presidential aspirations: Williams, *Defenders of the Unborn,* 219–24.

Congressional bills were introduced: Life Support Centers Act of 1975, S. 2360, 94th Cong. (1975); Equity in Health Insurance Act, S. 2359, 94th Cong. (1975). For a concise summary of the proposed bills, see "Fact Sheet on Alternatives to Abortion Package," box 3, folder 3, ACCL Records.

122   *former moderates like Mecklenburg:* Williams, *Defenders of the Unborn,* 233.

embraced a human life amendment: For a more thorough discussion of then candidate Reagan's embrace of a human life amendment, see Williams, *Defenders of the Unborn,* 231–32.

The overt political strategy: Michele McKeegan, "The Politics of Abortion: A Historical Perspective," *Women's Health Issues* 3, no. 3 (Fall 1993): 127–31.

arguing that the word "choice": Mary Ziegler, *Beyond Abortion: Roe v. Wade and the Battle for Privacy* (Cambridge, MA: Harvard University Press, 2018), 65–66; Post and Siegel, "*Roe* Rage," 418; Reva B. Siegel, "Constitutional Culture, Social Movement Conflict and Constitutional Change: The Case of the de Facto ERA," *California Law Review* 94, no. 5 (October 2006): 1389–402.

liberalized abortion access: Siegel, "Constitutional Culture," 1392–93.

On the ground: Ziegler, *After Roe,* 12–13; Post and Siegel, "*Roe* Rage," 420–21.

Fiscally conservative Goldwater Republicans: Williams, *Defenders of the Unborn,* 235–36.

123   *Sandra Day O'Connor's confirmation hearing: Nomination of Sandra Day O'Connor: Hearings Before the Senate Comm. on the Judiciary,* 97th Cong. (1981). See the following pages for exchanges about abortion with specific senators: Thurmond at 60–61, Kennedy at 78–79, Dole at 95, DeConcini at 98, East at 106–8, Denton at 124–27, Hatch at 150–51. Denton resumes questioning about abortion at 237.

seven pro-life Democrats and three pro-choice Republicans: The seven pro-life Democrats were Senator Bob Casey (PA), Representative Henry Cuellar (TX), Representative Conor Lamb (PA), Representative Dan Lipinski (IL), Senator Joe Manchin (WV), Representative Ben McAdams (UT), and Representative Collin Peterson (MN). The three pro-choice Republicans were Senator Susan Collins (ME), Senator Shelley Moore Capito (WV), and Senator Lisa Murkowski (AK). Senator Capito has said she opposes overturning *Roe,* but she consistently votes for anti–abortion rights bills, and in January 2020 she publicly offered her support for the March for Life. March for Life Education and Defense Fund, "Why Our Pro-life, Female Senators Are Marching for Life #WhyWeMarch," January 27, 2020, YouTube video, https://www.youtube.com/watch?v=NoX-mYKL3Zs.

pro-life Democrats were not welcome: Elana Schor, Associated Press, "Democrats Diverge on Outreach to Anti-abortion Swing Voters," *U.S. News and World Report,* February 18, 2020, https://www.usnews.com/news/politics/articles/2020-02-18/democrats-diverge-on-outreach-to-anti-abortion-swing-voters.

eight weeks and sometimes earlier: K. K. Rebecca Lai, "Abortion Bans: 9 States Have Passed Bills to Limit the Procedure This Year," *New York Times,* May 29, 2019, https://www.nytimes.com/interactive/2019/us/abortion-laws-states.html.

124   *Ruth Bader Ginsburg:* Ruth Bader Ginsburg, "Some Thoughts on Autonomy and Equality in Relation to *Roe v. Wade,*" *North Carolina Law Review* 63, no. 2 (January 1985): 381–83.

To opponents of abortion rights: Daniela Birkenfeld-Pfeiffer, "Abortion and the Necessity for Compromise," *German Politics and Society,* no. 24/25 (Winter 1991/1992): 122–23; Ursula Nelles, "Abortion, the Special Case: A Constitutional Perspective," *German Politics and Society,* no. 24/25 (Winter 1991/1992): 113; Tichenor, "Protecting Unborn Life," 628.

125   *main way for a woman:* Birkenfeld-Pfeiffer, "Abortion and the Necessity for Compromise," 123.

same as in East Germany: Tatjana Böhm and Diane Forman Kent, "The Abortion Question: A New Solution in Unified Germany?," *German Politics and Society,* no. 24/25 (Winter 1991/1992): 136, 140; Ferree et al., *Shaping Abortion Discourse,* 33–34.

More-Catholic, more-conservative Länder: Nelles, "Abortion, the Special Case," 114.

some of these Länder: Nelles, "Abortion, the Special Case," 114–15.

126   *forcing gynecological exams:* Ferree et al., *Shaping Abortion Discourse,* 37–38.

constitutional court's decision leaked: "Bonn Abortion Law May Be Overruled," *New York Times,* January 28, 1975, https://www.nytimes.com/1975/01/28/archives/bonn-abortion-law-may-be-overruled.html.

mass demonstrations: Paul Kemezis, "Top German Court Rejects Abortion," *New York Times,* February 26, 1975, https://www.nytimes.com/1975/02/26/archives/top-german-court-rejects

-abortion-bonns-1974-law-allowing.html; Ferree et al., *Shaping Abortion Discourse,* 34; Tichenor, "Protecting Unborn Life," 626.

themes of choice and autonomy: Margarethe Nimsch, "Abortion as Politics," *German Politics and Society,* no. 24/25 (Winter 1991/1992): 130.

Sociologist Myra Marx Ferree: Myra Marx Ferree, "Resonance and Radicalism: Feminist Framing in the Abortion Debates of the United States and Germany," *American Journal of Sociology* 109, no. 2 (September 2003): 316, 322–24. For a subsequent U.S. case emphasizing the autonomy of women in making abortion decisions and the accompanying lack of a state duty to support that decision in any way other than through legalization, see Maher v. Roe, 432 U.S. 464 (1977).

127   *opportunity for the Catholic Church:* Tichenor, "Protecting Unborn Life," 629.

Joseph Cardinal Höffner: Tichenor, "Protecting Unborn Life," 629–30.

Johannes Rau: Tichenor, "Protecting Unborn Life," 630–31.

128   *likening of abortion rights proponents:* Tichenor, "Protecting Unborn Life," 632.

A 1980 survey: Tichenor, "Protecting Unborn Life," 635.

Evangelical Church in Germany (EKD): Tichenor, "Protecting Unborn Life," 643.

failed to pass laws: Tichenor, "Protecting Unborn Life," 637–38; Birkenfeld-Pfeiffer, "Abortion and the Necessity for Compromise," 124.

women within the party: Tichenor, "Protecting Unborn Life," 636–40.

cooperation between the KFD: Tichenor, "Protecting Unborn Life," 640–43.

129   *Margarethe Nimsch:* Nimsch, "Abortion as Politics," 131.

almost derailed German reunification: Böhm and Kent, "The Abortion Question," 135.

130   *the liberal Free Democratic Party and the Christian Democrats:* Birkenfeld-Pfeiffer, "Abortion and the Necessity for Compromise," 126–27.

"group bill": Kommers, "The Constitutional Law of Abortion in Germany," 12–14.

struck parts of it down: Kommers, "The Constitutional Law of Abortion in Germany," 15–24.

131   *a revision in 1994:* Ferree, "Resonance," 313; Lynn Kamenitsa, "Abortion Debates in Germany," in *Abortion Politics, Women's Movements, and the Democratic State: A Comparative Study of State Feminism,* ed. Dorothy McBride Stetson (New York: Oxford University Press, 2001), 126–28.

fewer than ten thousand marchers: Micaiah Bilger, "Thousands of People Flood the Streets of Berlin for the March for Life to Protest Abortion," LifeNews.com, September 19, 2016, https://www.lifenews.com/2016/09/19/thousands-of-people-flood-the-streets-of-berlin-for-the-march-for-life-to-protest-abortion/.

March for Life in Washington, D.C.: Laurie Goodstein and Anemona Hartocollis, "Abortion Foes Aim to Compete with Turnout for Women's March," *New York Times,* January 26, 2017, https://www.nytimes.com/2017/01/26/us/abortion-foes-compete-womens-march-turnout.html.

The parties whose rhetoric: Jonathan Olsen, "The Left Party and the AfD," *German Politics and Society* 36, no. 1 (Spring 2018): 70–83; Kathleen Brown, "The Renaissance of Germany's Abortion Rights Movement," *Jacobin,* March 2018, https://jacobinmag.com/2018/03/germanys-abortion-rights-movement-afd-fascism.

132   *red state attempts:* For a roundup of these attempts in 2019, see Lai, "Abortion Bans."

133   *structure its political appeal:* Thomas Franks, *What's the Matter with Kansas?* (New York: Henry Holt, 2004); Gary Miller and Norman Schofield, "The Transformation of the Republican and Democratic Party Coalitions in the U.S.," *Perspectives on Politics* 6, no. 3 (September 2008): 433–50.

Hyde Amendment: For a brief summary of how the Hyde Amendment has evolved since its initial passage, see Julie Rovner, "Abortion Funding Ban Has Evolved over the Years," Morning Edition, National Public Radio, December 14, 2009, https://www.npr.org/templates/story/story.php?storyId=121402281.

quote from Robert Bork: Henry J. Hyde, "The Heart of the Matter," *Human Life Review* 3, no. 3 (Summer 1977): 94.

134   *the language of "choice":* Ferree, "Resonance," 331.

"post-abortion syndrome": Ferree, "Resonance," 336.

partial-birth abortions: Gonzales v. Carhart, 550 U.S. 124, 159 (2007).

The Cano brief: Brief of Sandra Cano, the Former "Mary Doe" of *Doe v. Bolton,* and 180 Women Injured by Abortion as Amici Curiae in Support of Petitioner at 22–24, *Gonzales,* 550 U.S. 124 (No. 05-380).

135   *a new Supreme Court:* The other new justices were Sandra Day O'Connor (replacing Potter Stewart), Antonin Scalia (replacing Warren Burger), Anthony Kennedy (replacing Lewis Powell), and David Souter (replacing William Brennan).

the unusual step: Deborah Peterson, "ACLU Wants Ruling on Abortion," *St. Louis Post-Dispatch,* November 12, 1991, 5A; Greg Henderson, "Supreme Court Asked to Hear Direct Challenge to *Roe,*" United Press International, November 8, 1991.

The petition urged the justices: Greenhouse, *Becoming Justice Blackmun,* 201–2.

Planned Parenthood of Southeastern Pennsylvania v. Casey: Planned Parenthood of Southeastern Pennsylvania v. Casey, 505 U.S. 833, 851 (1992).

136   *depoliticize abortion rights: Casey,* 505 U.S. at 868.

137   *top ten "life-protective" states:* In 2020, Americans United for Life identified the following ten states as having the best "law and policy protections for human life from conception to natural death," listed from first to tenth: Louisiana, Arkansas, Arizona, Oklahoma, Kansas, Indiana, Mississippi, Missouri, Alabama, and South Dakota. "Defending Life 2020," Americans United for Life, accessed May 27, 2020, https://aul.org/publications/defending-life/. Of these ten states, Louisiana was the only one offering some form of pregnancy leave as of 2020.

138   *bans on obtaining an abortion:* "Abortion Bans in Cases of Sex or Race Selection or Genetic Anomaly," Guttmacher Institute, June 1, 2020, https://www.guttmacher.org/state-policy/explore/abortion-bans-cases-sex-or-race-selection-or-genetic-anomaly.

"ensuring that a woman's choice": Casey, 505 U.S. at 873.

139   *Selective abortion of female fetuses:* Jason Abrevaya, "Are There Missing Girls in the United States? Evidence from Birth Data," *American Economic Journal: Applied Economics* 1, no. 2 (April 2009): 1–34; Giuseppe Benagiano and Paola Bianchi, "Sex Preselection: An Aid to Couples or a Threat to Humanity?," *Human Reproduction* 14, no. 4 (April 1999): 868–70; Christophe Z. Guilmoto, "The Masculinization of Births: Overview and Current Knowledge," *Population: English Edition* 70, no. 2 (2015): 185–243; T. J. Matthews and Brady E. Hamilton, "Trend Analysis of the Sex Ratio at Birth in the United States," *National Vital Statistics Reports* 53, no. 20 (June 2005): 1–20; T. M. Marteau, "Sex Selection: 'The Rights of Man' or the Thin Edge of a Eugenic Wedge?," *BMJ: British Medical Journal* 306, no. 6894 (June 1993): 1704–5.

exceptions for inherited sex-linked diseases: Rajani Bhatia, "Constructing Gender from the Inside Out," *Feminist Studies* 36, no. 2 (Summer 2010): 265; Miriam Wilhelm, Edgar Dahl, Henry Alexander, Elmar Brähler, and Yve Stöbel-Richter, "Ethical Attitudes of German Specialists in Reproductive Medicine and Legal Regulation of Preimplantation Sex Selection in Germany," *PLoS ONE* 8, no. 2 (February 2013): 1.

6. WHEN RIGHTS DIVIDE

140   *more than one hundred evangelical Christian churches:* Jeff Brady, "Colorado Springs a Mecca for Evangelical Christians," All Things Considered, National Public Radio, January 17, 2005, https://www.npr.org/templates/story/story.php?storyId=4287106; James Ridge-

way "Day Eight: Sunday Morning in the 'Evangelical Vatican,'" *The Guardian,* October 20, 2008.

an anti-abortion vigilante: Julie Turkewitz and Jack Healy, "3 Are Dead in Colorado Springs Shootout at Planned Parenthood Center," *New York Times,* November 27, 2015, https://www .nytimes.com/2015/11/28/us/colorado-planned-parenthood-shooting.html.

the city's dominant industry: Betty G. Lall and John Tepper Marlin, *Building a Peace Economy: Opportunities and Problems of Post–Cold War Defense Cuts* (New York: Routledge, 2019), 136; "Colorado Springs: Economy," City-Data.com, http://www.city-data.com/us-cities/The -West/Colorado-Springs-Economy.html.

lost the state of Colorado: "Colorado Results," Election 2016, *New York Times,* August 1, 2017, https://www.nytimes.com/elections/2016/results/colorado.

141   *"Go to Boulder":* Kyle Harris, "Clela Rorex Planted the Flag for Same-Sex Marriage in Boulder Forty Years Ago," *Westword,* August 13, 2014, https://www.westword.com/news/clela-rorex -planted-the-flag-for-same-sex-marriage-in-boulder-forty-years-ago-5882967.

live with his husband: John Frank, "Jared Polis Won't Move to Governor's Mansion, Will Remain at His Home in Boulder," *Colorado Sun,* November 21, 2018, https://coloradosun.com/ 2018/11/21/jared-polis-governors-mansion/.

Clinton won Boulder County: "Colorado Results."

never issued a marriage license: Grace Lichtenstein, "Homosexual Weddings Stir Controversy in Colorado," *New York Times,* April 27, 1975, https://www.nytimes.com/1975/04/27/ archives/homosexual-weddings-stir-controversy-in-colorado.html.

Clela Rorex: Harris, "Clela Rorex Planted the Flag."

its official response: Robert Barnes, "40 Years Later, Story of a Same-Sex Marriage in Colorado Remains Remarkable," *Washington Post,* April 18, 2015, http://wapo.st/1yFi2vZ.

142   *the Zax:* "The Zax" is a short story by Dr. Seuss featuring a north-going Zax and south-going Zax who refuse to compromise under any circumstances. Dr. Seuss, "The Zax," in *The Sneetches and Other Stories* (New York: Random House, 1961), 26–35.

Party conflicts: Chris Matthews, *Tip and the Gipper: When Politics Worked* (New York: Simon & Schuster, 2013). On the current state of political polarization in the United States, see Nolan McCarty, *Polarization: What Everyone Needs to Know* (New York: Oxford University Press, 2019); Lillian Mason, *Uncivil Agreement: How Politics Became Our Identity* (Chicago: University of Chicago Press, 2018); Christopher Hare and Keith T. Poole, "The Polarization of Contemporary American Politics," *Polity* 46, no. 3 (July 2014): 411–29; Nolan M. McCarty, Keith T. Poole, and Howard Rosenthal, *Polarized America: The Dance of Ideology and Unequal Riches* (Cambridge, MA: MIT Press, 2006), 23–24; "Political Polarization in the American Public," Pew Research Center, June 12, 2014, https://www.people-press.org/2014/06/12/ political-polarization-in-the-american-public/.

various Supreme Court decisions: For an exploration of the origins of contemporary political polarization, see Sam Rosenfeld, *The Polarizers* (Chicago: University of Chicago Press, 2018). In 1976, the Supreme Court held that the expenditure limits in the Federal Election Campaign Act of 1971 were unconstitutional. At the same time, the Court upheld the act's limits on contributions to individual candidates, campaign and political action committees, and political parties. Buckley v. Valeo, 424 U.S. 1 (1976). In 2010, the Court held that the provisions of the Bipartisan Campaign Reform Act of 2002 restricting corporations in their independent spending on political communications were unconstitutional. Citizens United v. Federal Election Commission, 558 U.S. 310 (2010).

144   *Amendment 2:* Romer v. Evans, 517 U.S. 620, 623–24 (1996).

folksy Colorado Springs car dealer: Dirk Johnson, "'I Don't Hate Homosexuals,'" *New York Times,* February 14, 1993.

In the wake of the law's passage: Ned Zeman, "No 'Special Rights' for Gays," *Newsweek,* November 22, 1992, 32; Marj Charlier, "Colorado Ad Campaign to Thwart State Boycott May

Be Misdirected," *Wall Street Journal,* January 19, 1993, B7; William Schultz, "How Colorado Did a 180 on Gay Rights," *Washington Post,* December 17, 2018, https://www.washingtonpost .com/outlook/2018/12/17/how-colorado-did-gay-rights/.

Perkins specifically brought up: Will Perkins, interview by Mike Kinsley and John Sununu, *Crossfire,* CNN, December 22, 1992.

145   *As Perkins told CNN:* Perkins, interview.

struck down Amendment 2: Romer, 517 U.S. at 623, 633.

permissible for states to ban sodomy: Bowers v. Hardwick, 478 U.S. 186 (1986). In the early 2000s, ten states still banned consensual sodomy (regardless of the participants' sex), whereas four states specifically banned same-sex couples from engaging in anal and oral sex. Associated Press, "Supreme Court Strikes Down Texas Law Banning Sodomy," *New York Times,* June 26, 2003.

146   *Justice Scalia's searing dissent: Romer,* 517 U.S. at 636–53 (Scalia, J., dissenting).

147   *Colorado's cultural politics:* "Key Ballot Measures," CNN.com, America Votes 2006, http:// www.cnn.com/ELECTION/2006/pages/results/ballot.measures/. In 2007, Governor Bill Ritter signed into law Senate Bill 07-025, which bans employment discrimination based on sexual orientation, gender identity, and religion, thereby revising the Colorado Anti-discrimination Act. Colo. Rev. Stat. § 24-34-402(1) (2019). In 2008, Ritter signed Senate Bill 200 into law, thereby extending protections to people from discrimination based on sexual orientation and gender identity in housing and public accommodation. Colo. Rev. Stat. § 24-34-601(2) (a) (2019).

walked into Masterpiece Cakeshop: Masterpiece Cakeshop, Ltd. v. Colo. Civil Rights Comm'n, 138 S. Ct. 1719, 1724–27 (2018).

148   *Unflattering comparisons:* Jamal Greene, "Foreword: Rights as Trumps?," *Harvard Law Review* 132, no. 1 (November 2018): 30–32, 81; Louise Melling, "The 'Gay Wedding Cake' Case Isn't About Religious Freedom or Freedom of Speech," op-ed, *Los Angeles Times,* December 4, 2017, https://www.latimes.com/opinion/op-ed/la-oe-melling-masterpiece-cakeshop -supreme-court-20171204-story.html; Newman v. Piggie Park Enterprises, Inc., 256 F. Supp. 941 (D.S.C. 1966).

submitted briefs: For comparisons to "landlords . . . refus[ing] rent to interracial couples" and "employers . . . [refusing] to hire women," see Brief of Respondents Charlie Craig and David Mullins in Opposition at 25, *Masterpiece Cakeshop,* 138 S. Ct. 1719 (No. 16-111). For comparisons to "a racist baker . . . refus[ing] to sell . . . cakes to African-American customers" and "a family portrait studio . . . enforc[ing] a 'No Mexicans' policy," see Brief of Respondent Colorado Civil Rights Commission at 4, 16. For a comparison to an anti-immigrant hairstylist refusing service to a girl preparing for her quinceañera, see Brief of Respondents Charlie Craig and David Mullins at 48. For additional comparisons to anti-miscegenation laws and school segregation, see Brief Amicus Curiae of NAACP Legal Defense & Educational Fund, Inc. in Support of Respondents at 9–10.

To hear the other side: Greene, "Foreword: Rights as Trumps?," 80–81. For examples of NRA and KKK comparisons, see Mike Rosen, "The Icing on the Masterpiece Cakeshop Case," *Colorado Springs Gazette,* September 5, 2018, https://gazette.com/opinion/columnists/ guest-column-the-icing-on-the-masterpiece-cakeshop-case/article_010e5b96-b04b-11e8 -b5d6-eff4b6d95085.html/. For arguments about involuntary servitude and the Thirteenth Amendment, see Brief Amicus Curiae of the Foundation for Moral Law in Support of Petitioners at 22, *Masterpiece Cakeshop,* 138 S. Ct. 1719 (No. 16-111); Brief Amici Curiae of Public Advocate of the United States et al. in Support of Petitioners at 31. For concerns over disbarring Christian lawyers and delicensing Christian doctors, see Brief Amici Curiae of Public Advocate of the United States et al. at 15–16. For the historical references to religious oppression, see Brief Amici Curiae of 34 Legal Scholars in Support of Petitioners at 17; Brief Amicus Curiae of the Becket Fund for Religious Liberty in Support of Petitioners at 24.

149 *At the oral argument:* For Justice Gorsuch's hypothetical regarding the Ku Klux Klan, see Transcript of Oral Argument at 87, *Masterpiece Cakeshop,* 138 S. Ct. 1719 (No. 16-111), https://www.supremecourt.gov/oral_arguments/argument_transcripts/2017/16-111_f314 .pdf. For Justice Alito's example about a cake honoring the anniversary of Kristallnacht, see Transcript of Oral Argument at 70. For Breyer and Kagan's likening of Masterpiece Cakeshop to Ollie's Barbecue, see Transcript of Oral Argument at 18–19, 37. The Supreme Court's decision in the Ollie's Barbecue case is Katzenbach v. McClung, 379 U.S. 294 (1964).

just how narrow the dispute: For Phillips's argument in full, see Brief of Petitioners Masterpiece Cakeshop, Ltd., et al., *Masterpiece Cakeshop,* 138 S. Ct. 1719 (No. 16-111).

150 *free custom cakes:* "Mullins and Craig were inundated by offers of free cakes from as far away as Japan." Nicholas Riccardi, "Religious Freedom and Same-Sex Marriage: How a Wedding Cake in Colorado Became a Cause," *Deseret News,* April 5, 2014, https://www.deseret.com/ 2014/4/5/20464315/religious-freedom-and-same-sex-marriage-how-a-wedding-cake-in -colorado-became-a-cause.

sites of numerous objections: Klein v. Or. Bureau of Labor and Indus., 410 P.3d 1051 (Or. Ct. App. 2017); State v. Arlene's Flowers, Inc., 389 P.3d 543 (Wash. 2017); Elane Photography, LLC v. Willock, 309 P.3d 53 (N.M. 2013).

152 *its own cake case:* Lee v. Ashers Baking Co. [2018] UKSC 49, paras. 1–3, 9–12 (appeal taken from N. Ir.).

"Bread from Asher": Genesis 49:20 (New King James Version).

153 *Hale's lead opinion:* Lee, [2018] UKSC 49 at paras. 22, 35, 62.

155 *Lillian Ladele was the registrar:* Ladele v. London Borough of Islington [2009] EWCA (Civ) 1357, paras. 4–15 (Eng.).

taken by Kim Davis: Adam Liptak, "Supreme Court Says Kentucky Clerk Must Let Gay Couples Marry," *New York Times,* August 31, 2015.

Obergefell v. Hodges: Obergefell v. Hodges, 576 U.S. 644 (2015).

156 *simply cannot be challenged:* Employment Div. v. Smith, 494 U.S. 872, 888–89 (1990).

"indirect discrimination": Ladele, [2009] EWCA (Civ) 1357 at para. 43.

157 *the borough's motivation:* Ladele, [2009] EWCA (Civ) 1357 at paras. 45–46.

didn't trivialize the burden: Eweida and Others v. The United Kingdom, 2013-I Eur. Ct. H.R. 215, paras. 104, 106 (2013).

159 *glimpse the problem:* Masterpiece Cakeshop, 138 S. Ct. at 1723, 1727.

most protective of freedom of expression: Ashutosh Bhagwat and Matthew Struhar, "Justice Kennedy's Free Speech Jurisprudence: A Quantitative and Qualitative Analysis," *McGeorge Law Review* 44, no. 1 (July 2013): 167–99.

a categorical way out: Masterpiece Cakeshop, 138 S. Ct. at 1729–31.

161 *"conscience clauses":* Claire Marshall, "The Spread of Conscience Clause Legislation," *Human Rights* 39, no. 2 (January 2013): 15–16.

Federal laws in the United States: Religious Freedom Restoration Act of 1993, Pub. L. No. 103-141, § 3, 107 Stat. 1488 (1993); City of Boerne v. Flores, 521 U.S. 507 (1997); Jonathan Griffin, "State Religious Freedom Restoration Acts," *Our American States* (podcast), National Conference of State Legislatures, May 4, 2017, https://www.ncsl.org/research/civil-and-criminal -justice/state-rfra-statutes.aspx.

arts-and-crafts chain Hobby Lobby: Burwell v. Hobby Lobby Stores, Inc., 573 U.S. 682 (2014).

163 *sterling partisan credentials:* Neil A. Lewis, "Bush Aide on Court Nominees Faces Fire as Nominee Himself," *New York Times,* April 28, 2004; Monique O. Madan, "New Supreme Court Nominee Kavanaugh Has Ties to Big Florida Moments," *Miami Herald,* July 9, 2018, https://www .miamiherald.com/news/nation-world/national/article214604235.html; Scott Shane, Steve Eder, Rebecca R. Ruiz, Adam Liptak, Charlie Savage, and Ben Protess, "Influential Judge, Loyal Friend, Conservative Warrior — and D.C. Insider," *New York Times,* July 14, 2018, https://www .nytimes.com/2018/07/14/us/politics/judge-brett-kavanaugh.html.

7. DISABILITY

171   *ventilator triage plan:* Amy Silverman, "People with Intellectual Disabilities May Be Denied Lifesaving Care Under These Plans as Coronavirus Spreads," ProPublica, March 27, 2020, https://www.propublica.org/article/people-with-intellectual-disabilities-may-be-denied -lifesaving-care-under-these-plans-as-coronavirus-spreads.
      elderly inmates at a geriatric prison: Jollie McCullough, "Older Inmates Sue Texas Prison System over Coronavirus Policies and Practices," *Texas Tribune,* March 30, 2020, https://www .texastribune.org/2020/03/30/texas-inmates-sue-prison-over-coronavirus-practices/; Defendants' Motion to Dismiss Pursuant Rule 12(b) at 2, Valentine v. Collier, 956 F.3d 797 (5th Cir., 2020) (No. 4:20-cv-01115).

174   *The leading case:* City of Cleburne v. Cleburne Living Ctr. Inc., 473 U.S. 432, 436–7 (1985); Richard Carelli, "Battle for Group Home Splits City," *Dallas Morning News,* April 21, 1985; David Hanners, "Home's Co-owner Rejoices: Cleburne Facility for Mentally Retarded Still Stirs Opposition," *Dallas Morning News,* July 2, 1985.
      "principled way": City of Cleburne, 473 U.S. at 445.

175   *lost his majority:* City of Cleburne, 473 U.S. at 449; William D. Araiza, "Was Cleburne an Accident?," *University of Pennsylvania Journal of Constitutional Law* 19, no. 3 (2017): 651.
      The ADA defines a disability: Americans with Disabilities Act of 1990 (ADA), 42 U.S.C. § 12102 (2008); Brumfeld v. Cain, 576 U.S. 305 (2015).

177   *The Screaming Bucket:* Gary L. Smith, "Stark County Board Chairman Suspended as Bus Driver After 'Screaming Bucket' Incident," Peoria *Journal Star,* May 31, 2019, https://www .pjstar.com/news/20190531/stark-county-board-chairman-suspended-as-bus-driver-after -screaming-bucket-incident; Ryan Jenkins, "Mother Says School Bus Aide Forced 'Screaming Bucket' over the Head of Her 7-Year-Old Autistic Son," WQAD.com, May 31, 2019, https:// wqad.com/2019/05/31/mother-says-school-bus-aide-forced-screaming-bucket-over-the -head-of-her-7-year-old-autistic-son/; Andy Kravetz, "Stark County Parents File Suit over 'Screaming Bucket' Practice," Peoria *Journal Star,* June 26, 2019, https://www.pjstar.com/ news/20190626/stark-county-parents-file-suit-over-screaming-bucket-practice; Complaint at 3, 5–17, Doe Child v. Stark County Community Unit Sch. Dist. #100, 19-cv-01215-MMM, 2019 WL 6702538 (C.D. Ill. Dec. 9, 2019).

178   *The End of Care's Life:* Asia Fields, "'Sorry for What Happened to Mr. Gray': DSHS to Pay $8M After Neighbors' Pleas to Help Vulnerable Seattle Man Brought No Action," *Seattle Times,* May 20, 2019, https://www.seattletimes.com/seattle-news/sorry-for-what-happened-to-mr -gray-says-dshs-about-to-pay-8m-after-neighbors-pleas-to-help-vulnerable-seattle-man -brought-none/; Antonia Noori Farzan, "A Developmentally Disabled Man Lived Alone with Hundreds of Rats. He's Now Been Awarded $8 Million," *Morning Mix* (blog), *Washington Post,* May 23, 2019, https://www.washingtonpost.com/nation/2019/05/23/developmentally -disabled-man-lived-alone-with-hundreds-rats-hes-now-been-awarded-million/.

179   *Joshua DeShaney:* DeShaney v. Winnebago Cty. Dep't of Soc. Servs, 489 U.S. 189 (1989).
      Castle Rock, Colorado: Town of Castle Rock, Colo. v. Gonzales, 545 U.S. 748 (2005).

180   *The Subminimum Wage:* Anna Schecter, "Disabled Workers Paid Just Pennies an Hour — and It's Legal," NBC News, June 25, 2013, http://investigations.nbcnews.com/_news/2013/06/25/ 19062348-disabled-workers-paid-just-pennies-an-hour-and-its-legal; Ashley DeJean, "Many People with Disabilities Are Being Paid Way Below the Minimum Wage, and It's Perfectly Legal," *Mother Jones,* August 8, 2017, https://www.motherjones.com/politics/2017/08/many -people-with-disabilities-are-being-paid-way-below-the-minimum-wage-and-its-perfectly -legal/; Fair Labor Standards Act of 1938 (FLSA), Pub. L. No. 75-718, § 14, 52 Stat. 1068 (1938).
      Virginia's sterilization of a woman: Buck v. Bell, 274 U.S. 200 (1927); U.S. Government Ac-

countability Office, *Special Minimum Wage Program: Centers Offer Employment and Support Services to Workers with Disabilities, but Labor Should Improve Oversight* (report #GAO-01-886, Washington, D.C., September 2001), https://www.gao.gov/products/GAO-01-886; National Council on Disability, *Subminimum Wage and Supported Employment* (report, Washington, D.C., August 23, 2012), https://www.ncd.gov/sites/default/files/NCD_Sub%20Wage _508.pdf; DeJean, "Many People with Disabilities."

182   *Civil Rights Act of 1866:* Act of Apr. 9, 1866 (Civil Rights Act), Pub. L. No. 39-26, 14 Stat. 27; U.S. Const. amend. XIV, § 5.

183   *an 1883 decision:* Civil Rights Cases, 109 U.S. 3 (1883).
Civil Rights Act of 1964: Civil Rights Act of 1964, Pub. L. No. 88-352, § 201, 78 Stat. 243 (1964).

184   *African-American interstate travelers:* 110 Cong. Rec., 88th Cong., 2d sess. (1964), 6531–32; Paul Brest, Sanford Levinson, Jack M. Balkin, Akhil Reed Amar, and Reva B. Siegel, *Processes of Constitutional Decisionmaking,* 6th ed. (New York: Aspen, 2015), 651; Heart of Atlanta Motel v. United States, 379 U.S. 241 (1964); Katzenbach v. McClung, 379 U.S. 294 (1964).
used to authorize a lawsuit: Seminole Tribe of Florida v. Florida, 517 U.S. 44 (1996).
gun possession near schools: United States v. Lopez, 514 U.S. 549 (1995).
provision of the Violence Against Women Act: United States v. Morrison, 529 U.S. 598 (2000).
first Affordable Care Act decision: Nat'l Fed. of Indep. Bus. v. Sebelius, 567 U.S. 519 (2012). The relevant ADA provisions are codified at 42 U.S.C. §§ 12112(b)(5), 12182(b)(2)(A) (2020).

185   *Patricia Garrett and Milton Ash:* Board of Trustees of Univ. of Ala. v. Garrett, 531 U.S. 356, 362, 367–68 (2001).

187   *requests for SAT accommodations:* "Learning Disorders," College Board, accessed June 7, 2020, https://accommodations.collegeboard.org/documentation-guidelines/learning-disorders; Miriam Kurtzig Freedman, "Have SAT Accommodations Gone Too Far?," *Education Week,* August 24, 2017, edweek.org/ew/articles/2017/08/25/have-sat-accommodations-gone-too -far.html.
One in four countries: Amy Raub, Isabel Latz, Aleta Sprague, Michael Ashley Stein, and Jody Heymann, "Constitutional Rights of Persons with Disabilities: An Analysis of 193 National Constitutions," *Harvard Human Rights Journal* 29, no. 1 (2016): 216, https://harvardhrj.com/ wp-content/uploads/sites/14/2016/09/Constitutional-Rights-of-Persons-with-Disabilities .pdf.
a twelve-year-old girl with cerebral palsy: Eaton v. Brant County Board of Educ., [1997] 1 S.C.R. 241, paras. 6–8, 17–20 (Can.); Canadian Charter of Rights and Freedoms, § 15(1), Part I of the Constitution Act, 1982, *being* Schedule B to the Canada Act, 1982, c 11 (UK); *Eaton,* 1 S.C.R. 241 at paras. 71, 76.

188   *relied on the detailed assessment: Eaton,* 1 S.C.R. 241 at paras. 72, 79; Diane Pothier, "Eaton v. Brant County Board of Education," *Canadian Journal of Women and the Law* 18, no. 1 (2006): 121, 131–36; *Eaton,* 1 S.C.R. 241 at paras. 73–76.

189   *come in for some criticism: Eaton,* 1 S.C.R. 241 at para. 77; Pothier, "Eaton v. Brant."
British Columbia hospitals: Eldridge v. British Columbia (Attorney General), [1997] 3 S.C.R. 624 (Can.).

190   *historical marginalization of people with disabilities: Eldridge,* 3 S.C.R. 624 at paras. 49, 56.
unintentional discrimination may: Eldridge, 3 S.C.R. 624 at paras. 61–64, 69–78.

191   *failed the third test: Eldridge,* 3 S.C.R. 624 at paras. 84, 87–89; R. v. Oakes, [1986] 1 S.C.R. 103 (Can.); *Eldridge,* 3 S.C.R. 624 at para. 90.

192   *such conjectural grounds: Eldridge,* 3 S.C.R. 624 at paras. 91–92.

193   *"it is not this Court's role": Eldridge,* 3 S.C.R. 624 at para. 96.

194   *significantly impair one's daily life:* Claudia Center and Andrew Imparato, "Redefining 'Disability' Discrimination: A Proposal to Restore Civil Rights Protections for All Workers," *Stanford Law and Policy Review* 14, no. 2 (2003): 321; Sutton v. United Air Lines, 527 U.S.

471 (1999); Bonnie Poitras Tucker, "The ADA's Revolving Door: Inherent Flaws in the Civil Rights Paradigm," *Ohio State Law Journal* 62, no. 1 (2001): 335; Toyota Motor Mfg., Ky. v. Williams, 534 U.S. 184 (2002); Atkins v. Virginia, 536 U.S. 304 (2002).

8. AFFIRMATIVE ACTION

195   *must be rationed:* Lenin is reported to have said that "liberty" is "so precious that it must be rationed." Sidney Webb and Beatrice Webb, *Soviet Communism: A New Civilisation* (London: Longmans, Green, 1936), 2:1036.
   accused Harvard of discriminating: Students for Fair Admissions (SFFA) v. Harvard College, 397 F. Supp. 3d 126 (2019).
   admitted to Harvard: SFFA, 397 F. Supp. 3d at 161–62, 178.

196   *maximum skepticism from courts:* Adarand Constructors v. Pena, 515 U.S. 200, 227 (1995). "All racial classifications, imposed by whatever federal, state, or local governmental actor, must be analyzed by a reviewing court under strict scrutiny." This standard constrains educational institutions that receive federal funding. Gratz v. Bollinger, 539 U.S. 244, 276 n.23 (2003).
   a more stringent standard: Government discrimination on the basis of sex is subject to a more forgiving standard than applies in the race context. United States v. Virginia, 518 U.S. 515, 533 (1996). While there is some uncertainty as to which standard would apply in a modern equal protection or religious discrimination challenge to a federal immigration ban based on religion, the Supreme Court has not overruled its 1889 decision holding that a federal decision to exclude particular classes of aliens is not reviewable by the courts. Chae Chan Ping v. United States, 130 U.S. 581, 609 (1889).
   not wealthy in economic terms: SFFA, 397 F. Supp. 3d at 156 n.37.

197   *a rupture in the demographics:* SFFA, 397 F. Supp. 3d at 178.
   Black and Hispanic disadvantage: Iris Marion Young, "Equality of Whom? Social Groups and Judgments of Injustice," *Journal of Political Philosophy* 9, no. 1 (March 2001): 2, 8–15; John Iceland, *Race and Ethnicity in America* (Oakland: University of California Press, 2017), 43–44; Patrick Sharkey, "Spatial Segmentation and the Black Middle Class," *American Journal of Sociology* 119, no. 4 (January 2014): 907, 918, 935; Glenn Firebaugh and Chad R. Farrell, "Still Large, but Narrowing: The Sizable Decline in Racial Neighborhood Inequality in Metropolitan America," *Demography* 53, no. 1 (February 2016): 139–64; Bruce Western and Christopher Muller, "Mass Incarceration, Macrosociology, and the Poor," *Annals of the American Academy of Political and Social Science* 647 (May 2013): 166; Bruce Western and Becky Pettit, "Incarceration and Racial Inequality in Men's Employment," *Industrial and Labor Relations Review* 54, no. 1 (2000): 8–9; Amanda Howerton, "Police Response to Crime: Differences in the Application of Law by Race," *Journal of Ethnicity in Criminal Justice* 4, no. 3 (August 2006): 53; H. A. Hewes, Mengtao Dai, N. Clay Mann, Tanya Baca, and Peter Taillac, "Prehospital Pain Management: Disparity by Age and Race," *Prehospital Emergency Care* 22, no. 2 (September 2017): 189–97; Imari Z. Smith, Keisha L. Bentley-Edwards, Salimah El-Amin, and William Darity Jr., *Fighting at Birth: Eradicating the Black-White Infant Mortality Gap* (2018), https://socialequity.duke.edu/wp-content/uploads/2019/12/Eradicating-Black-Infant -Mortality-March-2018.pdf; Clare C. Brown, Jennifer E. Moore, Holly C. Felix, M. Kathryn Stewart, T. Mac Bird, Curtis L. Lowery, and Mick Tilford, "Association of Medicaid Expansion Status with Low Birth Rate and Preterm Birth," *JAMA* 321, no. 16 (April 2019): 1599; Bolling v. Sharpe, 347 U.S. 497 (1954).

198   *"the majestic equality of the law":* Anatole France, *The Red Lily* (New York: Macaulay, 1898), 91.
199   *"disparate impact":* Washington v. Davis, 426 U.S. 229 (1976).
200   *first affirmative action case:* Regents of Univ. of Cal. v. Bakke, 438 U.S. 265 (1978).

"The 'white' majority": Bakke, 438 U.S. at 295–96.

the Court formally endorsed: Adarand, 515 U.S. at 227.

202   *high-profile litigation:* Fisher v. Univ. of Texas, 136 S. Ct. 2198, 2224–25 (2016) (Alito, J., dissenting).

only permissible motivation: Bakke, 438 U.S. at 314.

a "compelling" goal: Grutter v. Bollinger, 539 U.S. 306, 325 (2003).

203   *"the 'robust exchange of ideas'":* Bakke, 438 U.S. at 31–13.

"promotes cross-racial understanding": Grutter, 539 U.S. at 306, 330–33; *Grutter,* 539 U.S. at 355–372 (Thomas, J., dissenting).

204   *history of elite education:* Jerome Karabel, *The Chosen: The Hidden History of Admission and Exclusion at Harvard, Yale, and Princeton* (New York: Houghton Mifflin, 2005), 13–23.

twentieth-century elite college admissions: Karabel, *The Chosen,* 51, 101–2, 105, 108–9, 114–15, 130.

205   *"individualized assessment":* Bakke, 438 U.S. at 316–19.

advent of individualized assessment: Karabel, *The Chosen,* 484–86.

206   *Michigan's undergraduate college: Gratz,* 539 U.S. at 244, 254.

"nonindividualized, mechanical one": Gratz, 539 U.S. at 280 (O'Connor, J., concurring).

207   *as a "minus":* Complaint at 4–7, Students for Fair Admissions v. Harvard College, 2014-CV-14176, 397 F. Supp. 3d 126 (2019), https://docs.justia.com/cases/federal/district-courts/massachusetts/madce/1:2014cv14176/165519/1 (hereafter cited as *SFFA* Complaint).

Stuyvesant High School: Stuyvesant High School, website, accessed October 3, 2019, https://stuy.enschool.org; Josh Moody, "U.S. News Releases 2019 Best High School Rankings," *U.S. News and World Report,* April 30, 2019, https://www.usnews.com/education/best-high-schools/articles/us-news-ranks-best-high-schools; "List of Stuyvesant High School People," Wikipedia, accessed October 3, 2019, https://en.wikipedia.org/wiki/List_of_Stuyvesant_High_School_people.

nearly three-quarters: Eliza Shapiro, "How the Few Black and Hispanic Students at Stuyvesant High School Feel," *New York Times,* March 22, 2019, https://www.nytimes.com/2019/03/22/nyregion/stuyvesant-high-school-black-students.html.

208   *Under de Blasio's plan:* Sarita Subramanian, "Admissions Overhaul: Stimulating the Outcome Under the Mayor's Plan for Admissions to the City's Specialized High Schools," New York City Independent Budget Office, February 2019, https://ibo.nyc.ny.us/iboreports/admissions-overhaul-simulating-the-outcome-under-the-mayors-plan-for-admissions-to-the-citys-specialized-high-schools-jan-2019.pdf.

a court decision striking down: Hopwood v. Texas, 78 F.3d 932 (5th Cir. 1996); *Fisher,* 136 S. Ct. at 2205.

minimal scrutiny: Parents Involved in Cmty. Sch. v. Seattle Sch. Dist. No. 1, 551 U.S. 701, 788 (2007) (Kennedy, J., concurring in the judgment).

"top-seventh" plan: Karabel, *The Chosen,* 101.

210   *Only 2 percent:* Thomas D. Snyder, ed., *120 Years of American Education: A Statistical Portrait* (Washington, D.C.: National Center for Education Statistics, 1993), 64, https://nces.ed.gov/pubs93/93442.pdf; Bill Hussar, Jijun Zhang, Sarah Hein, Ke Wang, Ashley Roberts, Jiashan Cui, Mary Smith, Farrah Bullock Mann, Amy Barmer, and Rita Dilig, *The Condition of Education 2020* (Washington, D.C.: National Center for Education Statistics, 2020), 124, https://nces.ed.gov/pubs2020/2020144.pdf.

The U-shaped trend: Thomas Piketty, *Capital in the Twenty-First Century* (Cambridge, MA: Belknap Press, 2014); Emmanuel Saez, "Striking It Richer: The Evolution of Top Incomes in the United States," *Pathways Magazine,* Winter 2008, 3. Updated 2012 statistics are available at https://eml.berkeley.edu//~saez/saez-UStopincomes-2012.pdf.

an academic achievement gap: Sean F. Reardon, "The Widening Academic Achievement Gap Between the Rich and the Poor: New Evidence and Possible Explanations," in *Whither Oppor-*

tunity? Rising Inequality, Schools, and Children's Life Chances, ed. Greg J. Duncan and Richard J. Murnane (New York: Russell Sage Foundation, 2011), 91.

simultaneous developments: Karabel, *The Chosen,* 182–84, 186–89, 221–22, 239, 241–45, 251–52, 262–66, 332.

211 *stark differences:* Karabel, *The Chosen,* 266–70.

a federal investigation: Karabel, *The Chosen,* 507.

universities formulated: Karabel, *The Chosen,* 382–407; Lisa M. Stulberg and Anthony S. Chen, "The Origins of Race-Conscious Affirmative Action in Undergraduate Admissions: A Comparative Analysis of Institutional Change in Higher Education," *Sociology of Education* 87, no. 1 (January 2014): 40.

212 *In 1983, U.S. News and World Report:* Robert Morse, "The Birth of the College Rankings," *U.S. News and World Report,* May 16, 2008, https://www.usnews.com/news/national/articles/ 2008/05/16/the-birth-of-college-rankings; Robert Morse, Eric Brooks, and Matt Mason, "How U.S. News Calculated the 2019 Best Colleges Rankings," *U.S. News and World Report,* September 8, 2019, https://www.usnews.com/education/best-colleges/articles/how-us-news -calculated-the-rankings.

factors are self-reinforcing: Karabel, *The Chosen,* 520; Jeongeun Kim and Woo-Jeong Shim, "What Do Rankings Measure? The U.S. News Ranking and Student Experience at Liberal Arts Colleges," *Review of Higher Education* 42, no. 3 (Spring 2019): 954.

SFFA argued: SFFA Complaint at 102–18.

213 *Immigration and Nationality Act of 1965:* Immigration and Nationality Act of 1965, Pub. L. No. 89-236, 79 Stat. 911 (1965); Karabel, *The Chosen,* 500–13; Philip Yang, *Asian Immigration to the United States* (Malden, MA: Polity Press, 2011), 109–14, 125–27, 131.

well-developed affirmative action system: Vinay Sitapati, "Reservations," in *Oxford Handbook of the Indian Constitution,* ed. Sujit Choudhry, Madhav Khosla, and Pratap Bhanu Mehta (Oxford: Oxford University Press, 2016), 720–41.

214 *Markovits points out:* Daniel Markovits, *The Meritocracy Trap: How America's Foundational Myth Feeds Inequality, Dismantles the Middle Class, and Devours the Elite* (New York: Penguin Press, 2019), 132–51, 166–67.

subjectively experience their success: Markovits, *The Meritocracy Trap,* 87–88.

ranking algorithm: Morse, Brooks, and Mason, "How U.S. News Calculated the 2019 Best Colleges Rankings."

an alternative definition: Karabel, *The Chosen,* 251, 291–93, 317, 358–63, 369; Camille G. Caldera and Sahar M. Mohammadzadeh, "Record-Low 4.5 Percent of Harvard College Applicants Accepted to Class of 2023," *Harvard Crimson,* March 29, 2019, https://www.thecrimson .com/article/2019/3/29/2023-admit-numbers/.

216 *a Seattle school district: Parents Involved,* 551 U.S. at 701, 748.

217 *under the district formula: Parents Involved,* 551 U.S. at 724.

"ensuring all people": Parents Involved, 551 U.S. at 788 (Kennedy, J., concurring in the judgment).

218 *less judicial vigilance:* John H. Ely, "The Constitutionality of Reverse Racial Discrimination," *University of Chicago Law Review* 41, no. 4 (1974): 727.

219 *"outright prohibit":* SFFA Complaint at 6.

220 *banning all affirmative action:* Schuette v. BAMN, 572 U.S. 291 (2014).

9. CAMPUS SPEECH

221 *The SCV sued:* Walker v. Texas Division, Sons of Confederate Veterans, Inc., 576 U.S. 200 (2015).

222 *This absolutist posture:* New York Times Co. v. United States, 403 U.S. 713 (1971).

it is also what brought us: Citizens United v. Federal Election Commission, 558 U.S. 310 (2010).

no constitutional restriction: Walker, 576 U.S. at 207–8.

"Rather Be Golfing": Walker, 576 U.S. at 222 (Alito, J., dissenting).

223   *Vermont data miners:* Sorrell v. IMS Health Inc., 564 U.S. 552 (2011).

"Thank God for Dead Soldiers": Snyder v. Phelps, 562 U.S. 443, 448 (2011).

burning a cross: R.A.V. v. City of St. Paul, 505 U.S. 377 (1992).

rights to reproductive autonomy: Planned Parenthood of Columbia/Willamette, Inc. v. American Coalition of Life Activists, 41 F. Supp. 2d 1130, 1132. (D. Or. 1999).

"abortionists": Planned Parenthood of the Columbia/Willamette v. Am. Coalition of Life Activists, 290 F.3d 1058, 1063 (9th Cir. 2002).

224   *A man who had driven:* Jonathan M. Katz and Farah Stockman, "James Fields Guilty of First-Degree Murder in Death of Heather Heyer," *New York Times,* December 7, 2018, https://www.nytimes.com/2018/12/07/us/james-fields-trial-charlottesville-verdict.html.

an open-carry state: Va. Code §§ 18.2-287.4; 18.2-308 (2019).

Most U.S. adults: Peter Suciu, "More Americans Are Getting News from Social Media," Forbes, October 11, 2019, https://www.forbes.com/sites/petersuciu/2019/10/11/more-americans-are-getting-their-news-from-social-media/#3d1ed5913e17.

225   *eleven o'clock on Sunday:* Martin Luther King Jr., "The Most Segregated Hour in America," *Meet the Press,* NBC, April 17, 1960, YouTube video, https://youtu.be/1q881g1L_d8.

226   *graduate student named Cameron Padgett:* Alex Harris, "He's Not a Racist, He Says, Just an 'Identitarian' and He Books Richard Spencer's Campus Talks," *Miami Herald,* October 18, 2017,   https://www.miamiherald.com/news/local/education/article179559666.html;   Travis M. Andrews, "Federal Judge Stops Auburn from Canceling White Nationalist Richard Spencer Speech. Protests and a Scuffle Greet Him," *Washington Post,* April 19, 2017, https://www.washingtonpost.com/news/morning-mix/wp/2017/04/19/federal-judge-stops-auburn-from-canceling-white-nationalists-speech-violence-erupts.

impermissibly discriminated: Padgett v. Auburn Univ., No. 3:17-CV-231-WKW, 2017 WL 10241386, at *1 (M.D. Ala. Apr. 18, 2017).

227   *dissent analyzed the case: Walker,* 576 U.S. at 220 (Alito, J., dissenting).

The seminal case: Sweezy v. New Hampshire, 354 U.S. 234 (1957).

"The essentiality of freedom": Sweezy, 354 U.S. at 250.

228   *"It is the business of a university": Sweezy,* 354 U.S. at 263 (Frankfurter, J., concurring).

State University of New York at Buffalo: Keyishian v. Board of Regents of State of N.Y., 385 U.S. 589, 603 (1967).

"compelling" interest: Regents of Univ. of Cal. v. Bakke, 438 U.S. 265, 312–14 (1978).

229   *"it can hardly be argued":* Tinker v. Des Moines Independent Community School District, 393 U.S. 503, 506 (1969).

230   *Apart from a few bursts:* President's Commission on Campus Unrest, *The Report of the President's Commission on Campus Unrest* (Washington, D.C.: U.S. Government Printing Office, 1970), 20–21, https://files.eric.ed.gov/fulltext/ED083899.pdf.

the vast majority: Thomas D. Snyder, ed., *120 Years of American Education: A Statistical Portrait* (Washington, D.C.: National Center for Education Statistics, 1993), 64–66, https://nces.ed.gov/pubs93/93442.pdf.

"He wants very little": Richard M. Abrams, "The Student Rebellion at Berkeley: An Interpretation," *Massachusetts Review* 6, no. 2 (Winter–Spring 1965): 354.

"most prominent feature": C. Michael Otten, *University Authority and the Student: The Berkeley Experiment* (Berkeley: University of California Press, 1970), 21.

231   *That ended in 1959:* James A. Hijiya, "The Free Speech Movement and the Heroic Movement," *Journal of American Studies* 22, no. 1 (April 1988): 44.

As draconian as Berkeley's actions: Hijiya, "The Free Speech Movement," 45.

couldn't be suspended: West Virginia State Board of Education v. Barnette, 319 U.S. 624 (1943).

A number of students participated: Hijiya, "The Free Speech Movement," 48.

232   *The* Oakland Tribune: Hijiya, "The Free Speech Movement," 50–51.

newspaper's lack of diversity: Abrams, "The Student Rebellion at Berkeley," 361.

backfire more spectacularly: Robby Cohen, "Berkeley Free Speech Movement: Paving the Way for Campus Activism," *OAH Magazine of History* 1, no. 1 (April 1985): 16–17; Hijiya, "The Free Speech Movement," 51–52.

model for college student activism: Cohen, "Berkeley Free Speech Movement," 18.

233   *advocates for racial justice:* New York Times Co. v. Sullivan, 376 U.S. 254 (1964); National Ass'n for Advancement of Colored People v. State of Ala. ex rel. Patterson, 357 U.S. 449 (1958); Gregory v. City of Chicago, 394 U.S. 111 (1969); Lee C. Bolinger, "The Skokie Legacy: Reflections on an 'Easy Case' and Free Speech Theory," *Michigan Law Review* 80, no. 4 (March 1982): 620; Donald Janson, "Guards Bayonet Hecklers in Cicero's Rights March," *New York Times,* September 5, 1966.

234   *a Chicago man:* Beauharnais v. Illinois, 343 U.S. 250, 252 (1952); Ill. An. Stat., c. 38, § 471 (1949); Joseph Tanenhaus, "Group Libel," *Cornell Law Quarterly* 32, no. 2 (Winter 1950): 262.

The year before Beauharnais: Dennis v. United States, 341 U.S. 494 (1951).

"fighting words": Chaplinsky v. New Hampshire, 315 U.S. 568, 572 (1942).

most famous heckler's veto: Feiner v. New York, 340 U.S. 315, 317 (1951).

NAACP successfully opposed: Samuel Walker, *Hate Speech: The History of an American Controversy* (Lincoln: University of Nebraska Press, 1994), 83–86.

1965 Race Relations Act: Martin Adeney, *Baggage of Empire: Reporting Politics and Industry in the Shadow of Imperial Decline* (London: Biteback, 2016), 77; "Sentences Today on Four Colored Men, Ten Charges Under Race Act," *Times* (London), November 29, 1967; "Scuffles in Court at Race Case Hearing," *Times* (London), October 24, 1967.

235   *a series of decisions:* Cohen v. California, 403 U.S. 15, 16 (1971); Brandenburg v. Ohio, 395 U.S. 444, 447 (1969); Collin v. Smith, 578 F.2d 1197, 1199 (7th Cir. 1978); Miller v. California, 413 U.S. 15, 25 (1973); Stanley v. Georgia, 394 U.S. 557, 559 (1969).

At the University of Michigan: Doe v. Univ. of Mich., 721 F. Supp. 852, 854 (E.D. Mich. 1989); Eugene Park, "Racist Jokes Aired over 'U' Radio, Students Protest WJJX Broadcast," *Michigan Daily,* February 19, 1987.

at the University of Mississippi: "Ole Miss Chancellor Irate over Racial Incident," United Press International, September 20, 1989, https://www.upi.com/Archives/1989/09/20/Ole-Miss-chancellor-irate-over-racial-incident/7870622267200/.

236   *At Emory University:* Nancy Gibbs, "Bigots in the Ivory Tower: An Alarming Rise in Hatred Roils U.S. Campuses," *Time,* May 7, 1990, 104.

Between 1986 and 1990: Carnegie Foundation for the Advancement of Teaching, *Campus Life: In Search of Community. A Special Report* (Princeton, NJ: Princeton University Press, 1990), 18.

a code of conduct: Doe, 721 F. Supp. at 852, 854, 856.

"chill" his academic speech: Doe, 721 F. Supp. at 861.

is simply forbidden: Doe, 721 F. Supp. at 863.

237   *at the University of Wisconsin:* UWM Post, Inc. v. Board of Regents of the University of Wisconsin System 774, F. Supp. 1163, 1165, 1167–68 (E.D. Wis. 1991).

238   *"by establishing content-based":* UWM Post, 774 F. Supp. at 1176.

239   *not alone in this regard:* Corry v. Stanford University, No. 740309, slip op. (Cal. Super. Ct. Feb. 27, 1995); Dambrot v. Central Mich. Univ., 55 F.3d 1177 (6th Cir. 1995); Booher v. Board of Regents, 1998 U.S. Dist. LEXIS 11404 (E.D. Ky. Jul. 21, 1998); Bair v. Shippensburg University, 280 F. Supp. 2d 357 (M.D. Pa. 2003); Roberts v. Haragan, 346 F. Supp. 2d 853 (N.D. Tex. 2004); DeJohn v. Temple University, 537 F.3d 301 (3d Cir. 2008); Smith v. Tarrant County College

District, 694 F. Supp. 2d 610 (N.D. Tex. 2010); McCauley v. Univ. of the Virgin Islands, 618 F.3d 232 (3d Cir. 2010).

court case out of San Francisco: College Republicans at San Francisco State University v. Reed, 523 F. Supp. 2d 1005, 1009 (N.D. Cal. 2007).

240 *"A regulation that mandates":* Reed, 523 F. Supp. 2d at 1019.

We have come to see: Widmar v. Vincent, 454 U.S. 263, 267 n.5 (1981).

It is not: Christian Legal Society Chapter of the University of California, Hastings College of Law v. Martinez, 561 U.S. 661, 702 (2010) (Stevens, J., concurring).

The purpose of a university: Bloedorn v. Grube, 631 F.3d 1218, 1233–34 (11th Cir. 2011); Frederick Schauer, "Hohfeld's First Amendment," *George Washington Law Review* 76, no. 4 (June 2008): 921.

241 *Schools hire faculty:* Jamal Greene, "Constitutional Moral Hazard and Campus Speech," *William and Mary Law Review* 61, no. 1 (October 2019): 243–44.

Recent events on the campus: Kate Huangpu and Khadija Hussain, "Protesters Disrupt Anti-immigration Speech by Tommy Robinson," *Columbia Daily Spectator,* October 11, 2017, https://www.columbiaspectator.com/news/2017/10/11/protesters-disrupt-anti-immigration -speech-by-tommy-robinson-at-columbia/; Alex Hern and Jim Waterson, "Tommy Robinson Banned from Facebook and Instagram," *The Guardian,* February 26, 2019, https:// www.theguardian.com/uk-news/2019/feb/26/tommy-robinson-banned-from-facebook-and -instagram; Ross McCafferty, "Far-Right Activist Tommy Robinson Banned from Snapchat," *The Scotsman,* April 5, 2019, https://www.scotsman.com/news/uk-news/far-right-activist -tommy-robinson-banned-from-snapchat-1-4902298; Marc Fisher, John Woodrow Cox, and Peter Hermann, "Pizzagate: From Rumor, to Hashtag, to Gunfire in D.C.," *Washington Post,* December 6, 2016, https://www.washingtonpost.com/local/pizzagate-from-rumor -to-hashtag-to-gunfire-in-dc/2016/12/06/4c7def50-bbd4-11e6-94ac-3d324840106c_story .html; Olivia Nuzzi, "Mike Cernovich Pivots from Pizzagate to Not-So-Fake News," *The Intelligencer,* August 8, 2017, http://nymag.com/intelligencer/2017/08/mike-cernovich-pivots -from-pizzagate-to-not-so-fake-news.html.

242 *drew large protests:* Huangpu and Hussain, "Protesters Disrupt Anti-immigration Speech."

243 *"are laboratories* for *democracy":* Paul Horwitz, *First Amendment Institutions* (Cambridge, MA: Harvard University Press, 2013), 113.

universities are better suited: Greene, "Constitutional Moral Hazard," 244.

244 *But schools' decisions:* Christian Legal Society, 561 U.S. at 702 (Stevens, J., concurring). "As a general matter, courts should respect universities' judgments and let them manage their own affairs."

To the extent college students: Greene, "Constitutional Moral Hazard," 244.

Racist or sexist theories: Heidi Kitrosser, "Free Speech, Higher Education, and the PC Narrative," *Minnesota Law Review* 101, no. 1 (2017): 2038.

245 *ham-handed application:* Barry Siegel, "Fighting Words: It Seemed Like a Noble Idea — Regulating Hateful Language. But When the University of Wisconsin Tried, Its Good Intentions Collided with the First Amendment," *Los Angeles Times,* March 28, 1993, http://articles .latimes.com/1993-03-28/magazine/tm-15949_1_fighting-word/6.

A college platform can legitimate: Suzanne B. Goldberg, "Free Expression on Campus: Mitigating the Costs of Contentious Speakers," *Harvard Journal of Law and Public Policy* 41, no. 1 (Winter 2018): 182.

Minority students also spend: Louwanda Evans and Wendy Leo Moore, "Impossible Burdens: White Institutions, Emotional Labor, and Micro-Resistance," *Social Problems* 62, no. 3 (August 2015): 439.

246 *self-regulation by schools:* Dale Russakoff, "Penn Is Abandoning Speech Code," *Washington Post,* November 17, 1993, https://www.washingtonpost.com/archive/politics/1993/11/17/ penn-is-abandoning-speech-code/511a907f-f13b-400e-a3bb-c196b16f1b9c/.

247 *pressure from politicians:* Kitrosser, "Free Speech," 2003–6.

CONCLUSION

248   *There is such a thing*: Thatcher once said, "There is no such thing as society." The famous quote first appeared in a 1987 interview by Douglas Keay for the magazine *Woman's Own*, available at Margaret Thatcher Foundation, Interview for *Woman's Own* ("no such thing as society"), https://www.margaretthatcher.org/document/106689.

249   *a "nomos"*: Robert M. Cover, "Foreword—Nomos and Narrative," *Harvard Law Review* 97, no. 1 (November 1983): 4.

250   *how Frederick Douglass:* Frederick Douglass, "The Constitution of the United States: Is it Pro-slavery or Anti-slavery?" (speech, Glasgow, March 26, 1860), reprinted in *Frederick Douglass: Selected Speeches and Writings*, ed. Philip S. Foner, abridged and adapted by Yuval Taylor (Chicago: Lawrence Hill, 1999), 379–90.

    how Susan B. Anthony: Godfrey D. Lehman, "Susan B. Anthony Cast Her Vote for Ulysses S. Grant," *American Heritage,* December 1985, 25.

    how the Reverend Dr. Martin Luther King Jr.: Martin Luther King Jr., "The Negro Is Your Brother," *Atlantic Monthly,* August 1963, available at https://www.theatlantic.com/magazine/archive/2018/02/letter-from-a-birmingham-jail/552461/. This letter, which was printed in numerous publications, is commonly known as "Letter from a Birmingham Jail."

    changed his vote: John C. Jeffries Jr., *Justice Lewis F. Powell, Jr.: A Biography* (New York: Charles Scribner's Sons, 1994), 451–52; McCleskey v. Kemp, 481 U.S. 279 (1987).

251   *"inescapable network of mutuality":* King, "The Negro Is Your Brother."

    "we must never forget": M'Culloch v. Maryland, 17 U.S. 316, 407 (1819).

Index